Advance praise for

WILD FORESTING

Spectacularly encompassing, Drengson and Taylor's collection of essays and scholarly thought on Wild Foresting is plainly, even painfully, as much about the wildness in ourselves as in our ravaged landscapes. This volume is indeed aid and nurturance for the wild mind and one of its best habitats, the wild forest. The reader hungry for a substantial vision of human harmony with forests (and by extension nature and most self-realized humanity) will not be disappointed. Here are 40 nutrient-packed, highly digestible morsels from leading forest ecologists, ethnobotanists, ecopsychologists, philosophers of the wild, practicing ecoforesters, advocates of children's right to play outside, environmental visionaries, and Nobel prize winners. Drengson and Taylor strongly unite these works with the thread of Deep Ecology's principles of honoring the diversity of life and the diversity of carefully reflected personal philosophy, two great forces that synergistically carry us beyond the deconstructive post-modern impasse of nihilism. This book is a forest feast for the mind, heart and hands.

— Olin Eugene (Gene) Myers, Jr.,
Associate Professor, Huxley College of the Environment,
Western Washington University

Industrial forestry treats our forests as a globalized commodity. With the collapse of the world's financial industry, we have the opportunity to relearn the perils of an economy based on the fabricated value of currencies and commodities. *Wild Foresting* explores the contrary view, presenting our forests as real life, and forestry as real stewardship. This book reminds us that the knowledge exists to restore and sustain the ecological health of our forests, and to restore our relationship with the land. The next step is having the will to use that knowledge.

— Mitch Friedman,
Executive Director, Conservation Northwest

Alan Drengson & Duncan Taylor

WILD FORESTING
Practising Nature's Wisdom

NEW SOCIETY PUBLISHERS

Cataloging in Publication Data:
A catalog record for this publication is available from the National Library of Canada.

Cover design by Diane McIntosh.
Cover Image: Forest - istock/AVTG; Forest floor - istock/Ben Thomas

Printed in Canada.

New Society Publishers acknowledges the support of the Government of Canada through the Book Publishing Industry Development Program (BPIDP) for our publishing activities.

Paperback ISBN: 978-0-86571-616-2

Inquiries regarding requests to reprint all or part of *Wild Foresting* should be addressed to New Society Publishers at the address below.

To order directly from the publishers, please call toll-free (North America) 1-800-567-6772, or order online at www.newsociety.com

Any other inquiries can be directed by mail to:

New Society Publishers
P.O. Box 189, Gabriola Island, BC V0R 1X0, Canada
(250) 247-9737

New Society Publishers' mission is to publish books that contribute in fundamental ways to building an ecologically sustainable and just society, and to do so with the least possible impact on the environment, in a manner that models this vision. We are committed to doing this not just through education, but through action. This book is one step toward ending global deforestation and climate change. It is printed on Forest Stewardship Council-certified acid-free paper that is **100% post-consumer recycled** (100% old growth forest-free), processed chlorine free, and printed with vegetable-based, low-VOC inks, with covers produced using FSC-certified stock. Additionally, New Society purchases carbon offsets based on an annual audit, operating with a carbon-neutral footprint. For further information, or to browse our full list of books and purchase securely, visit our website at: www.newsociety.com

NEW SOCIETY PUBLISHERS
www.newsociety.com

Dedication

WE DEDICATE THIS BOOK TO ALL WILD FORESTERS and lifelong journeyers and the many companions who share the wild forest communities wherever they might be. May you all find joy and indigenous wisdom in your home places.

We are grateful for the help and support of Victoria Stevens in the preparation of this book for publication. We are also grateful for the skillful copy editing done to the manuscript by Betsy Nuse. Special thanks to the Board Members of the Ecoforestry Institute and to the Editors of the *Ecoforestry Journal*, Irv Penner and Davd Martin.

Contents

Foreword:
Life On Our Planet Is In Trouble — What Will YOU Do?

Georg Feuerstein and Brenda Feuerstein

When biologists, ecologists and other scientists predict biosphere collapse in 100 years or, far more likely, several decades from now, they are telling us that our planet is seriously ailing. While miracles can happen, we ought not to rely on them but resolutely go about healing Mother Earth, as we would attempt to heal ourselves.

Scientists are generally conservative. So, when seven out of ten biologists believe that we are facing a mass extinction today, we should take this very seriously indeed. In March 2005, a group of more than 1,300 scientists from 95 countries completed the Millennium Ecosystem Assessment project. In their report, they wrote:

> [A]pproximately 60% (15 out of 24) of the ecosystem services examined during the Millennium Ecosystem Assessment [2001–2005] are being degraded or used unsustainably, including fresh water, capture fisheries, air and water purification, and the regulation of regional and local climate, natural hazards, and pests ... The number of species on the planet is declining. Over the past few hundred years, humans have increased the species extinction rate by as much as 1,000 times over background rates typical over the planet's history ...[1]

If we are realistic, we might have just a few decades left before humanity could be added to the list of extinct species, except there would be no one around to record our species' demise. Given the proverbial lethargy of people and governments and the often destructive ways of corporations, pursuing profits come what may, there is not much time to turn things around.

If you are young enough to expect to live another 20 or 30 years, your life might be cut short by the increasing devastation of the biosphere. If you are in middle age, think of your children and grandchildren whose lives will be shortened. They might not even inherit a wasteland, because they might die of oxygen starvation, overexposure to ultraviolet rays from the Sun, hunger, thirst or flooding.

Clearly our collective situation is dramatic. Back in the 1960s when the first ecologists were warning the public of the baneful effects of environmental pollution, we thought we could afford to ignore them. By the 1980s, we should definitely have started to heed the chorus of environmental warning voices. Today we have a planet emergency!

We owe it to our children, future generations and to all life forms on this Earth to take incisive action immediately to help prevent the worst from happening. As rational beings, we must make our thinking and lifestyles radically green. We all must now embrace the Earth as dearly as we embrace our own life. Our love must be charged with great wisdom and compassion for all and with the will to make a difference for future generations from now on. Anything else is not responsible.

Unfortunately, too many people don't know how to tap into their innate wisdom and compassion. Modern civilization has neglected and largely forgotten the great teachings of its forebears and those who live quietly — and usually in a state of political suppression by the dominant culture — in sane enclaves that are still in touch with Nature. We must quickly relearn the ways of the sages and allow ourselves to be guided by their compassionate wisdom.

Often traditional wisdom is associated with Nature's most splendid habitat — wild forests abundant with life and wholeness. This anthology offers an in-depth examination of the integral relationship between wild forest environments and healthy communities. The various contributions all amount to an exercise in revealing the inalienable connection that exists between inside and outside, Nature and mind, ecosystem and human society — connections that have long been understood by traditional peoples.

Civilization is boxes within boxes within boxes. It gives us the illusion of at least relative certainty and security but largely robs us of the spontaneity and wholeness that are associated with Nature, with the wilderness. Unless we become willing to free ourselves from our addiction to all the little boxes that our civilization provides — house, car, career, TV, spectator sport, the mall, jet setting and so on — we will not be able to experience life as it really is. We will not see splendor of Nature or her present ailments. Perhaps for some people the step into reality will prove impossible and mentally devastating. Those of us who can still feel the life force circulating in our bones and have the survival instinct intact will have to squarely face humanity's greatest challenge.

For those who want humankind to survive and flourish, wild forests — offering the healing touch of Nature — will be a veritable life line. Therefore, we must do everything in our power to preserve, restore and multiply them as well as learn from them in all humility.

Alan Drengson and Duncan Taylor have for years bravely championed our forests. In 1997, they edited *Ecoforestry: The Art and Science of Sustainable Forest Use* which was the first comprehensive anthology focusing on the philosophy, policies and techniques of ecologically sound forest use. The present work, based on the rich lessons of the past decade, essentially introduces the idea that wild forests are reservoirs of wisdom and sanity. Anyone who has ever entered a wild forest and stood quietly amidst its solemn trees will know the healing spell that is woven in those moments. In view of the threat of imminent biosphere collapse and our increasingly insane civilization with its singular lack of balance and wisdom, this work serves as a beacon of wholeness and hope.

Introduction: Wild Foresting — A Vision Emerges

Alan Drengson and Duncan M. Taylor

In Wildness is the Preservation of the World
> — Henry David Thoreau
> (*Walking*, 1862)

When we try to pick out anything by itself, we find it hitched to everything else in the Universe
> — John Muir
> (*My First Summer in the Sierra*, 1911)

Wild foresting vision

A decade ago New Society published our book, *Ecoforestry: The Art and Science of Sustainable Forest Use.*[1] Since then, there has been continuing evolution in the paradigms of responsible forest use although the outmoded industrial removal of forests has continued unabated. Wild forests are now central to the convergence of community ecoforestry, wholistic forestry, permaculture, wild farming, place-based education, ecological restoration and the movement to stem global warming.

Wild foresting refers to any responsible use of forests that appreciates, is attuned to and learns from their wild energies and wisdom. Wild foresting activities are compatible with the evolutionary integrity and self organization of natural forest ecosystems. Wild foresting as a movement connects Indigenous knowledge systems with contemporary ecological knowledge; it reconciles the needs of the Earth with those of humans. It unites a great variety of practices tailored by local people to the characteristics and values of unique forest places around the world. It respects local adaptations uniquely suited to each forest stand and place, but it does not support large scale forest removal. *Thus, wild foresting is part of the broader movement for ecological responsibility.* It is especially in harmony with the platform principles of the deep ecology movement which stress the inherent values of diversity and of each being. Wild foresting is thus compatible with a vast diversity of cultural and personal worldviews ecologically adapted to specific places around the world.

Wild foresting practices sustain and promote deep forest wisdom, forest health and biological and cultural diversity. Wherever wild forests grow or are being restored, practitioners discover that health and life quality are intertwined with the integrity and resilience of diverse ecosystem processes that are uniquely expressed in local places. Wild foresting honors these processes, and it adapts human activities to the values these systems can sustain in perpetuity. Its diverse cultural adaptations evolve with forest systems. Instead of environmental crises, wild foresting leads to local control, personal freedom and rich cultural diversity. It also uses a more universal language found within the silence and melodious sounds of the natural and human world. It is in tune with the human heart and the creative love power flowing through all beings.

Global context and its challenges

Writings on the interactions of trees and people do not occur in a vacuum. This anthology addresses our profound social and environmental uncertainty and social dysfunction. A few years after the global media focused on the political and social crises brought on by the *war on terror* and the tsunami in Southeast Asia, two other tidal waves of greater long-term significance swept the planet. In March 2005 the *Millennium Ecosystem Assessment Report* stated that we are losing both species and habitat at unprecedented historical levels and are now on the brink of global ecological disaster. This Report was followed in 2007 by the Intergovernmental Panel on Climate Change (IPCC)'s Fourth Assessment Report. It underscored the threats that we now face from the global impact of climatic changes on both social and biophysical systems.[2] These changes are a direct result of human practices and industrial development based on fossil fuels.

Both reports pointed out that ecosystems, like other non-linear systems, do not always respond to stresses in incremental ways. They can alternate between periods of relative stability and periods of great instability and change. At times of great stress, systems can undergo sudden and dramatic shifts, with discontinuities from one state to another. An example of this is the rapid loss of Arctic ice and the melting of permafrost in the north. Here, a series of positive feedback loops have the synergistic link of increasing temperatures and releasing vast stores of methane from the melting of permafrost. This leads to further temperature increases and the loss of pack ice, as well as the loss of the reflective capacity of a diminished snow and ice pack to offset solar radiation (the albedo effect) — which in turn adds to the overall temperature increase — and so on in a faster and faster cycle. Not surprisingly, at the end of August 2007 the US National Snow and Ice Data Center reported the most significant loss of Arctic ice in recorded history.[3]

The loss of Arctic ice is one of a number of environmental stresses that have led even mainstream media to question many of the common values and assumptions about our lifestyles and development models. The industrial world's faith in progress, as unending growth and exploitation of nature for the satisfaction of ever-increasing material and energy demands, is now being seriously challenged. Recent findings on climate change and the loss of biodiversity have emphasized once again the value of more traditional notions regarding our need for respectful relationships to the Earth and its many beings. The modern global economy is based on consumerism, the idea of the totally separate self, the market as arbiter and the power of corporations. Its institutions define progress and economic health by continuing growth in Gross Domestic Product. These practices are all being deeply questioned, and new socially and ecologically responsible models of progress and development are appearing at the grass-roots level everywhere.

Because of the increasing power of technology and other global systems, the rate of consumptive change has continued to increase. This puts more of the basis of human life and cultures under extreme pressure. Regional and global ecosystems are undergoing severe alterations, with dire warnings from a wide range of empirical scientists and other observers. The realization that modern human civilization is on the verge of a collective tipping point that could send our support systems into rapid decline has become a common concern in current academic and popular literature. Thomas Homer-Dixon, Director of the Trudeau Centre for Peace and Conflict Studies at the University of Toronto, published *The Upside of Down* in 2006. He described five interlocking *tectonic* societal and biophysical stresses, including the widening gap between the world's rich and poor, the growing instability of the global economic system and the increasing loss of biodiversity and climate uncertainty — all of which are creating conditions for an immanent *perfect storm* of global environmental and social breakdown.[4] The abundant articles and books with similar themes all reflect the growing awareness that consumer industrial civilization, as it is now, is utterly unsustainable.[5] It cannot survive into the coming decades as it is, but it must undergo profound changes in practices and organization. It is all of these above conditions that have led us to create this book.

Just as *Ecoforestry* gave positive descriptions of alternative practices to use forests and trees in responsible, respectful ways, *Wild Foresting* brings a full range of forest uses into the center of cultural appreciation, education and valuing. The forests of the world, and of local areas, belong to themselves. They should be for the *respectful* use of all creatures and the humans that dwell within them. The industrial liquidation of wild forests and their replacement by plantations of clones is a moral outrage and crime against all creatures and people everywhere. Wild foresting is a partner of ecoforestry in honoring and caring for three great movements of global significance: for social justice, for peace and nonviolence and for *ecological responsibility*. Ecoforestry and wild foresting support flourishing wild forests and vernacular cultures, with their own unique wild forest dialects and creative ways to live in tune with the natural world. Ecoforestry and ecoagriculture are both shorthand for ecologically responsible uses of forest, crop and range lands.

Modern-postmodern detour and returning to perennial wisdom

We now must create local practices and global means of cooperation that do not undermine the cultural and biological diversity which are essential to long range resilience. These means and practices are part of an ancient assembly of values that make the Earth a treasure in the galaxy. In the West we tend to think and talk as if there is one solution, one metaphysics, one way of experiencing the world, rather than recognizing that our current problems offer a multitude of opportunities and rich choices for lives of deep and great quality. As Arne Naess points out, the deep ecology movement has a long and deep front. There are vast numbers

Modernism

1. Reality is not personal, has no inherent value, but is ordered by natural laws.
2. We can understand Nature by knowing these laws.
3. Specialized empirical science is the only way to know these laws.
4. Humans can live well by applying this objective knowledge to practical matters.
5. This theoretical and practical knowledge enables us to master Nature with technology.

Postmodernism

1. Reality is neither personal nor orderly.
2. All approaches to knowing the natural world are relative.
3. Nature has no inherent values transcending human subjectivity and culture.
4. Humans might not understand Nature, but their technological skill gives them great power.
5. There is no meaning or value in life other than what we ourselves create.

The Modern-Postmodern divide

1. Reality is personal and ordered.
2. Order is in part created by multitudes of beings striving to realize themselves in multi-dimensional relationships.
3. The powers of Nature are in us and other beings, and wise actions are possible through integration and unification of our many ways of knowing and powers of acting.
4. Nature is filled with diverse intrinsic values that can be discovered, as well as possibilities for creating new ones.
5. Completion and fulfillment are found in deepening ourselves through authentic dwelling in harmony with Nature and each other.

Ecological approaches and worldviews

ALAN DRENGSON. *CARING FOR HOME PLACES*

of ways to live in harmony with the natural world and each other.

We were both raised in the Euro-American context. We know that our particular cultural orientation, especially in the academic world, is still wrestling with the Modern-Postmodern divide and the *social construction of nature* that perpetuates a devalued natural world and an unacceptable nihilism. The main features of this divide are characterized by the five points at left.

Diverse ecological approaches transcend the shortcomings of this Modern-Postmodern impasse. These approaches are emerging in the Western nations and in other nations as well. In many places there are preexisting cultures, including those of our own ancestors, whose approaches to the world and relationships with all beings could be characterized broadly by the five features we list at left. These five features characterize a great diversity of shamanic cultures, the perennial wisdom of the traditions of nature spirituality (such as Shinto in Japan), as well as leading edge work in new cosmology of conscious living systems in the West described by writers like Ralph Metzner, Ervin Laszlo and New Story cosmologist Thomas Berry.

These figures show at a glance the main differences between the Modern, Postmodern and the diverse Ecological Approaches we describe. Note that the ecocentric narratives move across cultural differences and diversity as related to Nature and place. Pluralistic narratives based on culture-Nature ecology encourage mutual respect for diverse traditions and worldviews, ancient and new. They remind us that generations of humans and other beings will follow us. They encourage cross cultural communication to further global and local support for basic rights and the inherent values of humans, cultures, Nature and beings of all kinds. Their themes encourage the flourishing of all beings. They recognize that all life is one.

Since this book focuses on ecological approaches related to harmony with Nature and wild forests, we emphasize the cross cultural but locally diverse features of the Platform Principles of the Deep Ecology Movement. Here are those principles as articulated by Arne Naess and others.

Importance of personal and community philosophies

It is inevitable in individualistic societies for people to have different personal philosophies of life, even though they recognize certain general principles. Without honoring personal philosophies, we would not respect and care for the sanctity and rights of individual persons, but having our own whole sense for life enables us to be full community members and work together on shared aims.

Naess calls philosophies of life that honor ecological values, such as diversity and symbiosis, ecosophies. In principle there can be as many *ecosophies* as there are people. *Ecophilosophy* is the study of diversity in ecology, culture and personal worldviews. There is a major revisioning of spiritual traditions throughout the world inspired by the return of ecological and perennial wisdom and the importance of spiritual practices that engender unity and compassion. Nonviolent and respectful communication with all cultures and beings is based on respect, gratitude and the realization that we are all interrelated. This is at the heart, for example, of the teachings of Jesus as told in some of the *Gospels* and in the suppressed *Gnostic Gospels*. To know the beautiful in the world is to know deeply through the perennial

1. All living beings have intrinsic value.
2. The richness and diversity of life has intrinsic value.
3. Except to satisfy vital needs, humankind does not have the right to reduce this diversity and this richness.
4. It would be better for human beings if there were fewer of them, and much better for other living creatures.
5. Today the extent and nature of human interference in the various ecosystems is not sustainable, and the lack of sustainability is rising.
6. Decisive improvement requires considerable change: social, economic, technological and ideological.
7. An ideological change would essentially entail seeking a better quality of life rather than a raised standard of living.
8. Those who accept the aforementioned points are responsible for trying to contribute directly or indirectly to the realization of the necessary changes.

ARNE NAESS, LIFE'S PHILOSOPHY 6

Platform principles of the deep ecology movement

wisdom of the way of love. As Jesus taught, a loved world is filled with values that we know first hand. The power of love is a universal energy that can be actualized by each of us in our own personal way. This is our spiritual challenge and task — to become whole, complete persons — and as the world is always changing, we too must change with it.[7] Fixed dogmas sound a death knell to authentic spiritual life which is ever deepening in awareness, appreciation and compassion.

Cultural and ecological diversity

To solve our many international problems cooperation is necessary, and yet it is possible and necessary to maintain cultural and individual diversity. No one worldview or ontology will be held by everyone everywhere. Our world would be very impoverished if that were true. Even within countries such as India, Japan, China, Canada, Norway or the United States, there is considerable diversity in personal religions and worldviews. We each have our own unique way of experiencing, understanding and talking about the world. It is wrong to try to force others to think and feel the way we do, or to force them to use language the way we do. We each have our unique feelings and dialects that are interwoven with our place and personal history. Our right to this freedom to be ourselves is of course enshrined with obligations to respect the same freedom for others. This also applies to our judgments about the natural world with its great diversity of beings. We should recognize their right to flourish.

Nonviolent, respectful communication

Our communication should be nonviolent and respectful, especially toward those with whom we disagree. Nonviolent communication is compatible with direct action in support of ecological responsibility and caring for our home places and forests. Many supporting perennial wisdom distinguish between the small-s *self* of ego and the wider and deeper ecological sense of *Self* with which we each might come to identify. As we grow more mature we should become more tolerant and open to our differences and develop wider and deeper concerns that transcend narrow self-interests.

As we mature we care more deeply for our family, neighbors and place. Their welfare is even more important than our own. We become an expression of our people and place. A person might say, "I live in this place and for years have explored it on every level. I love and identify with it." Aboriginal friends say, "We are this land we live in and love. It tells us and others who we are." Our language and daily actions all have sense because our values and practices are deeply connected with knowledge of self and other, what our own local ecological Self is and so on. In this world there is still a great diversity of cultures and languages, as there has been for millennia. These should be respected locally and internationally, as should human rights, social justice and ecological responsibility. In the face of this great diversity and complexity of cultures and ecological communities, we become humble and realize our responsibility to be nonviolent in our communication from speech to direct action. We should have enlarging conversations rather than debates. In our highly technologized settings more and more of us lack contact with the natural world. Nowhere is this more critical than in the education of our children.

Nature deficit in learning

Wild foresting is a way to address the looming *nature deficit* in our children's education. It is critically important for us to address this deficit if we are to educate the younger generations to know and care for the natural world. In contemporary technological societies it has become increasingly obvious that the technological systems provide *virtual* experience as a substitute for authentic experience in the real world. It is no wonder, then, that many people educated within our systems from childhood through university have little actual deep personal experience in the natural world. Thus, some seem to believe that "nature is only a social construction," that there are only *subjective* realities and that only humans and their societies count. This is part of the postmodern legacy.

In countless studies we find that those who are defenders and eloquent protectors of the natural world and of wild beings are people whose deepest childhood experiences were in special places in the natural world. They played in such places without adult supervision and controlled programs. They created their own games, their own places, their own nests and huts. They dug caves, they lived in the trees and built tree houses, they made secret camps. They had special places they went to recover from childhood traumas and injuries. This is a key background in the setting of their childhood, and it is critical to processes of healing and wholeness for teens and adults.

Many traditional societies provide a context for this most important depth education in human life. It is through contact with the natural world that we connect with other beings, the plants and animals with whom we share our lives on a daily basis. They are in our dreams, they are our inner animals and plants that guide and tell us where we are, who we are, how to be whole and how to know ourselves in authentic ways. It is from such rich and complex origins in specific places that we are able to tell our own stories and weave our own personal place-based mythologies. In many cultures ceremonial initiations into a changed life with new names and stories are given in special places in vision quests and rites of passage, always rich with wild inner and outer plants and animals, forests and mountains, rivers and plains. It is all of these experiences and more that make us human dwellers on this Earth. It is from these rich experiences that our capacity to love all of nature is activated, and we become capable and competent whole humans who can care for and help others to find themselves. It is

how we know and become defenders of wild beings and forests. It is how we know our ecological selves.

In vision quests in traditional societies, in rediscovery programs, in outdoor adventure and therapy programs, in Norse *Friluftsliv*, in walkabouts and more, we find an emerging awareness of all that is said above. Some have systematized the central elements of these experiences and practices as they have surfaced in wilderness journeying in North America as the *Wildway*. All of these experiences resonate with practices related to the older shamanic journeying ceremonies and wild wandering which are done with focused intent or with open receptive searching; all of these and more are rich with mythologies and stories, filled with cross cultural symbols and complex values, grounded in wildness and the natural world. Forests and trees are prominent and of central importance. They are not merely a setting but a rich community of beings we are invited to join. We learn again and again from our own experiences, and from those of others whom we hear around the circle of firelight, that they and we ourselves have been nurtured and taught by this Earth and by its myriads of beings, rock, plant, tree and animal.

Perennial wisdom in nature and societies

The tree of knowledge and the world tree that supports the whole of reality are recurring themes in these stories and traditions. These animals and plants were often called helpers, or they can be called teachers too. They have many complex roles in cultures which live by nature spirituality and journeying. The more we learn about animals in their natural setting, the more we realize that they too learn from each other and share knowledge. A wolf might learn fishing from a bear, birds show other birds how to solve puzzles, capture certain prey or use a tool. Tool-using creatures become teachers to other creatures. Not only that, we find that animals too have cultures and make tools, have creative capacities that shows us that they are aware and feel, sense and know the world. They accumulate and pass on their knowledge to their young.

This great treasure of knowledge we are describing is in danger of being lost by the globalizing, monoculturing technological systems created by our modern industrial societies with their associated financial and marketing systems. It has often been claimed that technological systems are in themselves value-neutral, but we know now that value neutrality is impossible to attain. All systems throughout the human and nonhuman world are also systems of valuing; they are living processes and not fixed things. There are good value systems and bad value systems. They can be adaptive and have complementary impacts on the world, or they are maladaptive and have negative impacts on their users and their world. Many human societies went extinct because they developed systems that destroyed both their inner and outer ecology. Their selves and places were demolished by their systems of control and practice. Sometimes they learned before it was too late; sometimes they continued to do the same things that were making them ill, with even greater intensity, convinced that if they did so everything would be all right. But, of course, it was not, and these people and their societies perished.

Ways ahead

This book is not a rant about what is going wrong with the world; there are plenty of those. It is a clarion call for positive action and commitment; it is about love, hope and renewal. Indeed, all of the authors point to a silver lining that can lighten the breakdown and subsequent transformation of both our dominant expansionist consumer worldview and the exploitive ways it relates to most humans and the Earth. Our global systems of transportation and communication do not have to be instruments of central control, domination and destruction. Instead, they can help to spread awareness that we are all interconnected and that the fate of our local and regional ecosystems is also our fate. The fate of the systems we have created is in our hands. We *can* commit ourselves to work at the individual, community and regional levels to shape new practices and rebirth old ones that are in harmony with the great diversity of living beings with whom we are blessed to share this planet.

It is at times when complex systems are most unstable that they are supersensitive. It is at such times that even small fluctuations and pressures can give rise to large-scale consequences and outcomes. This is often called the *butterfly effect* whereby a butterfly flapping its wings in California shifts a highly unstable weather system, so as to cause a storm in Mongolia. Or again, like a climber at the top of a mountain peak, where any slight shift in route one way or another will lead her to any number of possible valley places. What directions can we shift in our own lives to help the many creative beings to be born around us? We each have far greater power and gifts to offer than we realize most of the time because we are disempowered by being deprived of free play in nature and subjected to passive conditioning and entertainment. As Arne Naess remarks "We each have far more capacity than we realize. We tend to seriously underestimate ourselves." We can be our own persons responding in unique ways to our own personal challenges, and we can dwell in our unique home places. This is also one of the deep insights of the shamanic ways whose ceremonies empower each person to connect with their own unique genius, starting from wild wandering and free play in nature. Do not require everyone to do the same thing, but invite all to contribute their unique gifts to our global efforts at nonviolent attunement to the natural world and each other. There are myriad positive ways forward.

Globally, we have reached a *decision window* with respect to our future. We need to celebrate and support those individuals and communities who are role models for living sustainably within their ecological communities. Over 60 years ago Mahatma Gandhi wisely noted that if we are to create a better world for all sentient beings, not only must the means and the ends for achieving this be of the same nonviolent quality, but we must also strive to "be the change that we want to see in the world." As Gandhi put it in another context, "We need more production by the masses and less mass production from big machines." Millions of local adaptations are rich sources of our salvation, not mega–power, monolithic monocultures.

It is with humility that we look at how a number of remarkable humans and communities in various parts of the world are currently acting as butterfly wings for setting in motion positive tipping for the renewal of one of this planet's most precious evolutionary manifestations — its forests. And while many of these articles are focused on forests and trees, they all are relevant to places beyond the edges of the forest. Indeed, the lessons contained here, in learning how to live responsibly with forest communities, are transferable to all other areas of human interaction with nature. For it is by learning to walk gently on the forest floor that we also learn to soften our ego boundaries and experience the universe as a vibrant living whole. This deep unity experience takes place in Merv Wilkinson's Wildwood forest in Canada and in the shamanic rituals of Peru, and these experiences can have subtle and profound effects on us all. It is in this spirit, and with the vision of a renewed and healthy planet with vigorous wild forests, that this book has been drawn together. It is given with gratitude and hope.

(Editors' note: Some of the material in this article is from the book manuscript *Caring for Home Places* by Alan Drengson, 2007.)

Khutzemateen grizzly bear sanctuary

VICTORIA STEVENS

Autumn Secret

Carolina Read

Orchard, ripe and ready, heave
your bounty, proudly laden
Landscape deva, dancing here
with Autumn's fairest maiden
So sweet your bite, such pips
to seed in me, a fruitful wisdom
I hold your hand and let you lead
me inwards to your kingdom
And there, I find benevolence
a healthfulness of old, where
looking out, I meet your glance –
a smile that's deep and bold
Sweet lady of these meadows
riding riches to the heart
Where bounty lies, in such disguise –
this, the greatest finding!

MARY JANE JESSEN

Red tideman apple tree

Part I

Wild Forests and Perennial Wisdom

Coastal British Columbia, Great Bear Rainforest

Values Deep in the Woods

Holmes Rolston III

In a forest, as on a desert or the tundra, the realities of nature cannot be ignored. Like the sea or the sky, the forest is a kind of archetype of the foundations of the world. Aboriginally, about 60% of Earth's land surface was forested; historically, forests go back three to four hundred million years. Humans evolved in forests and savannas in which they once had adaptive fitness, and classical cultures often remained in evident contact with forests. In modern cultures, the growth of technology has made the forest increasingly a commodity, decreasingly an archetype. That transformation results in profound value puzzlements. What values lie deep in the forest?

The forest primeval

The central goods of the biosphere — hydrologic cycles, photosynthesis, soil fertility, food chains, genetic codes, speciation, reproduction, succession — were in place long before humans arrived. The dynamics and structures organizing the forest do not come out of the human mind; a wild forest is wholly other than civilization. Confronting it I must penetrate

spontaneous life on its own terms. The genius of forestry as a pure science helps us to appreciate the biology, ecology, integrity of the forest primeval. Immersed in a nonhuman frame of reference, foresters know the elements, raw and pure. Applied forestry, making a commodity out of an archetype, is humane and benevolent at risk of prostituting the primeval. The principles reorganizing the managed forest do come out of the human mind. Seeking goods of their kind, humans modify the natural kinds. A domesticated forest, like a caged wolf, is something of a contradiction in terms. There remains what used to be a forest or wolf now reduced to something less. A tract of pine planted for paper pulp is not deep woods. The radical values are gone.

In the forest itself there are no board feet of timber, BTUs, miles or acre feet of water. There are trees rising toward the sky, birds on the wing and beasts on the run, age after age, impelled by a genetic language almost two billion years old. There is struggle and adaptive fitness, energy and evolution inventing fertility and prowess. There is cellulose and photosynthesis, succession and speciation, muscle and fat, smell and appetite, law and form, structure and process. There is light and dark, life and death, the mystery of existence.

Life support value

A forest is objectively a community. Only subjectively, with human preferences projected onto it, does it become a commodity. *Forest products* are secondarily lumber, turpentine, cellophane; the forest *produces* primarily aspen, ferns, squirrels, mushrooms. This life is never self-contained but incessantly ingests and eliminates its environment. Trees must photosynthesize and coyotes must eat. The flora, like the fauna, make resources of soil, air, water, nutrients.

Many species have found a home in the forest ecosystem, life-supporting niches into which they are well fitted. This objective satisfaction (= support) of life occurs with or without our human experiences. That the forest is able on occasion to satisfy human preferences seems a spin-off from its being valuable — able to satisfy organic needs — on its own.

Endangered species/ endangered ecosystem values

There can no longer be found about 500 faunal species and subspecies that have become extinct in the United States since 1600, and only rarely found another 500 that are (officially or unofficially) threatened and endangered. Hardly a stretch of forest in the nation is unimpoverished of its native species — especially those at the top of trophic pyramids such as otters and peregrine falcons. We have only scraps of undisturbed once-common ecosystems such as hemlock forests, and no chestnut forests at all. Acid rain is impoverishing the Adirondacks and the Great Smokies. An area of tropical rainforests the size of West Virginia is being destroyed annually.

All this ought not to be. Rather, forests ought to be optimally rich in native fauna and flora, in community types, and some forest ecosystems intact enough to support grizzly bears, wolverines, red cockaded woodpeckers, Chapman's rhododendron. What the forest produces is individuals, but at a deeper level what the forest has produced is species and ecosystems. Extinction shuts down forever lifelines that flowed over the continental landscape long before humans arrived and that might, apart from us — or together with us, were we more sensitive — continue for millennia henceforth.

Natural history value

A pristine forest is a historical museum that, unlike cultural museums, continues to be what it was, a living landscape. A visit there contributes to the human sense of duration, antiquity, continuity and our own late-coming novelty. The forest — we first may think — is prehistoric and timeless; world history begins with armies and kings. The perceptive forest visitor knows better and realizes the centuries-long forest successions, the age of sequoias or great oaks; she or he sees erosional, orogenic and geomorphic processes in rock strata, canyon walls, glacial moraines. The Carboniferous Forests were giant club mosses and horsetails; the Jurassic Forests were gymnosperms — conifers, cycads, ginkgoes, seed ferns. A forest today is yesterday being transformed into tomorrow.

Each forest is unique. Forest types exist only in forestry textbooks; what exists in the world is Mount Monadnock, Tallulah Gorge with its unique colonies of Trillium persistens, Mobley Hollow or Sinking Creek. Forests with their proper named features and locales — Grandfather Mountain or Chattahoochee National Forest — always exist specifically, never abstractly. When visited by persons with their proper names, the encounter is valued because it yields distinctive, never-repeated stories — the biography of John Muir in the Sierras or one's vacation hiking the Appalachian Trail.

Scientific study value

At least half of what there is to be known about forests remains undiscovered. Successive levels of biological organization have properties that cannot be predicted from simpler levels, and the least known level of organization is that of the *landscape ecology*. Do forests inevitably appear, given a suitable moisture and climatic regime? We are not sure why the tree line lies at the elevations it does, or why the balds in the Southern Appalachians are there. We are beginning to suspect that insect outbreaks sometimes convey benefits to a forest, something like those of fires, and of which we were long unaware. How do the nonfruiting mosses get propagated over long distances?

Does diversity increase over time? Stability? Do the species at the top of trophic pyramids rise in complexity? In neural power? All this seems to have happened, but why we do not know. Biologists are divided over whether intraspecific or interspecific competition is a minimal or a major force in evolution. Sizeable natural systems are the likeliest places to settle such debates. To destroy the relict primeval forests is like tearing the last pages out of a book about our past that we hardly yet know how to read.

Aesthetic values

Like clouds, seashores and mountains, forests are never ugly; they are only more or less beautiful; the scale runs from zero upward with no negative domain. Destroyed forests can be ugly — a burned, windthrown, diseased or clearcut forest. But even the ruined forest, regenerating itself, has yet positive aesthetic properties; trees rise to fill the empty place against the sky. A forest is filled with organisms that are marred and ragged — oaks with broken limbs, a crushed violet, the carcass of an elk. But the word *forest* (a grander word than *trees* in the plural) forces retrospect and prospect; it invites holistic categories of interpretation as yesterday's flora and fauna pass into tomorrow. This softens the ugliness and sets it in somber beauty.

One has to appreciate what is not evident. Marvelous things are going on in dead wood, or underground, or in the dark, or microscopically, or slowly over time; they are not scenic, but an appreciation of them is aesthetic. The usefulness of a tree is only half over at its death; an old snag provides nesting cavities, perches, insect larvae, food for birds. The gnarled spruce at the edge of the tundra is not really ugly, not unless endurance and strength are ugly. It is presence and symbol of life perpetually renewed before the winds that blast it.

In the primeval forest humans know the most authentic of wilderness emotions, the sense of the sublime. By contrast, few persons get goose pimples indoors, in art museums or at the city park. We will not be surprised if the quality of such experiences is hard to quantify. Almost by definition, the sublime runs off scale.

Recreation/creation values

The word recreation contains the word creation. Humans go outdoors for the repair of what happens indoors, but they also go outdoors because they seek something greater than can be found indoors — contact with the natural certainties. Forests and sky, rivers and earth, the everlasting hills, the cycling seasons, wildflowers and wildlife — these are superficially just pleasant scenes in which to recreate. They are the timeless natural givens that support everything else.

Those who recreate here value leisure (watching a sunset, listening to loons or to rain) in contrast to work for pay; they value being in a wild world that runs itself and need not be labored over. They value work (climbing, setting up camp) that isn't for pay; an environment with zest, in contrast to a boring or familiar job. They value an escape, if you like, but they value also being drawn to roots. They want to know the weather, protected by minimal enough cover and shelter as to leave rain or sun close at hand. They want to submit to the closing day at dusk, to be roused by the rising sun without benefit of clock. They want to know the passing seasons when migrants return or leaves fall without benefit of calendar. People like to recreate in the woods because they touch base with something missing on baseball diamonds and at bowling alleys — the signature of time and eternity.

Character-building value

It is no accident that many organizations that seek to form character use wildlands — Boy and Girl Scouts, Outward Bound, the National Outdoor Leadership School, church camps. Similar growth occurs in individuals independently of formal organizations. The forest provides a place to sweat, to push oneself more than usual, to be more on the alert, to take calculated risks, to learn the luck of the weather, to lose and find one's way. The forest teaches one to care about his or her physical condition. In the forest one has no status or reputation;

nobody is much or long deceived; nobody much has to be pleased; accomplishment and failure are evident. One is free to be herself or himself, forced to a penetrating sincerity.

It is no accident that forestry as a profession has a powerfully positive image; we do not expect a forester to be a sissy, lazy, complaining, naive, arrogant — certainly not one regularly in the field. Professional life and personal life overlap, and the probabilities are that a seasoned forester is genuine, competent, patient, wary. If, past applied concerns, a forester has an admiring respect for the woods we have yet the more evidence of character.

Nonhuman intrinsic values

Surrounded by politicians and economists, even by foresters at business, one gets lured into thinking that value enters and exits with human preference satisfactions. Surrounded by the forest, a deeper conclusion seems irresistible. The forest is value-laden. Trees use water and sunshine; insects resourcefully tap the energy fixed by photosynthesis; warblers search out insect protein; falcons search for warblers. Organisms use other organisms and abiotic resources instrumentally.

Continuing this deeper logic, organisms value the resources they use instrumentally because they value something intrinsically and without further contributory reference: their own lives. No warbler eats insects in order to become food for a falcon; the warbler defends her own life as an end in itself and makes more warblers as she can. A warbler is not *for* anything else; a warbler is for herself. From the perspective of a warbler, being a warbler is a good thing.

Biological conservation is not something that originates in the human mind, modeled by FORPLAN programs or written into Acts of Congress. Biological conservation is innate as every organism conserves, values its life. Nonconservation is death. From this more objective viewpoint, there is something subjective and naive (however sophisticated one's technology) about living in a reference frame where one species takes itself as absolute and values every thing else relative to its utility.

True, warblers take a warbler-centric point of view; spruce push only to make more spruce. But no nonhuman organism has the cognitive power, much less the conscience, to lift itself outside its own sector and evaluate the whole. Humans are the only species who can see the forest for what it is in itself, objectively, a tapestry of interwoven values. Forestry ought to be one profession that gets rescued from this beguiling anthropocentrism through its daily contact with the primeval givens.

Religious value

"The groves were God's first temples."[1] Trees pierce the sky like cathedral spires. Light filters down as through stained glass. In common with churches, forests (as do sea and sky) invite transcending the human world and experiencing a comprehensive, embracing realm. Forests can serve as a more provocative, perennial sign of this than many of the traditional, often outworn, symbols devised by the churches. Mountaintop experiences, a howling storm, a quiet snowfall, solitude in a sequoia grove, an overflight of honking geese — these generate experiences of "a motion and spirit, that impels ... and rolls through all things."[2]

Being among the archetypes, the forest is about as near to ultimacy as we can come in phenomenal experience. I become astonished that the forest should be there, spontaneously generated. There are no forests on Mars or Saturn; none elsewhere in our solar system, perhaps none in our galaxy. But Earth's forests are indisputably here. There is more operational organization, more genetic history in a handful of forest humus than in the rest of the universe, so far as we know. How so? Why? A forest wilderness elicits cosmic questions.

Deep values

Such values are, it is commonly said, *soft* beside the *hard* values of commerce. They are vague, subjective, impossible to quantify or demonstrate. Perhaps. But what is really meant is that such values lie deep. The forest is where the *roots* are, where life rises from the ground. A wild forest is, after all, something objectively there. Beside it, culture with its artifacts is a tissue of subjective preference satisfactions. Money, often thought the hardest of values, is nothing in the wilderness. A dollar bill has value only intersubjectively; any who doubt this ought to try to spend one in the woods. Dollar values have in the forest (and therefore in pure forestry) no significance at all.

What is objectively significant? The phenomenon of forests is so widespread, persistent and diverse, appearing almost wherever moisture and climatic conditions permit it, that forests cannot be accidents or anomalies but rather must be a characteristic, systemic expression of the creative process. Forests are primarily an objective sign of the ultimate sources, and only secondarily do they become managed resources. The measure with which forestry can be profound is the depth of this conviction.

Hardwood forest in fall

VICTORIA STEVENS

The Place and the Story

Ralph Metzner

Ecopsychology and bioregionalism are two fields of the emerging new ecological worldviews. Both are concerned with revisioning our understanding of human identity in relationship to place, to ecosystem and to nature. Traditional people had a much closer relationship to place. We need to learn to understand ourselves in relationship to a place, and to the story of that place.

Ecopsychology may be defined as the expansion and revisioning of psychology to take the ecological context of human life into account.[1] It is *not* a variation of environmental psychology, which deals mostly with the impact of institutional environments on psychological states. It offers a critique of all existing schools of psychology — including the psychodynamic, object relations, cognitive, behaviorist, humanistic and transpersonal — for focusing their research solely on the intrapsychic, interpersonal and social dimensions of human life and ignoring the ecological foundation. The most basic facts of our existence on this Earth — that we live in these particular kinds of ecosystems, in biotic communities with these kinds of species of animals and plants, in these particular kinds of geographic and climatic surroundings — appears to be irrelevant to our psychology. Yet our own personal experiences — as well as common sense — contradict this self-imposed limitation.

In that regard, ecopsychology parallels similar revisionings taking place in other knowledge disciplines: philosophy is being challenged by environmental ethics and deep ecology;[2] economics by green or ecological economics;[3] religion and theology by the concept of creation spirituality and other ecotheological formulations[4] and new ecological perspectives are emerging in sociology and history.[5] All of these foundational revisions may be seen as part of an emerging ecological or systems worldview, a worldview that can also be called ecological post-modernism.[6]

Underlying these fundamental revisionings of our systems of knowledge is a major paradigm shift in the natural sciences, a shift from physics to ecology and evolution as the foundational or model science.[7] Ecology has been called the *subversive science* because it deals with systemic interrelationships and is therefore in essence transdisciplinary and subversive of academic specialization. Ecological concepts are ideally suited for helping the knowledge disciplines transcend their specialized blinders and consider the wider contexts of ecosystem and Gaia.

Bioregionalism is one of four socio-philosophical movements that could be characterized as *radical ecology* movements, the other three being deep ecology, ecofeminism and social ecology (with socialist ecology a possible fifth). These movements are radical, and even revolutionary, in that they are not limited to advocating conservation or anti-pollution legislation. They challenge the very foundations of the modernist industrial worldview, its most cherished value systems and deeply engrained attitudes and habits of thought. The focus of the deep ecology critique is what is called *anthropocentrism,* but can more accurately be described as a humanist superiority complex. The ecofeminist diagnosis of our eco-cultural malaise is that it is based on patriarchal *androcentrism,* rather than anthropocentrism. The social ecology movement critiques all social structures of hierarchy and domination, whether toward ethnic groups, the poor, women or nature. For socialist ecologists, the crucial diagnosis is via the analysis of capitalist class oppression, which includes the domination and exploitation of nature.[8]

Bioregionalism offers a radical critique of the conventional approach to *place,* revolving around the idea of ownership of land and the attendant right to develop and exploit. Political control over the ecology and economy of local regions rests with the nation-state government, which is generally allied with and supportive of the interests of large industrial corporations. The bioregional approach advocates replacing the man-made, historically arbitrary political boundaries of nations, states and counties. It suggests instead using natural ecosystem features — such as watersheds, mountain ranges and entire biotic communities (human and non-human) — as the defining features of a given region. The primary values, from a bioregional perspective, are not *property rights* and *development,* but preserving of the integrity of the regional ecosystem and maximizing economic self-sufficiency within the region. Political control would thus rest with the community of people actually living in the region: this is the concept of *reinhabitation.*[9]

The bioregional movement, like the other radical ecology movements, contains within it a challenge to change our perception and understanding of the human role in the natural world. It encourages us to become aware of native plants and animals in the region where we live so we can feel and experience our actual place in the natural order. It encourages us to learn about the historical and present-day indigenous peoples of that region and how they sustained themselves before the arrival of European culture with its industry and technology. Bioregionalism thus forges an explicit connection and solidarity with existing native peoples, their cultures and their struggle for autonomy. These cultures are clearly bioregional in their explicit sense of rootedness in the land, and have been gently offering a radical critique of Eurocentric arrogance ever since the time of Columbus and the Conquest.[10]

Bioregionalism also involves something like a consciousness-raising practice or, we might say, an ecopsychological practice. Such a practice can affect our sense of identity, our self-image. By creating bioregional maps that depict watersheds, rivers, forests and mountain ranges rather than roads and cities, we come to a renewed appreciation of the ecological complexity of the place we inhabit. There is a bioregional self-questionnaire that tests our knowledge of the place where we live. My favorite consciousness-expanding question on it is: "could you direct someone to the house you live in without using any human-made buildings or signs?" When I first attempted to do this it led me to notice much more of the landscape through which I was driving mindlessly every day.

Another principal question is whether you can identify the four directions in the place where you live or where you are. This is reminiscent of the Native American practice (also found in other parts of the world) of beginning every meeting, whether political council or religious ceremony, with a prayer in the four directions. What better way to come into communion with the natural energies and features of a place or region, than by tuning in to the four directions? Here in California, for example, it is hard to escape the dominant presence of the Pacific Ocean in the West even when you can't see it.

The native practice of aligning ourselves with the four directions coincides with the bioregional practice of attaining a deeper sense of the place. It reminds us of ancient, pre-Christian European concepts of the spirit of place, the *genius loci*. Surely the spirit of a place is constituted by the whole system of interdependent relations in the bioregion. The biotic community is also a spiritual community — if we approach it from the intuitive, perceptual, subjective standpoint and do not confine our observations to those that can be quantified.

In doing so, we are back in the realm of polytheistic animism, a worldview in which all of nature is respected as imbued with conscious intelligence. This was the religion of our ancestors in the ancient world, prior to the ascendancy of transcendental monotheism. William Blake described the suppression of polytheistic animism in his visionary prose poem *The Marriage of Heaven and Hell.*

The ancient Poets animated all sensible objects with Gods and Geniuses, calling them by the names and adorning them with the properties of woods, rivers, mountains, lakes, cities, nations, and whatever their enlarged & numerous senses could perceive.

And particularly they studied the genius of each city & country, placing it under its mental deity;

Till a system was formed, which some took advantage of, & enslaved the vulgar by attempting to realize or abstract mental deities from their objects: thus began Priesthood; Choosing forms of worship from poetic tales.

And at length they pronounc'd that the Gods had order'd such things.[11]

Here we have a convergence of the ancient and indigenous spirit of place with ecological consciousness and a bioregional orientation. We also see how understanding the story of our religious beliefs can help us gain fresh perspective.

We can now use the combined perspectives of bioregionalism and ecopsychology to come to a deeper understanding of the nature and meaning of *place*. What is a place, and how does it relate to and differ from the concept of space? And, since time and space are the fundamental organizing categories of our knowledge of the external world, how does *time* relate to space and to place?

The koan or question I would like to pose is: *What is related to time, the way place is related to space?*

As space is to place

A place is a localized, particular region, whereas space is abstract and infinite. A place can be defined and delimited, mapped and described. In the unfathomable vastness of macrocosmic space, a galaxy, a solar system, a planet are localized, identifiable places. On the continental landmasses of planet Earth, we can map and identify local places of different size: deserts, mountains, lakes, plains, forests, cities, houses, trees, rocks, caves (which open into interior space). Speaking geographically or topographically, a place always has *boundaries.* They may be very definite or fuzzy and indistinct; and certain boundary regions or borderlands are themselves identifiable places, often of special significance. A key aspect of the bioregional agenda is to change the way we define the boundaries of a place.

Places always have a certain *size* or *extension.* A place of particular extent always forms the background for the Cartesian *res extensa,* the extended substance. Surveyors and cartographers measure and map the size of the place with all its details and features. The size of a place may be large, medium or small. From the perspective of size, we could say the bioregion is intermediate between the global and the local. If we are to think globally and act locally, should we perhaps learn to feel bioregionally?

There is another kind of space, less abstract, more psychological or psychic. For example, an individual may say to a partner "I need more space in this relationship." Or we may feel our personal space intruded upon in a crowded elevator. There is also the psychological notion of an altered state of consciousness, in which one may experience traveling, or being *on a trip* or a journey, traversing a kind of inner landscape. In traditional cultures such experiences are referred to as a shamanic journey or an otherworld journey, which clearly implies that consciousness is regarded as analogous to some kind of terrain or territory. In this interior world, the space of our subjective experience, there are also four directions, in which attention can move: forward and backward, left and right. One may contrast these with the four directions of objective space: East, South, West and North. The two coordinate systems, inner and outer, change in relationship to each other as our orientation changes.

A particular place always has *internal divisions* and structural features in which it resembles and differs from other places in a large variety of ways. These internal features and divisions can also be mapped, described and named. The exception to the principle of internal divisions occurs with the oceans (and to some extent certain deserts). The vast, undifferentiated expanse of oceans is often disorienting to land dwellers such as humans, precisely because we cannot find landmarks or other distinctive structural features. Scientists can map the ocean floor, with its ridges and troughs, and sailors can learn to navigate by the stars and instruments to traverse the ocean. But being at sea is similar to being lost, and even the sailor has to come home from the sea.

Most places, at least on land, also have a *center:* this is the fulcrum or hub around which the events and activities in the place organize themselves. Ayer's Rock is right in the dead center of Australia; the Black Hills of South Dakota are exactly in the middle of North America. Both places have an undeniable magnetic kind of power, and the native people have long regarded them as sacred and performed rituals in these centers. Towns and cities have centers, often marked by a plaza or other public structure, where people tend to congregate for trade and entertainment. In older towns the center of community life is usually marked by a church, cathedral, temple or shrine. In a dwelling, the center of family life is usually the living room, perhaps with a fireplace, or in some dwellings it might be the kitchen and eating area.

A place may also be said to have *inhabitants,* dwellers, those who are *from there.* Both human and non-human dwellers make up the community of that place, whether or not the humans recognize that. Inhabitants might be natives (humans, plants, animals), or immigrants or invaders. Part of the bioregional agenda is to raise consciousness about plants and animals that are native and therefore sustainably adapted to the regional environment. With this comes recognition that non-native plants and animals can sometimes be invasive and destructive to the ecosystem. It might be thought that this approach translates to anti-immigrant policies at the human political level. But it's just the opposite. In the Americas, it is white Europeans and their descendants who were the immigrants and invaders, who have had devastating effects on the land and native peoples. The bioregional philosophy advocates that we should learn from the surviving native people in a given bioregion how to live sustainably and in balance in that area. This is the project of reinhabitation: learning the habits of living

that will enable us to survive sustainably in the *habitat.*

Places have *names.* Names allow us to talk about places, and to talk about the spirits of that place, and about our own relatedness to that named place. In ancient times, the name of a place was related to the spirit of that place, the *genius loci.* As Blake pointed out, our ancestors associated spirits, gods and goddesses with particular places such as "woods, rivers, mountains, lakes, cities, nations." Indeed, the whole planet Earth was the home of the goddess named Gaia or Gaea, from which our words geology and geography are derived. The Sun, the Moon and the planets each were given the names of gods and goddesses.

In indigenous societies such as the First Americans and the Australian Aborigines, great importance attaches to the relatedness of a person to a particular named place. Such a person might introduce themselves by saying: "I am from this place, and my father's family comes from these mountains, and my mother's from this river." It is only after describing in some detail their relationship to that place, that land, that these indigenous people can proceed with the business at hand. In Euro-American society, we are much more likely to introduce ourselves and friends by saying what we *do,* our profession, accomplishments and the like. We don't know where we are from very often. Even if we own a house somewhere, we might not really be inhabiting that place with consciousness or feel at home and rooted there. The Indo-European tribes have always been nomads, wanderers, emigrants and invaders. They invaded Europe, conquering and dominating the aboriginal civilization known as Old Europe thousands of years before they set sail for the so-called New World. It has been aptly said that as the Euro-American descendants of the European invaders and colonizers begin to understand the true story of what happened, perhaps the time for the real discovery of America has now come.

So time is to story

Time, like space, is an abstraction of philosophers and scientists. If we want to localize and identify a particular segment of time, we do so by *telling a story.* "Once upon a time ..." begins the fairy tale. "What happened here before, what took place here?" we ask when we want to get to know a place. "What's your story?" we ask when we want to get to know someone. Or we might say, metaphorically, "where are you coming from, with that attitude or that point of view?" Just as time and space are really a continuum rather than separate categories, so place and story are intimately and mutually related. Wallace Stegner, that great interpreter of the American West, has written: "No place is a place until things that have happened in it are remembered in history, ballads, yarns, legends or monuments."[12]

Thus we study the history and mythology of our ancestors, our people, the places they inhabited and what happened there in order to understand how we have become who we are. Biologists study the evolution of species, the story of life on this planet, how species have adapted to changing environments and habitats. Cosmologists now speak of the Universe Story, the story of cosmic evolution starting with the Big Bang or the Primordial Flaring Forth.[13] As every place is defined by its boundaries, *every story is bounded* by its beginning and ending. Every life story is bounded by a birthing and a dying. Creation myths start with "in the beginning" and end with eschatological visions of the end times.

Just as every place has a certain size or extension that can be measured and mapped, so does every story, every temporal process, every developmental sequence, have a certain *extended duration* that can be measured and recorded using clocks and chronographs. Time on planet Earth is measured by reference to the orbit of the Earth around the Sun and by the rotation of the Earth itself — in other words, by the movements of planetary bodies through space. Some people and cultures have conceptions of time as a cyclical, recurring process, probably based on their perception of the rotations of planets and the recurrence of seasons. Others, impressed by irreversible events such as birthing and dying, have thought of time as a linear vector like a stream, moving ineluctably in one direction only. When Heraclitus said, "We can step into the same river," he was speaking about a place with boundaries; when he added "it is always different water flowing past," he was describing the irreversible stream of temporal process.

There is also a psychic experience of time, just as there is psychic space. In altered states of consciousness such as dreams and visions, time can seem to be shortened or lengthened or seemingly bypassed altogether. Everyone knows when we are excited and stimulated, time passes quickly; when bored or burdened, it crawls at a snail's pace. In near-death experiences and other extreme situations, people may have the experience of being suspended outside of time, of having ample time to make complex decisions even although only seconds may have elapsed in clock time. In the inner worlds of dreaming and shamanic out-of-body journeys, time is different: we can travel instantaneously across the globe, as well as backwards and forwards in time, on the wings of thought and desire.

Like places, stories too have *internal divisions,* structural features and parts. Every developmental sequence, for example in the growth and maturation of animals and plants, has its definite stages. The grand Universe Story contains nested within it innumerable other stories: the story of the galaxy, the story of the solar system, the story of planet Earth, the story of life on Earth, the story of animal and human life, the story of human culture. Continuing the lineage, we then come to the story of our ethnic group, our ancestors and family and our personal story. This personal story too has its subdivisions: the story of my childhood, my youth, my work, my relationships, children and so forth. Every story line or narrative has endless permutations of plot and subplot. Every cyclic process too has its crests and troughs: the seasonal cycle, the sleep-wakefulness cycle, hormonal cycles, the swings of mood between elation and depression and many others.

And stories have *centers,* the core issue or central theme around which the whole story is organized. One central theme in a person's life story is often the mid-life crisis or transition. The central theme in the Darwinian story of evolution is the principle of *natural selection.* When bioregionalists and deep ecology supporters advocate abandoning a homocentric perspective where everything is seen from our hopelessly muddled and arrogant human perspective, they advocate an ecocentric (ecosystem-centered) or biocentric (life-centered) perspective instead. Of course, in one sense we are always and inevitably looking at life and the world from the human-centered perspective — just as dogs have a canocentric and cows a bovicentric point of view. But perhaps this perspective need not remain as fixed as we think. Using empathy and identification,

we can perhaps learn to transcend our homocentric prejudice and understand the life story of another animal from the inside. Certainly this is what numerous myths and legends of native peoples seem to suggest: in ancient times humans and animals could understand each other's language and maybe even marry each other on occasion.

As a place has its inhabitants, so does a story have its characters, actors, heroes and antagonists, role-players and support crews. They are the agents in the dramatic action, performing the story or play as scripted by the laws of nature, the genetic code, the cultural tradition, the family upbringing, the karmic predispositions, the traits of character and temperament, our thoughts and our intentions. According to Rupert Sheldrake's theory of morphogenesis, the laws of nature are really more like *habits* that have developed over time than they are abstract principles existing in a timeless dimension.[14] The forms of the cosmos and nature develop the way they do by resonant similarity to previous forms. Thus organisms of different species inhabit the niches and habitats for which their ancestors have developed the habits of adaptation. The ecological crisis shows us that the human species has learned some extremely maladaptive and destructive habits in relation to the natural environment. The bioregional vision is that humans need to humbly learn reinhabitation — dwelling in a place in a balanced way, with respect for the stories of the other inhabitants.

Places have *names* and so do stories. Indeed, the name of a place is inextricably connected to the story of what took place there. We think of a place, say Egypt or Rome, and myriad images crowd our minds — the images of the history and peoples of those places. The life story of an animal or a plant cannot be told or even imagined separately from the place it inhabits. In the life story of humans too, biography and geography are intimately interwoven. The story of a city-dweller is different in spirit than that of a country-dweller. In medieval times, the difference was thought to be so significant that church-dominated city-dwellers asserted that country-dwellers, pagani or heathens, had no religion. For indigenous people, the name of the place often is the story, as in these lines from a poem by Kim Stafford called "There Are No Names but Stories."

> When the anthropologist asked the Kwakiutl for a map of their coast, they told him stories: Here? Salmon gather. Here? Sea otter camps. Here seal sleep. Here we say body covered with mouths.
>
>   How can a place have a name? A man, a woman may have a name, but they die. We are a story until we die. Then our names are very dangerous. A place is a story happening many times.[15]

Just as particular places each had a deity or genius associated with it, so did the divisions of time. The Babylonian calendar, which the West has inherited, invented the weekly cycle of seven days, each associated with the deity of one of the planets (e.g. Saturday with Saturn, Monday with Moon). The ancient science of astrology was based on the view that the spirit of the time and place of a person's birth can be determined by the pattern of the planetary positions at that moment. The rising or culminating of a given planet at the time of birth symbolically indicated something of that person's character and spirit. For instance, a person born when the planet Mars was rising might have a martial temperament; those born when Saturn was prominent were said to have a disposition to melancholia. During a given era, a whole society may be permeated by a certain mood, or feeling or spirit of the time, the *Zeitgeist.*

Every person's life story begins at a certain moment in time in a particular place; it ends at a certain time, also in a particular place. In the worldview and mythologies of many cultures, the life story is thought of as a journey, to and through a series of places. It might be a hero's journey of transformation, or the mystical path to enlightenment, or an exploration of hidden worlds or the quest for vision in wilderness. The very word *destiny* betrays its metaphoric kinship with the destination of the journey of our life. Ancient traditions tell us that as we come closer to the end of our life, we begin to gather the wisdom of old age, the understanding that comes from having dwelled fully in those places. As T. S. Eliot wrote

> We shall not cease from exploration
> And the end of all our exploring
> Will be to arrive where we started
> And know the place for the first time.[16]

(Editors' note: This original version of this essay was published in *The Trumpeter* 12#3 (summer 1995, pp.119-23) and in *Green Psychology: Transforming our Relationship to the Earth* by Ralph Metzner. Park Street Press, 1999.)

Forests and Sacred Groves

Sarah Laird

Every culture has narratives or beliefs which answer in different ways the fundamental questions about how we came to be, articulate how and where people originated, describe collective transformations undergone by the community and how people should behave towards one another and their environment (Elder and Wong 1994). Forests are the subject of a great deal of myth, legend and lore. Societies most closely entwined with forests tend to regard them with a healthy respect, awe at their splendor and majesty, sometimes dread and fear of the powerful spirits that lurk within them. Ancestors often find their resting places in forests, many wandering in various states of unease and spitefulness.

In European culture, the word *savage* was derived from *silva* meaning a wood, and the progress of humankind was considered to be from the forest to the field. Schama (1995) describes how from Ireland to Bohemia, penitents fled from the temptations of the world into forests, where in "solitude they would deliver themselves to mystic transports or prevail over the ordeals that might come their

way from the demonic powers lurking in the darkness." The "indeterminate, boundless forest" then was a place where the faith of the true believer was put to a severe test. The forests in European culture were also considered to be a more positive site of miracles, the source of great spiritual awakenings and the forest itself was held to be a form of primitive church or temple. The first temples in Europe were forest groves, progressively replaced with temples made of wood and subsequently by churches made of stone. Places of worship — particularly those of Gothic architecture — continue to evoke the forest with their design and proportions (Rival in Posey 1999; Schama 1995; Burch in Posey 1999).

Schama (1995) quotes a poem by Bryant called "A Forest Hymn" which expressed the American, or New World, version of the forest as a form of primitive church or temple.

> The groves were God's first temples.
> Ere man learned
> To hew the shaft, and lay the
> architrave,

And spread the roof above them —
ere he framed
The lofty vault, to gather and roll
back
The sound of anthems; in darkling
wood
Amidst the cool and silence, he knelt
down,
And offered to the Mightiest solemn
thanks
And supplication.

In other regions of the world there also exists a relationship to forests that combines fearful respect and awe at the beauty and mystical source of life held within forests. Buddha would sit alone in the depths of the forest lost in meditation, and it was in the midst of a beautiful forest that he was shown the four great truths (Porteous 1928). In Ghana, beliefs about forests include the belief that they are the home of dwarfs and the domain of the mythical Sasabonsam — a legendary figure responsible for all the woes of humankind and to which mishaps and everything evil are attributed (Abbiw 1990). The Dai people of Yunnan Province, China, believe that the forest is the cradle of human life and that forests are at one with the supernatural realm. They believe that the interrelationship of human beings with their physical environment consists of five major elements: forest, water, land, food and humanity (Pei Shengji in Posey 1999).

In sacred groves are manifested a range of traditions and cultural values of forests. Although they occur throughout the world, sacred groves share many similar features, which are summarized in part by Pei Shengji (Posey 1999) in his reference to the four hundred dragon hills (*lung shan*) in the Yunnan Province of China: " ... a kind of natural conservation area ... a forested hill where the gods reside. All the plants and animals that inhabit the Holy Hills are either companions of the gods or sacred living things in the gods' gardens. In addition .... the spirits of great and revered chieftains go to the Holy Hills to live following their departure from the world of the living."

Sacred groves are specific forest areas imbued with powers beyond those of humans; they are home to mighty spirits that can take or give life. These groves originate from a range of roots and include: sites linked to specific events; sites surrounding temples; burial grounds or cemeteries housing the spirits of ancestors; the homes of protective spirits; the homes of deities from which priests derive their healing powers; homes to a powerful animal or plant species; forest areas that surround natural sacred features such as rivers, rocks, caves and "bottomless" water holes and sites of initiation or ritual (Falconer, Pei, Bharucha, Zoundjihekpon and Dossou-Glehouenou, Pramod Parajuli in Posey 1999; Vartak and Gadgil 1981).

Sacred groves and biological diversity

Access to most sacred forests is restricted by taboos, codes and custom to particular activities and members of a community. Gathering, hunting, woodchopping and cultivation are strictly prohibited in the Holy Hills of China. The Dai people believe that these activities would make the gods angry and bring misfortune and disaster upon the community. A Dai text warns: "The Trees on the Nong mountains (Holy Hills) cannot be cut. In these forests you cannot cut down trees and construct houses. You cannot build houses on the Nong mountains, you must not antagonize the spirits, the gods or Buddha" (Pei Shengji,

Posey 1999). In Maharashtra, India, regulations and religious customs are set down by priests (known as *pujaris or bhagats*) with knowledge of the forest deities, their ties to the surrounding landscape and their influence on the daily lives of the community. Ancient folklore and stories are told which include fairly specific detail on the supernatural penalties that will result should the groves be desecrated, for example by felling trees. However, control over extractive activities in sacred groves varies by village, and in many places a complete ban is not in place. Limited collection of fallen wood, fruit from the forest floor, medicinal plant collection, honey collection, tapping of *Caryota urens* to make an alcoholic beverage and other activities are permitted, if strictly controlled (Bharucha in Posey 1999).

Sacred groves have survived for many hundreds of years and today act as reservoirs of much local biodiversity. The 40 contiguous groves studied by Bharucha (Posey 1999) account, as a whole, for most of the plant species present in the Maharashtra region. The forest structure is also unique, representing the least disturbed islands of old growth. The Holy Hills in China also make a significant contribution to biodiversity conservation on a number of levels: they contribute to the conservation of threatened forest ecosystems; they protect a large number of endemic or relic plant species and the large number of Holy Hills distributed throughout the region form "green islands" or "stepping stones" between larger nature reserves (Pei Shengji in Posey 1999).

Sacred groves as a conservation model

As a result of the high conservation and biodiversity values held in sacred groves, increasing attention is being paid to their potential as a tool and model for biodiversity conservation. For example, in its 1996 *Sacred Sites — Cultural Integrity, Biological Diversity* proposal, UNESCO found that

Sacred groves have served as important reservoirs of biodiversity, preserving unique species of plants, insects and animals. Sacred and taboo associations attached to particular species of trees, forest groves, mountains, rivers, caves and temple sites should therefore continue to play an important role in the protection of particular ecosystems by local people. Particular plant species are often used by traditional healers and priests who have a strong interest in the preservation of such sites and ecosystems. In some regions of the world, beliefs that spirits inhabit relict areas have served to quickly regenerate abandoned swidden plots into mature forest. In other areas, sacred places play a major part in safeguarding critical sites in the hydrological cycle of watershed areas. Furthermore, in a number of instances sacred sites have also been instrumental in preserving the ecological integrity of entire landscapes. For these reasons, sacred sites can help in assessing the potential natural vegetation of degraded ecosystems or ecosystems modified by humans.

Sacred groves have survived in many regions despite tremendous economic pressure on forest resources. In some parts of India, for example, sacred groves have retained high levels of biodiversity and remain largely intact, while government-controlled forest reserves are often in poor condition. Local level control has been vital to the protection of these areas, but economic pressures are mounting, and changing land-use patterns have contributed to a serious depletion of resources and a phenomenal rise in the price of land. This in turn has provided an irresistible incentive for some local people to sell the groves, irrespective of the sentiment that at one time was sufficient to preserve them (Bharucha, Pramod Parajuli in Posey 1999).

Even in cases where local communities are determined to retain sacred groves, they are often as vulnerable to outside political and economic forces as other forest areas. In East Kalimantan, for example, oil palm plantation and logging operations are clearing ancestral (*adat*) forest. The *adat* covers four types of forest: *Sipung Bengkut* (perennial tree gardens which have been developing since 1912), *Sipung Bua* (fruit tree gardens), *Sipung Payo* (swampy areas) and *Sipung Uwe* (rattan gardens). The companies promise in return to encourage "community participation," "the development of sustainable forest management," and "income generating schemes" which are considered "empty and pointless" offers for a priceless ancestral forest that cannot be equated with monetary and material conditions (Enris and Sarmiah in Posey 1999).

Although sacred groves undoubtedly contribute to the conservation of biodiversity, it is questionable whether the complex history and traditions that have created and maintain these areas can be operationalized as a tool or model for further conservation efforts. Conservation is often a side effect of customs that associate or dedicate forest resources to the deities. In the Western Ghats of India, rather than managing resources for future use, communities are instead attempting to benefit

from the protection and goodwill afforded by the deity in return for not disturbing the sanctity of the sacred grove (Bharucha in Posey 1999). This would be a difficult dynamic to reproduce in a conservation program. In Southern Ghana, Falconer (Posey 1999) argues that sacred groves exist as part of a system so complex and variable that a much clearer understanding of the spiritual, mystical and political functions and beliefs of sacred groves is needed before they can be incorporated into conservation programs.

In South India, sacred groves are populated by dead spirits prevented from transforming and hence remaining ghosts forever. Their life force engenders trees to grow wild and gives rise to highly fertile but extremely dangerous sacred groves, which are frightening and highly ambivalent (Rival in Posey 1999). Rival warns against environmentalists' views of sacred groves and trees as sanctuaries of biodiversity, home to benign and protecting deities. The suggestion that the belief systems that have protected these groves should be promoted to encourage the conservation of larger forest areas ignores the fact that — while both environmentalists and local peoples view trees as vital and holding regenerative power — trees in traditional India are not benign protectors: they are frightful, and the power of their life force is extremely dangerous. While important reservoirs of biodiversity, it is unlikely that with the exception of a few areas, the cultural beliefs and management systems that have led to the conservation of sacred groves could easily be incorporated into the Western cultural conservation ethos.

Tree lore and symbolism

Trees are universally powerful symbols, a physical expression of life, growth and vigor to urban, rural and forest dwellers alike. They can symbolize historical continuity and human society. They are often of frightening magnitude, linking earth and heavens, arbiters of life and death, incorporating both male and female aspects and home to both good and bad spirits, including the souls of ancestors. Trees provide protection from harm, cure disease and increase fertility. Trees preside over marriages, are planted at the birth of a child and at burial sites. In some origin myths, the first men and women were made of wood.

The Tree of Life in Mesopotamia and India brings fertility by linking death with life. The birds visiting its branches are the souls of the dead. The cross on which Jesus died grew into a tree on Mount Golgotha. The fig tree opened for Mary to seek shelter for the infant Jesus from the soldiers of Herod. The date palm was the staff of St. Christopher which helped him to carry the weak and small across a raging river. The birch in Scandinavia, larch in Siberia, redwood in California, fig in India and iroko in West Africa are widely revered and respected.

The Cosmic Tree, Tree of Life or *Axis Mundi* features in many of the world's religions. In Amazonia, the World Tree is often ceiba/kapok (*Ceiba pentandra*) or a yuchan (*Chorisia insignis*). The trunks of these tall emergent trees are characteristically bulbous, hollow and spongy, and the wood is rather soft. The ceiba has a life-span of up to 200 years and is arguably the tallest of Amazonian forest trees. It reaches maturity and starts to flower some time between its fortieth and sixtieth year, thus beginning its reproductive cycle at the oldest age people live to in the region. It lives a life corresponding roughly to four Huaorani generations. In Huaorani culture, the Amazon basin was born from the fallen giant ceiba tree (Rival in Posey 1999).

Sacred forest in Japan

ARIYOSHI ICHIRO

Ties to nature manifest themselves most notably in Turkish culture through attitudes to plants in general and trees in particular. After conversion to Islam, the importance of trees grew in local culture because Mohammed compared a good Muslim to a palm tree and declared that planting a tree would be accepted as a substitute for alms. Trees are planted after children are born, when a son is drafted into military service, after a wedding and as a memorial to the dead (Tont in Posey 1999). In one of the oldest collections of Turkish tales which make up the *Book of Dede Korkut,* the unknown poet agonizes over his failure to find a more exalted name for his beloved plant:

> Tree, tree, do not be embarrassed because I call you by that [after all]
>> The doors of Mekka and Medine are made of wood
>> The staff of Moses is also made of wood
>> The bridges spanning over big rivers are also made from you
>> The ships which roam the black seas are also of wood.

The oak tree was worshipped by Romans, Druids, Greeks and Celts as the home of deities. In Europe, fairies were said to make their homes in old oak trees, departing through holes where branches had fallen; it was considered healing to touch the fairy doors with diseased parts (T. Shanley 1997, personal communication). In Scotland in the last century, mistletoe growing on the famous Oak of Errol was bound up with the fortunes of the family Hay, acting as a "sure charm against all glamour and witchery" (Porteous in Posey 1999). Cowley and Evelyn in seventeenth-century England wrote about the oak (as in Schama 1995):

> Our British Druids not with vain intent
>> Or without Providence did the Oak frequent,
>> That Albion did that Tree so much advance
>> Nor superstition was, nor ignorance
>> Those priests divining even then bespoke
>> The Mighty Triumph of the Royal Oak

Conclusion

In forest culture we find the common threads of human experience. Whether the "dangerous and highly fertile" sacred groves of India, the oak tree in Britain, the graveyard forests in Côte d'Ivoire or in the fall of the great *Ceiba pentandra* which created the Amazon Basin: throughout the world we see a shared focus on the origin, force and power of life expressed in trees and in the forest.

Enrichment Forestry at Windhorse Farm

Jim Drescher

Although the name Windhorse was adopted in 1990, the forestry experiment commonly known by that name has been going on here since 1840 when Conrad Wentzell settled in this valley on what is now called Wentzell's Lake. After four generations of careful land management in the Wentzell family, this path of land stewardship was generously pointed out and handed on to Margaret and Jim Drescher in 1990.

Since that time, our understanding of the Acadian Forest has increased as our experience in this place has deepened. Some folks visit here and guess, "This must be 'sustainable' forestry?" Of course, it's far too soon to know about that. The experiment is less than 200 years old, just a blink of the eye in the life of a forest, even for the relatively young (less than 15,000 years) Acadian Forest.[1] All we can say is that the experiment is well under way. On the other hand, in terms of a human life span, the duration is quite extensive; in fact, it is the longest-standing experiment in sustainable forestry in Canada. As one friend puts it, "Windhorse is on the leading edge of something very old."

Forest description

The Windhorse Forest, in the beautiful and peaceful LaHave River watershed, enchants even the most objective visitors as they wander in the brilliant green softness of the forest floor, which comprises several dozen species of mosses and liverworts. The tall mixed-species tree canopy filters the sun and interrupts the rain drops; the clear brooks tumble over rocks in harmony with the melody of bird songs. For many people, the tranquility and natural energy of this place is directly perceived in one's body even before the brain thinks about it. This direct or non-conceptual knowing is a first key to solving the riddle of Windhorse Forest. Before our minds conceptualize how it feels, how it is or how it should be, we have a direct experience that there is nothing missing at all. There is no problem to be fixed and no one to fix it.

Although the forest includes 250 acres, only about 100 acres have been the subject of this project for the entire 168 years. Here are some facts about just that portion:

- In commercial terms, the annual growth increment is approximately 80,000 board feet.
- It has been logged 168 times, once a year since 1840.
- Approximately 7.5 million board feet of timber have been harvested.
- The standing merchantable timber volume is about two million board feet.
- If this 100-acre lot had been clear-cut in 1840, and again in 1890, 1940 and 1990, the total harvest would have been, at most, 5.5 million feet, and the quality of the second, third and fourth harvests would have been much lower than the wood harvested by the annual selection methods. Of course there would be no standing merchantable timber today.

You can do the math.

Guiding questions

Unfortunately, in today's culture of short-term profits, few people have learned to care about how to maximize the yield from a forest over a period of a century and a half. Usually the question asked is, "How can we maximize the return on investment over the next decade or two or — better yet — how can we get as much as possible in the next five weeks?" If we took that attitude about the Windhorse Forest right now, what would we do? Faced with this pervasive short-term economic argument, what logic is powerful enough to maintain this Windhorse experiment? What logic might change the course of forestry in Canada? What effect would a truly beneficial long-term forest policy have on Canadian society altogether?

Perhaps we have to look beyond the financial and the quantifiable. Can we be more open-hearted and open-minded? If so, we can begin to experience the forest in its own terms, and we begin to make some important discoveries: If this 100-acre lot had been clearcut every fifty years, it would be sadly deficient in diversity of flora and fauna; the long-lived, shade tolerant Acadian Forest species would be absent; there would be no heavy and dense trees so sought after by woodpeckers and woodworkers. If this 100-acre forest had been clearcut four times in the past 168 years there would no opportunity to see a 500 year-old hemlock, a pine board two feet wide or to bear witness to the harmony and interaction of countless life forms unable to reestablish their complex communities between 50 year rotations. How could these realizations fit into the logic of a Canadian Forest Policy?

At least since 1990, and I suspect long before that, Windhorse Farm has been less about how to make money, or even how to do forestry, than it has been about exploring human nature and the nature of the forested world. We often reflect on the ethical frameworks that motivate our lives and our activities in this world, and we have discovered that this place in the forest is very provocative in that regard.

Ecoforestry: A resource management ethic

Upon arriving here, we plunged into the project, guided by a resource management ethic strongly influenced by Aldo Leopold, a childhood hero from my home ground of Wisconsin. Leopold articulated a land ethic proclaiming, "A thing is right when it tends to preserve the integrity, stability and beauty of the biotic community. It is wrong when it tends otherwise."[2] The question that rose to the top for us was, "How can we make a living in this place while respecting, and not harming, the other life forms that are also trying to make a living here?" In these early days of our tenure, we called our forestry style *ecoforestry*, short for "ecosystem-centered economic forestry." In addition to working in the forest here and setting up a small-scale, labor-intensive sawmilling and wood products manufacturing business, I got involved in Forest Stewardship Council (FSC) Canada, serving on its initial Board of Directors as well as on the Acadian Forest regional standards writing committee. The motivation for all this early activity was a love affair with ecoforestry and a desire to demonstrate its forestry solutions. It was a time of intense learning about views different from my own, and about the virtues and frustrations of consensus decision making. In spite of recent disappointment with the direction of the FSC, Windhorse maintains its FSC certification, both for its woodlands (forest certification) and its manufacturing operation (chain-of-custody certification). In addition, we hold the much stricter regional certification with Nagaya Forest Restoration.

The economics of ecoforestry: wealth

One of the most important results of our engagement with ecoforestry in this experiment has been how we understand forest wealth. This has come out of much reflection on the economic part of ecoforestry. What is wealth from the forest's point of view? How is wealth created? How is it lost? How is it conserved? Early in the analytical process, we realized that wealth, from the forest's point of view, is biological material. The creation of

this wealth is both a cause and a result of a heavy, healthy forest. Key to long-term forest health is the retention of wealth after it has been created. Retention depends on the efficient and flexible functioning of the entire interdependent web of life, which is the forest itself.

Of course, forest wealth is only created at one point, the point of photosynthesis, where sunlight is incident on chlorophyll. After that, it can be redistributed, made more complex and diverse or lost, but it cannot be created. That means that the way to maximize the growth of forest wealth is to maintain a forest structure that optimizes the total surface area of chlorophyll. Interestingly, or perhaps obvious to keen and insightful observers, the natural structure of the Acadian Forest does, in fact, do just that. The species-diverse, tall and multilayered canopy, along with a great variety of ground vegetation, offers tremendous opportunity for the transformation of solar energy to biomass. This is what ecologists call primary productivity and what carbon accountants call sequestration. Conserving that wealth is dependent on the very slow decomposition of huge volumes of dead wood.

From the point of view of prudent long-term forestry economics, one wants to lose as little biomass as possible. Since forestry business usually involves selling biological material (e.g. stumpage, logs, lumber or other wood products), it actually is in the business of trading real wealth — forest wealth — for money. As long as one needs cash to buy what one doesn't make or can't do without (e.g. beer or gasoline), one must give up some wealth to get the cash. Ordinary logic dictates that one should give up as little wealth as possible to get the desired money. That requires maximizing "dollar-to-biomass" ratios for all wood products removed from the woodlands.

One of the slogans at Windhorse Farm is "Never sell cheap biomass," and this means we don't sell pulpwood, sawdust, firewood, logs or low-quality lumber. One might object to this, saying, "Don't you think making paper is important?" Actually we wouldn't have any reticence to sell pulpwood if the price were about 10 times higher than it is now, but at current prices we would have to give up a tremendous amount of forest wealth to get a little money, which is clearly not a good deal either for us or for the forest. We are continually working to add dollar value to, and subtract wood volume from, all products sold from Windhorse Farm. Needless to say, from this point of view practices such as burning brush or otherwise *cleaning up* the woodlot are like taking hundred dollar bills out of your bank account and burning them in your fireplace to heat your house.

Old forest

VICTORIA STEVENS

The economics of ecoforestry: Carbon budgets

Another critically important aspect of the economic side of ecoforestry, which is now talked about even in the mainstream press, is the carbon cycle. Carbon sequestration is moving carbon from a gaseous state (CO_2) into a solid state (complex organic carbon compounds) by means of photosynthesis in green plants. Remember that from the forest's point of view, this is the point at which wealth is created. Similarly, from the point of view of carbon budgets, this is *income*. After being sequestered, the carbon tied up in biomass could be thought of as in the bank or in the so-called *carbon sink*. In turn, as biomass is burned or slowly decomposes, the solid carbon compounds are transformed back into CO_2. This loss of wealth is the expense side of the carbon accounting statement.

Life-threatening climate change is largely a consequence of the accumulated deficit in the global carbon accounts: in other words more CO_2 being lost into the atmosphere than CO_2 being tied up in green plants. So, for both forest health and climate stability, it is advantageous to increase carbon sequestration and slow the flow of carbon through the carbon sink, thus reducing the loss of CO_2 into the air. The locking up of vegetation (later turned into coal, oil and gas) in the Carboniferous Period, roughly 300 million years ago, was a terrific way to reduce *expenses.* That provokes the question, "What forestry practices are most likely to do this today?" This is a critical question, just as important as the more common query about how to maximize carbon sequestration. At Windhorse Farm, we are actively investigating both these questions. What have we found?

First, maximizing carbon sequestration over the long-term involves determining what forest composition and structure will maintain the greatest surface area of chlorophyll over the long term. It just so happens that the natural Acadian Forest came up with the optimum solution on its own over its 15,000 year evolution. Good forest management will maintain that natural composition and structure.

Second, the best method for reducing the loss of carbon as CO_2 is to maintain the forest that holds the greatest amount of carbon in the sink at any one time. It should be no surprise that this is the same composition and structure that maximizes sequestration and is the same thing that maximizes biodiversity. Another way to slow the flow through the sink is to turn harvested wood into products that have a long lifespan, e.g. fine furniture or musical instruments. The possibility having perhaps the greatest promise is the small-scale, low-temperature production of charcoal for agricultural fertilizer. In addition to tying up carbon, this could greatly reduce the use of petroleum-based fertilizers, further reducing carbon *losses* by reducing the use of oil.

What I am trying to point out in this brief discussion is that a clear understanding of the economics of ecoforestry is essential if one is to engage effectively in the public discussion of forest policy.

Restoration forestry: An environmentalist ethic

While our economic ecoforestry enquiry at Windhorse Farm was quite fruitful in terms of the insights it inspired, we found the term ecoforestry gradually lost its usefulness in the same way *sustainability, stakeholder* and *model forest* lost much of their meaning when they came to be used widely as promotional rather than technical terms. When this erosion became apparent to us, we started focusing on one aspect of ecoforestry which we always considered primary — forest restoration.

An historical aside, not unrelated to the Windhorse Forestry experiment, is that one of the two fundamental themes of the Acadian Forest Regional FSC Standard, as endorsed by FSC Canada and the International FSC Board, was restoration of the pre-contact (before the European invasion a few hundred years ago) Acadian Forest. Along with the other dominant theme (full cost accounting) in the originally-endorsed regional standard, forest restoration has recently been expunged. This is unfortunate from the point of view of climate change as well as forest health and community well-being. This is part of a long and fascinating story about the development of regional FSC standards, which has been recounted in detail elsewhere. It is mentioned briefly here because of the mutually beneficial exchange of insights and experience between Windhorse and the regional FSC standards-writing committee.

The next phase of thinking in the Windhorse experiment was "Forest Restoration and Restoration Forestry." In other words, our question became, "How can forestry practices be used to accelerate the natural processes of restoration of indigenous ecological diversity?" In certain respects, this represented an ethical shift from "How can I make money without doing too much damage?" (a resource management ethical framework) to "How can I use forestry methods to restore the natural Acadian Forest?" (a forest environmentalist ethical framework).

Interestingly, what we actually did in the forest didn't change much as our view shifted, however, what we removed from the forest became more clearly a by-product of our restoration work, and the purpose of our work came into clear focus: to restore the fully functioning mature Acadian Forest that existed here before European contact. We examined the few remaining vestiges of old growth on sites similar to ours and tried to hone our understanding of the forest parameters that best embodied total ecological diversity.

This brief chapter cannot accommodate a complete description of this restoration forestry philosophy, but here is its essence:

The forest, itself, is the primary product. The forest is an infinitely complex interdependent web of life, which is well described in terms of its ecological diversity. The practice is to restore and protect the total indigenous ecological diversity, which has four components: species diversity, genetic diversity, structural diversity and age/size diversity of trees.

Restoration forestry: Five management principles

In order to make forest restoration simple enough to be manageable, we had to find a few diagnostic parameters. Structural diversity, the distribution of biomass above and below the ground, turns out to be more directly correlated than the other three components with total ecological diversity. Within structural diversity the three most important parameters are canopy height, canopy closure and dead wood. If we add in species diversity and connectivity (unobstructed pathways for travel of animals and spread of plants and other organisms) we have only five things to think about and manage for. These five have become the Windhorse management principles.

Maximize canopy height. The thicker the forest layer, from the tops of the tallest trees to the depth of the deepest roots, the more opportunity there is for abundance and diversity of life. Reducing the height of the canopy, for example by cutting the tallest trees, reduces existing ecological niches.

Keep canopy closure, a measure of how much sunlight is intercepted before it can reach the ground, to the natural range in the mature Acadian Forest. The natural canopy closure, 65% – 80% closed, has evolved in synchronization with the existing biodiversity. Abruptly changing it will automatically reduce the diversity.

Maintain volumes and distribution of dead wood very close to those found in the old-growth reference points. Our slogan is "Dead wood is the life of the forest." Almost half the animals in the Acadian Forest live in or on or from dead wood. Reducing the volumes or changing the natural distribution of dead wood degrades the habitat for much of forest life.

Don't do anything to reduce species diversity. For example, don't harvest or disturb relatively rare species, even within very small areas.

Maintain connectivity, or enhance it where it has been diminished. Corridors of connectivity are the pathways along which animals and plants travel and disperse. Allowing ecosystems to become fragmented (the opposite of connected), at any scale, is the beginning of ecological collapse.

Forestry methods based on these restoration principles are very doable and very effective. We teach the many details of how to implement these management principles at Windhorse Farm. The *restoration* hypothesis is that on all land where these methods are practiced carefully and effectively, there will be a steady movement toward a more naturally diverse, structurally mature, fully functioning Acadian Forest.

Enrichment forestry: A buddhist ethic

A few years ago, I was in the midst of writing a book on Forest Restoration and Restoration Forestry with Tegan Wong, a land stewardship colleague from New Brunswick. We were putting all the chapters together when both of us, independently, recognized our discomfort with something we couldn't really put our minds on. After a period of reflection, we came to similar realizations: the whole restoration thesis was based on the dynamic of guilt and pride — guilt that we humans had messed things up in the first place, and pride that we thought we could fix the problems we had created. This is a classic environmentalist syndrome: "We are guilty of having created a problem and now we are obligated to fix it." Tegan and I reflected on whether we really

wanted to base our thesis on these principles rather than on the more fundamental truth of "no problem." In other words, were there other principles more appropriate to our understanding and our intent? From that point on we started thinking and talking less about restoration. I also began to reflect on the moralism in Aldo Leopold's land management ethic as a root of this environmentalist syndrome.

What? Is someone finding fault with Leopold's Land Ethic? That's blasphemous! How could this sensible moral approach inhibit us as environmentalists in our aspiration to benefit this world? Well, it encourages the divide between camps of right and wrong and perpetuates the battle between the forces of good and the forces of evil. By finding an enemy in other, it tends to obscure the unaligned basic goodness of each human being and the underlying sacredness of the phenomenal world. In other words, moralism does little to dissolve the aggression that lies at the heart of all the suffering which was the root cause of environmental degradation itself. In fact, dividing the world into the good and bad can even become a further cause of painful ecosystem unraveling by solidifying conflicting opinions and oppositional behavior.

Friends poked a bit at this change of view, asking, "Now what are you going to call this forestry you do here?" Of course, before knowing what to call it, we had to reexamine the philosophy or *view*. I felt a bit like a serial divorcee, first becoming separated from ecoforestry, then undergoing the split-up with restoration. What is the alternative to seeing a problem in the situation, and setting out to fix it? Is it seeing clearly that there is no problem — that is, no *fundamental* problem? This is the principle of "Nothing Missing". If one's perception is not ambushed by seeing a problem, then it can experience the fundamental richness that underlies the so-called problem.

What is required, then, of our forestry practices is to reveal or uncover that underlying health, beauty and wealth *within our own minds* and within the forest itself. In other words, what appeared as a problem was, in fact, mere confusion about the fundamental reality. Rather than fixing a problem, the challenge became one of unwrapping our direct experience of the undeniable *isness* or *sacredness* of the forest. The forest is as it is, and our feelings or opinions about it exist only within our own habitual ways of seeing. Therefore, the primary forest practices at Windhorse Farm have become ones that tend to connect us with the fundamental reality, which is experienced before we resort to judging and conceptualizing. This is the view of what we have come to call *Enrichment Forestry*.

Windhorse forest practices

So the view continues to evolve, but it is interesting to note what, in addition to the fundamental richness of the forest, hasn't changed. Our actual forestry practices, on the ground, have remained pretty consistent even while their articulated logic, in terms of the

Horses working, Windhorse Farm

WINDHORSE FARM

view, has evolved somewhat. The following are examples of practices consistent with all three of the aforementioned views.

- Select trees for harvest based on which tree in a crowd is the slowest growing (maximize wealth creation).
- Never cut the tallest trees (increase canopy height).
- Don't open things up too much (maintain natural canopy closure).
- Don't cut trees of species underrepresented in that particular stand (conserve species diversity).
- Don't cut dead trees or trees that have fallen naturally (respect dead wood as the life of the forest).
- Don't harvest trees that have a relatively low dollar-to-biomass ratio, and move to the log brow only the most commercially valuable parts of the trees that are cut (conserve the wealth).
- Girdle many low dollar-to-biomass trees each year (increase the standing dead volume).
- Build and maintain slabwood/sawdust roads and slab walls (avoid fragmentation and enhance connectivity).

In fact, at a quick glance it seems that nothing on the ground has changed.[3] Care and restraint still appear to be dominant themes, as they have been since the days of Conrad Wentzell. So was all this thinking about the view just useless philosophizing?

Perhaps it was; on the other hand, maybe it brought some useful clarification, a look beyond our conceptual blinders. Has this clarification led us to believe that the Windhorse forestry practices should be modified? At this point it seems that they don't have to change very much — not on the ground, at least. The important changes are in how we understand and experience mind and nature. That will require diligent study, keen observation, insightful analysis, resourceful generosity and deep stillness practice. This stillness practice allows the body, breath and mind to rest peacefully within the depth of natural forest energy. These additional practices that attend this view of *nothing missing* involve foresters, woodlot owners and other landscape lovers hanging out in the forest a lot more: studying, observing, reflecting, working and investing lots of time doing as close to nothing as possible. Should these be called forestry practices or forest practices? Or are they simply the practices of being fully human in the forest?

What is the result of this path of stillness practice? Since much of the experience is non-conceptual (before we think about it and before we speak about it), it is impossible to express precisely what it is, but it is how ordinary people can rediscover an intimate heart connection with the self-existing energies of *forest mind*. When we make ourselves available, simultaneously wakeful and relaxed, we begin to live in that place of nothing missing, where there is no fundamental problem. The process of uncovering the underlying richness of a situation is much more delightful than working to make a living or working to fix a problem, even if the forestry techniques may look the same from the outside.

We learned the view of *nothing missing* and the practice of stillness from the Buddhist tradition. So in this Windhorse forestry experiment we have moved from a resource management ethic to an environmentalist ethic to a Buddhist ethic. Of course, these ethical frameworks are not mutually exclusive. In fact, there is some of the other two in each of the others, and although our journey through these different views has been presented here as linear, that is an oversimplification. Sometimes it is circular, and increased awareness is one result of thinking in circles, not coming to a conclusion. Although this may sound unscientific, inefficient or even wishy-washy, this patient curiosity is what allows surprising insights to arise. Our experience at Windhorse Farm has been a journey of increasing relaxation and delight, although certainly not without its gritty challenges occasioned by the habitual unwillingness to let go of preconceptions and self-importance.

Evaluation of the experiment: The five filters analysis

This forestry experiment has evolved over the years and has served to clarify some forestry principles. We think it has more to offer in the future, but how can we really know whether we are learning anything, getting anywhere or if this makes any sense at all? Any experiment needs to be periodically evaluated to ascertain its ongoing usefulness and benefit. Recognizing this, we have developed an evaluation method we call the *Five Filters Analytical Process,* a fancy name for a common sense technique. In working through this process, we ask questions relevant to each of five filters (ecological, social, economic, spiritual and magical). Although this can be a subtle and complex enquiry, a few basic questions can be asked quite simply. The following are examples drawn from a much more extensive list.

- Ecological Filter: Are we causing harm to the non-human beings in this place or elsewhere? Is there tangible enrichment of the lives of other beings?

- Social Filter: Does this experiment contribute to community harmony or to its opposites — divisiveness, animosity and territoriality?
- Economic Filter: Does the forestry practiced here tend to build economic stability for this community (human and non-human) or does it pose undue hardships or financial risks that are likely to destabilize the local economy? Does it reflect ecological economics rather than market economics?[4]
- Spiritual Filter: Can we notice an increase in kindness, compassion and awareness among the humans involved in this experiment? Alternatively, do we see an increase in covetousness, aggression and ignorance?
- Magical Filter: Do the human beings here seem to be more connected to the peacefulness as well as the hair-on-end zing of forest energy, experiencing each tree and rock as alive and distinct, or do they tend to be isolated, dulled out and cut off from that direct knowing or non-conceptual experience of forest mind?

Conclusion

While our evaluation is incomplete and our questions still alive, today we wonder where this investigation and journey may take us. We really don't know, but it does seem possible that more will be revealed regarding how this experiment might bring benefit to human and non-human beings. The question we first posed when we came here remains unanswered. "Can the forestry view and practices in Canada be transformed in ways that result in less harm and more benefit?" As a result of our work at Windhorse, our question is now more focused, "What do the contemplative and meditative practices of this Windhorse experiment have to offer to individuals, communities and our Canadian forestry culture?" and "How can Enrichment Forestry, and recognition of the reality of Nothing Missing, contribute to the creation of a healthy and peaceful society altogether?"

One thing can be said for sure: each day's walk in the forest is a fresh and enriching experience. Never have I taken the same route, returned to the same place or perceived the same light, smells or orchestration of sounds as I did the day before. Somehow the depth of this forest mind keeps beckoning, enticing and inviting us deeper into the experience of nothing missing.

So, for all of us engaged in this journey, the old adage holds true: the more we learn, the less we know. As foresters and land stewards, this is our constant reminder to be very cautious in our harvesting practices and other activities on the land. While we have no final conclusions to offer to other land stewardship practitioners, our aspiration is that this Windhorse forestry experiment, begun by Conrad Wentzell 168 years ago, may continue to offer insights and inspiration for many generations to come. May many beings benefit, and may the natural richness and energy of forest communities provide support for a healthy and harmonious society.

Ecoforestry — Doing the Right Things

Ray Travers

What is needed on our part is the capacity for listening to what the Earth is telling us.

— Thomas Berry

Conventional forestry is driven by efficiency — doing things right. That is why this kind of management results in simplification and uniformity of the forest and why its advocates have favored conversion of ecologically diverse forests into conveyer belt plantations. Ecoforesters have a different view. Ecoforesters are driven by effectiveness — doing the right things — actions which flow from a clear vision and sound judgment.

This critical distinction between efficiency and effectiveness was made famous by North America's leading management guru, Peter Drucker, is his 1967 book *The Effective Executive.*[1] Ecoforesters want effective, fully functioning natural processes which capture energy, which cycle water and nutrients in an ecologically diverse forest. To be efficient, one simply minimizes the cost of whatever is being done. This has survival value in a competitive economy, which explains why some resource managers have become obsessed with it. Unfortunately, this obsession can blind forest managers to the larger issue of effectiveness, which means doing only those things which produce results worth having.

The gospel of efficiency was widespread in many of the forestry schools in the 1900s. Any forestry student opening a textbook in the 1950s and 1960s would find information on how to convert old-growth stands into even-aged regulated forests, how to prevent and suppress fire, create habitat for early successional game species and how to calculate the financial rotation of a forest. In those days, the forester could take up a job in the woods, plan for a sustained yield of timber to maximize the annual allowable cut, reduce the obvious negative impacts of logging and feel secure in the knowledge he had exercised his professional duty.

The single most common theme of ecoforestry is complexity — moving forestry from a worldview of simplified concepts involving uniformity and predictability into complex concepts of ecological and human systems. The discovery and recognition of complexity, through the study of ecological principles and processes, is providing dramatic new insights into how forests actually work. For example, instead of seeing forest insects and fungi as pests and pathogens, it is now realized that these organisms are fundamentally important to maintaining the health, diversity and productivity of the forest. As one writer said, "Microbes are the little things that run the world!" Ecoforestry's challenge is to understand the interdependencies of these species and to move away from simply trying to eradicate them to trying instead to manage a delicate balance between their positive and negative characteristics.

We now know that a forest is not just an assemblage of trees, plant and animals. Like friendship between two people, it is a complex of interactions involving the past, present and future and also involving others. Interactions are at the source of all the forest's processes, creating the qualities we value: ecological integrity, stability and beauty.

One of the images of conventional forestry was that clearcutting mimics fire. Now we know that fire and other natural disturbances do not destroy everything in a forest. Foresters previously assumed the new forest was established by seeds and other organisms from the surrounding area filling the new openings. We now know natural disturbances leave behind a wide array of biological legacies which provide strong linkages between old and new forest ecosystems.

Gaining an appreciation of ecosystem complexity and self-organization, and then managing for wholeness rather than for efficiency of individual parts, places ecoforestry in a much broader social movement, embracing systems thinking which has become well established in physics, education, business and medicine. The power of systems thinking is that it opens up new possibilities for creativity, social and economic opportunity.

In the past, forestry consigned social issues and related matters outside efficiency and production to a secondary role — an approach that in 1993 resulted in global controversies like Clayoquot Sound and shook the foundations of forest management in BC and elsewhere.[2]

This is why forestry has changed. It can no longer be built on biology and technical science alone. Forestry now will only succeed to the degree that it can integrate complex ecological, economic and social concepts and methods into forest policy and practice.

Doing the right things has enormous positive implications for the current move towards results-based forest management in BC.[3] It means working within the limits of natural patterns and processes, stabilizing human needs within the carrying capacity of the forest and living at nature's pace. Doing the right things involves a compelling vision of the future, making sound judgments which incrementally maintain and enhance the health, productivity and diversity of the forest.

Doing the right things will also reverse the degradation resulting from a century of biotic impoverishment brought on by the ill-conceived forest practices based on simplification and uniformity. It will do much more — it will help keep options open, address uncertainty, reduce risks, reduce value conflicts among people and it will maintain flexibility to meet future needs. It will also support ecoforestry's core values of ecological integrity, community vitality and economic opportunity.

(Editors' note: This article was originally published in *Ecoforestry* Vol. 16#3 (Fall 2001), pp. 2-3.)

Part II:

Wild Forests, Trees and Diversity of Values

West Coast
rainforest

Ecological Principles for Responsible Forest Use

Alan Wittbecker

An agenda for ecoforestry can be presented through a number of principles. Broad principles enable us to formulate fundamental rules based on the characteristics of specific forest ecosystems. These in turn can be used to create models to meet stated objectives — that is, the goals towards which our actions are directed, e.g., a healthy forest or strong beautiful lumber.

The principles presented are derived from typical characteristics of forests. Characteristics are qualities that distinguish unique individuals, systems or patterns; Gregory Bateson refers to characteristics as differences that make a difference. From these principles, standards for our activities in forests can be established. Standards are models or examples of quality or value, established by authority or mutual consent, that can be repeated as procedures.

For example, one characteristic of a mature forest is its wildness. The corresponding principle is that a forest is self-making and self-ordering, without human control and management. Our objective for any forest is to allow the foresting process to continue, whether we take resources from the forest or not (forests can be influenced by human effects such as acid rain, pollution and other industrial effluences). We can set standards that are likely to keep mature forests wild: limit biomass removal to 2% of the total forest; use appropriate techniques, e.g., single tree selection or horse skidding; retain mature forest structure, e.g., leave a good number of snags and downed trees and preserve surrounding landscape patterns.

The principles of ecoforestry are based on a number of fundamental philosophical, historical, scientific and cosmological principles that were first presented in other contexts by thinkers such as Whitehead and Einstein. Very few of these principles are absolute or universal; in fact the further one gets from physical or chemical principles, the more likely there are significant variations or exceptions. Nevertheless, these principles are essential to understanding forests and quite useful in application.

General, metaphysical and historical principles

At the most general level these global principles apply to the universe and to various facets of the universe.

Being

This is an ontological principle that states that everything has its source in existence. Simply, forests are. When they disappear, they are not. Many archaic peoples living in forests accepted their existence; in fact the forest was often considered another being, as a god or mother.

Change

Although botanists recognized that change was inescapable as a principle of the new science, Frederic Clements insisted that change was not an aimless wandering, but a steady flow (he thought it was towards a stable final state, however). Continuous change has been identified recently by ecologists and evolutionary biologists as the context for ecosystems and species; in fact, biodiversity is an expression of continuous change. Individuals change, patterns change, forests change. Neither tree plantations nor old growth forests can remain unchanging.

Of course, thousands of years ago Heraklitus noted that everything changes. And Alfred North Whitehead made change the basis of his metaphysics. In his *process* view, organisms are dynamic structures immanent and simultaneous with process, rather than a simple consequence of the natural selection of random mutations.

A forest is a process. It grows; it is not made like a model or a plastic tree. It smells, it cools, it involves. It is not a form or a web of human words that we can manipulate into endless imaginary variations (as the deconstructionists are intent on doing in their nihilistic ecology).

Organism

Whitehead regards organism as a universal principle, applicable in every field of reality from metaphysics to ethics. Everything that exists has its place in the order of nature. This does not mean that reality is an organism or that everything is reduced to biological terms. It does mean that every thing resembles a living organism since its essence depends on the pattern in which it occurs, and not on its components. The organism is what it does. The organism expresses an order particular to its place and time, within limits. In Whitehead's metaphysics of experience, the world is an ecosystem, an intertwining of all things.

An organism is characterized by wholeness. Wholeness is the organizing principle in nature, according to J. C. Smuts (1912). Wholes are self-making systems composed of subwholes (or holons) in a hierarchical system. All well-unified wholes are organic; all wholes are involved in organic wholes. Life refers to complexes in which parts are modified according to principles derived from the whole. Organism can refer to molecules and ecosystems, or to any general sense of organic unity. Each individual organism is only a partial, however. They are like Arthur Koestler's concept of the holon (1969): from above each is a whole; from below each is a part.

Forests are composed of living organisms; the forest itself changes, lives and dies in ways similar to a living entity or organism. The forest as a whole remains the same, according to W.S. Cooper (1913), "the changes in various parts balancing each other." Partly this is because the whole is a nested system that turns over at a rate much more slowly than the parts.

Field

The ideas of field and particle were indispensable to physical inquiry by the end of the

19th century (Faraday developed the concept in the 1860s). Although Whitehead noted that though the two concepts were considered antithetical, they are not logically contradictory. Ordinary matter was considered atomic, whereas electromagnetism was conceived as arising from a continuous field. A general space/ time/ energy/ matter (STEM) field has many characteristics: discretion, participation, connection, consistency, limitation, wholeness and self-development. No component of this field is ontologically subordinate to another: energy matter and pattern all have equal status — or, put another way, process is not more basic than structure or function.

By the time Alexander Gurwitsch (1922) used the term field in biology, gravity was also regarded as a field (then, nuclear interactions were described in terms of fields). The field concept was useful in Gurwitsch's investigation of mushrooms where nondifferentiated structural units resulted in highly regular and specific shapes. The source and extent of a field was not confined to an organism, but was the result of geometric properties.

Paul Weiss saw the field as a symbolic term for the unitary dynamics underlying the ordered behavior of the collective. Field denotes properties lost in the process of analysis. In living organisms, the patterned structure of the dynamics of the system as a whole coordinates the activities of the parts. The parts of the organism are not assembled, but integrated. In the operation of a field, every part knows the activities of every other and responds to a collective equilibrium.

Although recent experiments support the existence of some kinds of biological fields, scientific descriptions are still unsatisfactory. Waddington regarded his own concepts of chreods and morphogenetic fields as descriptive "conveniences." The topological, qualitative models of Rene Thom (1975) depend on fields, but Thom admits that the use of local models implies nothing about the ultimate nature of reality.

The forest acts as a field, containing organisms. David Perry notes that any removal, even a single tree, sends ripples through the forest system; this ripple effect may be good or bad for the health of the system, depending on the chain of consequences. Thinning produces a larger ripple effect; because more light reaches the ground level, it stimulates herbs and shrubs which may compete for moisture and slow tree growth or increase the rate of nutrient cycling and enhance tree growth.

Fields exist on many scales. Every field is limited by what can happen within a unit of time — its locality. Thus, fields are independent of, although not unaffected by other fields. The principle of locality is biological also; that is, each tree or owl interacts primarily with other organisms in its local neighborhood — not with all organisms under all conditions. One thing this means to forestry is that global approaches may not always work.

Patterning

Patterns are the key to understanding the nature of a forest. Nature, for Whitehead, consists of patterns whose movement is essential to their being. These patterns are analyzed into events. Everything that exists has its place in the order of nature. The essence of every thing depends on the pattern in which it occurs, and not on its components. In some ways, patterns are prior to things in helixes, light, fields and ecology. Ecology attends the overall pattern of relationships. Paul Shepard and others have written that relationships are as real as the objects that result from them.

The genotype determines the physical and chronological pattern of an organism within the limits of an environment and interactions — that is, an organism unfolds as an embedded part of an overfolding environment. The being of a species is the reality of the pattern of its members — that is self-sustaining, self-organizing, reproducing units (compared to the idea of other holons at other levels). Selection operates as a survival filter that passes any structure with the integrity to persist.

Richard Hart suggests that the actual substance of which the forest environment is made consists of patterns rather than things or individual species. The forest environment is generated by a patterning of the ecological ebb and flow of energy, substances, individuals and species across a suitable landscape. Successful adaptation to this complex system requires an enormous amount of minute local adaptations by a large number of individual organisms from a large number of species. The distinction between growing and declining patterns is not arbitrary, and can be arrived at objectively, through monitoring.

Based on a broader metaphysical foundation, with more comprehensive values, measuring and monitoring need to address patterns of being in a forest and not just a few commodities dictated by economics. One challenge to eco-forestry is to set up long-term programs to identify and study patterns and relate them to a healthy sustainable human use of forest ecosystems. But, the tools have to be used in new ways in a new framework, perhaps with topology and holograms as metaphors (topology provides the mathematical model for processes; a hologram provides a model for wholeness).

Monitoring is crucial to understanding forests. Until we understand how forests change and move around the landscapes, we will not know which changes are important and inevitable and which are the unhealthy result of human interference. Until we understand the changes, we will not be able to adjust our needs to the limits of forests.

The principle of patterning has several subalterns that refine its definition.

- *Limits.* All patterns are defined by their limits. Limit gives form to the limitless (Pythagoras).

- *Polycentricity.* The universe has more than one center; it has multiple frames of reference. Having multiple frames of reference means that things can only be fully described through an idea of complementarity (after Bohr). Things that in nature may seem contradictory are functions of perspective or the tools we use for examination.

- *Continuity.* Forests proceed through distinct continuous steps in relation to past environments and disturbances;

Nurse tree

VICTORIA STEVENS

that is, a tree plantation cannot become an old growth forest without developing through intermediate stages of continuity.

- *Connectivity.* Everything is connected, however weakly, to everything else. In a local system the connections are often strong. In a global system, connections between local systems may be weak or invisible. Reactions often propagate like ripples through the systems, or like a tug on a spider web.

- *Participation.* The human species participates in its environments. Interactions and interrelationships are undeniable. Cobb and Griffin state "The whole of nature participates in us and we in it." By the act of observing the observer influences the outcome of a phenomenon, as Wheeler says, taking part in the construction of reality. And, of course, every individual observes, from fungi to trees and humans.

- *Complexity.* As it continues, the universe becomes more complex; things change, patterns build. Evolution increases the levels of complexity through the operation of natural events.

- *Historicity.* History creates unique patterns, especially in forests. Each forest is unique in its parts and structure, in its matter, energy, forms, information and in its dynamics and history. An individual entity, according to Whitehead, whose own life history is part within the life history of some larger, deeper, more complete pattern, is liable to have some aspects of that larger pattern dominating its own being, and to experience modifications of the larger

pattern reflected in itself as modifications of its own being.

- *Irreversibility.* Forests pass through stages that are never repeated, despite superficial similarities; that is, treeplanting cannot reverse clearcutting (although another old-growth forest may develop in time).

- *Indeterminacy* (after Heisenberg). Some part of nature is always fuzzy. Heisenberg's uncertainty principle states that predictions about location and velocity are just statements of probability. The effect of this principle on epistemology is that our exact interpretation of forests has to be abandoned.

- *Novelty.* As an ordering/disordering process, a forest continually creates new forms and new patterns. Every forest is unique. Forests decay, as well as become more complex.

- *Creativity.* The process of nature is not merely rhythmic change, it is a creative advance, producing new forms everywhere. "There is an all-embracing fact which is the advancing history of the one universe," Whitehead states. Ecoforestry embraces creative complexity, as opposed to the simplification on which industrial forestry is based.

- *Surprise.* The interactions of billions of small actions cause a change in quality; that is, quality emerges from quantitative action. Thus, rare events may shape the entire course and texture of the universe and its systems. Where does rarity go in our understanding? Unusual and exceptional events, such as the origin of life on earth, must be factored into scientific understanding.

- *Intrinsic Value.* Value is mentioned sometimes as if it is just one thing, the economic market value of forest commodities indicated by price, but there are different kinds of value. Every species has some value (Deep Ecology Platform Principle 1). These values are independent of the usefulness of the nonhuman world for human purposes. The value (intrinsic worth) each being has for itself is shared by others. Each exists for itself and for others; is a value in itself and for others. Value is achieved through an ongoing process in nature, not a static one.

Physical and energy cycles

There are laws that have been identified by physicists and chemists which form the basis of life. Some laws have been called "impotence principles" by the biologist E. T. Whittacker. They cannot be proved true as laws, but they limit what we can do, i.e., we cannot use all the energy in a system, and we cannot return the system to a previous state. The first two principles here are the same as the first two laws of thermodynamics, which are impotence principles.

Energy

Energy can be transformed but not created or destroyed; energy is not created in the sun, just changed from its state in matter, mostly hydrogen and helium. "You cannot win," one of my professors used to say. A forest, which grows only from solar energy, is just a stage in the transformation of energy into production of flesh. This principle is why old growth

forests have no extra energy in the form of net primary productivity.

Entropy

Energy transformation cannot occur unless some of it is degraded into a dispersed form where it cannot be used again in the same system. "You must lose," the professor would add. The biosphere and forests obey the law of entropy only as a general limit. The entire process is exentropic since energy flows from sun to earth, and long wave radiation flows from earth to the sink of space.

Waste

That quantity of energy and material no longer of use to the system is wasted (for that system). Often it goes through another system, where a percentage of it is used (energy is not considered to recycle, although it can be used several times within a system and by several systems), but eventually it is lost to the interplanetary space surrounding the earth.

Cycles

Chemical elements, especially those used by life, circulate in the biosphere in characteristic paths known as biogeochemical cycles. Very little is actually lost to space, but often the elements concentrate in sinks, where they may be unavailable for ecological or geological periods of time. Forests, for instance, act as sinks for carbon; the ocean bottom acts as a sink for phosphorus. The rapid release of sinks can affect other atmospheric or terrestrial cycles.

Limits

Biological order is built on physical and chemical orders. That is why life is limited to such a narrow range of conditions. And that is why the most complex orders are vulnerable to changes in their substrates; energetic radiation can alter and destroy an individual, a small change in climate can destroy forests and civilizations. The earth is suitable for life because of three kinds of limits: (1) solar radiation has stayed within certain limits for 4 billion years; (2) the biogeochemical cycles of oxygen, carbon, nitrogen, phosphorus, sulfur, water have stayed within certain limits; (3) the environment has been constant enough for organic evolution, but variable enough for natural selection to be challenged. Life is limited by elements and physical factors (light, water, gas, salt); too little of an element limits life (Liebig's law); too much of an element limits life (Shelford's law of tolerance). Regardless of how plentiful nutrients are, for instance, without water a forest cannot exist.

Productivity

Energy is bound into organic material and is measurable as productivity. This energy can be partially used by living beings or released by disturbances, such as fires. The gross primary

Mt. Douglas coastal Douglas fir

VICTORIA STEVENS

productivity is the capital of a forest ecosystem; the net ecosystem productivity is the interest. The kinds and numbers of organisms in a forest are limited in varying degrees by the productivity of the system.

Energy relation

Within a range, biological activities increase with increases in temperature. Metabolism and respiration increase in animals; reproduction and growth increase in plants. Rapid, introduced changes in temperature, however, shorten life cycles and increase microorganisms. Sudden modification of a forest, such as from clearcutting, can cause changes in temperature and other unexpected effects.

Food chains

The transfer of energy and materials through organisms is referred to as the food chain. It is of various lengths, depending on the system but is rarely more than seven or eight layers deep. Mature forests have longer food chains than young forests.

Trophic structure

The interaction of individuals in a food chain in a local physical environment results in the trophic structure of communities (ecological pyramids), which interacts with material cycles. Mature forests generally have more steps on the trophic pyramid.

Maturity

The energy required to maintain an ecosystem is inversely related to complexity; succession decreases the flow of energy per unit biomass until the system reaches maturity (Margalef's concept of maturity). In a mature forest almost 100% of the energy is required to maintain the state of the forest. Any system formed by reproducing and interacting organisms must develop an assemblage in which production of entropy per unit of information is minimized. It is a general property of some systems that acquired information is used to limit further inflow. A mature system needs less information, since it works toward preservation.

Synergy (Fuller's concept)

Reactions at the chemical, organism or ecosystem level, when combined, produce unexpected positive results from the sum of single reactions. The forest ecosystem has emergent properties that are different from the sum of community interactions. They also affect biogeochemical cycles. Health is a dynamic quality of the whole, the result of a harmonious interaction of all the analyzable parts that comprise the whole forest with the surrounding larger environment.

Summary

Most of these principles are global principles; some principles may apply to a particular region; others may exist at a very local scale. The global provides the framework for the regional, which provides the framework for the local — the level of detail and participation.

These principles, whether we accept or deny their applicability, influence our interactions with forests, from clearcutting to preservation. They influence our objectives, our standards and our operations. The interplay of these principles with examples and exceptions will refine our approach to and understanding of forests. This is part of the process of living with and understanding forests.

GUS DiZEREGA

A Tree is a Quintessential Plant

Chris Maser

Someone's sitting in the shade today because someone planted a tree a long time ago.

— Warren Buffet

He plants the tree to serve another age.

— Cicero

If you were to ask me directly what a tree is, I could not answer. I don't know what a tree is; I only know what a tree is not. It's not a horse, it's not a mountain, it's not lightning; yet it has something in common with all three. A tree, like a horse, is a living being. Like a mountain, a tree is a historian, recording Earth's history in its annual growth rings as a mountain archives cosmic events in its geological strata. And like the electrical soul of lightning, a tree's impulse to live is transmitted throughout its being by electrical current. But a tree is much more than this, for a tree travels the world in time, its roots growing out of the same soil in which lies the seed of our human heritage. If I followed my ancestral lineage back some 5,000 years, the life span of one

bristlecone pine that was cut down at Great Basin National Park in the US state of Nevada, I would be looking at the history of 100 generations (if the average life span of my ancestors was 50 years) or 71 generations (if the average life span was 70 years).

These generations are a bridge across time within the lineage or ancestral tree of a single human family. As such, the shape of a deciduous tree in winter without leaf is a cosmopolitan motif. Consider, for example, the branching behavior of a tree, be it maple, oak, chestnut, elm or beech. As a tree moves from Heaven to Earth collecting into branches, consolidating into trunk and outflowing into roots, it forms a great repetitive dendritic pattern seen everywhere in the waterways of the world (dendritic comes from the Greek *dendron* meaning tree).

This dendritic pattern appears across the surface of the Earth's landscapes as the arterial system guiding rain and melting snow from mountain and plain to valley and sea. As raindrop and snowflake become trickle, stream and river, gathering into main stems (trunks) like the Mississippi, the Amazon and the Nile, they come together in their flowing only to dissipate again over the great deltas where river and sea meet. Here the waters spread out over the submerged land of the continental shelf and maintain the integrity of their past flowing when the glaciers of ancient times hoarded unto themselves the water and lowered the level of the sea. Today, with the death of the Pleistocene glaciers, these rivers flow in secret, sandwiched between the pulsating sea and the continental shelf, building their deltas, expanding their ever-changing network of channels as each discharges the fresh water of its being into the salty body of the sea.

It is impossible for me to reduce a tree to a mere intellectual abstraction. I shall therefore endeavor to paint for you a word portrait of a tree in but a few of its myriad forms. Although I discuss the parts of a tree as separate components, remember that a tree is a living being, an integrated living system in constant motion, and as such is surrounded by and infused in a large system called the biosphere, which includes you and me.

Leaves

With the advent of each spring, there comes forth a soft green halo on the trees of my garden as the sleeping leaves of winter awaken and grow. I love the leaves of spring, for they are bright and tender with the innocence of a new year. With the passing days, however, the leaves mature in the warmth of the sun and become home and food to insects. And it is while watching a wee caterpillar climb a leaf on my pear tree that I find myself contemplating what a leaf really is.

Leaves come in limitless sizes and shapes, no two of them ever exactly alike. They have many functions, be they the broad leaves of a maple, the needles of a noble fir or the small leaves and long thorns of a desert acacia. They are, for example, amazingly compact energy converters, which use chlorophyll to harness the sun's energy, to convert carbon dioxide, water and elemental nutrients from the soil into simple sugars that are in one form or another distributed throughout and among ecosystems, where they are a critical part of the world's food web.

Leaves also transpire water, creating a humid microclimate around their individual surfaces within a tree's crown and within a forest. As they filter the sun's light passing through their bodies, the leaf community of a tree's top creates an ever-moving dapple of lights and shadows on the forest floor in response to the sun's daily passage across the heavens.

A forest spider can find shade from the sun and a roof from the rain under a single leaf. Although considerably larger than a spider, some tropical bats chew partway through certain leaves, causing them to fold over and create an instant shelter in which the bats pass the daylight hours sleeping. As far as we humans are concerned, however, it takes the combined shadows of many leaves to cast one large enough to protect us from the sun's heat and ultraviolet rays. But in the distant Congo where the Pygmies live, there are leaves large enough for these forest folk to thatch their huts with roofs of green.

And leaves create beauty not only in form and function as they grow and mature in spring and summer but also in color as they change hue with their dying in autumn. For it is autumn's warm days and crisp, clear nights that begin calling the leaves back to earth to share the atoms they have so briefly borrowed from the atomic interchange of the ages. As autumn matures and the winds blow colder and harder, the dying leaves break loose their bonds to bump and bounce and float to earth. Others, clinging stubbornly to dormant twigs, rustle in the teasing wind. Each passing day sees more leaves collect beneath trees, forming a brittle, crunchy blanket over the ground.

And then comes winter, the season of leafless trees and bare-limbed shrubs, of withered bygone flowers and dead grasses. It is a time for hibernating, for being snug and sleepy in a cozy nest as wind-driven rain and sleet and snow buffet the outside world. What about the leaves of spring and summer? Where are they? Have you ever looked closely at a leaf bud on a tree in winter? Inside the frozen bud is a miniature leaf just waiting for spring to release it from bondage to begin again the dance of leaves exemplified by the trembling ballet of quaking aspen as they rustle softly in summer's breezes.

Unlike the leaves of maple and oak, of beech and ash, the needles of coniferous trees do not dance in the breezes, for they tend to be narrow and stiff, designed with the rigidity of soldiers clinging to limb and twig in orderly file. Although they do not dance, they sing. And to me, the greatest love song of all time is the wind playing its melody through the orchestra of needles high in the crowns of ponderosa pine. Although the needles of coast redwood trees do not sing like those of pine, they collect precious water. The great redwood forest of northwestern California would not exist if not for the coastal fogs. Most of the redwoods' summer moisture is gleaned from fog flowing inland from the Pacific Ocean, where it collects on needle after needle. Here it forms into crystalline mounds that converge into fluid pendants that drip with the persistence of Chinese water torture from

lofty crowns to saturate the forest floor, where salamanders depend on it for the breath of life because they absorb oxygen through their skin and must therefore remain moist or they suffocate. Beyond the salamanders, deeper in the soil, wait the thirsty roots of the giant trees that for millennia have gathered their own drinking water along the edge of the sea.

To the north, in western Oregon, lives the small red tree vole, a mouse-like denizen of the stately Douglas firs. Building its nest anywhere from six to 150 feet above the ground, it depends for life on the needles of Douglas fir and along the coast on western hemlock and Sitka spruce. In addition to eating the needles, however, these little tree-dwelling mammals lick the dew off of them and thus quench their thirst. Their ability to use this source of water allows them to extend their geographical distribution eastward into the hot interior of the land along major rivers, which create their own fog that in turn envelops the Douglas firs growing along their banks to the benefit of these small voles.

Halfway around the world, in the deserts of Egypt, grow acacia trees whose tiny leaves and rapier-like thorns conserve precious moisture as they endure the scorching heat of a relentless sun, the hot breath of desert winds and the choking clutch of howling sandstorms. Yet even here, leaves must produce the essential sugars from the sun's harvested light if they are to live. Here, too, lives the shrike or butcherbird. The butcherbird is so called for its habit of fastening extra food securely to the acacia's thorns by impaling its prey thereon for another day's feast. Thus a thorn, which on some plants is an anatomically modified leaf in Nature's scheme of things, not only conserves moisture and protects its bearer from being eaten by most large herbivores but also serves as a pantry for so deft a hunter as the shrike.

Unlike deciduous trees, which lose their leaves seasonally and stand in naked slumber for part of each year, such conifers as Douglas fir and western hemlock shed about a third of their needles annually. As the needles die and turn yellowish, they loosen from their moorings and spin quietly to the forest floor or ride the gusty winds to their final resting place. There, they serve as food for a host of organisms and thus through many circuitous routes are eventually incorporated into the forest soil only to rise again in some future microbe, flower, mouse or tree, each of which in turn completes its cycle and passes on the atoms it borrowed from needle and leaf.

Thus, while a deciduous tree or forest annually produces two entirely different habitats, one in full leaf and another following leaf fall, a coniferous tree or forest produces a continuous habitat of relatively similar characteristics throughout the year. In addition, broad leaves decompose rapidly and pass into the soil within a year, which makes them ideal mulch and compost for my garden, whereas coniferous needles may take a decade or more to break down and recycle through the system.

However one looks at leaves, they are a graphic symbol of life's cycle, from their emergence in spring, through their maturation in summer, to their decline and death in autumn and their apparent absence in winter. But the leaves of trees are more than that. They are also a barometer of the harmony with which human society coexists within its environment, for they simultaneously produce the oxygen we breathe and monitor our trusteeship of the world's air, soil and water, which affect the tree's flowers and fruits in my garden as well as in the forests of the world.

Flowers and fruits

The creation of a thousand forests is in one acorn.

— Ralph Waldo Emerson

Some flowers are bright and showy, some drab and secretive; some are large while others are tiny; some transmit from place to place wonderful perfume on the pathways of the air, and others do not. Some flowers are pollinated by wind, some by insects, others by birds and bats. Brightly colored flowers always cheer me, regardless of circumstances. And some flowers scent the air in such a way that on smelling them I am transported to another world.

Some trees have both male and female flowers on the same individual plant, whereas others have them on separate plants. Some flowers contain both male and female parts in the same blossom; others have separate blossoms. Some flowers are self-fertilizing when cross-pollination fails, whereas other flowers accept pollination only from different blossoms.

In addition, some male flowers, through their wind-borne pollen, have left a multi-millennial climatic record and through it given society a glimpse into its own evolution before language made recorded history possible. The time-encapsulated secrets of a world lay archived in the sedimentary strata of lake bottoms, peat bogs and glaciers before humans even knew how to question their existence. Here is secreted the drama of migrating trees and forests, of great fires and raging floods, of glaciers and drought-ridden deserts. Here, too, resides the ancestral lineage of communities of trees whose pollen chronicled their comings and goings even as their blooms brightened the day with color and tinted the air with odor in their bid to bring forth fruit and seed — the trees of the future.

But most of all, I marvel that so small a cone, so tiny a seed as that of the western red cedar can produce the ancient trees I remember from my youth, when a fallen monarch was so big that I could not climb over it when it blocked the trail as I hiked along the Green River in western Washington State. And the coastal redwoods of northwestern California live even longer and grow larger than the cedar.

The first time I saw a redwood tree, I pressed my cheek against its bark in an effort to look up the straightness of its trunk to the place where its top and the sky met. I failed, however, because the tip of the redwood's crown was far loftier than I had ever imagined. While I was awed by the sheer size and majesty of this ancient tree, I was comforted by it as well. This redwood, close to 3,000 years old, also arose like the cedar from a seed so fragile that I could squash the life out of it between my fingers.

As flowers provide food for such animals as honeybees, butterflies, hummingbirds, sunbirds and nectar-eating bats; fruits, seeds, and nuts offer food to others, such as squirrels, mice, deer, bear and fruit bats, some of which have wingspans approaching four feet. The flowers and fruits eaten by animals are not, however, free of service to Nature. Many species of trees in the tropical rainforests, especially those that germinate in the dark understory, have large seeds that carry enough stored energy to grow leaves and roots without much help from the sun. Such fruits and seeds are often so large that only proportionately sized birds and mammals can swallow or carry them. In Gabon, for example, monkeys may disperse 67% of the fruits eaten by animals.

Seed-dispersing animals, such as large birds and monkeys, are critical in replacing the large trees and lianas (high-climbing vines) of the tropical forest canopy. By eating the fruits and defecating the seeds some distance from the parent plants thereby improving the seeds' chances of landing in a favorable place for germination, the birds and monkeys are helping the trees and lianas, as species, to survive. These animals are the first species to disappear, however, when humans hunt for food and, along with elephants, have already been hunted so heavily that they either have been drastically reduced in numbers or eliminated completely over vast areas of the African forest, as well as in the tropical rainforests of Central and South America.

For the most part, foresters have overlooked how the interdependency of plants and animals affects the biodiversity of a plant community. Elephants, for example, disperse the seeds of 37 species of trees in the Ivory Coast. Of those, only seven species have alternate means of dispersal (by birds and monkeys). Of the 201 individual trees in one study area, elephants dispersed 83 species. In one forest where humans had eliminated elephants a century earlier, few juvenile trees of the elephant-dispersed species were left, and the two major species had no offspring at all. Once the large species of birds and mammals are gone, the stunningly rich tropical rain forests will change and gradually lose species of trees, lianas and other plants. Smaller seeds dispersed by wind will replace large seeds dispersed by large animals. Those species of plants whose seeds grow in the shaded understory will not survive, and the land will gradually be forested by fewer, more common species.

Branches

The leaves, flowers and fruits of a tree are simultaneously nurtured, held for a time securely in place, united and ultimately allowed to fall from branches. January and February are the months each year during which I must attend to the branches of my fruit trees and, if necessary, those of the maples. It is the time of year when the sleeping trees are ready for pruning, when last year's growth is cut and the trees shaped to keep them under a semblance of control. When Zane, my wife, and I bought our house, the pear and apple trees were unkempt and in need of attention. Arriving at our new home in late summer, our first harvest needed to be done by climbing into the trees to reach those fruits whose locations were beyond the capacity of my ladder. But over the next three years, I pruned the branches shorter and shorter each winter, and I can now reach almost every pear and apple from a six-foot stepladder.

It is during the activity of pruning that each year I revisit the concept of a branch and how humanity has endowed this portion of a tree with a variety of symbolic meanings. Branches, for example, are like the arms of a tree, the shape of which often conjures its human-envisioned demeanor — a gnarled oak, a weeping willow or a stately ash. Beyond space, in the realm of time and human imagination, a tree offers a symbol of Creation and the balance between the spiritual (branch) and material (root) aspects of life in the *tree of life,* of the continuing evolution of life's infinite variety in the branching of the *phylogenetic tree* and of the continuity and divergence of personal lineage in the branching of the *family tree.*

But what does a spider whose sole intent is to fasten its web from branch to branch or a warbler seeking a suitable location for its nest know of time or human imaginings? To the spider, one branch may be much like another as an anchor for its web, but to the nesting bird or sleeping bat, branches are as varied as the trees themselves. A Douglas fir, for example, offers many suitable nesting sites for a variety of birds among its horizontal branches and abundant, stiff needles and a secure place for the hoary bat to hang by day; but a western red cedar or Alaska yellow cedar, with its drooping branches and tiny scale-like leaves, has little that a nesting bird or sleepy bat requires. The same is true of a Pacific yew with its zigzagging branches and often scraggly form, of a western hemlock whose branches are sparsely clothed in lacy needles or of a tamarack, whose branches are covered with little pegs to which are attached whorls of soft, pliable needles offering little protection from sun, wind or rain.

But the same limber, downward sweeping branches that are unsuitable for a nesting bird, such as those of a grand fir, can shelter a snowshoe hare. A grand fir's boughs with their flat needles often become weighted down and frozen into snow as it continually piles up around the fir's base during a long mountain winter. In the cavity created and maintained under the fir's bough as it becomes roofed over by snow, a hare is safe and warm, out of the bitter cold wind.

As a boy, I thought branches were made for climbing. But even then, I discerned that there were safe and unsafe branches and that some trees, because of the characteristics of their branches, were easier to climb than others. I learned to *read* a tree's branches, taking none for granted before placing my weight on them or using them to pull myself upward. Some branches, such as those of the hawthorn, locust or acacia, are not readily climbable because of their thorns. Some branches, such as those of the South American monkey-puzzle tree, are protected by sharp, scaly leaves which can confound even a monkey. Others, like beech, are smooth and difficult to grasp. Spruce branches are covered by tiny, rough pegs; whereas rhododendron branches at the timberline on Phulung Ghyang, Newakot District, Nepal, have exfoliating bark which is continually self-peeling. And the branches of the true fir, which grow between 11,000 and 12,000 feet on the same mountain, are strong enough to give the common langur, a large monkey, safe purchase for a good night's sleep because they are simultaneously too limber to support the weight of the heavier clouded leopard, which hunts the monkeys at night for food.

Old growth cedar

VICTORIA STEVENS

But whatever a branch is like, it is somehow synonymous with campfires.

Fire was my only constant companion in years bygone, as it was that of my boyhood heroes, the American Indian and the mountain man. My first fire was intensely spiritual and private, known only to me and to the silent forest. The wisp of fir smoke, the heat, the tiny licking flame, the crackling branches became part of my spirit — and still are. Since the days of my youth, fire has warmed me during cold winter nights in interior Alaska and during chilly desert nights in North Africa. Fire has cooked my food in the jungle of northern India and in the Himalayas of Nepal. And it has lifted my spirit on days of seemingly endless rain and shrouding fog in the coastal mountains of western Oregon and Washington.

Each fire is a reflection of the past, of the dawn of humanity, when the first purposefully made fire united humans and branches in a cultural dance the world over, a dance to remove the darkness and its terror, to heat a protective shelter, to cook food and to alter the landscape for hunting, gathering, agriculture and war.

Trunk

Although there is nothing that I must do with the trunks of the trees in my garden or with those of the maples just outside except be careful not to injure them, I am reminded while pruning the branches each year that it is the trunk of a tree that has in so many ways influenced humankind. The trunk, in this sense, is the main ascending axis of a tree, a stalk or stem. To me, however, a tree's trunk has always been more than simply the stem of a plant, especially one trunk— that of a giant noble fir on Marys Peak, the highest mountain in the Coast Range of western Oregon, whose campground near the summit is only 25 miles from my home town of Corvallis.

The campground was at the end of a narrow gravel road that made a short loop through blue-tinted grandparent noble firs that ringed the lower edge of the grassy meadow atop the peak. And it was here, near the last picnic table at the meadow's edge, that in 1943 at age four I discovered the huge trunk of a fallen noble fir. The trunk, which had already lain on the ground for some decades, was so large that I had a difficult time climbing on top of it. Nevertheless, I never got enough of climbing on it, exploring its nooks and crannies and examining the mosses, lichens, mushrooms and various insects and centipedes that lived in, on and around it. And sometimes, if I managed to lie quiet long enough, a squirrel or Townsend chipmunk would scamper over the top of me as though I was part of the trunk.

I visited the old trunk as the years passed. While I matured in stature, the old trunk became smaller and smaller as it gradually rotted away, returning to the soil from whence it had grown in times before my birth, when it had stood for centuries as a sentinel along the edge of the ancient, powdery-blue forest. In the summer of 1964, when I was 25 years old, I visited the old trunk, sat on it while enjoying the warmth of the sun and stepped over the top of it as though it were now the child. I felt sadness in so doing, however, because the old trunk, now mostly collapsed in on itself, had given me as a child a measure of stability that I could not find in my family. As a child, I could talk to it, confide in it and be safe with it. I wonder if the sadness I felt was in part a premonition that this was to be my last visit to the old trunk. In any case, it was; a severe early winter storm blew down that whole portion of the forest, and the old trunk all but disappeared under the impact of neighboring trees as they fell on it.

Thinking back to the trunk of that ancient noble fir, I wonder how the first humans might have begun a purposeful relationship with the trunks of trees. Was it the discovery of hollow trunks as shelter or drums? Was it the leaping flames, far-flung light and long-lasting heat of a trunk burning? Or was it when the first human hollowed a tree's trunk with fire and the canoe was born, and so might have begun the purposeful exploration of the world's waterways?

Without trees, the peoples of the great continents would still be separated from one another; the oceanic islands, such as Hawaii, New Zealand and Australia, would be barren of people and the oceans and the skies of the world would still be unknown. The world and human culture would be very different without the sounds of the Stradivarius and all other musical instruments crafted from the trunks of trees. Without heat from wood there could be no metal, and the face of the moon would still be without the footprints of humanity. And I, as a boy, would not have had my ancient Douglas fir to climb on windy days, where near its top, reveling in its supple strength, I could ride with the wind as it blew the ancient tree hither and yon.

But the influence of a tree's trunk reaches far beyond human history into the eons of life's web as it grows, matures, declines, dies, falls and recycles into the soil. An old Douglas fir tree in its 810th year dies in the mountains of western Oregon and falls to the floor of the forest. For 525 years, the forest grows up around the decomposing giant until its last vestige is incorporated into the soil. Over the decades and centuries, the tree's atoms become parts of bacteria, fungi, earthworms, insects, birds, mammals and green plants as each in turn has borrowed, used and given up the atoms of its being to the next in line. Some atoms may go from insect to mother bird, to her offspring and be carried away on wings and wind to a distant land, there to enter a different strand in life's web.

Suppose, for instance, that a young warbler matures and dies while over-wintering in South America, where it falls into a jungle stream and is eaten by a scavenging fish. The fish is caught by the son of a poor slash-and-burn farmer, who builds a small fire and cooks and eats the fish. A year later, the boy leaves the jungle and goes into a city to attend school. After some years of wandering, he goes to sea as a merchant seaman and dies an old man on a far distant shore where the atom of the ancient tree that became part of the insect that became part of the warbler that became part of the fish that became part of the boy now enters yet another strand of life's web.

Thus from seed to soil, the old fir's trunk influenced the site on which it grew and fell for 1,335 years, but its atoms will travel the world forever. As I mentioned earlier, I know of a bristlecone pine in Great Basin National Park that was finally cut down at an age of more than 5,000 years. How long would its trunk have influenced the site on which it grew had it been allowed to fulfill its entire ecological role? Where might its atoms travel could we but follow them through the corridors of time — to the root of another tree?

Roots

To examine the notion of a root, we will venture into a largely unknown, hidden world with the slightly buried seed of a Douglas fir as our guide. It is spring, and the seed begins to swell as it absorbs moisture from the warm soil. The seed's coat splits, and a tiny root begins to penetrate the bosom of the Earth as small, green seed leaves reach toward the sun. Thus the seed of the tree becomes the seedling of the tree in its first spring of life.

As the seedling's roots spread through the soil, the new nonwoody root tip of a tiny feeder root comes in contact with a week-old fecal pellet of a deer mouse. The deer mouse had dined on a truffle (the belowground fruiting body of a fungus) the night before it deposited the pellet. The pellet, packed full of the truffle's spores, is still soft from the moisture in the soil, and the root tip has little difficulty penetrating it. Inside the pellet, the root tip comes in contact with the spores that have passed unscathed through the mouse's intestinal tract. Meanwhile, the yeast (a fungus) in the pellet is growing and producing a substance called yeast extract that is food for nitrogen-fixing bacteria. (*Nitrogen-fixing* means to capture gaseous nitrogen and convert it into a form usable by the plant.) As the root tip contacts the spores, the yeast helps stimulate the spores to germinate and grow into and around the root tip; the nitrogen-fixing bacteria and yeast become enveloped in the fungal tissues. Once inside the fungal tissue and in the absence of oxygen, the nitrogen-fixing bacteria are nurtured by the extracts of both the yeast and the truffle's non-reproductive tissue. The bacteria in turn fix atmospheric nitrogen that can be used by both the fungi and the host tree.

The non-reproductive tissue of the truffle, called *mycelia*, forms a mantle around the tree's feeder root; this symbiotic association is called *mycorrhiza*, which literally means, fungus-root. As the mycelia grow into and around the root tips, they also grow out into the soil where they join billions of miles of gossamer threads from other mycorrhiza-forming fungi. These mycelial threads act as extensions of the seedling's root system as they wend their way through the soil absorbing such things as water, phosphorus and nitrogen and sending them into the seedling's roots. As the seedling grows, it produces sugars that feed the fungus, which in turn expands through the soil as it is nourished by and nourishes the seedling. The tree is therefore a product of both the sun's light and soil's darkness; the nutrients of darkness feed the tree's top in light and the sugars of light feed the tree's roots and their fungi in darkness.

Although as a young man I knew nothing about this tree/fungal association and doubt that I had ever really considered the functional aspects of a tree's roots, I learned about their tenacity the year I was confronted by an old cottonwood stump on a ranch in northwestern Colorado where I worked as a ranch hand. This particular cottonwood stump was in a small grove of its kind along the little stream that supplied water to the main ranch house. I forget the reason now, but the old rancher wanted the stump taken out, and removing it fell on my shoulders.

"Well," I thought to myself with the surety of youth, "this will be easy. All I have to do is chop through its roots with my ax, and I can pull it out with a team of horses." That's what I thought until the first day I hacked unceremoniously at the stump and the blade of my ax got so deeply buried in the soft wood that I couldn't get it out no matter how hard I tried. The upshot is that I had to dig out each root on which I then cut, hacked and sawed. In addition to my physical assault on its roots, I muttered at that infernal stump for the better part of the summer and autumn until the

day came when I thought that I could in fact pull it out with a team of workhorses.

With the team hitched and anchored securely to the stump by a chain, I gave the word and the horses began to pull. I had, over the course of time, dug so far under the stump that I thought it would snap out in a twinkling. The old stump groaned and shivered, rose and fell until the chain broke, but would not release its grip in the soil. It had, I found, a monstrous taproot, which I could see only when the horses were pulling on the stump. I therefore had to dig the hole deeper.

Then came the day in early October when the old stump finally relinquished its hold, and the horses pulled it free of the soil. That was a bittersweet moment because it wasn't just a stump anymore; it had become a stump with a personality. I had unknowingly developed an honest-to-goodness relationship with it, one that challenged not only me but also technology and a team of powerful horses. But I don't think I really ever conquered it, because I have long had the distinct feeling that at some point in our relationship the old cottonwood stump decided, for whatever reason, to let me cut it out. That stump, perhaps more than any other, caused me to focus on roots. Yet as I chopped at the old stump's roots, I had no inkling of how vitally important tree roots are to the health of the forest beyond the individual trees.

Decomposing woody roots of tree stumps have distinct functions. Tree roots contribute to the sheer strength of the soil, which is a root's ability to hold soil in place. Declining sheer strength of decomposing woody roots increases mass soil movement after such disturbances as catastrophic fire and clearcut logging. Another related function of decomposing tree stumps and roots is the frequent formation of interconnected, surface-to-bedrock channels that rapidly drain water from heavy rains and melting snow. The collapse and plugging of these channels as roots decay may force more water to drain through the soil matrix, which reduces soil cohesion and increases hydraulic pressure, which in turn may cause mass soil movement. Because these plumbing systems are necessary to the stability and sustainable productivity of the soil in a forest and cannot be replaced by young trees with their relatively small roots, grandparent trees are necessary to mediate the relationship between water and soil.

Although the pear and apple trees in my garden hardly qualify as a forest, their roots perform similar functions in the soil, many of which I know nothing about. What I do know, however, is that the care I take of my fruit trees aboveground affects directly the health of their roots belowground. In addition, how I choose to participate with the aboveground environment of my garden is a choice, my choice and nothing more. But the consequences of my choices will in many unknown and hidden ways affect not only the trees but

Old growth tree

THE LAND CONSERVANCY

also the next person to call this small piece of ground "my garden."

Mark Collins, of the World Conservation Monitoring Center, says that, "forest destruction is the key threat to species worldwide," including 10% of the world's species of trees. One-tenth of the known species of trees in the world are in danger of extinction, yet fewer than one in four species benefit from any kind of protection, according to the 650-page report *World List of Threatened Trees*. According to the study, which was financed by the Dutch government and released in Geneva, Switzerland, on August 25, 1998, 8,753 of the world's estimated 80,000 to 100,000 species of trees are vulnerable. Of these, 1,000 are classified as critically endangered, reduced to less than 100 living individuals. Some of the species threatened with extinction have yet to be investigated scientifically. What will society lose with these secret extinctions?

It is my hope that whoever reads these words will pause for a moment before putting his or her saw or ax to a tree and in that moment pay homage to the being whose life is about to be severed. I say this because it is through the consciousness with which we act, and not the acts themselves, that we honor the Creation of which we are all an inseparable part.

(Editors' note: This essay is based on a chapter from Chris' book *Ecological Diversity in Sustainable Development: The Vital and Forgotten Dimension.* CRC, 1999.)

Salmon Nutrients, Nitrogen Isotopes and Coastal Forests

Tom Reimchen

The yearly return of salmon from the open Pacific Ocean to coastal waters of Western North America is one of nature's grand displays, and recent investigations by researchers in Washington, British Columbia and Alaska indicate that the signature of salmon finds its way into both aquatic and terrestrial ecosystems as far inland as the Rockies. The most widespread species associated with these formerly immense schools of salmon are black and grizzly bears, which migrate from alpine and distant habitats to congregate along streams and rivers during the spawning migration. Recent studies show that these predators play a much more significant ecological role in coastal forests than previously recognized.

During an investigation begun in 1992 on the foraging behavior of Queen Charlotte Island black bear, I found that bears individually captured about 700 largely spawned-out salmon over the six-week spawning period and carried the majority of these into the forest where they could feed relatively undisturbed. At Bag Harbour, where most of the data were collected, eight bears transferred 3,000 salmon

into the forest over the more than half a mile of stream where salmon spawned. On average, about one-half of each salmon carcass was consumed by the bears, and the remnants were scavenged by eagles, marten and flocks of crows, ravens and gulls. A diversity of insects including flies and beetles were found with the carcasses and typically within five days, all carcasses were a seething mass of maggots, which consumed all remaining soft tissues, leaving the bone. The cumulative effect of decomposing carcasses combined with the fecal and urine discharge from bears and other animals produces a highly odoriferous riparian zone.

Expansion of these studies on the Queen Charlottes indicates that transfer of salmon carcasses into riparian zones is widespread throughout the British Columbia coast wherever bears and salmon are common and that these nutrients represent a significant part of the nitrogen budget of vegetation and soil invertebrates. The use of stable nitrogen isotopes allows us to identify the relative contribution of salmon to the ecosystem.

Researchers have noted that 15N, the heavy but rare isotope of nitrogen, is more abundant in marine algae than in terrestrial vegetation. Theodore Rasmussen at McGill University and others have shown that the isotope is further enriched with each successive trophic level.

Salmon, occurring at the 4th trophic level in marine waters, are very enriched in 15N. Consequently, comparisons of 15N levels in vegetation beside a salmon stream with control plants nearby without access to salmon provides a direct measure of the contribution of salmon-derived nitrogen to the plants. Researchers in Alaska and Washington, such as Kline, Bilby and Ben-David, have shown evidence for 15N enrichment in aquatic and streamside vegetation. My student, Deanna Mathewson, has looked at needles or leaves from 10 riparian plant species, including western hemlock, devil's club, false azalea, red huckleberry, salmon berry, buckbean and false lily of the valley from some 20 watersheds throughout the British Columbia coast that differ in abundance of salmon. These data demonstrate that up to 40% of the nitrogen used by the riparian plants is derived from salmon nutrients, with values dependent on the salmon density in the stream, abundance of bears, plant species and distance from the stream.

Another student in my lab, Morgan Hocking, is examining isotope signatures in insects and other invertebrates and has shown major amplification of 15N at multiple trophic levels, including herbivores, omnivores, carnivores and detritivores. This amplification does not extend from direct consumption of salmon carcasses but rather from indirect food web effects. Dr. Jonathan Moran, another member of our group, has examined nitrogen isotopes in soil at increased distance from the stream at each of six watersheds differing in the numbers of salmon and finds a direct relationship between soil 15N and salmon density.

That riparian plants or insects are using salmon-derived nutrients does not itself provide evidence that this source of nutrients is required or essential for the plants. One line of evidence that plants directly benefit from salmon nutrients would be evidence for improved growth rate in trees. Nitrogen is usually limiting in coastal forests, as can be readily seen by the positive effect of adding fertilizers. At Bag Harbour, the salmon carcasses contribute up to 120 kg nitrogen per hectare into the forest, comparable to applied fertilization rates by industry in coastal forests.

As a preliminary test of this, I examined yearly growth rings of Western Hemlock at Bag Harbour of 13 trees of similar size from sites differing in carcass density. Average growth rate over the last 50 years was 0.1 inches per year within 32 feet of the stream where carcasses were most abundant and less than 0.04 inches per year where carcasses were not present. Furthermore, individual trees grow more rapidly following years with high salmon abundance, while control trees nearby without access to salmon show no changes in growth for the equivalent period. These data are at best ambiguous, as multiple factors influence plant growth, including light, moisture and nutrients. I am currently examining yearly growth in Western Hemlock and Sitka Spruce from 80 watersheds throughout the British Columbia coast differing in abundance of salmon and a variety of physical parameters in an effort to partition the influence of salmon from other factors. Some of our study sites are particularly useful as they include comparisons of trees immediately above and below waterfalls that are impassable to salmon.

One of the empirical observations emerging from the Bag Harbour studies was that the amount of salmon transfer into the forest each year varied directly with the yearly numbers of spawning salmon returning to the stream. As such, it seemed plausible to me that yearly differences in this nutrient pulse might be reflected in the 15N levels in yearly growth rings of the conifers. If so, the rings might retain evidence for past fluctuations in salmon nutrients and potentially allow a reconstruction of movement of salmon into the watershed into past centuries. This has proved, however, logistically challenging due to the difficulty in detecting 15N in wood. Standard mass spectrometers, the instruments used to measure isotopic ratios, work well with leaves or needle in which the carbon to nitrogen ratio (C:N) is about 40:1. Yet, the C:N ratio in wood is about 1000:1, and as such, the signature of 15N is masked by the large amount of carbon. Over a three-year period and in collaboration with colleagues at McGill University, wood samples were sent out to four different mass spectrometer laboratories, but none could produce a repeatable 15N signature. In 1998, I sent some wood samples from Bag Harbour to a mass spectrometer researcher from California, and he was able to gradually solve technical constraints and measure 15N on yearly growth rings of Western Hemlock and Sitka Spruce. The excess carbon in the samples remains a constraint, and progress is slow. To the present, I have sent wood samples from 25 trees and the results can be briefly summarized:

- Comparisons among watersheds show that the 15N levels in the wood of trees adjacent to streams is directly proportional to salmon numbers. The highest values, near 10 parts per thousand, occur in ancient Sitka Spruce at a mid-coast stream near Bella Bella that has

Bear in coastal BC

TIM IRVIN

the highest salmon spawning density identified in our studies (60,000 salmon/ 0.6 mile). Up to 80% of the yearly nitrogen budget in some years in these spruce appears to have been derived from salmon nutrients.

- Comparisons within watersheds show that the 15N levels are highest in trees near the stream and decline with increased distance into the forest, concordant with the decline in salmon carcasses and bear activity. Even in small watersheds, vegetation 164 yards from the stream still has the signature of salmon. This suggests a much broader riparian zone than the 10-32 yard zone suggested in government policy on fish streams. Recent studies by G.V. Hilderbrand in Alaska suggest that the salmon signature in vegetation occurs some 874 yards into the forest where grizzly bears are common.

- Comparisons within trees demonstrate a correlation between 15N signatures among yearly growth rings and DFO records of salmon escapement over the last 50 years. The peaks in salmon can take from one to three years to show up in the tree rings.

- Older or larger trees exhibit higher 15N levels in growth rings than younger or smaller trees. This could reflect either increased transfer of salmon nutrients to larger trees or increased isotopic fractionation (reduced uptake of 15N) of young trees when the static nitrogen supply in the soil may exceed the requirements.

The research is ongoing, and we have taken cores from 750 trees at 80 watersheds along the coast that will be analyzed for dendrochronological and isotopic data. The results will provide a detailed historical assessment of nutrient cycling in watersheds throughout the coast.

Our research over the last decade, combined with those of other investigators in the Pacific Northwest, has yielded previously unrecognized linkages between the open ocean and forests and these may be important to our understanding of forest ecosystems. The available evidence currently suggests that these linkages occur from the estuaries and small streams that fringe the North Pacific through to the headwaters of the major rivers that penetrate far into the continents. The estimated 80-90% reduction in salmon returning to streams over the last 100 years, largely the result of deforestation and overfishing, will have ecosystem-level consequences for the remaining forests. What these are remain largely unknown, but more of these effects will emerge from the ongoing research programs.

Acknowledgments

This research is financially supported by the David Suzuki Foundation, Friends of Ecological Reserves and the Natural Sciences and Engineering Research Council of Canada. I also thank my graduate students D. Mathewson, M. Hocking, D. Klinka, my collaborators D. Harris, Bristol Foster and J. Moran, volunteers including D. Coopland and I. Jacobs and, for sharing their lab space, B. Hawkins, N. Livingston and D. Smith .

(Editors' note: This paper was originally published in *Ecoforestry* 16(3):13-16.)

GUS DiZEREGA

Life With Carnivores in the Great Bear Rainforest — Notes From an Autumn Diary

Chris Genovali

It was still dark when the bark of a wolf woke me up. I got up with my sleeping bag draped around me and crouched behind the blind of the observation platform, listening intently. I had gone to sleep watching stars emerge and listening to seals chase after salmon. It was my birthday, and I was secretly hoping something special might happen; I wasn't disappointed.

A cacophony of howls suddenly reverberated through the valley, almost as if in an echo chamber. Just as quickly the howling came to a halt. In anticipation I grabbed my binoculars. Then in the slowly advancing light of day the wolf pack began to appear on the beach, one by one, then a pair at a time. The pack's play and roughhousing went on for a good part of the sun-drenched morning.

It was fall on Canada's Pacific coast, and Raincoast Conservation Foundation's wolf project team was conducting a ten day expedition on our research vessel *Achiever* to collect genetic samples from areas on the north coast of the Great Bear Rainforest we had not sampled in the past and to revisit wolf home sites

we had previously identified. Arriving after sunset, we anchored in a system known to us to be a wolf hot spot. As was my wont on this trip, I slept on deck up in the observation platform that was still attached to *Achiever* from our marine mammal surveys that had recently concluded for the season. It would prove to be a good spot for viewing terrestrial wildlife too.

After the wolves had finished their romp on the beach, my colleagues and I waited until we were certain they had retreated into the rainforest so as not to disturb their normal routine. I hiked quickly up the system to where the salmon stopped spawning. All along the banks of the stream were headless pinks, the missing heads a telltale sign of wolf predation. Only past the spawning reach was there black bear sign — the bears knew who was boss in this valley. I heard a high-pitched whistle far downstream; it was time to go as tides and schedules dictated. As my jog back to the beach turned into a sprint, I marveled at the surgeon-like precision the wolves exhibited in chomping the heads off of so many fish.

As we pulled into the north coast inlet I glassed the port side shoreline with my binoculars, checking for wildlife. It was that magical time of day right before dusk when unexpected and unusual things often manifest in the coastal fall alpenglow. No one else was on deck. I was standing in the observation tower. On the port side of the inlet, at the water line, was a bear. As I focused in I could see this was "not your average bear," to paraphrase a well-known cartoon bruin. Everything about its appearance was distinctive. The coat was a champagne color I had never seen on a coastal bear. At first I thought it might be a spirit bear, but as I peered through my binoculars I could see it had the physical characteristics of a grizzly: dish-shaped face, hump between the shoulders, the size of the feet and length of the claws. But the perplexing factor was that this bear's skin color along with the pads on the feet, the fleshy end of the snout and the skin around the eyes — were all pink: all signs of albinism. Was I looking at an albino grizzly?

I called my colleagues to come up on deck from down below. They all emerged with binoculars in hand, and we proceeded to go back and forth speculating on exactly what kind of bear we were observing. There was no doubt it was an albino, but whether it was a grizzly or not was discussed at length. To this day I am certain it was *ursus arctos,* but in the end I suppose it doesn't matter — seeing an albino bear of any species is a once in a lifetime experience. More importantly for me, it was yet another confirmation of the power and mystery of the Great Bear Rainforest in the half-light before sunset.

The pale afternoon light that is so peculiar to autumn filtered through the trees, refracting through the flowing water to the tessellation of river rocks below, giving the entire landscape a golden hue. A haunting wind blew up the valley, alternating gusts of comforting warmth and icy chill. The alder and cottonwood leaves floated crazily to the water, landing on the tattered backs of the returning salmon holding in the river. My Raincoast colleagues and I sat motionless on the bank, hypnotized by the beauty laid out before us in this river valley located on the central coast of the Great Bear Rainforest. We were doing a reconnaissance of the watershed as there was talk that it was slated for logging.

As I silently stood up, still watching the river, a marten appeared from nowhere and walked across my foot. The marten quickly realized that my shoe was not a root and scrambled up the nearest tree in a state of extreme panic. He had been headed down to the river, no doubt to feed on dead salmon.

The weather had been perfect all day, not a cloud in the sky, comfortably warm with just a hint of a cool breeze. At the apex of our hike we stopped, basked in the sun, dried out our gumboots and lunched on salmon sandwiches and organic oranges. For dessert we grazed on huckleberries growing along the bear trails.

On our way back down the river approaching the estuary we crossed over to the opposite side. Quietly making our way through the bush there was bear sign aplenty; grizzly tracks and fresh piles of scat seemed to appear around every corner. I began to feel an adrenalin infused hyper-awareness of my surroundings, being fully immersed in each movement and each step taken, being keenly attuned to each sound in the bush, knowing that we were in the presence of the temperate rainforest's largest predator.

We followed tracks in the loamy soil and kept moving along down the river until we came to a large side pool bordered by several downed logs. I stood silently on a high point looking back into the bush. As I leaned over to peer over the shrubby growth that was about waist high at the bank, my field of view was filled by the back of the enormous head of a grizzly. I was close enough that I could've reached out with the stick I was holding and scratched the bear behind his fuzzy ears. The grizzly had his back to us looking for salmon that had been trapped in the pool. He was huge and healthy looking and had a beautiful coffee colored coat. He methodically moved around the pool and then calmly looked up at us with a slight turn of the head, his big rump pointing toward us.

We stood there looking back at him, trying not to stare directly into his eyes, taken aback by his beauty and bulk. He casually made his way out to the middle of the river, doing a balancing act on slippery rocks and logs, and began fishing in earnest. We watched from our perch as he deftly caught a salmon returning up the river and dragged it over to the far bank and rapidly ate it. He dropped the mostly eaten carcass on the forest floor and headed back into the river to snag another one. Eventually the bear moved up the river and disappeared into the bush. The sun was sitting low on the horizon and we reluctantly hiked back toward the estuary.

The next day we awoke to another beautiful morning and we hiked the bear trails along the river full of anticipation. We staked out a mossy bench overlooking the river and watched the salmon in their return up the river. Pink, chum, coho and a lone sockeye. It's an event that never fails to mesmerize me.

VICTORIA STEVENS

Bear bags in the forest

My salmon-induced reverie was abruptly interrupted, however, as we spotted a large grizzly walking up the opposite side of the river. As the bear approached we could see that he was massive, appreciably bigger than yesterday's grizzlies. This had to be the bear that left the Sasquatch-like tracks on a sandy spit farther up river. He waded into the river and began snorkeling for salmon, sticking his snout and eyes underwater, but leaving the rest of his huge head above the surface. He caught a prize, ripped it open and ate the salmon head first as he floated on his back not unlike a sea otter.

Now he was dog-paddling closer to our side of the river bank. All the while he was calmly and methodically fishing for salmon. We stayed stone silent. He knew we were there. Swimming closer to us, he was almost directly below us under the bank, not more than ten feet away. This was an immense bear. I don't think I've ever seen anything more beautiful in my life. His milky brown coat shone in the bright morning sunlight. My head was reeling. It was like having pure energy injected directly into my veins.

The big grizzly king moved up the river, climbed over a couple of huge logs and was out of sight. Unexpectedly we spied another grizzly. The bear was a younger male with a dark brown coat, smaller than the previous bears we had seen the past two days. The younger grizzly was catching salmon that had started to run aground in a couple of shallow side channels. We stood behind some cedars in the shade and watched him munch a few fish.

Soon the younger grizzly was padding along a gravel bed headed right in our direction. Because we were down wind and partially obscured he hadn't picked up on our presence. As he came parallel with us he suddenly figured out someone, or some thing, was ten feet away from him on the bank. He stopped dead in his tracks, the hair on his back stood straight up and he turned to face us. Then he took a couple of steps in our direction and began to growl. But once he deduced that we weren't a threat and realized who and what was on the bank, the younger grizzly turned and walked away in that slow motion gait grizzlies often use when they know you are close. As soon as he reached the other side of the river he stood still, sniffed the air and took a lengthy pee. I walked into the bush to do the same.

The Spirit Bear's white fur chest was covered in bright red blood, as if he'd been spattered with paint. The blood red dye job

Wolf in Great Bear Rainforest

CHRIS DARIMONT

was from all the salmon he had been eating. For about an hour we had been watching him catch fish at river's edge and then bring them back into the forest to consume. This bear was a prolific fisher as I timed him snagging and devouring a salmon about every eight minutes. He had a variety of angling styles from the one leg reach (appearing as if he was sticking his paw down a hole) to the submerged snatch-in-jaws chomp, but the one that was most fascinating was the belly-flop. There was a large swirling pool created by an assemblage of rocks amongst the fairly fast flowing water, and the pinks were gathering in it before heading further up stream. The white bear would launch himself from a rock, legs splayed out, and land with a thunderous splash. When all the spray and wave action stopped he would emerge from the pool, fish in mouth and would pad back up into the bush to feed.

We were in a small runabout, tenuously anchored, actually just edged up to a rock in shallow water, near the mouth of the river and quite close to shore. A young black bear who had been wandering down the rocky shoreline strolled right across the bow of our boat as if it were just another boulder. The black bear circled round again. We were getting too far into the shallows, so my colleague had hopped out of the boat and was balancing on a rock pushing us out into deeper water when the bear padded right up behind her to observe what was going on.

In my most casual tone of voice I said, "Better not take another step backward." When my colleague asked why, I gestured with my thumb to indicate she should take a peek over her shoulder. We both had to stifle the urge to laugh uproariously.

Having never seen a wolverine before, my initial impulse was to rub my eyes in disbelief. We were sitting in a zodiac with the engine turned off as we had just made our way up the long winding river and into a spectacular lake. There waddling along on shore was a wolverine, compact and stout with dark brown fur that almost looked black. Little if any information currently exists on wolverine populations in coastal ecosystems throughout the Great Bear Rainforest.

Wolverines are well-known for being peripatetic, and the one we were watching was clearly on its way somewhere and wasn't about to wait and pose for a couple of awestruck humans. The wolverine quickly vacated the open shoreline and tromped into the forest. In the aftermath of our wolverine moment, we sat there quietly floating, the surface of the lake shimmered under the mid-day sun and the eerie call of a varied thrush echoed from the trees.

Postscript:

The scientific study and conservation of large carnivores has long been a focus of the Raincoast Conservation Foundation. It was with this in mind that Raincoast purchased the largest commercial trophy hunting tenure in the Great Bear Rainforest, covering approximately 8,000 square miles of precious wildlife habitat. This creative approach has put large carnivore conservation as the priority in a vast area of BC's central coast. With the support of local First Nations and the coastal eco-tourism industry, it has become an integral part of what is both a national and international effort to protect the Great Bear Rainforest's top predators.

Why Preserve Wild Forests?

George Wuerthner

Is there any need for wild forests, especially if society were to adopt sustainable forestry practices? This is not just a rhetorical question. At least some proponents of sustainable forestry and adherents of the working forest paradigm believe that if we managed forests in a sustainable manner, there is little reason to protect wild forests. In fact, there is even the implied message that wild forests, i.e. non-working forests, are somehow inferior to those doing real work (nearly always defined as producing timber and/or other forest products) for society.

While sustainability is an admirable goal and something as a society we ought to strive to attain, most of what I have seen peddled as sustainable forestry practices are far from ecologically sustainable, especially when compared to wild forests. Wild forests protect, preserve and provide many values that I have yet to see fulfilled by forests that advocates suggest are managed sustainably.

Today with a growing awareness of our global environmental impact, finding ways to sustain ourselves while sustaining the planet is imperative. The question for me is whether *sustainable* practices really exist or are they just another piece of propaganda used to sell more products to unwitting consumers to assuage their guilt.

Sustainable forestry operations that I have observed fail to ask a fundamental question: how does a wild ecosystem function and how can we emulate it and preserve natural ecological processes? Instead promoters of sustainable exploitation tend to start with the premise that they are going to log the forest and then attempt to make the land fit the needs of the industry, while doing less ecological damage. Typically what is touted as sustainable is an economic measurement rather than an ecological one. Sustainable forestry, as it is usually practiced, is more about making sure that there is a sustainable supply of wood for the mill over the long haul, and only secondarily about preserving forest ecosystems. As far as I have seen anywhere, we have only succeeded in preserving forest ecosystems by preserving wild forests. All other attempts at sustainability to achieve *ecological* sustainability have fallen short of this goal and criteria.

Two forests in California

To illustrate the point let me relate a recent experience I had with sustainable forestry in California. I toured a highly touted sustainable forestry operation in California. The company whose property we viewed was certified as a sustainable forestry wood producer by the Forest Stewardship Council. Certification by FSC permits a company to sell its wood for a premium and presumes to give consumers reassurance that the wood they are buying is environmentally benign or may even enhance ecosystem function.

The land we visited still had trees, but did it have a forest? For many the mere presence of trees is taken as proof that logging on the site was sustainable. But a continuous supply of trees for the mill doesn't necessarily mean you are preserving or sustaining a forest ecosystem.

I don't want to imply by the following critique that we should abandon forest certification or the goal of sustainability. The forestry procedures I saw on the tour were a vast improvement over the cut and run practices of the past. The company practiced selective cutting of trees over clearcuts. They maintained buffers of unlogged strips along streams. They typically did not cut existing old growth trees. However, whether they are truly ecologically sustainable as is often implied is questionable.

For instance, the company owner showed the group growth rings of a tree that grew on the site before his company began to manage the area. Because of the competition with other trees in the wild forest, the rings were close and tight. Then he showed us a segment of a tree after they had selectively cut some trees. The growth rings were wide and spaced far apart, demonstrating in his mind how thinning *improved* the forest. Now he was growing more wood on the land than when it was a wild forest. But my first thought when I saw the two tree segments was "what good are trees that grow under slow conditions?" Do trees with tight growth rings resist rot longer? If so, would they remain as a biological legacy on the site far longer than a tree grown under sustainable forestry practices, if that tree grown on a sustainable forest site was even allowed to die a natural death and molder back into the forest soil? While a fast growing tree may be good from the lumber company's perspective, a fast growing tree is not necessarily good from a forest ecosystem perspective.

Though the company does not clearcut its land, the company forest management plans call for the eventual cutting of all trees on any particular area — just not all trees at the same time as in a clearcut. You might call this a *rolling clearcut*. Because of this practice, no trees will ever again attain old growth dimensions or status — except for the small percentage of existing old growth that is scattered about its lands which the company has agreed not to cut.

So how does this affect forest ecosystem sustainability? After the tour, I visited a large state park nearby that had wild (unmanaged) forests. Though the differences might not be apparent to the casual visitor, I saw substantial physical differences between the managed company lands and the wild forest.

First, the wild forest *felt* different. It was striking to walk through the ancient cathedral-like groves. Not only were these trees in the wild forest significantly larger than the trees found on the managed lands, but they had a different effect upon me as observer. The forest seemed quieter. The ground beneath my feet was spongier with accumulated litter.

And on the whole there were far more large trees. On the lands managed for sustainable forest production, trees are cut well before they attain what we would call old growth size. Furthermore, these disparities will grow ever greater the longer the company lands are managed for sustainable timber production. Over time on the company lands the few remaining stands of old growth forest will die and will not be replaced because all non-old growth trees are scheduled to be cut at some point as part of its sustainability plan. By contrast in the wild forest, the percentage of old growth will vary over time depending on things like wildfire or insect attacks, but no matter what disturbs the forest — over time a wild forest will gravitate towards old growth.

Given what we know about the value of older, bigger trees, this can't help but affect the forest ecosystem. For example, big trees take longer to rot. They remain longer on the ground, in streams, and provide structural diversity to the forest floor and stream channels. One of the noticeable things about the managed forest we visited was the absence of big woody debris (logs) on the forest floor compared to the nearby wild forest. And though the company foresters had a prescription that left a few snags per acre, the number of large snags was considerably less than what I observed in the wild forest.

Another difference between the so called sustainable forestry site and the wild forest were the number of logs, particularly large logs, in the streams. In the wild forest there was an abundance of logs that had fallen into the creek, sometimes in a tangled clump that created small check dams or armored the banks against erosion. These logs also created fish habitat. By comparison on the sustainable forestry sites, there were far fewer downed logs in the creek, despite the fact that the company did maintain some narrow buffers of unlogged land along all creeks.

Spotted owls and marbled murrets are both native residents of this part of the California coastal forests. Because of their dependence on old growth forest, these species as well as many others that are dependent upon old growth forest ecosystem, not just a few big trees, were present in the wild forest but absent from the sustainable forest. Because thinning the forest opened up the canopy permitting more light to reach the forest floor, the sustainable forest had more shrubs and small trees growing in the understory. These shrubs and small trees were natural ladders for fires to carry the flames of any fire that should occur into the canopy of the trees. By contrast the understory of the old growth wild forest was open and had much less ladder fuel; this openness holds soil moisture longer due to the heavy shade.

In addition to these physical differences, there were other potentially important losses. Among other things, the timber company did not permit wildfires to burn through its sustainable forest tracts. Yet in this particular part of California, wildfire was an important ecological factor to the long-term health of wild forests that on occasion would normally burn at least some of the forest stands. Typically such fires would create a mosaic of burned and unburned forests, release nutrients and clean the forest.

In the sustainable forest, the company representatives admitted that the disturbed habitat created by logging roads and skid trails facilitated invasion by exotic weeds — but they handled it by spraying herbicides along roadways. In the nearby wild forest there were no roads and even few trails. Weeds were far less of a problem as a consequence.

Soil erosion, particularly that from logging roads, was also an issue at the sustainable forestry site and one that never disappeared because once they constructed their main roads for timber management access, they did not remove them. Roads remained as a long-term source of sedimentation. In the wild forest sedimentation of streams was less of an issue. When sedimentation increased due to natural factors like wildfire, a healthy wild forest is able to restore the balance quickly, typically restoring sedimentation levels to pre-fire conditions within a matter of a few years.

Suffice to say it is premature to claim that such forestry practices are sustainable. While they may be an improvement over the kind of butchery that occurred in the past and is still the dominant paradigm on many timber lands including public forests, I question whether such techniques are sustainable from a forest ecosystem perspective. And in the long run that is the only perspective that really counts. After all on most forest lands we have only gone through two-three rotations (cuttings) and like a corn field, we can get a few harvests from the land before the soil productivity is depleted. Whether we can cut trees indefinitely on timber company lands, even those managed for sustainable cutting, remains to be seen. My guess is that far too many ecological impacts are externalized and uncounted.

Reasons for preservation

There are a number of important reasons to preserve wild forests. The first is scientific value. In order to know whether sustainable

forestry ever works, we need the scientific control provided by unmanipulated forests as a comparison. Only by measuring physical and other attributes against a wild forest can we be assured that sustainable forestry is truly sustainable.

Secondly, wild forests provide many ecological services for free that we are only beginning to appreciate — from protection of genetic diversity to preservation of intact watersheds. Wild forests protect wild fish with study after study demonstrating that the most

Redwood forest in California

intact fish populations are those found in wild forests. They can even reduce the extent and intensity of forest fires by reducing evaporation and wind speed, creating conditions less hospitable for the spread of fires. The value of these forests to society is worth more to society than any timber that may be produced from a forest.

Landscape amnesia

But we must preserve wild forests for another reason that may not be obvious to everyone. In Vermont where I am residing, the forests were systematically logged and cleared for farming. At one point more than a century ago, 85% of the state had been cleared for farming. What wasn't turned into sheep pastures and corn fields was logged for timber, charcoal and firewood, so that there are few patches of wild forest left in the state. However, today's residents do not mourn the loss. Indeed, they suffer from landscape amnesia. Nearly everyone, including most of the state's environmental organizations are champions of the working forest and see it as the ideal. Few see any reason to preserve wild forests, because the working forest does it all — provides timber, protects watersheds, provides wildlife habitat — or so they think. Yet when I walk through these Vermont woods, I see a degraded landscape, much like the sustainable forestry operation I visited in California. There are few snags and little woody debris on the forest floor. There are very few large trees. And the lack of large trees was not a consequence of climate and other natural factors. Indeed, there are very large trees in front of old farmhouses where they have provided shade for centuries — just not in the forest itself. A few large trees do not make a forest ecosystem. Unfortunately in Vermont, unlike in California and much of the West, there are few wild forests left intact for people to visit so that visual and other comparisons can be observed. In the West people tie themselves to trees to protect old growth. In Vermont, people do not miss, and therefore do not protect, the forests they have never experienced.

Spiritual and ethical value

Do we turn every last acre of the planet's forests into a woodlot to serve human ends or do we permit at least some parts of the wild forests to be self regulated, and self directed to at least some degree? Some critics might argue that with global warming, acid rainfall and other human influences, no truly wild forests remain. But this is all a matter of degree. The state forest I visited in California was infinitely wilder than the sustainable forest managed for timber production. And if we have learned anything from conservation biology and other sciences, it is the need to preserve large chunks of wild nature if we are to have nature survive at all.

As much as wild forests fulfill such values as watershed protection or non-extractive purposes, we may need them even more for what they can teach us about humility as well as spiritual and ethical values. Whether wild forests survive may ultimately depend on human self-discipline and sense of ethical responsibility. To the degree that we limit our inclination to manage all forests, leaving some to function as wild (meaning self-willed), will be a full measure of our own humility and commitment to restraint. Preservation of wild forests is a magnanimous action that seeks to preserve options and opportunities not only for ourselves, but for the forests themselves.

Buddhism and Global Warming

Bill Devall

How do we Buddhists practice during an era of global warming, global deforestation and rising rates of species extinctions due to human causes?

For some Buddhists the answer is simple. Practice like we always practice, breathing in and breathing out. Living in the present moment. Giving away the merit of our practice.

While some Christian religious teachers advocate nonviolent direct action to change personal and community practices, even presenting teaching materials on global warming for congregations to use (Evangelical Climate Initiative 2006), very few Buddhist teachers have presented teaching materials on global warming for local congregations.

A few Buddhists have searched in the history of Buddhism for sources of Buddhist environmentalism. Daily practice and renewing our vows based on the interpenetration of beings is manifest, for example, in the Ecological Precepts of Green Gulch Zen Center (Kaza and Kraft, 2000).

Zen teacher John Daido Loori in his book, *Teachings of the Earth,* concludes that the Buddhist precepts guide us to wise action. Loori writes:

> The precepts are about creating activity in the world in a way that is in harmony with it. It is what we call compassion. The first realization of unity is wisdom, the realization of oneness. The manifestation of that wisdom in the world of separation is compassion, which is the functioning of the precepts. The bottom line is that these precepts are yours, and no one else's. Please practice them well. In so doing, you take care of this magnificent, great earth of ours. And that is no small thing (Loori 2007, 102).

Following the precept of *do no harm*, I am caught in the conundrum of keeping warm by burning wood pellets in the stove in my home and walking in the woods near my home. Dwelling on the rugged northern coastline of California, I walk through the forest and receive energy in my body, mind and spirit. Walking through the woods during the Autumn, I observe mushrooms growing in abundance. Walking during the winter, I realize that Spring must follow. Walking during the Spring I participate with salmonberries blooming and trillium and other native plants bringing forth their blooms. Walking during the Summer I pick berries of native plants and enjoy the cool shade of the forest.

When I asked Buddhist teacher Alan Senauke if we can find guidance in the Pali scriptures, he replied. "… I don't think the Pali Canon is our source for views on climate change, or Dogen or others. Our ancestors point towards our responsibility for sustaining life. But we are responsible for figuring out what that looks like and means in the world we have to live in and leave for the next generations. Developing such understandings is the real challenge of engaged Buddhism" (e-mail May 17, 2006).

Some Buddhists attempt to place right action during an era of global warming, deforestation and species extinction in the context of social justice. These Buddhists base their call for redistribution of wealth to poor nations on the consensus among scientists that negative effects of global warming, including increasing drought, will be felt by people in the poorest regions of the earth including Africa.

When I asked some of my colleagues in the local Buddhist community for their responses to global warming, deforestation and species extinction, they either said that the issues have been exaggerated or that it is a lifestyle issue of people in rich countries. They said that Buddhists who practice right livelihood or the Buddhist middle way will be drawn to buy hybrid vehicles, reduce their personal consumption, eat a vegetarian diet and invest in mutual funds that specialize in companies offering alternative energy production. Some of my Buddhist colleagues encourage mindfulness practice and spending more time sitting zazen.

Buddhist teacher Stephen Batchelor comments on this response. "While 'Buddhism' suggests another belief system, 'dharma practice' suggests a course of action. The four ennobling truths are not propositions to believe; they are challenges to act." (Batchelor, 1997, 7) Batchelor concludes, "Dharma practice today faces two primary dangers: through resisting creative interaction, it could end up as a marginalized subculture, a beautifully preserved relic, while through losing its inner integrity and critical edge, it could end up being swallowed by something else, such as psychotherapy or contemplative Christianity." (Batchelor, 1997, 113) When American Buddhism becomes an extension of individualistic psychology, the interpenetration of social dukkha is diminished. Individuals come together in therapy sessions to address their personal suffering, not the suffering of the world.

In a society that emphasizes individual suffering, how do Buddhists come together as community as we adapt to rapid change during this era of global warming? Batchelor emphasizes the importance of community. "Community is the living link between individuation and social engagement. A culture of awakening simply cannot occur without being rooted in a coherent and vital sense of community, for a matrix of friendships is the very soil in which dharma practice is cultivated" (Batchelor, 1997, 114).

David Loy, a Buddhist scholar, argues that Buddhist teachings can lead to social theory. American Buddhists are required to develop our own Buddhist social theory of community because we live in a radically different culture from that of the Shakyamuni Buddha, 2,500 years ago. The Shakyamuni Buddha held his meditation retreats in the forest, during the rainy season. The simple lifestyle of forest dwelling monks and nuns is radically different from the lifestyles of the middle classes in India, China and European nations today.

Loy argues that "loving the world as our own bodies" enables us to use our cognitive power to develop patterns of behavior that help us adapt to current cultural and environmental conditions. He concludes that "Taoism and Buddhism also emphasize 'letting things be' in order for them to flourish: not for our sake, and not even for their own sake, but for no sake at all — because questions of utility and justification no longer apply. That challenges the basic principle of our technological and consumerist society, and it also subverts our sense of ego-self. To admit that natural objects (or natural events) have an inherent value independent of any awareness or appreciation of other beings is to question our commonsense dualism between the conscious self and the objective world. The ecological catastrophes that have now become common make it evident that resolving the duality between ourselves and the natural world is necessary if we — not only humans, but the rich diversity that constitutes the biosphere — are to survive and thrive in the new millennium." (Loy, 2003, 51)

Where can Buddhists dwelling in California and across America look for teachers in what Loy calls "the great awakening?" Some Buddhists dwelling in California look to Governor Arnold Schwarzenegger as a teacher. The Governor brings together people

from across the political spectrum, and he signed landmark legislation on global warming in 2006. He has made lifestyle choices confirming his practice of the middle way. He changed his large SUVs into alternative energy vehicles. He is active in moving energy to encourage ecological sustainability.

Moss in BC rainforest

Bo Martin

I am dwelling in the Humboldt bioregion of California. This bioregion is rich in forests, mountains and rivers and rich in people who are peaceful, active and creative.

Laypeople dwelling in Humboldt County are actively developing communities of local food production, renewable energy, social organizations that care for members of the community, and new organizations continue to emerge. During the next several decades we envision Buddhist centers in various watersheds in this bioregion, monasteries in the forests, where nuns and monks contribute to the social life of the community through their productive labor raising food, harvesting timber in sustainable ways, living simple lives rich in experience and teaching children the ways of peaceful interrelationship.

We live in an era of challenge and opportunity. We bring forth our positive energy and creativity and live our lives in simple ways but with rich experiences in the Buddha, the Dharma and Sangha.

Part III:

Case Studies Here and There

TREES FOR LIFE

Volunteers planting trees in Scotland

Lessons from the Old Growth —
Merv Wilkinson and Wildwood Forest

Jay Rastogi

> Our forest managers have studied economics, but they haven't studied the forest ecosystem, which is the basis of this whole thing.
>
> — Merv Wilkinson

Merv Wilkinson has shown people what is possible with forestry in British Columbia and beyond. Thousands of people visit Wildwood each year to experience the forest and benefit from the lessons Merv has learned over his tenure here. Merv (95 years old as we go to press) has spent most of his life stewarding Wildwood, a 77 acre forest on the edge of Quennell Lake plus other properties in the vicinity on southeastern Vancouver Island.

Merv began managing the forest in 1938 after a year and a half stint at a pulp mill. "I was looking for an escape plan," he says referring to the difficult circumstances of working in a non-unionized industrial setting in the depression years, "and this was it. Growing up here I saw my friends across the lake farming and figured I might do the same." Hoping to raise poultry or livestock but not knowing

much about it, "I decided to take a non-graduating course the province offered at UBC (University of British Columbia). There I met Dr. Paul Boving. He had asked us all what our land was like, and when I told him he said, 'Good Lord, you need to study forestry!' A few weeks later he asked me to stay behind after class and said he had just received the most recent forestry course from Guttenberg and that it was a good one. Was I interested in taking it? Well, going to Europe was out of the question for me, but he said he would translate it and help guide me — it wouldn't be official, but I'd get the main points. So on one side of my desk I studied agriculture and on the other forestry. For the practical bit I would mark out roadways or select trees, and he would come over occasionally on the weekends, go fishing and would look it over. He always asked, 'Now, why did you select this tree and not that one?' and he wanted a good explanation — because often times it doesn't matter too much if you select this tree or that one — as long as you don't take both. At graduation time his wife made up a beautiful certificate and when he handed it to me he said the wisest thing I think anyone has ever said to me. He said, 'Don't think this has made a forester out of you. It has given you the tools to become one.'"

The system of forestry Dr. Boving taught was single tree selection or what Merv has sometimes called "sustainable selective forestry" — the underlying guiding principle being one of sustained harvest (sustained yield). "Sustainable means that you don't destroy the forest in order to harvest trees. You need to be sure you don't cut over the annual growth or else you drain the bank account." The standing volume of the forest is seen as being equivalent to the capital in a bank account and the annual growth as interest. This analogy is helpful, however it is not completely correct. The forest has needs which need to be met for ecological processes to function. "Much of this I didn't realize until foresters and ecologists started visiting. I was always interested in and believed in working with nature, so I always wanted a multi-age, multi-height and multi-species forest, but it took 40 years for me to see that dead wood on the ground was necessary for soil building, moisture retention, habitat for fungi and insects and other ecosystem functions. Without healthy soil, you can't have a healthy forest — it is the real resource."

"It is important to realize that relationships exist between all things and no one thing can exist in the forest alone — and that includes us. The forester has a legitimate role when he's working with nature. He's an illegitimate bum when he's trying to kill nature. We've got too much of that. Rows of trees represent blind stupidity and a one track mind."

Pileated Woodpeckers also played a role in encouraging Merv to incorporate ecological criteria into his decision making by illustrating the relationships and connections in nature. "When I realized how important they are to keeping insect populations in balance I decided I better leave some snags for them to nest in so that they would always be around. I also leave cedar trees with carpenter ants because that is a favorite food." We now view all indigenous organisms as being important and view their welfare and the maintenance of ecological processes as our primary goal. Therefore before any harvest critical ecosystem elements are identified first so that they can be retained in the stand. These include wildlife trees and downed wood, seed trees and tall trees.

Wildlife trees and downed wood

Any tree or group of trees with more than average wildlife use should be retained. Dead and dying trees are particularly attractive to fungi, insects, birds and small mammals. In addition to providing food and habitat, downed wood releases nutrients and moisture slowly, moderates temperature and moisture fluctuations and builds soil. In this way in our region, over the long run dead and dying trees also reduce the intensity of any potential fires and in times of fire and drought provide fungi, bacteria, insects, amphibians and plants with potential refuge.

Even after valuing wildlife trees Merv "used to think dead trees on the ground was wasteful, but in fact they have an important role to play and for 15-20 years now I've been leaving some to go back to the soil." One method for increasing downed wood is to retain wind thrown trees on the ground. This also has the beneficial effect of retaining small hummocks where the trees have been uprooted. These areas create micro-site differences in moisture holding and nutrient pooling, and the exposed soil increases the probability of Douglas fir regeneration. Where possible downed trees should be left full length as they don't desiccate and decompose as quickly as smaller sections. Trees decomposing over a longer period of time tie up the least amount of soil nitrogen (a limiting nutrient). Thus the benefits of downed wood are expressed over a longer time period.

Creating snags by girdling some trees is also valuable (especially in small groups). Pick areas where you want more light (i.e. pick areas with bare ground but no tree regeneration and understory shrubs or pick dense areas with a lot of inter-tree competition). If the risk of fire hazard from human use is high, branches on downed trees could be cut and dropped to the forest floor. Most fires Merv believes are caused "by carelessness — smoking or using equipment in the wrong season. Fire in the hands of our aboriginal people was a useful tool, but white man doesn't know how to use it properly. There hasn't been a fire here in my lifetime but you can still see charcoal on the older trees. By burning they got better berry crops and also more deer."

Seed trees

Natural seeding is preferred because locally adapted genes are retained in the stand. It is also inexpensive. The dominant trees are good candidates to consider as seed trees. At the end of their lives they also become good wildlife trees. Merv feels "a good forester manipulates the canopy, opening it up to light when necessary." This benefits the trees that remain and also lets new seedlings get started. "By simple observation you learn to recognize what is a normal growth rate and when a tree is suppressed or has too much light. The rule of thumb is: enough light to make a tree grow; enough shade to make it reach for the light." In addition to providing light competition, which promotes the lower limbs of trees to self-prune, the surrounding canopy also

Merv Wilkinson in Wildwood forest

THE LAND CONSERVANCY

protects younger trees from snow damage and especially wind damage. A tree grown in an open area "is shorter, is bushy — has a lot of knots, has a lot of taper and crowns off too soon. They are only good for pulp. I choose to leave my best trees for seeding. The ones the squirrels like the cones from always have the best germination."

Tallest trees

"When I went out East ten years ago, I found they had a rule of thumb to never cut your tallest trees. Only in areas of uniform canopy heights should co-dominants be considered for harvest." Retaining the tallest trees in the stand is beneficial in reducing wind velocities and therefore damage to tree leaders (particularly those approaching the top of the canopy). The tallest trees are often the best seed trees as well. Retaining the tallest trees means the stand height will remain high or get taller — thus better economically in the long term, and also better ecologically because more habitat opportunities exist.

Candidates to harvest

Our understanding of ecosystem functioning is not sufficient to say with certainty what can be maintained for hundreds or thousands of years. But "any time you cut more than the growth you are in a deficit position. Because of the forests needs I now realize the cut cannot be the growth rate, because your soil will wear out. How much below the annual growth rate one has to go I don't know. It takes a long time to build soil back up, but trees like alder are good for that."

It is desirable to allow sufficient light to reach the forest floor in a patchy fashion to allow for the regeneration of the desired plant species. This criterion will have to be balanced with the desire to keep the stand sufficiently dense so that the trees lose lower limbs and develop less juvenile wood. A helpful way to decide which trees to remove is to consider what in the stand would be next to die naturally. This may include some (but not all) diseased or suppressed trees. Typically trees with less than 25% of their length in live foliage have a higher probability of dying next. Lack of foliage density and a poor (yellowish) color are also indicators of our native conifer trees in decline. In Douglas fir as the tree grows its red inner bark becomes exposed. Those trees showing a lot of red between the grooves of bark are faster growing. Those trees showing little red in the grooves of bark are slower growing and could be considered for harvest. One should keep in mind that some of these trees should be left for wildlife use and nutrient cycling. Also, diseases are a part of the forest too and should not be eliminated. Many diseases are fungal and play an important role in recycling nutrients. "I no longer worry about diseases. In 1945 I cut trees in an area with root rot. But some trees didn't show any signs of disease, so I left them. For some reason they weren't vulnerable and now I think of them as good seed trees for that area."

"Wildwood is a managed forest, where I've lent a helping hand. My interference is minimal, and I'm learning all the time that the process of growing a forest is very complex. Forests operate on a very different time frame than do governments and businesses. Clearcutting reduces a forest to zero. It will be hundreds of years at best before that area will be close to being a real forest again. But the balance sheet of a company does not consider hundreds of years. The refusal to do a proper job in the interests of foreign investors is criminal. Unions and operators have blinded the workers and the public to this. BC forestry has always been corrupt."

The 1980s and 1990s in British Columbia saw considerable conflict around views on the values of forests and the public's role in guiding the development of forest planning policy. Merv's contempt for industrial forestry, his outspokenness and his willingness to allow access to Wildwood illustrated that another way was possible. Merv's involvement in this debate also benefited him with an injection of ecological knowledge from experts which contributed to changes in his stewardship practices — and which continues to influence Wildwood's trajectory today.

Merv also was involved in large civil disobedience actions at Clayoquot Sound (blockading a public road used for transporting logs out of the area) and was among the 850 arrested and charged with contempt of court for ignoring a BC Supreme Court injunction against the blockade. A logger, protesting logging methodology, representing himself at trial and being called "magnificently unrepentant" by the sentencing judge proved captivating and thus propelled Merv and his work at Wildwood to greater prominence. Merv continues to refer to that action as the "proudest moment" of his life. "Nothing is ever accomplished without some form of popular action. Here we had bad laws, a bad cabinet, a bad premier, attorney general and a disgusting justice; all the ingredients for civil disobedience. It happened, and the reaction was global. I would have been a traitor not to have challenged an injunction which gives industry the right to destroy. It's simply not necessary. You don't need to destroy the forest to get timber — it's a matter of method and greed. Rather than seeing my operation as an advantage we were viewed as the enemy. We need more people and fewer companies involved in forestry. We have people who would and could do what is needed. The reason industry doesn't practice alternative forestry is because then they would be admitting they know how. It was not acceptable to save trees to cut later. I was laughed at, ignored and threatened but I was not dislodged. But that is in the past."

With Merv's increasing age and declining physical condition it was becoming a concern to a small group of friends and academics that the example would not continue beyond Merv's lifetime if plans could not be made to purchase Wildwood (now in an area of rapid residential development). TLC-The Land Conservancy (a charitable land trust) and the Ecoforestry Institute became involved and purchased Wildwood. Their primary purpose is to use Wildwood as a learning site for those wanting to bridge the gap in our culture between humans and nature and for those wanting to explore other models of forest stewardship which do not degrade forest associated ecosystems. "We need to understand our relationship with the planet on which we live," says Merv. "We have to live with the earth. The earth does not have to live with us."

GUS DIZEREGA

Renewing Our Forest Culture —
The Art and Practice of Natural Forests

Iliff Simey

Our once great forests

My forest in Wales, Coed Nant Gain, I described in the *Ecoforestry* journal (Simey 2002) and addressed the question of just what is ecoforestry. Since then I have made significant progress in understanding the holistic nature of the forest and the role we humans play in forming a new harmonious relationship with the forest in this 21st century.

The triple problems of overpopulation, material greed and loss of our connection with the land have brought things to a head, and this degradation which is worldwide is leading to the universal disappearance of the forest. This is a matter of urgency, rethinking our whole attitude and relationship with the forest; that something so complex and beautiful yet apparently timeless can be willfully and deliberately destroyed is a terrible indictment of our generation.

Nature evolved on a broad scale, yet our woodlands in Britain are but small disparate fragments of the original wild forest. Mostly in poor health, abandoned, they are derelict, suffering inappropriate and heavy-handed intervention that is tree-focused yet which claims to foster conservation. In restoring these fragmented woodlands we must therefore encourage diversity creating a mosaic in miniature of the original forest structure. People are amazed by how much variety there is in my relatively small forest for it feels enormous (20 acres is a reasonable size for Britain), greatly encouraging me in what I am doing. Interestingly they comment on its peace and tranquility saying "I feel better already!" I sense a refreshing peace of mind. By comparison, most forests in Britain lack this spiritual quality.

I enjoy taking people on conducted tours as it's a great opportunity to explain and experience the forest, rather than regard it simply as fresh air for dog exercise. We've lost our forest culture yet people interact as if something is stirring in them. One great success was a party of young people from a city allotment project who on arrival announced, "We know nothing about woodland." Inspiration struck and I responded "Great, your mind is not cluttered — just observe and learn." They did. Being well versed in genetics, seed origin and so on, we explored together the evidence of two sources of genetic stock in a single species of oak. As a result their visit became a serious interchange of ideas, and they departed feeling harmony with the forest.

The best part of visits (rain permitting) is sitting round the campfire where I have used a historic feature to create a small woodland amphitheater. People bring sandwiches and discuss issues of their choice, the peace and tranquility of the forest providing a new perspective on the world and for children an exciting opportunity to experience the woods on their own. Amazingly few children know how to kindle an open fire, the thrill of burning their fingers or getting smoke in their eyes! I'm very careful to maintain the wild forest setting as if the bear or wolf is right there watching us, for it could all too easily become open, tidy and denuded like a public park. I'm making a small bunkhouse so that people can stay over and experience the sounds in the night, rain on the roof, wind in the trees, animals hunting in the dark, the dawn chorus and smell the forest in the morning air. Our imagination is the only limitation! There are also special places —focal points where everything comes together — where I have placed flat topped rocks to make seats to contemplate the peace and tranquility enclosed by the forest, views, running water, a pond, with posts to screen my silhouette from passing animals. It feels, one visitor commented, as if Shakespeare had been here the night before writing A *Midsummer Night's Dream*.

A new relationship with the forest

I previously explained to visitors about growing trees for timber, forest flowers, wildlife hotels, indeed whatever was visible. Recently however I've discovered that people love my describing things that stimulate their imagination; large mammals roaming the forest — bear, beaver, wolf for example (no matter that many are long extinct) — ancient trees and great birds, the sound of melt water from the retreating glaciers and gold in the stream. I use two aluminum dishes to let the bear know we are coming (recently a 15-foot python was seen roaming free in south Wales); I've snakes in my compost heap (some plastic) and trees obviously scratched by the bear (it couldn't be anything else). Footprints in the snow could be a wolf. One visitor capturing the spirit caught a distant view of the bear on camera. By the time people leave, fact has become blurred with fiction for the forest is such an exciting place to explore.

There is a serious side to all this, for it illustrates how the forest must have been 300 years or more ago and how what we see has changed. I am increasingly aware that my intervention should be working towards compensating for the extinctions of fauna, flora and place. The beaver is one obvious example, making a significant contribution to the holistic health of the forest, old large trees with hollows and decay another. Visitors are very happy to become beavers for a while, damming the stream or making artificial hollow trees.

I see the forest as existing past, present and future, all at the same time. This becomes apparent as we learn to interpret what we see and sense around us, the past living in the present, carrying its genes forward to the next generation. Sessile Oak for example (*Quercus petraea*) grows from the stump and so conforms to the original genetic stock. The stump may date back to the original forest before being downgraded by indiscriminate felling and the importation of new seed. Thus I'm trying to propagate cuttings so that it may be possible to reinstate the oak growing here in the ancient forest. The oldest oak we estimate at about 400 years or more and — wow — the energy flowing in that tree is amazing (just try placing your hands on trees of differing age).

I talk about *we* not *I-* because our intervention in the forest must work *with* nature rather than *impose* upon. *I* implies I know best, whereas nature has millennia of experience to contribute and together we can restore the forest in a new working harmony. Using terms such as *thinning* (not a natural event and damaging to holistic health) and *coppicing* deludes me into believing that I alone know how to *manage* the forest. I have found it immensely refreshing to quit using such terms and stick to plain English which everyone comprehends. Thus we begin to appreciate that the forest consists of rather more than trees and is a self-sustaining and self-regulating community that includes ourselves.

My Interpretation of the Deep Ecology Platform Concepts Governing my Relationship with and Intervention with the Forest

1. *The forest has intrinsic value in its own right irrespective of its use to us.* On the one hand, the forest belongs to the forest community, not to human society. On the other, of necessity humans are responsible for the land, to protect and represent.

2. *The forest is a rich, diverse, holistic community that is self-sustaining.* Humans have for centuries taken of the intrinsic value; they are therefore obliged to participate in restoring the health of the forest both physically and spiritually.

3. *This richness and diversity in the forest must not be abused by our need.* Humans may take only where there is a local abundance and for their our own need.

4. *The forest will only flourish if the human population is reduced.* Humans are now in serious conflict with the forest and are eradicating the forest all together so that future generations of humans will not know the forest.

5. *Human interference in the forest is excessive and rapidly getting worse.* There is no longer enough forest to meet the need of the human population so that human access to the forest is now a privilege not a right. Humans enter the forest with respect for the forest community.

6. *Hence, all policies affecting the forest must be reviewed and strengthened.* We will produce a deeply different solution preventing the destruction of forest communities — conserve essential skills, experience and tradition — re-educate governments, bureaucracies and corporations — renew our woodland culture.

7. *Change must move away from increasing material expectations* to concern for the well-being of the forests.

8. *In supporting the above we are obliged to try to bring about changes* both locally in our own forests and globally in the forests of the world.

This interpretation forms the basis for an ongoing process.

Deep ecology principles applied in the forest

When I first came across Deep Ecology I immediately sensed its relevance but could not find anyone who had applied its concepts in the forest. This kept on surfacing with me but it was some time before I seriously gave it thought and began to ask questions. Why protect the native fauna that took the farmer's sheep? Should I cull non-native species like grey squirrels? Deep ecology principles pose difficult questions concerning these issues, challenging my thoughts and ideas. Questions raise more questions. To some there is no clear answer, for example regarding our attitude and response to non-native species. Each of us must decide for ourselves our response to such problems. Thus my attitude is developing, and even as I write this my relationship with the forest is constantly maturing.

The forest as one harmonious community

The Deep Ecology Platform Principles have thus opened my eyes to the full breadth of my relationship with the forest and underlie all that I do there. Implied in the Platform Principles is a hands-on practical approach of a scale that is harmonious with the functioning of the forest. Thus intervention in scale with the forest decade on decade achieves considerable progress, whereas one major intervention then nothing for three or four decades is unnatural and actually harms the holistic health of the forest. Like the universe, the forest is complex beyond our comprehension; we understand so little in spite of experiencing it at first hand! I'm learning to observe this interacting whole in my own forest; it is beautifully illustrated in Joan Maloof's collection of essays *Teaching the Trees* (Maloof 2005). That she holds her student seminars in the forest has particular appeal, for too many people are lectured in the classroom rather than actually experiencing firsthand what is being discussed.

A parallel history

Our countryside must have been very different in previous centuries, hugely richer and more diverse than anything we have today. I sense that much of the experience I am now acquiring must have been known to our peasant ancestors. I recall working with a friend in Oregon. We went to see the tallest surviving Douglas fir (*Pseudotsuga menzii*) in 80 acres of natural unlogged forest. On return to his logged-over forest, we realized that large mounds of decaying debris were indicators of where great trees had stood. We were astonished, and suddenly our vision of his forest as a living entity over millennia became meaningful to us.

Looking back through history, the conflicting needs of silviculture and the needs of peasants have gone largely unrecognised. This divergence goes back through history: the profound influence of two world wars (grow more trees at home); John Evelyn's *Silva* of 1642 (totally tree-focused); the medieval land enclosures (self-sufficient rural economy); Spanish Armada (felling oaks on a vast scale); Forest Charter of 1217 (Magna Carta apparently made such a mess of forest management that a new charter had to be quickly introduced) and more. The practical evidence in buildings and forests is even more tantalizing: in Britain for example where did they get so much oak from which to build the timber frame farm houses, church roofs and so on? In our own time ecoforestry on one hand and government and multi-national corporations on the other illustrates how this divergence still exists. Behind a silvicultural facade, bureaucracy is imposed on us — the new generation of forest peasants.

Learning from the natural forest

Walking in the Oregon forest, the old-growth trees clearcut three or four decades previously — dense, dark, hardly a sound, trees all the same age — I unexpectedly entered a natural glade. From canopy to ground, wildflowers bloomed, creepers climbed, birds sang, insects danced in shafts of sunlight, seedling trees competed for light — the forest was alive and vigorous, renewing itself! Without any intervention by us, nature was putting right the disaster of the clearcut and forest health was recovering.

Here in Wales nature works in the same way. Glades, each quite different and unique, neither too big nor too small, created as if a large tree had fallen in a gale, with wet snow, root decay, old age or topped for a power line, allow shafts of sunlight to penetrate and fallen branches to decay. To the untrained eye this looks untidy and chaotic, but to nature this complexity is essential to restoring forest health. Nature left on its own would take centuries to achieve this, but by our working *with* nature, we can accelerate natural processes of recovery the full effect of which may not be apparent for decades. Glades should be small enough to maintain humidity and protect the soil from drying out, yet large enough for shafts of sunlight to penetrate. A rich and diverse flora and fauna arises; there is an abundance of food and shelter; birds nests, insects abound; small mammals, like stoat and weasel, shelter in the ground cover; flowers bloom,

make scent, seeds ripen and dormant young trees start growing in competition for the light. Fallen trees decay, insects and fungi recycle nutrients. Most importantly the mycorrhizal fungi in the soil are alive. Thus the forest is harmonious, at peace with itself. As with organic farming it takes time to convert to natural practices. The changeover requires

Woodland amphitheater in Wales

ILIFF SIMEY

at least a decade to implement so great is the change required in our thinking.

Coed nant gain — demonstrating our helping hand

CNG has been here since the retreat of the glaciers 12,000 years ago and is thus exceptionally rich and diverse. I term forests like these *Old-Growth Ancient Forests,* distinguishing them from *Ancient Woodlands* defined technically as a mere 400 or more years old. CNG was trashed twice (probably clearcut in 1801 and in 1919 when timber trees were felled and the forest abandoned as waste probably for the first time in its history). In 1919, I'm told, the woodland flowers were prodigious. Then, as the canopy closed over, the forest became dark, quiet, still and cold. Nature endeavored single-handed for almost eight decades to turn this around. It was then that I began to grasp how I could assist, indeed accelerate this natural process, working with and giving nature a helping hand, recognizing the intrinsic value of the forest to realize its full potential. Now its health is bouncing back, a mosaic in miniature reflecting the ancient wildwood of which it was once part, be it on a much larger scale.

Living in the forest enables me to experience intimately its moods and respond to times of day, weather and seasons. Increasingly wildlife is beating a trail outside my window: owls, badgers, dragonflies and foxes look for scraps of food; it's becoming something like an African safari park. Their comings and goings provide a constant source of interest reminding me that I am in their forest, not mine.

No trees survive in Coed Nant Gain large enough to have hollow trunks, decaying cavities or major broken branches, and few have nest sites or decaying bark to harbor insects and beetles. I am constantly seeking means to compensate for this. I value ivy clad trees as *wildlife hotels,* providing shelter, food and nest sites; volunteers install nest boxes; I create *beetle houses* when felling a tree by leaving the stump 4" or 6" higher than normal and slotting the stump horizontally providing a home for spiders, slugs, worms, bugs, even baby lizards. I replicate *artificial hollow trees* using clean 50 gallon drums filled with forest debris — sticks, woodchips, leaves, bark, even the odd dead squirrel. Where nature selects a weak tree for removal I accelerate its decline by slotting the base vertically and leave it standing to encourage fungi to penetrate the heartwood and so increase the decaying wood. These actions are all experimental, and in a few years time we will open one of the artificial hollow trees to see who is living there.

Nature and I together are learning where to make glades. I choose a dark, retarded part of the forest that needs invigorating; nature selects a weak tree to take out. Recently, with the help of a couple of professional tree surgeons who offered freely of their skills, we cut the tops off trees rather than felling to create standing decaying trunks. We slotted the base (in preference to ringing) so that the tree dies slowing over a decade or more, replicating the natural forest. In the process the dying tree makes dense stubby side growth providing great nest sites and shelter. In due course I hope the number of woodpeckers will increase. Larger trees are left as grandparent trees to provide seed, nest sites and decay for insects. Thus the potential to create glades with minimal intervention is maturing, and some of the early glades are now responding with seedling trees that will grow on for timber.

Long-term Coed Nant Gain will again be productive, valued for quality not quantity. Wildlife will spill over into the surrounding countryside; we will have organic logs for the stove, spiritual refreshment and timber to offset the running costs. In Britain there is no provision for land trusts as in North America; separating land ownership from whatever stands on the land for this might well meet my needs. I am concerned that whoever follows me in caring for this forest may not understand my approach, and so it is essential that I leave a record of how I've been working so that hopefully they carry on where I leave off. I plan to have my likeness carved in the trunk of a tree overlooking the valley so that anyone again felling trees will court trouble!

Conclusion —
from rhetoric to reality

Today I acquired three beautiful tropical rainforest beams, discarded from a conservatory, replaced with plastic and now on their way to the landfill — one brief use since the destruction of the ancient forest from which they came. Have we the right to destroy the remaining ancient forest with all that this implies for our planet and humanity? What of the peace and tranquility, the refreshment we so need in our stress-filled lives and of which nature has such abundance? Without forests humanity will indeed be impoverished, both globally and within ourselves.

Coed Nant Gain provides a working demonstration of what Natural Forest Practice has to offer and how it works in practice, namely:

- Creating a truly self-sustaining, self-sufficient forest where all the parts are essential to the whole

- Demonstrating how natural systems work in practice and how we can compensate for that which is missing
- Rediscovering and developing forest skills that are rewarding and fulfilling
- Giving forests a role in the local economy, providing regular employment and wide ranging produce which contribute to the well-being of the global environment year after year
- Relieving our stress in this difficult world in which we live
- Empowering small-scale owners to be responsible for their forest land

The next logical step is drafting a *Forest Bill of Rights.*

Invitation

I'm setting out a range of guides describing the principles and practice of Natural Forest Practice. My next step is to establish a website that I will constantly update as experience accumulates. Please send relevant articles and observations. Visitors are most welcome to see what I'm doing at Coed Nant Gain. I may be contacted at organic.forests@btopenworld.com.

Glossary of my terminology

Forest and Woodland: I use forest to refer to that which relates to the natural, and woodland, especially in Britain, to indicate that which is the result of human intervention.

Ancient Forest: I use forest to differentiate from Ancient Woodland (actually ASNW) a technical term used in Britain referring to woodland that is 400 or more years old.

Old-growth Forest: Original forest with large old trees.

Wildwood: The original natural forest in Britain.

14

Restoring a Forest — A Remedy for Our Ills

Nitya Harris

"I am only a gardener," says Joss Brooks. Joss is director of the Pitchandikulam Bio-Resource Center (PBRC). We are sitting in a rustic kitchen hut in the pouring rain. We hardly need a fire in this 77°F weather, but it feels comforting. This kitchen is one of the few buildings in this dry evergreen tropical forest — full of lush vegetation, birds and some large snakes they say — that has been rehabilitated by Joss and the PBRC.

I arrived in Pitchandikulam in the state of Tamil Nadu during my travels in south India at the end of 2001. I had been wandering through the state looking at environmental projects. After meandering through windmill farms and bio-villages, I headed towards the reforestry project in Pitchandikulam. Well, I soon found out that there was no easy way to get to this forest. I started off in Pondicherry on the coast of the Bay of Bengal and walked for an hour until I found a local bus that I hoped was going in the right direction. After another hour on the bus I disembarked in a small village hoping to find some other transportation to the forest which was still 6 miles

away. It was fairly easy to see that the village was not going to provide me with a conveyance in the near future, and so I started walking along the red clay road. Just as the rain started, I managed to flag down the only car that I had seen so far, which turned out to be the local politician touring his constituents. Amidst a very interesting conversation on the concerns of the local people, I was let out at a crossroad half a mile away from my destination.

I remember that approach well. Walking along a narrow trail, I was surrounded by lush tropical forest. The air was perfumed with the smell of damp foliage and the musky scent of rain-washed earth. The trees were full of bird song. Ahead of me was an elderly lady from the village gently taking her cow for a walk. And to think that in 1973, Joss and a number of others arrived in this area to find a dry and desolate site with only a few scattered palm trees. The land had been covered by a tropical forest at one point but had been degraded by logging and agriculture. Through vision and hard work, it is now a flourishing self-generating forest with a wide diversity of fauna and flora.

The area is home to the Tropical Dry Evergreen Forest (TDEF) — a forest type found only in south India and Sri Lanka — which provides rare biological richness due its very high species abundance. In this subtropical environment a tremendous wealth of biodiversity flourished in the past. The bioregion is home to at least 735 vegetative species including 400 plants that have medicinal properties. Today, due to pressures of population, modern agricultural practices, technology and politics, the bioregion is close to extinction as only 0.01% survives. If action is not taken to preserve and restore this forest, this ecological wealth will be lost forever.

The major work in the rehabilitation of this forest has been on erosion control, watershed management and extensive reforestation work. Over 2 million trees have been planted in this and other nearby areas. Seeds are collected from remnant forests, sacred groves and sanctuaries and are propagated in nurseries and then transplanted in appropriate sites. After 25 years of this work, Pitchandikulam is now a diverse ecosystem containing more than 400 species of plants covering a mere 50 acre area.

As the forest grew, so did the efforts to include and interact with the local villagers on the importance of this forest and of the uses provided by the indigenous plants. The Pitchandikulam Bio-Resource Center (PBRC) was established in 1993 to become the focal point of the forest rehabilitation work being done in the area. The PBRC is active in conserving and regenerating of sacred groves in collaboration with local communities. It is also an environmental education facility for the local community with a focus on the teaching of conservation, identification and use of indigenous medicinal plants. Along with

demonstration and thematic gardens, the Bio-Resource Center provides documentation of local healers, a display of photos, seeds, herbarium sheets, raw drugs and traditional technologies and a library and database to help with sustainable community planning. The center provides training for various target groups like women, school children, teachers, youth clubs, NGOs and government departments in all aspects of eco-restoration work with an emphasis on the revitalizing of local health traditions. During my short time there, the center was visited by a group of architecture students from the local university, who not only had the chance to personally see and feel the forest, but who were also able to hear Joss's views on nature in design.

One of the areas that Pitchandikulam has focused upon is on the regeneration of endangered medicinal plants. India has a long and honored tradition of using traditional medicines. This particular bioregion is home to at least 400 species of medicinal plants that have been used for centuries by traditional practitioners of herbal medicine. However these species are being rapidly depleted by the continual destruction of the Tropical Dry Evergreen Forest. Some causes of this include monoculture planting by the Forest Department and the over-exploitation by the pharmaceutical industry which collects its plant materials from these wild sources. A key accomplishment has been the development of the Pitchandikulam Medicinal Plant Conservation Park. There is continuous work with the traditional healers of the local villages in identifying the medicinal plants and collecting seeds for propagation. The seeds are grown in nurseries and transplanted into the correct habitats. There is hope that these will serve as the gene banks for the future. The PBRC has painstakingly collected and documented the knowledge of over 200 local healers and are now working on methods to transfer this knowledge to others through meetings and visits to remnant forest areas. Information is provided on groups of plants that cure poisonous bites, bone fractures, headaches and stomach problems. One example is *Rauwolfia tetraphylla* which is stated to cure most snake and scorpion bites. Classes are held to demonstrate the preparation of herbal remedies to cure common ailments using plant material from the Pitchandikulam nurseries and gardens.

I am sitting on the floor of the Bio-Resource Center with Joss and four village women at their weekly meeting. The women are traditional healers from neighboring villages, and now they work with Joss to educate the people of the villages about medicinal plants and their traditional uses. As a part of their work, the women visit other traditional healers to document many of the traditional healing systems. These methods have slowly been lost as modern methods take hold in the villages. But there is now an upsurge of bringing back the traditional medicine in India, and Pitchandikulam is playing a part in it. The village women are learning about planting kitchen gardens that have food and medicinal plants, the children are learning about their traditional medicines and as the forest grows back, everyone is able to directly experience the effects of these plants. What is important here is that as the forest is being regenerated so is the knowledge and value of the traditional medicine that has been a part of the people for centuries.

Just as I was set to leave this part of India, Joss received word that the European Commission had approved PBRC's grant application to implement the same Tropical Dry Evergreen Forest rehabilitation process on a larger land base — that of the entire bioregion of nearly 300 square miles. Now, there's a job for our gardener!

Ferns in Garry Oak-Douglas Fir forest

VICTORIA STEVENS

Editor's note: This article was originally published in *Ecoforestry* 17(2): 34-37.

15

The Vision of Trees For Life

Alan Watson Featherstone

The vision of the award winning charity Trees For Life is to restore a wild forest, which exists for its own sake, as a home for wildlife and to fulfill the ecological functions necessary for the well-being of the land itself. Trees For Life is not aiming to regenerate a forest that will be utilized sustainably as an extractive resource for people, although it recognizes the need for this in Scotland. It endorses the efforts of other organizations in seeking to establish a new, ecologically sustainable system of forestry, and strongly believes that this utilitarian approach must be complemented by the restoration of large areas of truly wild forest. Trees For Life is unique in being the only organization working specifically towards this end.

Scotland is a prime candidate for ecological restoration work, as it is one of the countries to have suffered most from environmental degradation in the past. The Highlands in particular have been described as a *wet desert* as a result of centuries of exploitation, which have reduced them to their present impoverished and barren condition. With most other countries now

repeating the same ecological mistakes, Trees For Life believes that a great opportunity exists for Scotland to provide examples of how we can reverse the damage that has been done here. Thus Trees For Life envisions its work to restore the native Caledonian Forest as not only helping to bring the land here back to a state of health and balance, but also having global relevance, as a model for similar projects in other countries.

The Caledonian Forest

The Caledonian Forest originally covered much of the Highlands of Scotland, and gets its name from the Romans, who called Scotland *Caledonia,* meaning "wooded heights." The native pinewoods, which formed the westernmost outpost of the boreal forest in Europe, are estimated to have covered nearly 4 million acres as a vast primeval wilderness of Scots pines, birch, rowan, aspen, juniper and other trees. On the west coast, oak and birch trees predominated in a temperate rainforest ecosystem rich in ferns, mosses and lichens. Many species of wildlife flourished in this forest, including the European beaver, wild boar, lynx, moose, brown bear and the wolf as well as several notable species of birds — the capercaillie, the crested tit and the endemic Scottish crossbill, which occurs nowhere else in the world apart from the pinewoods.

However, there has been a long history of deforestation in Scotland, and clearance of the land began in Neolithic times. Trees were cut for fuel and timber and to convert the land to agriculture. Over the centuries, the forest shrank as the human population grew, and some parts were deliberately burned to eradicate *vermin* such as the wolf. More recently, large areas were felled to satisfy the needs of industry, particularly after the timber supply in England had been exhausted. The widespread introduction of sheep and a large increase in the numbers of red deer ensured that once the forest was cleared, it did not return. Today, less than 1% of the original forests survive, and the native pinewoods have been reduced to 35 isolated remnants. Gone with the trees are all the large mammals with the exception of the deer. Species such as the brown bear and the wild boar had become extinct by the 10th and 17th centuries respectively. The last to disappear was the wolf when the last remaining individual was shot in 1743.

The surviving fragments of the native pinewoods are links with the past; they are the last vestiges of Scotland's forests as they existed from the end of the last Ice Age until around 2,000 years ago. However, those remnants are running out of time, as the majority of them consist only of old trees. About 150 years ago the forest reached a critical point of no return; since then there have been too few trees and too many deer eating them, so that no young trees have become established. As a result of this human-created imbalance in the ecosystem,

the remnants have become *geriatric* forests. As the trees die, the forest continues to shrink, and without protection from overgrazing most of the remnants will disappear in the next few decades. Thus, we are the last generation with the opportunity to save the Caledonian Forest and restore it for the future.

In the last 30 years, work has been done to protect some of the remnants, and where the deer numbers have been reduced or where they have been fenced out of the forest, natural regeneration of the trees is taking place. The results of these initiatives are encouraging, but they only cover a small part of the original forest area and have been largely uncoordinated. While they are enabling a new generation of trees to grow and take the place of the old ones, they will still result in just a few relatively small, scattered stands of pinewoods. To restore the true Caledonian Forest however, requires vision and action on a much larger scale. The forest is a complex, living community of interdependent plants and animals, many of which require large areas of habitat in which to live.

Practical solutions

Trees For Life is working to restore the native forest in a target area of about 600 square miles. We have a threefold strategy to facilitate the return of the forest. The first part of its strategy is to encourage the natural regeneration of the trees by fencing deer out of areas on the periphery of the existing remnants, so that seedlings can grow naturally to maturity again without being overgrazed. This is the simplest and most effective way of regenerating the forest, as it involves the minimum of intervention and allows nature to do most of the work. This is one of the basic principles of ecological restoration. However, this only works for locations where there is an existing seed source nearby, which is not the case in the treeless expanses that make up most of the Highlands today.

The second part of its strategy comes into effect in these situations, and it involves planting native trees in barren areas where the forest has disappeared completely. To do this, seed is collected from the nearest surviving trees to maintain the local genetic variation in the forest. The resulting seedlings are then planted in a random, non-linear pattern inside fenced exclosures, replicating the natural distribution of the trees. Trees For Life is working with all of the native trees from the forest, paying particular attention to the pioneer species, such as birch, rowan and aspen, as they have an important role to play in the succession of the forest as it gets re-established.

The third part of the strategy involves the removal of non-native trees, which in some areas have been planted as a commercial crop amongst the old trees of the Caledonian Forest remnants, thereby preventing their regeneration.

Combining these three strategies, the charity's intention is to re-establish areas, or islands, of healthy young forest scattered throughout barren, deforested glens. As these new trees reach seed-bearing age they will form the nuclei for an expanded natural regeneration in the surrounding area. While the trees in these islands are growing, it will be important to reduce the numbers of deer so that the forest restoration process can become self-sustaining, without the need for further fences.

After several years of preparation, Trees For Life began practical work to regenerate the Caledonian Forest in 1989. Since then, thanks to fencing funded by Trees For Life, over 150,000 naturally regenerating Scots pine

seedlings and other native trees have been protected from overgrazing. To date more than half a million Scots pines and native broadleafed trees have been planted by staff and volunteers. Thousands of volunteers, from teenagers to seventy-year-olds, have taken part in this forest restoration work. The volunteers receive a powerful experience of working together in a group with like-minded people to do something practical and positive for the planet.

Many of the trees planted are grown in Trees For Life's own nursery at Plodda Lodge, (purchased in 1996) where propagation is particularly concentrated on the scarcer species such as hazel, holly and juniper which are difficult to obtain from other sources. The charity has also initiated special projects for the regeneration of rare trees in the forest, such as aspen, by running the largest program of aspen propagation in Scotland, growing this rare species from root cuttings for planting out in the Highlands. It has also carried out an extensive survey of the target area for

Scots pine

TREES FOR LIFE

aspen trees, having mapped out over 350 sites where it occurs.

Trees For Life also runs projects focusing on specific threatened parts of the forest ecosystem, including riparian or riverside woodland and the montane shrub community. Over a period of several years, it has carried out the most extensive surveys in Scotland for dwarf birch, a key component of the montane shrub vegetation community. This is part of Trees For Life's program to facilitate the regeneration and recovery of this community, which has been almost entirely eliminated in Scotland by overgrazing and burning.

Cooperation and influence

Much of the work of the charity is carried out in close cooperation with other organizations seeking to establish a coherent, integrated strategy and action for forest regeneration. In particular, Trees For Life has been working

Hand and sapling in Scotland

TREES FOR LIFE

with Forestry Commission Scotland since 1989 to expand the area of native pinewoods in Glen Affric, where the majority of its work to date has been carried out. In 1993 Trees for Life acted as a catalyst for the purchase, by the National Trust for Scotland (NTS), of the West Affric Estate which encompasses the entire headwaters of the Affric River. In partnership with NTS it is working to facilitate forest restoration on West Affric through a series of exclosures for natural regeneration, some planting of native trees and a reduction of deer numbers. It also works in cooperation with the Royal Society for the Protection of Birds on their lands at Corimony, which fall within our target area, as well as with private landowners.

Further afield, the vision and practical work of Trees For Life have played an important role in inspiring several other projects to become established, for example — the Carrifran project, which aims to restore native forest to an entire valley in the Borders region of Scotland; Moor Trees, which aims to restore native forest to Dartmoor in the southwest of England and the Yendegaia project in Tierra del Fuego, Chile, where a substantial area of land which lies the same distance from the equator as the Caledonian Forest has been purchased for the restoration of its degraded forests and protection of its wilderness qualities.

In recognition of Trees For Life's work, the Conservation Foundation declared it the UK Conservation Project of the Year in 1991. In 2000, after five years of monitoring and assessment, Trees For Life received the prestigious Millennium Marque Award, which was given to projects that "demonstrate environmental excellence for the 21st century." And in 2001, the charity's founder and Executive Director, Alan Watson Featherstone, received the celebrated Schumacher Award for "his inspirational and practical work on conserving and restoring degraded ecosystems."

The future

Now in its 18th year of planting, Trees For Life continues to grow, attracting more interest than ever in its work both from the public and from companies wanting to get involved. This surge in interest has partly come about with the increased profile of the environment in the media and the public arena, and is also the fruit of many years of hard work. Each season of planting is more ambitious than the last, with the number of volunteer Conservation Work Weeks doubling over the last few years. There are plans to run 47 in 2008 — a record for the charity.

In 2007, Trees For Life pledged to plant 100,000 trees as part of the United Nations Environment Program's *Billion Tree* campaign, representing a massive up-scaling of the work and one which looks set to continue. Trees For Life has an agreement to purchase the 10,000 acre Dundreggan estate in Glen Moriston, which will be the first piece of land to be wholly owned by the charity, providing a unique opportunity to expand its reforestation work and establish a native woodland link between Glen Moriston and Glen Affric. In the long-term, the charity's vision is to continue to identify suitable areas for reforestation within its target area in order to expand the practical action on the ground, and

to continue to raise the profile of the charity's work. Trees For Life combines an important vision with practical action and visible results. It plays an important role in ecosystem restoration not only in the UK, but throughout the world.

Oregon coast

ALICE DRENGSON

16

Learning From Trees

Wangari Maathai

Between 1973 and 1974, I was in the National Council of Women. I listened to the problems of Kenyan women: "We need clean drinking water." "We need firewood [their main source of energy]." "We need food." "We need building materials." "We need fencing materials." "We need to protect our soils." The more I listened to those issues, the more I connected them to the land.

Then I asked the women, "Why can't we plant trees?" and they said, "We don't know how to plant trees." I decided to solicit the support of foresters. I went to the Conservator of Forests, who said we could have all the trees we wanted. Later the Conservator changed his mind because we were collecting more trees than he could afford to give us free of charge, so he asked us to pay for those trees. Eventually, we decided that instead of spending too much time and money collecting seedlings from the foresters we would ask them how to establish our own tree nurseries. The women were creative and established tree nurseries as best they could. They nurtured those seedlings until they were about a foot or two high, and then they planted them on their own land.

They needed to take care of those trees. Once the trees had survived, the Green Belt Movement would compensate them with a little money that we had fundraised. This became a transformation for the women because the treeplanting became an income-generating activity. You could put money in the hands of women because they had raised several thousand trees. And although the money was very little per tree, when you multiply that several thousand times, women could make enough to pay school fees, to buy clothing and to meet some other domestic needs, which was wonderful. That became a very important token and a very important reason for them to plant trees. When they had planted trees on their farms we said, "Now talk to your neighbors. Tell them why they should plant trees. And give them trees free of charge. And when they have planted and the trees have survived they will be compensated for the work they have done."

Fortunately, in the tropics trees grow very fast. So within a very short time trees grow up; they become tall. And it becomes a very interesting experience for those who plant because it's as if trees talk to them. The trees become their own ambassadors. As the trees grow they give hope, they give self-confidence, they transform the land. Once the landscape is transformed even birds come back, smaller animals come back; there is not so much dust; as you walk along the path there is shade and suddenly there is a good feeling in the community. And you don't have to persuade people any more to plant trees. They know the value of trees.

Now that would have been a wonderful experience if that was all we did. And that, in many ways, is all that people see — women planting trees. And so people ask, "Why would anybody arrest a woman, beat her up or put her in jail for planting trees?" Now, the reason why I got myself into trouble is that I realized that you need to mobilize a lot of women, a lot of men and children; that you can never really make an impact if you do not have a very large number of people involved.

So we decided we must educate people. We set up a Civic and Environmental Education program. We wanted to make people internalize the many reasons why trees are important to us, both in protecting the environment and in helping us meet our own needs. And that's when I was first confronted with violation of human rights, because the government said, "You can meet, but if you are more than nine, you need a license." And I said, "Why would I need a license to talk to another person, to persuade that person to dig a hole and plant a tree?" And the government said, "Because that's the law. Nobody is allowed to gather more than nine people."

Now that definitely was the beginning for me in understanding the role that democracy plays in maintaining, protecting or destroying the environment. So we decided to challenge that law. We decided to say we must have the freedom to meet, the freedom to move from one place to the other, freedom to associate. But instead of talking about it we acted it out. We met where we had the tree nursery, and we insisted that we have a right to meet and discuss the possibilities of protecting our environment and improving our environment. Well, occasionally we would be beaten, we would be disrupted and we would be refused permission to meet. But in order to help women, so that they are not too disempowered by these disruptions, we advised them to go and register as societies or as groups (the government allows groups to have a license to meet).

We then saw the need to intensify the education on governance. In the course of our studying we realized that one of the reasons that the politicians did not want us to get together to inform each other is that they were some of the most destructive members of society! They logged illegally in the forest, they privatized forests, they stole from the treasury: they practiced corruption at every possible opportunity. So we knew that what they really did not want us to understand was how they govern us and why we are governed that way.

By studying and understanding the structure we decided that one thing we must do is change that structure. But we knew we could not change that structure with that government in place. So we started working on how we would change that government. And we knew that one way to change that government would be to participate in the elections. So we started preparing how we could all participate in the elections and try to put in power people we could trust — people who have their integrity in place — because we learned that if you don't have people of integrity in power, they destroy the environment. We did it under the pretence that all we were doing was planting a tree. And quite often when the government came where we had gathered, it would say, "We know you have a license to meet, but what are you talking about?" and we would say, "We are talking about how to plant trees effectively." And so we became part of the pro-democracy movement in Kenya.

Good management of the environment is linked to democratic governance. We also saw that when you have bad governance it thrives because it is able to create factions among communities. In Africa it is able to set one tribe against another tribe. This usually happens very easily between, for example, farming communities and pastoral communities. If you look throughout the world today and assess the reasons why many people are fighting in different parts of the world, in Africa and elsewhere, you will find that most people are fighting over natural resources. When people are fighting over those resources, because bad governance facilitates it or allows it, there can be no development.

(Editors' note: This is an extract from Wangari Maathai's Nobel Prize Acceptance Speech, given at the Nobel Peace Prize ceremony on December 12, 2004 at Oslo City Hall. Copyright: Nobel Foundation 2004. To read the whole speech visit wangarimaathai.com, or to see a video version visit nobelprize.org/nobel_prizes/peace/laureates/2004/maathai-lecture.html.)

17

Gaviotas — Lessons From A Global Classroom

Doug Skeates

It seems that only in very recent times have we humans examined critically our ecological footprint and, beyond that, started planning to reduce it to a manageable and hopefully sustainable size. Extremely rare are those communities that have been intentionally pre-planned at the outset to have minimal adverse environmental impact and that have actually succeeded. Gaviotas is one such place. This small village located on the plain east of the Andes, a difficult 16 hour drive inland from Bogotá, Colombia, is setting an example from which the rest of the world might gain a great deal.

It all began more than 30 years ago in the mind of university professor Paolo Lugari, a visionary who felt that with rapidly rising world populations and ever more crowded cities, it would be necessary to find new places for people to live. An engineer by training, Palol reasoned that because these new places would of necessity be in areas that were currently sparsely or entirely uninhabited owing to difficult environmental challenges, the best environmental science and technology was needed. Colombia, common with much of the tropics, has vast areas of savannahs, essentially uninhabited and infertile wastelands. Paolo was sure these semi-deserts could be transformed into habitable situations. Starting from scratch in an area largely isolated from the resources of the so-called civilized world, the community would have to be self-sufficient. New technology would have to be developed which was appropriate to the conditions. They would have to find ways to feed and house people, provide for energy, water supply, medical facilities, schooling and so on.

> They always put social experiments in the easiest most fertile places. We wanted the hardest place. We figured if we could do it here we could do it anywhere.
>
> — Paolo Lugari,
> founder of Gaviotas

Today, what started out as a scientific experiment has become a successful village with thriving industry that continues not only to achieve zero emissions but turns innovative new ideas into environmentally-sound, marketable products. Gaviotas needs to be seen by the world but unfortunately, ironically, it is virtually impossible to visit there because of political upheaval that makes travel in the more remote areas of Colombia a life-threatening venture. One can, however, learn a great deal from *Gaviotas: A Village to Re-Invent the World* written by Alan Weisman (Chelsea Green, 2008).

From a forester's or ecologist's perspective probably the most exciting part of the Gaviotas story has been a tree planting project in the low productivity lands around Gaviotas. After considerable research, it was discovered that a foreign species, a Caribbean Pine from Honduras, was best suited to the difficult growing conditions of the savannah. The community developed a seedling nursery and embarked on planting one million trees annually in the thin, highly acidic soil. In a few short years, the result was a rapidly developing forest of pines covering 27,000 acres. Before long, rather than harvesting the trees for wood fiber, residents were instead able to collect tree resin without killing the trees. Using a method similar to maple sap or rubber tapping, the resin collected can be processed and substituted for petroleum-based ingredients in paints, cosmetics, perfumes and medicines. With refining and processing done onsite in a zero emissions facility, resin has become the financial mainstay of the community, particularly turpentine production.

Frog

JANE DRENGSON

In addition to the economic benefits, this new exotic forest has brought something else that many biologists consider nothing short of miraculous. Under the sheltering canopy of the pines, a tropical forest not seen for millennia in these savannahs has begun regenerating, restoring long lost wildlife habitat that has allowed deer, hawks and anteaters to colonize and expand. No less than 250 native plant species have been identified providing the inspiration for Gaviotans to convert their pharmacy into an herbal apothecary as well as launch an ethno-botanical research lab in collaboration with local Guahibo Indians. Today many Guahibos and rural peasants live in Gaviotas, riding to work on Gaviotas-designed bicycles especially made to negotiate the sand of the savannah. Keeping with the zero emissions philosophy, bicycles are the official mode of transportation. New projects made possible by the success of the reforestation efforts include a purified water bottling plant and a musical instrument factory that uses wood culled from the pine forest.

From an ecological perspective, it will be most interesting to watch this new rainforest as it continues to develop from an understory to an overstory complete with once indigenous trees and shrubs, insects, birds and animals which, though not seen there for hundreds of years, were nevertheless components of the pre-existent rainforest. Recreating the ecosystems of the region is possibly the most important development of Gaviotas, a lesson for the rest of the world. There is undoubtedly pertinence here not just for the tropics but for temperate and boreal regions as well.

I had the opportunity to attend an information session, held in Colorado by an informal group, Friends of Gaviotas. There I met Paolo Lugari. When asked about the future of Gaviotas, Paolo basically said it isn't necessary for the village to grow. What is needed is to grow more and better Gaviotas's around the globe. This was thrown out as a challenge to the rest of us. The building of new communities from scratch in the same manner as Gaviotas is hardly practical anywhere in North America and arguably on most of the planet at this time. The challenge is how we can add some of the elements Paolo has demonstrated to our existing communities. We too could innovate, reduce our dependence on imported resources; become more self-sufficient and develop a wider range of products from our own environment in the process creating new business opportunities based on the resources we are blessed with in our local environments wherever they may be. This is a real challenge for all of us, but one full of exciting possibilities.

18

A Letter from Victoria

Brenda R. Beckwith

After the founding of Fort Victoria on Vancouver Island, British Columbia, in 1843, many descriptions of the landscape were recorded in the forms of journal entries, professional correspondence and personal letters. Since this time, the landscape has changed dramatically, and the now nationally endangered Garry oak ecosystems that were once described as a work of art are highly threatened by habitat loss and degradation, the introduction of invasive species and the suppression of indigenous land management activities. Today, most ecosystems with Garry oak (*Quercus garryana*) are located in shallow soil sites such as rock outcrop and coastal bluff communities. According to the Garry Oak Ecosystems Recovery Team, these ecosystems are listed at less than 5% remaining. Less than 1% remains of the deep soil oak savannahs that were perpetuated for millennia by the ongoing stewardship by First Nations peoples, largely to maintain the productivity of their staple root food, the blue camas lily (*Camassia spp.*).

The following letter borrows from early writers of the Victoria region. The ecological restoration of this cultural landscape will require good landscape reconstruction of the past interrelationships between ecological process and cultural practice and the even better use of our imaginations. The year included in the letter written below, ends in 57; it is up to us to decide if it begins with a 20 or will remain forever with an 18.

23rd Aug -57

Dear Kathryne,

On this day, my darling, I write a special letter to you. I must relate a story about this place, of what I have learned about the blue savannah here. It is a remarkable parkland and worthy of putting pen to paper. The open savannah of this clime, unobstructed for a large part from tree or shrub, is interspersed with other open and cleared lands across the patchwork of this place.

There are noble oaks dotted about this undulating countryside. Their great arching canopies are formed by the tangle of gnarled and lichened limbs. Their trunks are thick and stout. The trees appear as guardians of these gentle slopes, providing sanctuary to shrubberies of snowberry, rose and fern. To the oaks come the deer, providing a place of rest and camouflage, and the lark and the bluebird that forage under the heavy low branches. They depict centuries of proud solitude through their enormity and resilience. By moonlight or under the sun's rays, their very presence captivates the imaginations of visitors and reminds the locals of time-honored customs.

A stately forest exists, yet it appears to stand aside for the savannah. The fir, berry and black haw wait at its boundary for direction, for pause to enter. They linger singly, some in thickets, to be welcomed into this district. Many years ago such vegetation was here and it could gain hold again. But this is not their time. This savannah's performance is for the blue lilies. Their cerulean show compares well to deep lakes and many explorers have been fooled by these tricky lilies when traveling at the right time of year through the wet meadows of the west. When the flowers fade, the round esculent roots wait, buried, for the people of this place. Which roots will be placed into the bag or basket and which ones will hold their ground? That audition was some time ago, before the season's heat hardened the soil and sent the lilies and their kin into their summer slumber.

Before the rains return, the people of this place will come again to this parkland, kindling fire. I am told it is a sight to behold. The flames tease the dry, tan capsules of the blue lilies until they rattle and fall. The shiny black seeds disappear into the crevices of the churned, blackened soil and the singed clumps of the bunchgrasses. They tell

Ancient oak

BRENDA BECKWITH

me the flames run along the crackling savannah like the brisk canter of the mustangs back home, light and snappy. The flame of the savannah asks for so little and gives renewed life in return. The fire will eddy and twirl leaving merely a dusting of black upon the oak's craggy bark. It will dance across the savannah's stage in a grand finale, and then into the forest it retreats. As the oaks cast long ghostly shadows over the ash, the timber looks on. They will remain at nature's edge for a little while longer.

Then the rains arrive, as they always do on the west coast. The water penetrates the quiescent soils of the savannah slowly at first. Through the cavities left from this season's stalks drops of water will seep until halted by clay and bedrock. The fire will be long burned out by this time and the verdure of the savannah returned. The bunchgrasses flush out more green, the roots of the blue lilies swell and sprout. The oaks will shed their hard-shelled crop. The jays hop and jab stealing away their prize to another cache, to another wood. They came early last year; they know of changing weather. Oak leaves will gather on the ground until the fall winds send them tumbling into the rocky clefts along with the whirling winged seeds and leaves of the maple. Eventually the winter storms will come and flatten the leaves into a layered mat, closing the doors on the open stage while the savannah's players rehearse for the coming year, remade by flame and water.

I have been in this place for only three days, my darling. Each day I have walked the savannah and listened to its stories. I sat amongst the seed capsules of the lilies and imagined a flood of blue blossoms. I saw bumblebees and checkerspots. I roll the lily stalks between my fingers and wonder if the capsules' rattle is what the savannah fire will sound like. What can it give that cannot be found elsewhere? What magic lies in its breath?

Yours truly,
Levi Legg

The Future of Ecoforestry in Western Australia

Robert Hay

Australian forestry is still engaged in shifting its paradigm of forestry management from production (industrial) forestry to one based on *ecologically sustainable forest management* (ESFM). There is also an ongoing battle to internalize a moral approach in forest management.

The policy approach in Western Australia (WA) to protection is interesting. Forest management is usually left to the professionals, while the booming economy and excellent quality of life lulls the rest into a laissez-faire *she'll be right, mate* attitude. Ecoforestry pilot projects are needed, as is higher visibility for its platform. Much is therefore left to be done on the western frontier of this large continent.

Status of forests, woodlands and the forest economy

In Western Australia (WA) the forest industry is very small compared to the dominant mining industry. The forest industry contributed only $88 million for hardwood and plantation production from Crown lands in 2006, with more income from private plantations and value added industries. The *WA State of the Environment Report 2007* states that there are approximately 64 million acres of forest in WA, about 10% of the total land area. However, the *WA Forest Management Plan 2004-2013* (FMP) only applies to 2,754,978 acres of State forest in the southwest.

At the time of the Comprehensive Regional Assessment (CRA) for the Regional Forest Agreement (RFA) in 1998, there were 2,745,340 acres of jarrah (*Eucalyptus marginata*) and 232,279 acres of karri (*E. diversicolor*)/marri (*Corymbia calophylla*) available for harvest; this has been reduced to about 1,977,000 acres presently (WA SOE, 2007). The original old growth forest was estimated to be about 8.6 million acres of jarrah, karri and wandoo (*E. wandoo*); in the southwest region there are approximately 855,000 acres of old growth, primarily jarrah and karri (WA Forest Alliance, 1998). These two species are the most common trees used for timber, with jarrah dominating in the drier regions of the forest belt.

The other eucalypti such as wandoo and marri, that are used for forest production are

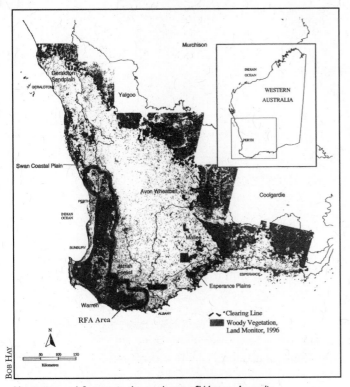

Vegetation and forestry in the southwest of Western Australia

hotspots): the eco-region contains at least 9,000 vascular plant species (almost one-half that of Australia), with a very high rate of endemism (at least 70% — Burbidge, 2000; Pittock, 2007). However, there had been a lot of cutting of old growth forest prior to 2001: 90% had been cut at least once already, affecting biodiversity (WA Forest Alliance). Anti-logging NGOs also claim that the majority of forest products were exported as woodchips (85%).

The RFA process was designed to minimize forest conflict by involving the community (Lane, 1999). The goal was 15% (per ecosystem type) of pre-1788 forest area preserved, as well as 60% of remaining old growth forests; a comprehensive, representative and adequate system of ecologically viable protected areas was to be established to protect various forest types. However, the RFA process in WA was too secretive: data was not available for public scrutiny/critique. Few felt that a proper consultation process had occurred (see Horwitz and Calver, 1998; McKenna et al, 2006). Prior to the WA State election of early 2001, there was 80% support in political polls to halt old growth logging in the southwest. As a response to this development, the WA Labor Party changed their position in mid-2000, stating that it would preserve old growth forests if elected. Partly due to this stance, Labor was elected in February 2001, and immediately started a process to protect these forests. As part of that process, $41 million was promised to assist displaced forest workers as more parks were made, and a review of *high conservation value* forests was also undertaken, to ascertain if these should be protected as well. By March 2001, 99% of old growth forests had been protected. This was similar to the protection of west coast native forests on the

minor in scale, with these not replanted either; tingle trees (*E. jacksonii* and *E. guilfoylei*) are found near the wetter south coast and tuart (*E. gomphocephala*) near the southwest coast. There are 3,123,659 acres reserved under the FMP, with an additional 482,000 acres to be added due to old growth forest protection (WA SOE, 2007). Note that Alcoa removes extensive stands of jarrah annually (about 420,000 acres/year) to access underlying bauxite. The plantation industry in WA has the second largest plantation area of all states (21% of total), covering 978,000 acres in 2006 (WA SOE, 2007).

The biodiversity in the southwest of WA is very high (it is one of world's 25 megadiverse

South Island of New Zealand in June 2001 and the attainment in 2000 of 12% protection of the land of British Columbia, Canada.

Forest and biodiversity conservation policies

The development of the new FMP in WA began in earnest in 2002/03, led by the Conservation Commission. The intention of the Commission was to embed ESFM principles in forest management. There was a struggle between those in the business of practicing forest management versus others trying to improve failings in that management. Several publications were produced from each camp, with those by government researchers (e.g. Abbott and Christensen, 1994; Abbott and Christensen, 1996; Underwood and Bradshaw, 2000; Burrows et al, 2002; Lee and Abbott, 2004) contrasted by ones promoting a new view of forest ecology and ecosystem management (e.g. Norton and Mitchell, 1994: Ferguson, 1996; Hobbs, 1996; Lindenmayer and Franklin, 1997; Calver and Dell, 1998; Calver et al, 1998; Lindenmayer and Recher, 1998; Lindenmayer, 2000; Calver, 2003; Calver and Wardell-Johnson, 2004; Soule et al, 2004).

The EPA reviewed the draft FMP in 2003, and it was approved by 2004. It has many explicit *key performance indicators,* similar to those of the Montreal Protocol and the Australian Forestry Standard, which will make it easier for the EPA to review its implementation. ESFM especially needs to be properly practiced, including reducing the cut rate overall, as stressed by Sharp (2005) and outlined by Lindenmayer and Franklin (2003, 2004). Private forests also need management (Bradshaw, 2005), as do private contractors on Crown lands (Ryan et al, 2002).

An assessment of risks versus opportunities

Risks

Complicating the forestry situation in WA is an ever-worsening salinity problem, declining precipitation due to climate change and forest dieback. Salinity is primarily affecting the Wheatbelt region of the southwestern interior (Figure 1), due to large-scale land clearing in much of the 20th century (Beresford et al, 2001). This is one of the largest cleared areas on Earth; more than 90% of the woodlands have been cleared with government support. The EPA released a position statement on the *Environmental Protection of Native Vegetation in Western Australia* in 2000, noting its opposition to land clearing in the agricultural area. Note that the cleared land is mostly privately owned, whereas the mallee shrubland that remains east of the clearing line is on Crown land. Saline rivers also flow from agricultural regions through the forested areas of the southwest, having an effect on riparian zones there. The National SOE (2006) stated that there were 3.9 million acres affected by salinity in WA; this total is projected to increase to 13.3 million acres by 2050 (WA SOE, 2007).

Oil mallee (*E. polybractea* and *E. horistes*) is being promoted by the WA Department of Environment and Conservation as a new shrub to be planted as extensive monocultures in the Wheatbelt to help combat salinity. The benefits of this, including carbon sequestration and utilizing these trees as a crop (for eucalyptus oil production), are considered to outweigh their faults; 25 million trees had been planted by 2003 (see Shea, 2003). Drains are also being advocated by many farmers in this region to channel salt water away.

More difficult to resolve is forest dieback, which is caused by a water mould (*Phytophthora cinnamoni*). There are restrictions on vehicle use in the southwest logging areas, but dieback has become widespread, especially affecting jarrah and banksia species (a shrub) and perhaps tuart. Bushfires have also become worse in the past decade due to a decline of rainfall, particularly in the southwest. The previous suppression of fires led to a buildup of fuel load, so that when fires do occur they are often more serious. Eucalypti are adapted to a periodic fire regime, but unusually hot fires during the summer season exacerbate this ability (see Abbott and Burrows, 2003).

Declining precipitation in the southwest has been researched recently by the Indian Ocean Climate Initiative (IOCI), which has documented an average annual rainfall decline since the mid-1970s of 15 to 20%, as well as a rise of temperatures of 14°F in the 20th century (IOCI, 2002). It is likely that this warming and drying trend will continue, including droughts in the southwest which would result in the loss of many species (see CSIRO and Australian Bureau of Meteorology, 2007; Pittock, 2007). The loss of biodiversity due to such rapid changes cannot be ameliorated. Such change is coming on top of ongoing salinity and forestry pressures (see Calver and Wardell-Johnson, 2004; Sharp, 2005) and the natural cycle of droughts and bushfires.

Opportunities

The history of forestry in WA and Australia has been uneven, with the story yet to be played out. In the midst of difficulties are opportunities, with promise for the future. This includes nature-based tourism, the psychological benefits of forest retreats and outdoor recreation activities, with a *Nature-Based Tourism Strategy* released in 2004 to support planned development and marketing. An example of a prime tourist attraction in the southwest is the Tree Top Walk near Walpole, which celebrated its 10th anniversary in 2003. This walk is in the Valley of the Giants, a national park. The walkway is 656 yards long, and takes visitors to the tingle forest canopy, 43 yards above the ground. It won a national award in 2000; over

A giant karri tree on the tree top walk

BOB HAY

2 million visitors have now done the walk. A visitors' center and guided walks help to showcase this unique forest type, which is a remnant of ancient Gondwanaland.

Related opportunities involve biodiversity incentive programs. There are programs such as Wetland Watch and Woodland Watch, promoted by the WWF. The latter builds on the community collaboration in the Wheatbelt that began with Landcare, enhancing the community's capacity for bush conservation (WWF, 2005). Living Landscapes is a Greening Australia project that encourages farmers to rehabilitate their local landscape while maintaining their productive agricultural capability. Bush Bank is a fund set up to buy bush blocks of high conservation value on private land. Bush Brokers helps farmers to manage and protect private bushlands by linking owners with conservation minded individuals and groups. An example of such an initiative is Gondwana Link, stretching across 621 miles of southern WA to restore ecological connectivity by re-planting degraded private bushland. Conservation covenants limit the clearing of native vegetation, with landowners putting these restrictions onto their land title.

The psychological benefits of being in native forests are only recently being realized in WA, with a shift lately toward forest retreats for healing and wellness, as in ecotherapy (see Clinebell, 1996). This therapy can be accessed on a weekend away or by a *tree change,* moving to forested estates in the southwest. An opportunity that is only now beginning to be realized is retaining forests as a carbon sink. The Commonwealth Government has resisted carbon emissions trading, but as a result of a Federal election in late 2007 and international pressure for actions on climate change, it is making more solid gestures at last.

Steps toward a more ethical future

A certain *forest consciousness* developed in Australia over the past two centuries of European-dominated immigration which was at first exploitative and then oriented towards resource conservation. Stewardship, in the form of the AFS and the practice of ESFM, is now taking hold, but its implementation will need to be carefully managed. With severe impacts on biodiversity and water availability in the southwest due to climate change looming in the next few decades, adaptive management is urgently needed. The cut rate for native forests will have to decline, with greater reliance on plantations and imports. Ecoforestry could become widespread in this scenario, as private woodlots are managed more carefully. Such a change could help to instill a more ethical approach to forests and to nature in general. This approach would be more akin to that of traditional indigenous views. But, until recently, indigenous approaches have been marginalized, except for some ranger programs, NRM regional planning and the co-management of major national parks.

What is lacking is both a moral compass and leadership to take us boldly into the 21st century. This dearth of informed direction is happening at a time of resource scarcity (e.g. water), climate change, biodiversity loss, immigration pressures and an economic upturn. The last point should provide the wherewithal for change, with the other points providing the impetus. And yet, Australia remains poised on the cusp of unrealized opportunity, with WA mimicking the national trend.

For a revolutionary shift in forest consciousness to incorporate morality, towards what some have stated should be *conscientiousness* (see Calver et al, 2005), both passion and a real choice are needed. Ecoforestry is an unrealized concept at this stage. Most have not heard of the term here and there are few (if any) pilot projects in operation. Permaculture is much better established in this regard. The promise for a holistic view of forestry that is effectively practiced, within a more enlightened society, is still there. There are excellent collaborative examples to build upon and a slow realization of the wide-ranging values of forest lands. What is needed now are active champions to help educate people and raise awareness, to get beyond our *monocultures of the mind*.

Pilot ecoforestry projects are needed to build the case for an evolved form of forest management here. In other words, the art of ecoforestry can help sway the science in Australia — the philosophy can outshine the limited pragmatic views of our present generation of forest practitioners. But for that to occur, we need some help ... anyone want to come down under to promote ecoforestry before it gets too hot? Let me know — I'll throw another shrimp on the barbie for you!

(Editors' note: This chapter is revised from a presentation made in 2003 to the Australia and New Zealand Institute of Forestry Conference in Queenstown, New Zealand.)

Eco Tipping Points —
How a Vicious Cycle Can Become Virtuous

Amanda Suutari and Gerald Marten

The cicadas are in full voice on a sultry morning in May as we make our way along a rickety wooden boardwalk that snakes through a community mangrove forest near Thung Dase village in southern Thailand. The mangroves offer welcome shade near a dock where a small boat is moored. Handmade bamboo traps are set to catch mud crabs when the tides go out. In a flash of orange and turquoise, a kingfisher swoops to a low-hanging branch.

It's hard to imagine that three decades ago the area's lush abundance was collapsing into a wasteland. "At one time," recalled Nom Ham Yak, chair of the forest's management committee, "our economic base was crabs, fisheries and rubber. Then areas were leased as concessions to private contractors to clear for charcoal, and the forest became badly degraded." The prospects for the area's villages were so bleak that a revival would have seemed a fantasy. What brought them back from the brink was an *Eco Tipping Point*.

Eco Tipping Points offer a new paradigm for restoring our communities, both natural and human. Conventional approaches to ecological problems — from piecemeal micromanagement, to techno-fixes, to top-down regulation — often fail or generate new messes. But Eco Tipping Points show how the same forces that endanger environments and communities can be harnessed to heal them. To demonstrate what Eco Tipping Points are and how they work, consider two very different stories from two continents: the mangrove forests of Trang Province and the marshes of Arcata, California.

From charcoal to pink gold

Five hundred and thirty-five miles south of Bangkok, Trang Province is located on Thailand's southwest coast at the western shore of the Andaman Sea. Thung Dase and its neighboring villages lie in the watershed of the Palian and Trang Rivers, which drain into the sea from the Bandthat mountain range. The villages cluster along the mangrove-lined coastal wetlands, providing a fertile buffer zone for marine and terrestrial life. Besides offering a rich variety of foods, mangrove forests supply medicinal plants and materials such as thatch for housing and fishing gear. They are also refuges and nurseries for juvenile fish, crabs, shrimp and mollusks.

Big changes came in the 1960s, when the Thai government embraced the Western model of export-led development. Industrial trawlers freely violated the no-fishing zone two miles from shore. They ravaged the sea bed and coral reefs, swallowing fish stocks faster than they could regenerate. As their coastal fishery waned, fishers spent more time on their boats and went further from shore. Some used explosives or poisons to harvest the remaining fish or invested in better fishing equipment — causing stocks to plummet even faster.

Meanwhile, the government had granted mangrove concessions to the private sector to make charcoal briquettes. As mangroves dwindled, so did the diverse and useful products they provided. "Plants and animals, especially crabs, became scarce," explained Nom Ham Yak.

Their options narrowing, fishers began accepting menial jobs cutting mangroves for charcoal, working on commercial trawlers or migrating into nearby cities for work. "Fishing incomes went down," Ham Yak said. "The people in the village had to leave for towns to find work in fish-canning factories, rubber-tapping plantations, general day labor or construction. When the men went out to work and the wives stayed in the village, family relations would suffer. People also started selling pieces of land because there was no work at that time."

Worse, development agencies and banks had begun promoting shrimp farming in the mangrove forests. Unfortunately, the pink gold of shrimp aquaculture can be a classic boom-bust venture in which the production from a shrimp pond declines drastically after the first five years. Local people discovered that initial quick returns were supplanted by mounting debts and environmental ruin as abandoned shrimp ponds spread across the landscape.

In 1999, a team led by economist Suthawan Sathirathai did a cost-benefit analysis of shrimp farming on a coastal village in Surat Thani Province, southern Thailand, to compare the monetary value of mangroves versus shrimp farms. When taking into account only marketable products, shrimp farms brought higher returns, with a net value of $9,335 US per acre compared to $1,665 for mangroves. But calculating in the indirect value of mangroves dramatically reversed these figures. When they assigned a monetary value to environmental services such as nurseries for fish and protection from erosion and storms, the value of the mangroves rose to $14,428, more than 50% higher than shrimp aquaculture.

The positive tip

As university students, Pisit Charnsnoh and his wife, Ploenjai, were part of a generation of democracy activists. After graduating from Khon Khaen University, Charnsnoh got involved with rural development and urban labor rights. In 1985, the couple moved to Ploenjai's hometown in Trang Province, where they started a small organization called Yadfon Association (Yadfon means *raindrop* in Thai), aimed at helping the coastal villages in the region. At that time, Trang province residents were locked into a vicious cycle of increasing poverty, unraveling society and a deteriorating ecosystem.

Yadfon members spent nearly a year in dialogue with the villagers of Ban Laem Makham, working hard to gain the community's trust. The approach was to support residents' own insights into their shared crisis. Charnsnoh pointed out that this method was more powerful than giving the villagers lectures. "We couldn't go in as outsiders and tell them, 'This or that species is disappearing, you have to be careful,' or 'You have to protect these forests.'" Over time, and with some success with micro-credit, well-digging and other rural development schemes, Yadfon began to earn the villagers' respect.

Through a series of meetings with Yadfon, villagers developed the idea of reviving the badly degraded mangrove forests around Ban Laem Makhamand Thung Dase. Because the land was under government control, Yadfon staff acted as a go-between to obtain consent from provincial authorities to create a community mangrove forest. The first of its kind in Thailand, the forest covered 95 acres of land. It later became part of a 235-acre area that combined the mangrove forest with a sea grass conservation zone.

An emerging inter-village network created a system to manage the forest. Allowing use of some areas of the forest helped to get buy-in from a community that would otherwise break rules if the whole forest were declared off-limits. The network prohibited shrimp farms inside the forests, set up no-fishing areas, discouraged the use of cyanide and dynamite and banned push nets altogether. They replanted some areas of the forest and designated others untouchable to allow for natural regeneration. The network also began replanting the seagrass beds in the coastal waters of nearby Chao Mai village.

Their efforts paid off. There was an increase in the near-shore fish catch, and a species of fish thought to have disappeared returned. These early results boosted the villagers' commitment and motivated them to further

action. An endangered dugong spotted in the waters near Chao Mai village helped win government support for their seagrass protections zones; the dugong became a living symbol for conservation progress in the area.

Cycles and tipping points

Creating community mangrove forests was an Eco Tipping Point. It tipped the local community and environment from a vicious cycle to a virtuous cycle, and the momentum switched from destruction to recovery.

Vicious and virtuous cycles are feedback *loops*. These mutually reinforcing cycles of cause and effect are the heart of Eco Tipping Points. In the negative tip, as mangroves were cleared, fisheries began to decline. As fish stocks fell, fishers worked harder to get them, causing stocks to fall ever faster. In this way, they were locked into a vicious cycle of declining resources and an accelerating race to get what little remained.

After the positive tip, the fishery began to restore itself. In a study of 500 families between 1991 and 1994, total catch rose by 40%. Fishers spent three to four fewer hours per week on the water, while their net incomes increased by 200%. They could return with full boats without using dynamite or push nets. In this virtuous cycle, less pressure from fishers allowed fish stocks to recover faster, making the fishers' jobs even easier.

The revival of the fishery spawned other virtuous cycles. Better incomes meant there was less need to migrate from villages. Instead of being locked into depletion, villagers were now locked into conservation, as the financial incentive to preserve mangroves now outweighed the incentive to destroy them.

Most importantly, investing in their future motivated people to fight for it. A sense of ownership gave them the grit and confidence to confront encroaching trawlers and to lobby the government to enforce the two-mile no-fishing zone. It also made them less likely to sell off their land, which often ended up being converted to resort development. Reviving the forests also helped to put zoning limits on shrimp ponds. Charnsnoh explained that while many of their villages have shrimp ponds, they have kept the ponds outside the boundaries of the forests.

While the community mangrove forests started small, the virtuous cycles rippled out over time. Today, these districts include 10 community forests and four sea grass and dugong conservation areas totaling 50 square miles. Meanwhile, Yadfon has extended its involvement to some 60 villages in the three districts. Through a growing network of grass-roots organizations, Charnsnoh is involved with influencing policy at the national and international levels, lobbying for stronger legal standing for the forests and gathering support to stop the practice of intensive shrimp farming. Meanwhile, Ploenjai is connecting with villages further inland, discovering new links between inland and coastal regions. "I was working with the fisher folk since the beginning," she explained, "and have moved up [the watershed]. Now we work with the whole ecosystem."

Treating wastewater with wetlands

Across the Pacific Ocean, a small university town nestled in the northern California coastal redwoods may seem worlds away from a fishing village of southern Thailand. But Arcata's pioneering wetland and wildlife sanctuary reveals a similar underlying story: tipping a coastal ecosystem from a vicious cycle into a virtuous one.

Home to Humboldt State University, Arcata is a vibrant little community some 280 miles north of San Francisco. Historic charm is visible in the thriving downtown, and green space abounds with the community forest and wetland areas framing the vista of Humboldt Bay. Arcata's Eco Tipping Point arrived when the community faced a sewage treatment crisis. Until the early 1950s the city discharged unchlorinated primary effluent into Humboldt Bay. Secondary treatment and chlorination were not added until the early 1970s. In 1974, federal water quality standards were revised, and state and regional authorities began cracking down.

The community faced a thorny dilemma: buy into a proposed $25-million regional sewage processing plant to discharge treated, up-to-standard wastewater into Humboldt Bay — or devise a more environmentally acceptable alternative. The former would be a costly undertaking for a community whose population at the time was just 12,600. Also, the sewer pipeline was a potential nightmare, since ruptures under the bay could make pollution worse.

Most importantly, the regional plant would have unleashed a vicious cycle of runaway sprawl. By laying the pipeline along

Blue camus

ALICE DRENGSON

undeveloped land between Arcata and its neighbors, Arcatans believed developers would soon follow with strip malls, big-box retail zones and subdivisions. More development would have affected the thriving downtown and locked residents into car dependency. The sewage plant itself, along with the roads and infrastructure needed to support the development, would have demanded an unprecedented outlay from municipal coffers and taxpayers' wallets.

The problem is the solution

The idea to treat the wastewater as a resource rather than a problem first came from Humboldt State University fisheries professor George Allen. In 1969, he had begun testing whether Pacific salmon and cutthroat trout could be raised in ponds of seawater and partially treated wastewater. Bob Gearhart, another Humboldt State University professor, expanded on Allen's idea. Why not use a marsh to treat municipal sewage more easily, more sustainably and more economically? "The whole issue is the ownership of the wastewater — what you have control over," explained Gearhart. "It's not about disposal — it's a resource issue."

After a protracted and divisive political and legal battle known locally as *The Wastewater Wars,* regional authorities reluctantly allowed the city to create a small version as a pilot project. If it was successful, the community would be free to expand to a fully functioning system. The chosen site was a derelict brownfield that included a sealed landfill, two defunct logging mills and a log pond. Creating the marsh first meant breaking up concrete where lumber had once been stacked and stored on the old lumberyard site. National Guard engineers blew up the concrete and

carted it off. Next, a bulldozer terraformed the ground, creating a micro-terrain similar to that of a wetland. Volunteers from the community planted several kinds of native marsh plants in order to have alternating areas of open water and vegetation. They took care to plant more densely in the farther reaches of the marsh in order to fully remove any solids that remained in the water. In 1986, the treatment system was completed and became operational.

Today, the Arcata Marsh and Wildlife Sanctuary covers 154 acres of freshwater and saltwater marshes, tidal mudflats and grasslands. Wastewater is piped from homes and buildings to the *headworks,* where debris is removed and solids settle. The solids are sent to digesters for use as compost on the town's community forest. The sewage is sent to oxidation ponds before entering a series of treatment and enhancement marshes. Naturally occurring processes progressively purify the water, then two rounds of chlorination bring it up to state standards before its release into Humboldt Bay.

When Eco Tipping Points launch virtuous cycles, they employ nature's own processes to do most of the work. Instead of a multi-million dollar treatment plant, Arcata has used the

Fawn lilly

ALICE DRENGSON

free services of a wetland to purify its wastewater. Roots and stems of wetland plants form a dense, netlike filter that removes suspended solids. Plants and algae remove nutrients such as nitrogen and phosphorus, while bacteria and fungi decompose solids and remove dissolved organic material. Bulrushes provide a canopy of shade, controlling the growth of algae and helping to slow water flow so the microorganisms can do their job.

Plants and microorganisms pass organic material up the food web to small aquatic animals and insects, and ultimately to top predators such as hawks, foxes and otters that have come to symbolize the wildness of Arcata's wetland. As plants, animals and microorganisms break down organic material to extract energy, the residue passes out of the wetland ecosystem and into the atmosphere as carbon dioxide and water. Meanwhile, larger animals, birds and flying insects move out of the wetland, carrying organic material and nutrients and distributing them around the surrounding countryside. They also bring in seeds from other areas, promoting and supporting biodiversity. The end result is a wetland and wildlife sanctuary that supports 300 species of birds and mammals, 100 species of plants, and six species of fish.

As the wetland regenerated nature's systems, it spun off virtuous cycles for humans as well. Arcata's wastewater and derelict brownfield became economically and socially valuable. *Recycling* gave Arcatans access to their formerly blocked-off waterfront. They gained a community space for leisure and recreation that draws as many as 150,000 visitors a year. Walking through a pathway surrounded by the songs of thrushes hidden in dense foliage, it is hard to imagine that the wetlands are actually working to break down household

sewage. By creating a physical barrier to development, the wetland became a de facto *zoning restriction* that was more effective than any government regulation. Students at Humboldt State University gained a research site. In the process, they provided a level of technical support, data collection and monitoring that the town could not have afforded on its own. More critically, choosing this unorthodox path set Arcata apart from its more conventional neighbors and fed the city's sense of pride. The marsh became a shared symbol that has helped to shape local identity. The community's motto today is *Flush With Pride.*

"I think the marsh has become symbolic of [the idea] that we can do things our way," said Julie Fulkerson, a former Arcata mayor and councilor. "Thinking of this community without the marsh is very depressing. For one thing, if the massive [treatment] system had been built, it would have cost millions of dollars, and we'd be paying for it. And with a pipeline between Eureka and Arcata, I just can't imagine why there would not have been development in that entire strip. It would have looked like any other blended community in California."

Common ground

In spite of their obvious differences, a deeper look at both Arcata and Trang Province reveals Eco Tipping Points at the source of each community's revival. Both communities had found leverage points in the vicious cycles where targeted actions could reverse them. Feedback loops that created and reinforced environmental degradation were replaced by feedback loops that rescued the ecosystems. By allowing mangroves to regenerate, and by designing a system that could treat waste with very little external manipulation, the communities let nature do the work of restoring their shared resources. The cohesion that emerged as a result gave them the impetus to rise to new challenges.

Despite their successes, these communities are not utopias. Both are on steep learning curves towards sustainability, and new challenges emerge as old ones are tackled. But they show how human and natural systems can tip together out of decline and towards greater health and sustainability. They show that local citizens can devise their own environmental solutions without elaborate government regulations or high-cost technologies. Sharing the stories of these Eco Tipping Points can demonstrate that achievements often considered unrealistic, costly or otherwise unfeasible are not just desirable alternatives. They are practical ones.

ALICE DRENGSON

Red tree buds

Editor's note: This article was first published in *Earth Island Journal* 22(2):26-31 (Summer 2007). Steve Brooks and Ann Marten provided editorial contributions. The authors thank members of Yadfon Association, Arcata City Hall and Humboldt State University for their extensive assistance.

Part IV

Indigenous Knowledge, Meeting Human and Wild Forest Needs

Yawar panga —
sacred plant, Peru

A First Nations Perspective
on Ecosystem Management

Richard Atleo

A First Nations perspective on the current environmental crisis on earth must speak about the disharmony and imbalance between people and nature. More importantly, this perspective implies that the earth's environmental crisis has been created by disrespect. There is a true story in my family that helps to illustrate this point about respect. It is as follows:

My Grandfather Keesta

Every protocol had been observed between the whaling chief and the spirit of the whale. Keesta had thrown the harpoon and the whale had accepted it, grabbed and held onto the harpoon according to the agreement they had made through prayers and petitions. Harmony prevailed; whalers and whale were one, *heshook-ish tsawalk.*

All of a sudden something went wrong, some disharmony took place, some disunity intruded, and the whale turned and began to tow Keesta and

his paddlers straight offshore. Keesta took inventory. Everyone in the whaling canoe remained true to the protocols, cleansed, purified and in harmony. Prayer songs intensified. Still, the great whale refused to turn towards the beach but headed straight offshore. Keesta and the paddlers had kept true to their agreements, and now there seemed nothing left to do except to cut the *Atlu,* the rope attached to the whale.

Keesta took his knife and as he moved to cut the rope *Ah-up-wa-eek,* Wren, landed on the whale and spoke to Keesta: "Tell the whale to go back to where it was harpooned." Keesta spoke to the whale, and immediately the great whale turned according to the word of Wren, the little brown bird, and returned to where it was first harpooned and there it died.

After the whale had been towed ashore Keesta discovered, as he had suspected, that the disharmony and disunity intruded at home. When his wife heard that the whale had taken the harpoon, she roused herself and broke away prematurely from her ritual to make preparations. At the point when she began to go about her life in disharmony from the rest is exactly when the great whale had begun to tow Keesta and his paddlers offshore.

The story of my grandfather Keesta illustrates a First Nations perspective to ecosystem management. Through fasting, cleansing rituals and petitioning prayers Keesta respectfully observed protocols among life forms.

This story is one of thousands of First Nations stories that can be told to indicate a perspective to ecosystem management that turns around the development of a special relationship between humans and the natural world. While the connectedness or holistic nature of the ecosystem may be taken for granted, the nature or quality of the connectedness is not. Keesta well understood that, if he took the whale for granted, he would in all likelihood endanger himself and his crew. All relationships have spiritual dimensions that may be latent or potent, depending upon the perceptions and decisions of the human. Clearcutting is an example where the spiritual dimension of relationships between loggers and trees is latent, dormant and completely ignored. What are the origins of these perspectives?

A philosopher, Clement C. J. Webb, has said that modern civilization began when European thinkers *left off telling tales* (1959). He dates this to the time of the ancient Greeks, but modern civilization did not gain universal prominence until the development of the Age of Science, or the Age of Reason, as John Ralston Saul has termed this period (1993). But where modern civilization left off telling tales is where First Nations perspectives originate. In the Western world tales are usually called myths, fables or origin stories. While the Western world may consider these stories to be untrue because they are apparently unscientific, many First Nations people can and do consider these stories to contain dimensions of actual truth about the nature of reality.

The stage for the origin stories is set by *Qua-ootz,* a Nuu-chah-nulth word for Creator or God. *Qua-ootz* when translated means Owner of Reality, that is, owner of all of existence. *Qua-ootz* is the context for all of creation. The story "How Raven Captured the Day" illustrates the origin of First Nations perspectives to ecosystem management.

In the beginning only half the world had light. Across the waters a Chief owned the light of day that he kept carefully guarded in a box. The people who lived in darkness grew tired of it and wondered what to do. Raven suggested that they try to capture the day.

"How can we do that?" he was asked.

"We will entertain the chief with a dance. Deer, who cannot only run fast but also leap far, will dance. If we are to capture the day, Deer must dance as one who is inspired, as one who captivates an audience."

"And then what will happen?" they asked Raven.

"Deer will have soft dry cedar bark tied behind him. When no one seems to expect it, he will dance close to the day box and dip this bark into the fire."

"Yes, that's a good idea!" they said.

Spiritual truths hidden from the physical eye are made plain in this story. The waters represent the great divide between the physical and spiritual realms. Clearly the source of light comes from the spiritual realm where the chief (*Qua-ootz*) resides. The two realms are connected, but the quality of the connection is left up to beings on earth. Raven's first efforts to capture the light are unsuccessful. Each failed plan is characterized by an attempt to outdo or to outwit the spiritual realm, usually through egotistical means. For example, Deer is unsuccessful because, although Deer is fast, the people on the other side are faster. Twice Raven blunders because he has transformed into a giant salmon and giant salmonberry shoot rather than transforming into an ordinary sockeye and ordinary salmonberry shoot, outlined in Wren's original plans. Raven has a great vision to capture the light but an equally great ego. Not until Wren devises a plan for Raven to become a tiny leaf does the plan become successful. Raven situates himself in the Chief's spring water where his daughter comes to drink. The insignificant leaf is swallowed and the daughter becomes pregnant. The rest is a long story that culminates in Raven bringing light into the world. A successful relationship between the spiritual and physical realm is to be marked by humility, exemplified by the tiny leaf, rather than boastful self-importance, exemplified by the giant salmon and giant salmonberry shoot.

In the beginning, all lifeforms were of one common species. The Transformer, or Trickster, changed all that — and that is why we have biodiversity today. Science is able to measure the inaccuracy of this worldview in the physical realm. Clearly the salmon and the deer have a very different set of genes from each other and from other species. However, in the spiritual realm, all have a common origin. In the physical realm, it is known that Wren is not able to speak any human language — but in the spiritual realm, Wren is not limited by the physical. In this worldview the two realms are intimately connected. Wren is able to speak and does speak for ears that will hear. Keesta had ears to hear, and this is why the whale turned towards the shore.

Origin stories set the tone and quality of all relationships. In the First Nations perspective, the tone and quality is one marked by respect. This tone and quality is actually *Qua-ootz*, the Owner of Reality, who is characterized as sacred in the Western view and characterized by respect in a First Nations view. *Sacred* is primarily a vertical relationship, while respect is inclusive in the First Nations perspective, it pertains to the relationships between *all* lifeforms.

Although the practice of respect among all lifeforms was an ideal, it could not always be upheld. There are forces of disrespect that seek to upset the balance and harmony among lifeforms demanding respect. Origin stories teach the truths that are reflected in daily newscasts around the world today. The balance and harmony among lifeforms on earth today have been severely upset. Wars and conflict are the chief characteristics in all of Earth's relationships. However, there was a time when balance and harmony was achieved among some peoples. The first missionaries to the Americas during the early 1600s recorded this feat of genius.

> [T]hose of their Nation … offer reciprocal Hospitality, and help each other so much that they provide for the needs of all so that there is no poor beggar at all in their towns, burgs and villages, as I said elsewhere, so that

they found it very bad, hearing that there were in France a great number of needy and beggars, and thought that it was due to a lack of charity, and blamed us greatly saying that if we had some intelligence we would set some order in the matter, the remedies being simple. (Jaenen, 1988, p.121)

The value of respect is one discernible theme or thread in a complex web of life and existence. In the modern world, this theme has been completely replaced by science and technology. At the moment, the themes of respect and the applications of science appear to be at odds. They are at odds when one or the other is denied. They can be balanced and harmonized if both themes are accepted as part of one whole within the human.

The applications of science and technology that magnificently express human cognition can complement the human spirit. The two working together can create ecosystems that are not only sustainable but also beautiful, bountiful and glorious, as it was in the beginning.

(Editors' note: This article was originally published in *Ecoforestry* 14(4):8-11.)

Heiltsuk youth swim off the central coast of British Columbia

DUNCAN M. TAYLOR

The Culture of Forests — Haida Traditional Knowledge and Forestry in the 21st Century

Nancy J. Turner and Barbara Wilson (Kii'iljuus)

Haida culture is our relationship to the land in its totality — *Ginn7waadluwaan gud7ahl Kwaagiidang* — everything depends on everything else. The old forests of Haida Gwaii have sustained and continue to sustain our way of life. In the past 50 years, industrial logging has transformed the landscape of Haida Gwaii from diverse old forest to young, even-aged stands of one or two species. The major river systems that once provided Haida villages with salmon; large cedars for longhouses and monumental art and plants for food, medicines, fiber and animal habitat have been eradicated by logging without consideration for these values (Council of the Haida Nation, quoted in Cathedral Grove, 2004-2007).

Traditional ecological knowledge and wisdom

The philosophical underpinnings and values reflected in traditional knowledge systems, while they may vary in specific detail from one cultural group to another, are widely held among indigenous peoples in different parts of the world. Embedded within peoples' belief systems is a recognition of a spirituality and power emanating from all lifeforms and from entities like rivers and mountains relegated to the *non-living* world in prevailing Western thinking. Trees, fish and other life are widely seen in indigenous societies as persons in another form, having their own societies and capable of influencing the lives and well-being of their human relatives or relations. Kincentricity is one term that has been applied to the prevailing indigenous peoples' view towards plants and animals as kin or family, deserving of the same considerations that would be given to one's grandparents, parents, aunts, uncles or siblings (Salmón 2000 A,B; Senos et al. 2006). Bears, salmon, trees and other species are regarded in traditional worldviews as generous relatives, willing to give themselves to people within a reciprocal system that demanded proper care and respect in return. This approach is reflected in traditional narratives, ceremonies, vocabulary and artistic representations of other lifeforms, for the Haida as for many other indigenous groups.

Other aspects of traditional ecological knowledge systems include practical knowledge about the environment, the life cycles of various species and their interrelationships: how they grow, their behavior, how they reproduce and regenerate themselves, their seasonal variation, their response to various types of disturbance and harvesting, their varying needs for shade, sunlight and moisture, and the specific habitats they require. The table on page 132 presents a list of important tree species of Haida Gwaii and the applications that reflect the deep practical knowledge and ingenuity of the Haida in their use of local resources, as well as their ability to identify and name the diverse lifeforms they encounter. Traditional knowledge systems also incorporate means of acquiring and passing on knowledge and experience through daily life over generations. This knowledge is embedded in indigenous language, vocabulary and stories; concepts of conservation and respect are lived and conveyed by example, within families and clans and through observation and teachings (Swanton 1905; Turner et al. 2000).

An excellent example of how Haida Traditional Ecological Knowledge and Wisdom is reflected in their approach to forestry is in the *Culturally Modified Trees*, or CMTs, that can be found in standing forests throughout Haida Gwaii, at least in places where commercial forestry has not destroyed them.

Culturally modified trees of Haida Gwaii

A beautiful convergence of the three overarching aspects of Traditional Ecological Knowledge and Wisdom — spirituality and worldview, practical knowledge and technique and intergenerational transmission of knowledge and practice — is reflected in the

PAINTED BY GIITSXAA

Mask

culturally modified trees of Haida Gwaii. These trees, at some time past, provided materials in the form of wood, food, bark, pitch, medicine, roots, withes or branches to the Haida. Culturally modified cedars, some of them centuries old, show evidence of: selection of potential canoe trees by test holes into the heart of a tree; harvesting one or more wooden planks of clear wood from the trunk; harvesting rectangular sheets of bark for roofing or house siding; harvesting strips of bark for the fibrous inner bark used in weaving mats, hats or baskets or as cordage or harvesting branches for implements, basketry or rope. Examples of these various types of culturally modified

Trees Haida Name (Note: S = Skidegate dialect M = Massett dialect)	Common & Botanical Names	Uses/Applications
sgaahlaan (S); **sgahlaan** (M)	Yellow cedar (*Chamaecyparis nootkatensis*)	Specialty wood; canoes; bark fiber for clothing, rope, mat, hats, baskets; role in story
hlgiid (S,M)	Pacific yew (*Taxus brevifolia*)	Tough, resilient wood used for digging sticks, bows and other implements; edible flesh around aril (otherwise toxic); medicine
kayd, kaayd (S), **kiid** (M); edible inner bark: **sgaalaak'uu ts'ii** (S); spruce roots **hllnga** (S), **hlii.ng** (M)	Sitka spruce (*Picea sitchensis*)	Edible inner bark, specialty wood, pitch for medicine, adhesive, role in narratives; roots for woven baskets, hats, cordage
ts'ahl (S); **ts'ahla, ts'ahl** (M) ('pine')	Lodgepole pine (*Pinus contorta*)	Specialty wood; pitch, bark for medicine
ts'uu (S, M)	Western red cedar (*Thuja plicata*)	Houses, house posts, large beams and rafters and the planks; canoes; storage boxes; cedar withe rope; fuel; medicine; role in narrative
k'aang (S, M); edible inner bark: **xi** (S) **xiga, xig, xi** (M)	Western hemlock (*Tsuga heterophylla*)	Edible inner bark; boughs for herring egg harvest, temporary shelters and hunting blinds; pitch; wood for fuel; bark for dye, medicine; role in narrative; roots for cordage
kaal, kal (S, M)	Red alder (*Alnus rubra*)	Light, easily carved wood used specifically for making bowls and masks; fuel; red dye; medicine
k'aahl7a (S), **ka7as, ka.as, ka7aj** (M)	Green alder (*Alnus crispa*)	Specialty wood
k'anhl7l, k'aanhll (S), **k'ayanhla, k'a7inhla** (M); fruit: **k'ay** (S, M)	Pacific crabapple (*Pyrus fusca*)	Edible fruit; tough, resilient wood used for digging sticks, bows and other implements; medicine; role in narratives
tsaanaang (S), **sgiisga, sgiisg** (M)	Scouler's willow (*Salix scouleriana*)	Leaves used as tobacco, medicine
tsaanaang (S), **sgiisga, sgiisg** (M)	Willows (*Salix hookeriana, S. lasiandra, S. reticulata, S. sitchensis*)	Leaves used as tobacco, medicine

Haida Names and Uses of Forest Trees of Haida Gwaii

TURNER 2004

cedars can be seen on the trail around Spirit Lake above the village of Skidegate. The trees are recognized by distinctive scars where bark or planks were removed, exposing the underlying wood. Sometimes the marks of adzes or chisels can be easily seen on the wood, and usually the scar shows some stage of the tree's healing process, with overgrowing edges of living growth reclaiming the area that was cut. Rectangular scars indicate removal of planks or sheets of bark from the tree, while long, tapered scars — some extending up the trunk for 32 feet or more — result from harvesting lengths of the soft, flexible inner bark. Most of these scars reflect the removal of bark or wood from no more than one-third of the circumference of the young tree. Some CMTs show removal of bark and/or wood on several successive occasions, sometimes decades apart, from different sides of the tree. This important evidence of sustainable harvesting over long periods of time is highly significant and often represents the most compelling proof of people's past occupancy and use of forests. Cedars on Hanson Island in Kwakwaka'wakw territory are exemplary of long-term sustainable cedar use (Garrick 1998).

Other types of culturally modified trees include those whose inner bark was harvested as food (e.g. western hemlock — *Tsuga heterophylla*), those cut or notched to produce pitch for chewing gum, medicine or as a waterproofing or caulking agent (e.g., Sitka spruce — *Picea sitchensis*), those showing removal of strips of bark used in medicinal preparations (e.g. red alder — *Alnus rubra*), those whose limbs are taken for implements or basketry (e.g. western red cedar or Pacific yew — *Taxus brevifolia*), and those whose roots are harvested for basketry (e.g. Sitka

ROBERT D. TURNER

spruce) (British Columbia, Province of 2001; Mobley and Eldridge 1992; Stryd and Feddema 1998; Turner 1995, 1998, 2004).

Culturally modified tree

Other culturally modified trees can be found showing a wedge-shaped undercut, evidence of partial cutting that was for some reason abandoned, leaving the tree notched but still living. For trees that were actually cut, stumps with telltale chop marks from stone, antler or metal tools, sections of logs topped from the tree and remains of skidders used to transport them as whole logs or partially finished canoes to the water's edge or wherever else they were to be used. Traditionally cut stumps are often quite high, since there is less wood to cut through well above the root flare, and they vary in shape according to the felling technique used (Stewart 1984; Stryd and Feddema 1998).

Harvesting activities of the Haida and other First Peoples reflected the utmost care and attention to the tree as a living and generous being, whose life would not be forfeited unnecessarily. The harvester would negotiate with the tree, through a respectful request, and an explanation as to the purpose of harvesting by those undertaking the task. (Boas 1930; Clayoquot Scientific Panel 1995; Deur and Turner 2006; Stewart 1984; Turner 2004). This approach, and the actual technique of partially removing the materials required from the tree while still allowing it to continue to live and grow, would have been carefully conveyed to any younger people who would be assisting their elders in their tasks and learning about proper harvesting protocols at the same time. These teachings remain an important part of Haida cultural knowledge today, although it is much more difficult to access trees to harvest and to pass on this important knowledge under the present circumstances.

Protecting CMTs:
A clash of values

Culturally Modified Trees are by definition human-created artifacts, constituting significant physical evidence of traditional occupancy and use of trees and forest habitats (Garrick 1998; Stryd and Feddema 1998; British Columbia, Province of 2001). Groups of CMTs are known to archaeologists as *forest utilization sites*, and these are protected by the Heritage Conservation Act of the province of British Columbia if one or more of the trees in the group were modified prior to 1846.[1] If the ages of the trees are not known but there is a reasonable likelihood that the modification was previous to this date, protection through the 1996 Act still applies (British Columbia, Government of 1996; Stryd and Feddema 1998). The dates of cultural modification of still-living trees can often be determined

through tree-ring dating, if a core into the center of the tree can be taken. However, coring living trees is sometimes prohibited because of potential injury or damage to the tree. Some of the oldest documented CMTs in British Columbia date back to the middle of the 12th Century AD, and the ages of CMTs range from that time right up to the present, since contemporary indigenous people continue to modify trees in various ways as they continue their practices of basket material collection, medicine harvesting and other types of tree use.

Thus, the cultural and legal significance of CMTs is recognized both by the British Columbia government and First Nations. Guujaaw, Michael Yahgulanaas Nicoll and Captain Gold (formerly Wanagun) are three Haida leaders who have spoken out about the importance of CMTs for their people and the land. Guujaaw (1990, cited by Stryd and Feddema 1998:14) characterized these trees as sacred memorials to "... our ancestors who worked in the forests and created the canoes and totem poles for which the Haidas are known worldwide." To him, culturally modified trees provide "... a sense of communion with the old canoe makers." Elsewhere, Guujaaw, Yahgulaanas and Captain Gold (1991:2, cited by Stryd and Feddema 1998:14), described the CMTs at S'yall (the Collison Point site) as "...'living archaeology' [that] presents a unique opportunity to get close to the activities of our ancestors in a live and dynamic setting" and explained that, "... to our people the spiritual effects of being in the footsteps of our ancestors is the primary significance of the site." Thus, for many people, places where culturally modified trees can be found have spiritual significance because they represent simultaneously people's direct connections to their ancestors and to their ancestral lands (Clayoquot Scientific Panel 1995). CMTs also provide wonderful teaching and learning opportunities, and important windows into past practices and techniques of selecting wood, harvesting planks and bark, felling trees and canoe building (Guujaaw 1990, cited in Stryd and Feddema 1998). Moreover, CMTs can also serve as concrete evidence of an Aboriginal Right, as enshrined in the Canadian Constitution.

There are, however, limitations to the protection of CMTs, even those that qualify for protection under the Cultural Heritage Act. Old Growth forests, where most CMTs occur, are increasingly subjected to industrial logging. Many CMTs have been cut for timber because they were overlooked or unrecognized.

Furthermore, it is possible for companies to obtain permits that allow them to cut CMTs. This is what happened in a recent case at Naden Harbour in the spring of 2007, when a group of ancient and known CMTs were cut down by a logging company (see Husby 2004), all of them authorized through site alteration permits from the Archaeology Branch. Naden Harbour has long been recognized as a place where Haida have gone to harvest sheets of cedar bark for roofing, used directly by the Haida or traded with neighboring groups such as the Nisga'a (Turner 2004).

The Husby Group of Companies expressly recognized the importance "to the Haida Nation and the Province" of identifying, assessing and managing CMTs and the need to create Reserve patches for them (see Husby

Skang Gwaii pole and building

ROBERT D. TURNER

2004, p. 23, 3.9 Cultural Heritage Resources). Regarding the CMTs in the Naden Harbour area, they noted: "Archeological Overview Assessments were conducted in 1996 and again in 1999/2000 for the Naden Harbour area. This plan [to log] adheres to provisions of the Heritage Conservation Act." (Husby 2004). They also claimed, "As a final precaution [against damage of CMTs], fallers for the HGC are primarily local residents and have been trained to identify potential CMT's. When there is a doubt, operations are halted until further assessments are completed" (Husby 2004:23). Yet, against the expressed and clear objections of the Council of the Haida Nation (Guujaaw 2003; Munt 2007), they applied for and received approval to cut at least 18 CM Trees in cutblock NAD120 (including, it was learned afterwards, one dating back to 1555, and others of ages representing each century from that time).

Ongoing issues in Haida forestlands

The recent cutting of CMTs at Naden Harbour is just one of countless incidents in which Haida perspectives, values and knowledge have been downplayed or overlooked in industrial forestry. On many occasions, the Haida have stood up in opposition to clearcutting and other encroachments on the lands and waters of their territory. In November 1985, Haida protestors and their supporters formed a human blockade across a logging road on Lyell Island, preventing the trucks from passing, and as a result, 72 Haida, including many elders, were arrested. The resulting media coverage brought the situation of serious logging damage on Haida Gwaii and the Haida's opposition to it to the world stage, and ultimately (in 1993), Gwaii Haanas National Park Reserve and Haida Heritage Site was created. At this time, too, the Haida Gwaii Watchmen program, initiated by the Haida in 1981 to help protect Haida ancestral villages, was supported and formalized as part of the co-management agreement between the Haida Nation and the Government of Canada. A world famous protected area, Gwaii Haanas was recently voted the best park in a survey of 55 national parks in Canada and the US by the National Geographic Sustainable Destinations Resource Center (Hamashige 2005)

Another major impact on the forests of Haida Gwaii is that of introduced species, both plants and animals. The species of Haida Gwaii has evolved in relative isolation for thousands of years. There are unique endemic species, remnants of the islands' status as a glacial refugium during the last ice age. Even for species that occur both on the islands and the mainland, their genetic composition is often different because of the separation of these populations. Within the last century or so, however, many new species and populations have been introduced, some unintentionally, but many others on purpose.

One of the most pervasive and contentious of the introduced species is the Columbia black-tailed deer. Deer were introduced to the islands first in 1890 and again around 1910 and 1920 to provide game for hunters. The deer have multiplied to the point where their browsing has depleted the diversity and productivity of the islands. Tree seedlings, branches and many shrubs and herbaceous plants have been heavily browsed to the point where they can no longer grow and reproduce. Devil's club, an important Haida medicine plant, is one of the species impacted by the deer. Throughout much of Haida Gwaii, the deer have devoured virtually all the herbaceous and shrubby browse within their reach, with the only berry bushes left intact being those growing on the top of tall stumps. Pollinating insects, songbirds and other native wildlife have also been affected through the food web.

Some trees brought to the islands as ornamentals, including cottonwood (*Populus balsamifera*) and maples (*Acer* spp.), have spread locally. Trees not occurring naturally on Haida Gwaii — most notably Douglas fir (*Pseudotsuga menziesii*) — were planted in plantations following clearcutting of the original forests in some places. However, recently, increased efforts to replant with local indigenous trees are in evidence. Programs for culling and removal of the deer and other introduced animals have been established in some areas, and in these cases, the original ecosystems have been noticeably restored and renewed. The Haida Forest Guardians have undertaken a research program in which deer are excluded from some sites through fencing; these provide evidence of the impacts of deer browsing, by demonstrating the dramatic increase in growth and diversity of native species in the exclosures. Introduced species remain an ongoing and potential future threat to the Haida and their forestlands.

Conclusions

Forests continue to sustain and inspire the Haida and other residents of Haida Gwaii. Today more than ever, the Haida rely on their forest ecosystems to maintain and renew their culture. The newly opened cultural center at Qay'llnagaay near Skidegate is just one example of the critical importance of forests: in the construction of the buildings, which are modern manifestations of ancient architecture; in the magnificent story poles that stand before each structure in the complex; and in the myriad ferns, shrubs and trees that surround the buildings, bringing beauty, richness and educational possibilities to all those who come to this place.

The relentless industrial logging that has taken place on the islands over the past century has, by some calculations, reduced the ancient forests of Haida Gwaii by two thirds of their original state (Cathedral Grove 2004-2007). The forest industry on the islands has not been sustainable: too much has been removed, too quickly, with too much damage to other species including salmon and marine life, not to mention the monumental cedars and giant old spruce trees. Yet, the newest Haida poles stand symbolically as a reflection of a different value system, one that can sustain the forest ecosystems and respect the integrity of complex relationships they foster. The Haida count themselves as a part of the intricate web of life nurtured and shaped by the forests. For them, the survival of the forest is essential if they themselves are to flourish.

Acknowledgments

We are grateful to the Haida elders and leaders who have spoken out against the destruction of the forests of Haida Gwaii, particularly to Guujaaw (President, CHN), Captain Gold, Michael Yahgulanaas Nicoll and all those who stood up to protect the forests at the blockades and through negotiations. *Haawa* to the Council of the Haida Nation and the Haida Forest Guardians for providing us with some of the information presented here, and to Jaalen Edenshaw, Gwaai Edenshaw, Marguerite Forest, Audrey Pearson, Elizabeth Bulbrook, April Churchill Davis, Giitsxaa (Ron Wilson) and Karen Wonders for their important contributions.

Plant Teachers as a Source of Healing
in the Peruvian Amazon

Gonzalo Brito and Claire Sieber

Cultivating healthy relationships between humans, environments and the spiritual realm is fundamental to much indigenous knowledge pertaining to community and environmental health and has much to contribute to what we know about health in modern, Western or biomedical medicine.

The forest as source of healing

As ecological studies have demonstrated, the health of the ecosystem depends upon many symbiotic and reciprocal relationships between plants, animals and non-biotic elements. Studies in psychology demonstrate that there are similar requirements for individual human health. The intuition that psychological problems arise not only from internal variables, but rather that they also depend upon the contexts in which people live, work, relate and change is not new. To better understand patients' suffering, and to find ways out of this suffering, psychology has drawn from the application of systems theory in the therapeutic field. In particular, psychologists have focused on contextual variables such as the familial and social dynamics in which patients are situated.

More recently, we have come to understand that it is not only our social systems, but also the ecosystems in which we live that have a profound impact on our psyches and our general sensations of well-being or illness. It becomes obvious that there are environmental contexts that facilitate the appearance of psychopathologies and others that favor health. According to eco-psychology reports, access to nature acts as a protective resource to maintain psychological well-being. In contrast, the alienation of human beings from nature (such as the loss of direct contact with forests, rivers, mountains) seems to be related with the sensation of alienation from oneself and the loss of a sense of meaning. The high rates of anxiety, depression and addiction to legal and illegal substances prevalent in large urban populations seem to correlate with the lack of access to nature. This deprives many of the fundamental human experience of feeling a sense of connection to, as though we are a part of, nature.

Addiction to drugs is a psycho-social problem of special relevance, contributing to our understanding of the complex relationship between psychological well-being, direct contact with nature and spirituality. To approach the subject of addiction and the potential for rehabilitation through direct experience in contact with nature, we refer to the experience of a Center for Drug Rehabilitation and Research of Traditional Medicines, Takiwasi,[1] located in the city of Tarapoto, in the department of San Martín in the Peruvian Upper Amazon. Takiwasi provides an interesting example of how wild forests can be a source of healing and how local medicinal knowledge can have global significance by restoring a respectful relationship with nature.

Takiwasi Center is a non-governmental, not for profit organization that since 1992 has offered treatment to patients dependent on drugs. Patients proceed through a protocol of treatment that integrates the tools of psychology and Western medicine with the knowledge and practices of Amazonian medicine. In practice, this is realized through the collaborative work of psychotherapists who are responsible for both group and individual therapeutic interventions, curanderos or healers who administer medicinal plants according to traditional Amazonian medical practices and Western-trained doctors who supervise the general state of health of the patients in their process of detoxification and recuperation.

Takiwasi has a *chacra* (local word for a piece of land in the jungle) of 124 acres on the edge of the San Martín jungle. This land is used with three principal objectives: to conserve the native forest; to have an adequate place for patients, therapists and healers to complete their *dietas* (healing retreats and apprenticeships explained below), and to cultivate medicinal plants endemic to the region and used in the treatment of patients.

Generally, a person who takes drugs looks for an experience that would bring them out of their habitual perceptions, feelings and thoughts — usually because in ordinary reality they perceive an intolerable level of suffering or lack of meaning. This necessity to feel extraordinary experiences which offer meaning contrasts with a notable lack, in our post-industrial society, of ritual spaces that provide youth with the important experience of belonging to a community and access to the sacred — or, in other words, to feel that one's own life is not trivial but significant. Unable to access this initiation into community, the addict lives in a state of counter-initiation, experimenting, without adequate guides or protective rituals, with modified states of consciousness through transgressive, inadequate use of sacred plants.

Apart from synthetic drugs (which are often also modeled after active plant compounds), many addictive drugs we know are derived from plants that have been used as sacred or medicinal plants in indigenous traditions. In their original environmental and cultural contexts, plants such as the coca leaf have been used for millennia by Andean cultures, *cannabis* has been used in northern India and tobacco in the shamanic traditions of North and South America, to name just a few examples. *Ayahuasca* is a principal medicinal and sacred plant among the indigenous peoples who live in the Amazon Basin from Peru, through Colombia and Ecuador. Its continued use for millennia as a source of healing and wisdom without any documented cases of addiction is a testament to the healing potential of Ayahuasca and the cultural knowledge surrounding its use.

In Takiwasi's view, addiction to drugs implies a transgressive relationship of a person with a plant; the plant is not respected in a sacred dimension, but rather is treated as a simple object of consumption. The healers at Takiwasi explain that when a person disrespects a sacred plant through irresponsible use, the *anima* or spirit of the plant takes revenge on that person by taking their spirit captive through addiction. Some examples of disrespectful or irresponsible use include refining a plant to extract the alkaloids, not respecting the numerous abstinences that are required for working with plants or taking them outside of appropriate, spiritually protective rituals. The cost of these transgressions is the loss of a person's liberty.

Rehabilitation for addicts and the therapies offered to the local population and to visitors provide a tangible possibility for patients to repair their relationship with the world of plants, the world of the spirits and consequently, their relationship with themselves. This is realized through experiencing personal contact with the forest and its medicinal resources following the ethical rules and specific behaviors observed in the local healing tradition. Thus, the forest is presented as a double therapeutic resource: first, as a source of a rich variety of medicines and secondly, as a healthy context in which one can retreat to find oneself.

The immersion of the patient into the exuberant nature of the jungle, with very few belongings at hand besides a change of clothes and a flashlight, usually turns into a fundamental experience of healing for the patient. Specifically, this experience is the radical opposite of drug consumption. More broadly, it is contrary to consumption in general. Without anything to do during this time, the patient has the opportunity to simply be and to open their perception to the gifts of nature. Regularly, with this experience of extreme austerity and introspection, a great recognition and gratitude emerges for that which one has and, for many, this recognition takes a spiritual form.

The experience of Takiwasi, with 15 years of work, more than 600 patients who have passed through the resident therapy program, and some 1000 patients who have received ambulatory treatment, shows how the forest can be an effective source of physical, emotional and spiritual health.

Experiential knowledge

Experience as a way of knowing is basic to many traditional knowledge systems. Healers apprenticed in Amazonian medicine must dedicate years of their life to prolonged *dietas* in the jungle to learn from the *plantas maestras*[2] the skills for healing. Healers experience the medicine that they learn to prescribe to their patients. They accompany their patients through healing ceremonies having ingested the medicine themselves. Healers also have intimate knowledge of the plants that they work with because they have learned to harvest, prepare, ingest and administer them, and through the *dietas* they learn the sacred songs that the *plantas maestras* impart to them. This close relationship with the plants demonstrates how healers' experience of nature is vital to their healing practice.

At Takiwasi, therapists are also required to participate in healing rituals, to take plant medicines and to complete *dietas* in order to understand and relate to the patients' experiences. Visiting researchers are encouraged to experience first hand the medical knowledge that they have come to observe. Health practitioners at Takiwasi express a need for more research that includes an experiential perspective of Amazonian medical practices. They explain that researchers often come to observe medical practices and document knowledge systems without knowing, experiencing or explaining how these knowledge and practices actively work upon and change the individual.

Claire visited the Takiwasi Center from May to November of 2006 to conduct research for her masters in anthropology. What follows blends an outline of Takiwasi's healing regime with Claire's personal experiences there.

Experience, insight and responsibility

Although not addicted to drugs, I found treatment at Takiwasi for many emotional anxieties that have been afflicting me on a physical, emotional and spiritual level. Participating in weekly purges, *Ayahuasca* sessions and one *dieta* of eight days gave me an opportunity to discover the health benefits of Amazonian medicine combined with therapeutic follow-up.

The purgas

Purge plants are administered in a ritual setting at Takiwasi, led by an experienced healer. They involve the ingestion of a designated *purga* plant accompanied by the *ikaros*, or healing songs, of the healer. After one to two hours of vomiting, I would return to my home in Tarapoto to rest and contemplate the experience. Often, as I was vomiting, memories of past anxiety, guilt or insecurity would surface. The physical force of vomiting felt like a cathartic release of those emotions. The memory stimulation continued for hours after the purge, and although they seemed

random and insignificant, these memories linked to significant experiences in my life. I recognize that I am exposed to memory triggers constantly, but as the healers explain, plants help us to remember these memories *passing them through the heart*. I was able actually to feel and afterwards to integrate the emotional meanings linked to these memories. The following is an excerpt from my fieldnotes, June 5th, 2006.

This small Chinese bowl was a simple object that took on enhanced significance after my *paico* purge, digging up memories about a close childhood friend from whom I had grown apart. Remembering my brother and his interest in Chinese and Japanese traditions also brought back memories of how much I admired and have been greatly influenced by my siblings. As a child, I felt a great loss when my siblings left for university, unable to understand at the time the distance that came between us.

Contemplating this bowl helped me to get at the root of some of my fears about losing contact with friends and family. I could see

Chinese bowl

CLAIRE SIEBER, JUNE 2006

why I keep myself distant and non-committal with people in my life, but I was also reminded of how these people have supported and inspired me, which gave me deep gratitude.

Ayahuasca

Guilt, insecurity, fear, envy and doubt: these were the main emotional anxieties that I felt emerge from my experiences with *Ayahuasca*. Talking to other visiting patients, I surmised that these were common feelings that arose in *Ayahuasca* sessions. There are also a few corresponding illnesses that are identified among local Amazonian healers, including *susto* (fear), *nerviosidades* (stress), nervousness and *envidia*, *mal ojo* (envy or evil eye). The ability to see images and memories relating to these emotions helped me to confront them, to reflect upon how they influence my life and to release some of the tension surrounding them from my physical system through vomiting and diarrhea. The visions inspired by *Ayahuasca*

provided visual tools to creatively overcome my anxieties of guilt, doubt, insecurity, envy and fear.

Tiny flecks of light appeared in the periphery of my darkened vision. The more faith I gave, the more elaborate the visions … I started to imagine and let the visions flow. Feeling skeptical, I asked "Is this just my imagination?" As a response, *Ayahuasca* showed me a big clay belly with a window into it, then, while clearing another moon-shaped window into the belly, a voice inside me asked "Just your imagination? Isn't your imagination a way to see? An insight?" I was amazed and relieved at the same time, realizing that I could trust my intuition and my imagination, and that so many fragments of my past could be stitched together now with these visions — that the plant was showing me how valid my imagination is for processing my thoughts, my anxieties, my insecurities — my problems. The clay belly became a recurring symbol, and each time I worried that I was making up the visions myself, *Ayahuasca* reminded me that my imagination is a means to understanding and that I need faith to create my reality.

Although not educated in psychotherapy, I recognized immediately that the images produced by *Ayahuasca* surrounding my emotional anxieties, were very healing. Through visualization of these anxieties I could accept them, take responsibility for them, release them or consciously work through them in my daily life outside of Takiwasi. The psychotherapeutic follow-up definitely confirmed and elaborated

Ayahuasca — sacred vine, Peru

CLAIRE SIEBER

upon this, and I began to see how these medical knowledge systems are complementary.

The dieta

The *dieta* at Takiwasi is eight days in duration, a time in which the person maintains exclusive contact with the forest, protected by a rustic construction of cane stalk walls and a palm thatch roof. During the *dieta* patients must avoid all perfumed products, excessive heat through sun exposure and contact with anyone else besides the healer. This permits the energetic body of the patient to open up and allow the *planta maestra* to do its work.

> Removed from daily anxieties, small details become precious revelations. The delicate petals of a fallen flower after heavy rain hold a perfume that fills my head with blissful serenity.

This was an insight that I had after six days of isolation in the jungle. My therapist at Takiwasi suggested that I take the plant *Ajo Sacha* (*Mansoa alliacea*), which is meant to address physical problems of general discomfort, pain and heat and on a psychological level reinforce strength and will power (Giove 2002: 48). It was also explained to me that *Ajo Sacha* helps to develop one's spiritual connection.

During my *dieta*, I connected with the writing of Thich Nhat Hanh, a renowned Zen master, poet and peace activist. Among the few things I had with me was his book *The Miracle of Mindfulness*. The writings of this book complemented what I was learning about Amazonian medical practices and psychotherapeutic attention to dreams and visions. Thich Nhat Hanh advocates contemplative meditation and mindfulness in every act. Through attention to my breathing, my thinking, my dreams, my every little action, I became painfully aware of the cacophony of my mind — always leaping to think of something else. In the setting of my jungle tambo, or shelter, I was able to practice calming my mind, and appreciate the interdependence of everything around me. I read:

> Recall a simple and ancient truth: the subject of knowledge cannot exist independently from the object of knowledge … the practitioner meditates on mind and, by so doing, is able to see the interdependence of the subject of knowledge and the object of knowledge (Nhat Hanh 1975:70).

This passage resonates with increasing global awareness of the interconnectedness of all systems. It helped me to cultivate compassion, empathy and patience in my thoughts about my life and the people I know. During the *dieta* I had the luxury of seemingly limitless time to sort through my memories, to reflect upon my relationships with people and places in my life, to dream about decisions that I needed to make about my life and to take those dreams seriously. I drew pictures, I wrote down thoughts I have never been able to articulate about my relationships with family, friends and environments in my life. It was as though I could finally be myself, and not be distracted by all of the things I had to do or consume.

Daily meditation became my way of connecting to something deeper that had been pushed aside by all the daily tasks I obsessed about. Now, I was learning to practice mindfulness in those daily tasks, which would prove to be a skill I needed to draw upon when I returned to my daily routines. In that jungle *tambo*, with only one simple meal of boiled plantain and rice, one change of clothes, one book to read, my journal, my camera and some watercolor paints — I felt intense joy over a fallen flower, baths in the river, a beautiful river rock, the sound of wind and rain and the music I was learning to pull from a small bamboo flute. I knew that when I returned to cities and my regular routines that I could easily be convinced that my happiness depends upon the consumption of material things, obscuring the basic joys that I had during the *dieta*. Mindfulness and meditation have helped me to reconnect often to that deeper happiness that simplicity uncovers.

Conclusions

The plants, systems of knowledge and healing, and the local communities of the Upper Peruvian Amazon are in a relationship of dynamic and interdependent health. Urban development strategies, usually based on centralized and decontextualized decision making, threaten to destroy this delicate socio-spiritual and psycho-biological balance (Ibacache et al. 2002) that has been maintained for centuries.

With growing international interest in and awareness of the use of Amazonian medical knowledge comes the responsibility to respect the community and environments within which these knowledge systems have emerged, changed, and been maintained through the relationships of many healers with their plant teachers, and their communities. Through our experiences at Takiwasi and in the region of San Martín, we have come to understand the paramount importance of nature and spirituality in the Peruvian Amazonian medical practices and ways in which these practices complement psychotherapeutic practices. Takiwasi provides an example of how the perennial wisdom maintained and cultivated by people living in contact with nature can have global significance in repairing the social and environmental impacts of modern, post industrial and capitalist consumption. Specifically, these medical knowledge systems demonstrate how cultivating healthy relationships of reciprocity and gratitude among humans, nature and the spirit world can be a source of healing for our communities.

Chacruna — used in healing, Peru

CLAIRE SIEBER

Tree Meditation Meets Shamanism

Alan Drengson

Spring day with trees on a ridge

We were on a Sunday climb of Mount Ellinor in the southern Olympic Mountains. When Japanese living treasure Masanobu Fukuoka visited the Olympics several years ago, he got very excited once outdoors there. He said that, "this is a land that is fully alive." Spending time there is always revitalizing for me and others I know. It was a splendid day with perfect spring weather. The blue skies were filled with high, billowy, cumulus clouds; there was warm sun with cool breezes that blew at times in moderate gusts. We climbed from the road end at about 2,500 feet to almost 6,000 feet above sea level, passing through an impressive range of forest and plant growth patterns. From the top of the mountain we had a 180 degree view of snowy mountains and, behind us, the hills, rivers, bays and lowlands of Puget Sound. Most of the foothills of the Olympics were still clothed in forest to the North, but to the East and South the clearcuts of industrial forestry had removed most of the old-growth forests. The clearcuts formed brown and light green checkerboards across the landscape. Looking to the interior of the Olympics we could see ridge after ridge of mountains and forests, a landscape still primal in its qualities.

On the way down we glissaded to the bottom of a long snow chute into subalpine forest. The subalpine gave way to taller woods the rest of the way down. We followed an animal trail that went down a steep, heavily forested ridge. As the ridge descends it narrows and one side falls steeply to a rushing creek. Just before you can hear the creek, the ridge reaches a high point that stands out from the mountain, with the sky visible above the trees.

I was ahead of the others and stopped on the crest of the ridge. Standing among the conifers with my heavy climbing boots planted firmly on the ground and tree trunks all around me, I looked up through the trunks to the limbs and needles and the sky beyond. The trees were swaying rhythmically together in the wind. Once in a while a harder gust swayed them more vigorously.

As I stood I became entranced and *Earthed*. I began to sway without intending to.

Looking up through the trees to the sky, my mind was empty and I was intensely aware of the trees, the sky, the sounds — but blending and merging with the surroundings. The boundaries between my normal sense of self and the rest of Nature fell away. I experienced the trees' spirit-power — an extensive, inclusive and immediate presence. I was aware of each tree as separate and yet unified, interdependent, vibrating, moving and harmonizing together. They are an ecological community where diverse life thrives. There is a unity in diversity. Years after this experience, I learned a word from Arne Naess to describe my feelings of harmony: *ecosophy* literally means ecological harmony and wisdom. Ecosophies are diverse evolving lifestyles. As a way of life an ecosophy is something we can theorize about even as we seek to cultivate a good way of life or to consciously change. Ecosophies are enlivened by spontaneous spirituality and guided by primal practices. They are personal and place based.

The tree meditation I have been describing is similar to those practiced by some Taoist monks as described in ancient Chinese literature. It is also important to note that according to legend Buddha achieved enlightenment under the Bo tree, which literally means the tree of light. In ancient traditions and Shamanic practices in many places, the tree with its roots represents the cosmic systems with the medicine circles representing cosmic cycles and concentric circles of relationships. In the Old Norse traditions, for example, the tree of reality had nine distinct levels. In Shamanic traditions living trees in the forest have their own spirit and wisdom. An old tree is like an elder human who has the wisdom of the tribe or forest, holds the perspectives of age and senses above and below

the ground. My own tree meditations came first from spontaneous experiences as described above, but these were enriched by learning formal meditation practices from Taoist, Zen and Shinto (Aikido) traditions. These were further enriched by a series of workshops I did on *The Way of the Shaman*.

An old tree joins a forest

Michael Harner led a Tree Meditation Ceremony at a *Spirits of Nature* workshop in the Spring of 1988 in the hills near Bellingham, Washington.[1] In one exercise, Harner told each of us to find in the vicinity of the meeting house a tree that appealed to us. We were to sit by and be with that tree, to feel its bark and limbs, study its leaves, listen with it, hug it and let ourselves merge with it. I walked until I felt a particular tree pull me toward it: a large, old, gnarly cedar tree. It was in the middle of a natural area spared of lawnmowers, herbicides and chainsaws.

My tree friend overlooked the first tee on a semiwild golf course. The golfers chatted as they waited their turn to play. The tree's energy field encircled them. The tree often has quiet nights, and is so tall that its limbs feel the sky, sun, moon and stars and the nearby lake. I hugged the tree, stroked its bark, felt its shape and wondered at its age, looking up its trunk to the sky, merging with it, sensing its slightest movements, swaying with it ever so gently. I was aware of the forest beyond the developed area, as well as the logged-over lands on some of the distant hills. My tree had stood a long time. It had escaped cutting because it is not in the way of human interests, and it was not a good tree for lumber or pulp. This survivor was loaded with well developed seeds almost ready to go. Squirrels and birds loved this tree. It was settled in place. Its great roots went deep into the mineral soils of the earth and spread out in all directions. Its limbs were intertwined with the limbs of trees around it on most sides. I sensed much more to the tree than I can say or logically understand. The energetic tree spirit was fully there in all its details connected through its living presence with the life force shared with other lives in a Great Spirit Circle. As on the ridge before, I was rooted with the tree in a trance. This is a transbiotic energetic field of awareness.

Hi! An insistent drumming was calling us back. I emerged from the tree's energy and walked, part tree, back to the ceremonial drumming circle in the octagonal conference building. Once back in the circle we human trees stood as a forest. Harner and two assistants started the entrancing ceremonial drumming. Once more my feet firmly rooted to the ground, once more slipping deeply into my tree, once more swaying with the rest of the forest, just one in a community of living tree spirit beings, enjoying the sound of the drums becoming the wind, waterfalls, birds and other creatures calling, river-talk, wind-talk, children singing, the sun and rain, darkness and fog, just standing there out of modern time; not living in human history. *Wild time!*

This primordial peace was shattered when Harner shouted, "Here come the chainsaws!" The drums increased in tempo and grew louder. They produced a hideous sound, an ugly whine, a frightening violent noise, from which we could not run like animals. Coming like a forest fire, undaunted by shifting winds — ugh! — visions of chainsaws, gas and oil smells, machinery noise, trees falling, being sawed again and again, cut off from their roots, their limbs removed, cut off from one another and the rest of the forest, falling, sighing, moaning, calling, crying out as they fell, crying as they lay on the ground, visions of cables wrapped around their trunks and pulling away their parts and saws coming again and again — a chainsaw massacre. Our communal mind shuddered. Some still stood after the saws had passed. They would seed a new forest, patiently regrowing what was lost, loving the Earth and living creatures, sharing with them some needles, seeds, limbs, canopy and more.

When the saws passed we felt sorry for those who wielded them. We were aware of the compulsion and enslavement to systems cut off from the ecological community of trees in the spiritual forest. The drums called us back and we streamed tears of grief. Blocked grief later becomes a flood. Denuded hills change life-giving water into an erosive and destructive power. Forested hills give life, and elder tree spirits live on in old trees.

Shamanic worlds

Shamanic cultures the world over describe journeying as involving three different interconnected realms, and in each there are many levels or dimensions. There is journeying done in the *middle world*, or the world of our daily lives, working in the garden or walking on the seashore. It is possible to journey in this daylight world to distant places through shamanic techniques. You can use these to see from the sky like an eagle, for example. There are many other examples involving shapeshifting, night travel and the like. These are things that any of us has the capacity to do, even if we have not used it. The ability to shift perspectives is a natural one. The ability to create and improvise is a gift we all have, even small children. This is what Socrates referred to as his daemon or spirit, the creator within.

There are shamanic journeys to a *lower world*. One can experience going there in lucid dreaming and in ceremonial drumming. It also can happen spontaneously when you are wilderness wandering. You are aware of going through a dark tunnel or being drawn down into a whirlpool to the lower world. Sometimes people go into a hollow tree and find themselves falling down a shaft into this lower world, as in *Alice in Wonderland*. There is an actual experience of going down. The lower world is populated with animal, plant and other natural spirit beings. In my experiences the light is subdued with no obvious source like the sun. It is like a twilight realm. The colors vary from time to time. Sometimes the ground is green like beautiful meadows; other times it is dark in color. The animals, like a white bear I encountered, have a glowing quality. They also can communicate without making any sound. All types of animal and plant beings are encountered, even ones people often don't like such as spiders and snakes. Other people say they have been quite scared by creepy crawlies, but then spiders are powerful helpers and messengers. All of the creatures one meets have many levels of significance. Many people find cures for illnesses in the lower world; they learn what to do by listening to a bird who shows them a plant to use, where to look for it and what to do with it once obtained.

The *upper world* in my experience is a world of light and sun. Here the feeling of the journey is very much going up, an ascent. The upper world is where we meet angels, sages, teachers and ancestors. We were invited to journey to the upper world and instructed in how it could happen for us. We each were lying down with our eyes closed, listening to the beat of the drums. We had a question to ask whatever person or being we met there. Sometimes we would journey with a completely open or empty mind, with no questions. In other journeys we asked questions helpful in healing ourselves or someone else. We also did some journeying acting as therapists to each other. The drumming circle was the foundation of the other things we did, and it was in drum journeys that we consistently experienced the upper and lower worlds. We did not decide beforehand whom we would meet. This was something that just happened spontaneously while journeying. In journeys to the upper world I met people like the founder of Aikido, Morihei Ueshiba, and other people who had been my teachers before they died. I met ancestors and beings I don't recall encountering before. I met guardians and angels. All kinds of questions about healing and other matters can be taken to the upper world.

Shamanic arts

In addition to the drumming circle journeys, participants in Harner's programs were also given instructions in how to read the signs of Nature and how to do divination using a rock. For signs of Nature we were shown how to formulate a series of questions related to solving some specific personal problem for a *client* (one of the other workshop participants). With our four or five questions we would then go out walking in the surrounding area waiting to see, hear or feel signs from Nature in answer to each question. The results were amazing!

In a similar way, we were taught to go out looking for a rock of a certain size and shape, one that appealed to us. We were to be very careful to note where it was and how it was oriented, so that we could return these rocks to their original places after our work with them. We took our rocks back to the drumming circle, and then as we looked at each side we were asked questions to consider. We drew on paper what we saw on the rock as an answer to the question asked for each side. The six drawings were combined to tell a story that had some overall significance for us. Again, the results were astounding. The six sides, I might add, correspond to the six directions of the medicine circle: the four cardinal directions of north, south, east and west, plus the sky and earth or up and down.

In each weekend workshop the 30 or so people involved became a tribal community.

Over a period of a few days we gained significant knowledge and generated an incredible number of stories. Harner asked us to consider what would happen if we did this every day, while living together, so we could keep building on our results year after year. It was easy to see how in a short time we could have a very rich and evolving culture with its own stories and narrative traditions connected to our place and its denizens. Many of the participants later formed their own drumming circles to journey with others in their neighborhood.

Ceremonies and other practices are a way to combine the incredible power and memories

Shaman's drum made on Vancouver Island, BC

ALAN DRENGSON

Seeing the Ikaro in healing ceremony

CLAIRE SIEBER

of a group of people, who when joined are more powerful than the most sophisticated computers. This is a communal, not a managerial, way of organizing physical, mental and spiritual powers. There are other ways that also use trance and more structured programs. The shamanic arts are primal and free. No one controls them. Everyone in a drumming circle is on the same footing. No one is superior to anyone else. The shaman is a master ceremonialist with a lot of journeying experience who helps others, who sets the stage and leads the drumming.

Wild experiences in the primal poetry of life help us to be in communion with the communities of spirited life. They are all around and run through us without end. They help us to appreciate Lao Tzu's saying that "the greatest cutting does not sever," "returning to one's roots is known as stillness," that to "bow down is to be preserved."[2] Through ceremony we return to our roots; by respect and compassion we are preserved, and through the spiritual journeys we are renewed. Wild forests and trees are outstanding settings for such spiritual journeying.

Wild Humans

Davd Martin

A Canadian mayor went to Sweden quite a few years ago now and came back full of praise for their forestry, those neatly lined up pines "like carrots." I wondered for a moment if she'd discovered *Waldsterben* and didn't know what color a living tree is! But even the Mayor pretty certainly knew that. I figured she didn't know the difference between a plantation and a forest. Mme. Mayor was praising tamed woodlots at about the same time the Swedish and Finnish forest ecologists were confirming that they weren't sustainable (cf. Lähde 2007; Maser 1994).

What I liked least about the whole notion was that the Mayor seemed to think humans should also be tamed, lined up in neat rows, punched in to work at 8 or 9 A.M. and out again eight hours later. Too many people think that. Human nature isn't mechanical, it's ecological; we are pack animals like wolves and dolphins and both the forest (Angus 2006) and the sea (Morgan 1973) can be home to us.

The late Helvi and Einari Pölkki of Hänniskylä, Finland, were considerably less tame than the Mayor and the forest industry of her time in office. The Pölkkis' pines were of all ages and intermixed with birch and spruce; some reached the impressive height of 100 feet before being carefully selective-cut for sale to Egypt as high-voltage utility poles. The Pölkkis kept their forest beautiful and spent thousands of happy hours in it each year, some working, some as long-married lovers, some with children and grandchildren. The forest furnished them lingonberries and bilberries for winter food and steam-extracted *mehu*; game and mushrooms for their table; birch-bark for crafts; fuelwood and timber to sell.

I mention those two because they were, in their traditional lifestyle, North-European indigenous people. I don't think anyone knows exactly when the ancestors of the current Finns took possession of their land; it's that long ago. The speech and manner of Helvi and Einari conveyed a freedom of self-conception that few North Americans exhibit today — though my good Métis grandfather was as wild as they, and I thank our Creator for my boyhood hours with him. He didn't have a forest; the Pölkkis did.

Their forest was much influenced by the work they did in it; but still, it was not so much tamed as guided ... and yes, the Finns were known as *wild men* to people farther south in Europe — men, because the women generally stayed home before the mid-20th century, while the men soldiered and traded and sometimes went abroad as experts. Imaginably, they as well as Native Americans contributed to Jean-Jacques Rousseau's concept of the *Noble Savage*.

So the contest between ecoforestry and plantation silviculture can fairly be seen as a contest between Noble Savages (humans in their wild state, before the Fall into various evils of which the Soviets showed us an almost ideal type of bureaucracy[1] and the clearcut an almost ideal type of pecuniolatry[2]) and those evils which began their modern form with the Enclosure of English common lands and the industrialization it forced upon the yeoman poor. If the yeoman gardens were even half-wild, the farms that fed the poor who worked in those "dark Satanic mills" were far too tame.

Tame agriculture

Wheat is Canada's best known and largest grain crop. It comes from the other side of the planet and is so thoroughly domesticated that I know nothing of the ecology of wild wheat; I don't even know if wild wheat still exists. The wheat varieties that are grown on the Canadian Prairies are all bred for monoculture farming; the wheat varieties that are grown in Southern Ontario are quite different from the Prairie varieties, and no one I have ever spoken with, including at least ten wheat farmers, seemed to know which varieties are closer to the wild plants from which wheat was bred many centuries ago.

I could say much the same thing about barley, maize, oats and rye (and about beans, canola, lentils and peas — especially canola, but let's not complicate the comparison too much). Our farm crops are so far removed from their wild ancestors that we can't readily trace some back. These crops grow in Canada mainly because the land where they are grown is forced into a state hospitable to them by chemicals, machinery and even considerable human labor. They grow as well as they do because that land is tilled, fertilized and weeded — whether mechanically or chemically — to provide the plants with hospitable soil and few competitors or predators. Grain farming is not the management of natural prairie, nor of any close variation on the theme of natural prairie. It is monoculturing large plantations of cultivars of species whose wild forms are either unknown or very different from what farmers now grow.

Rows of tame trees are not forests

Much silviculture is modeled on industrial agriculture: large plantations of a single species — usually a single strain to the extent that cultivar timber strains have been bred — planted in neat rows like wheat, fertilized, weeded and treated chemically against pests and diseases. Ecoforestry is more romantic — and more natural. It is modeled on the ideal state of natural forests. We start with natural tree species; we get to know what other species associate with them and how those associations help or hinder their development. We tend groups of timber species, not single species.

My woodlot, and the occasional even-better woodlots I see here-and-there where men and women who have been practicing ecoforestry for decades in the same place, is far wilder. It is not what would result from leaving the land untouched. We do select for the best timber specimens; we do encourage symbiotic fungi and discourage parasitic and pathogenic fungi, and as Merv Wilkinson observed about his famous woodlot, we arrange species associations and tree spacing better than Nature does, because Nature has a large random component.

Ecoforestry improves on wild forests by choosing the best trees, spacing stands for good timber growth but also for diversity and often improves the diversity of stands.

Eventually, we cut some timber, and we decide what to cut in terms of the forest more than the market. An ecoforester's logging adheres almost completely to the principle *Every cutting is an improvement cutting*. Every cutting leaves the forest better suited to grow during the next several years than if it had not been made (cf. Ontario Ministry of Lands and Forests, 1969).

The Creator has given us an eye for beauty which, while it can appreciate His handiwork in other species even when they are caged in zoos or lined up in plantations, recognizes that the full beauty of any species is to be found when it has some self-determination. The Pölkkis' pines were *P. sylvestris*; the neat rows beside the New Brunswick Forest Ranger Station at New Jersey — Village St.-Laurent are *P. resinosa*. *Resinosa* is generally the more impressive species, but they are less beautiful partly because they are lined up against their nature. Trees were created to associate with trees of other species as well as with their own kind; and that's how they look their best.

Humans were created to live in tribes and small villages, in packs if you want the nearest ethological term. Lone humans are as untypical as lone wolves — which is why we cooperate easily with canines and generally have less complete relationships with cats.[3] *Wild men* hunt and fish together more happily than alone. Women tending their babies and their quilting together are more wild than women sitting alone — even if they are sitting alone in surroundings we tend to call *wild*.

Unlike wolves, we humans have the power to modify our environment beyond preying

Sequoia in California

GUS DiZEREGA

on food species and digging dens. We can and do prey on food species from moose to strawberries; we can and do dig dens (but today, it's more a game than a subsistence skill). Industrial civilization lined humans up and undertook to tame us. It exercises more control than is healthy (cf. Morgan 1977), whether in the name of a Soviet state (Komarov 1980) or market forces.[4] During the Soviet years, it was a truism among Europeans trading and studying in the USSR that the people who worked in their state bureaucracy were ugly and officious on the job and delightfully human off the job. They managed somehow to be tamed part-time as Canadians are enslaved part-time by the demands of bureaucracies here today.

Eichenberger (2007) reports that as tamed hired hands for the market corporations Gaspésiens drive great big machines and devastate the interior of their peninsula, often weeping as they do. As natural human beings, they say "je ne veux pas voir d'esti d' ingnegneur (a pejorative pronunciation of ingénieur) sur mon terrain!"[5] *My land* need not mean marketable ownership (Martin 1998), and indeed salability is contrary to the holy books of Christianity, Islam and Judaism.[6] If we can transcend the *I-dollartry* of salable land ownership, perhaps we can recover the harmony of a genuinely long-term relationship between a household and its home place.

Markets do not free people: even in ideological sales copy, it is the markets and not the people who are called free. *Free markets* serve to tame more than to liberate human beings. Freedom in nature is limited, and the limits are not fought. They are pondered and worked with: the maples and the pines do not move to better spots, they make the best of the ones they have. The wolves do not change to eating acorns and forbs. Even we clever humans know better than to try growing oranges in Acadia or to fish on dry land. Perhaps we shall yet learn better than to prefer money over reality. The word *wild* has been abused, and human nature with it, by tamers who load wildness with a connotation of the berserk. Berserkers were Viking warriors who prepared for battle by going mad (taking poison — whether or not it was the mushroom *Amanita muscaria* — or inducing a trance). They were not tame nor were they wild as the Creator made us. Wild is not weird. Battle is not a common expression of human nature, either; by nature we cooperate a whole lot more of the time than we fight. Canadians were wise and accurate to choose Tommy Douglas as the greatest of us.

We can cooperate with forests as we can with dogs. I can take the burs from my canine helper's coat; I can take the dead limbs from a young maple's main stem and in each act I affirm and complement the nature of another species. The dog and the maple will do better for my ministrations. I have honored the nature of each; neither has been tamed. Each I leave more beautiful than I found it. Neither would I sell for mere money.

Wild need not be neglected; humans need not be tame. We can leave forests better than we find them — and it is in our nature, in our very sense of beauty, to do so.

Kingley Vale

Carolina Read

Chalk down soil of centuries passing
In vale where druids joined in drove
praising nature's everlasting —
Aged in sheltered grace, this grove

Of Yew of hallowed prayer time air
Cathedral with all mighty stance
Limbs of stature, roots that flare
In contemplation's timeless dance —

And yet, one need not travel deep
Herein to delve into her lores
Where unseen generations sleep
Midst elf and gnome, the arils and spores —

See! Bounty in Yew's fluted girths
The whorls of script upon her grain
The sticks and rods the Celts did birth
For divinations purpose gain —

And holy quiet lives in the birds
Who veil the blue-green canopy
Bringing to light in purest word
This love of immortality —

Gazing at yew

155

Part V

Wild Foresting, Healthy Children and Lifelong Learning

Child in nature

26

Nowadays We Idolize Nature — or Fear It

Richard Louv

In the mid-19th century, a boy ran along a beach with his gun, handmade from a piece of gas pipe, mounted on a stick. The pipe was loaded with gunpowder and slugs made with "gleaned pieces of lead," as the boy recalled later. The boy aimed, a companion "applied a match to the touch-hole," and he "fired at the gulls and solan-geese as they passed." Today, such activity might be cause for time spent in Juvenile Hall, but for young John Muir, shooting sea gulls was just another way to connect with nature.

"Whenever I read Muir's description of shooting sea gulls to my students, they're shocked. They can't believe it," says David Sobel, director of teacher certification programs at Antioch University's New England graduate school and co-director of the Center for Environmental Education. Muir, of course, was responsible for saving the mountains surrounding Yosemite Valley from development by helping to establish Yosemite National Park, and was the father of modern environmentalism.

Sobel tells this story to illustrate just how much the interaction between children and nature has changed. Practitioners in the new fields of conservation psychology (focused on how people become environmentalists) and ecopsychology (the study of how ecology interacts with the human psyche) say that, as Americans become increasingly urbanized, their attitudes toward animals move in paradoxical ways.

To urbanized people, the source of food and the reality of nature are becoming more abstract. At the same time, ironically, urban folks are more likely to feel protective toward animals — or to fear them. The good news is that children today are less likely to kill animals for fun; the bad news is that children are so disconnected from nature that they either idealize it or fear it — two sides of the same coin. Indeed, it's a truism: humans tend to fear or romanticize what we don't know.

Sobel focuses on *ecophobia*, which he defines as fear of nature. In its older, more poetic meaning, the word means fear of home. That older definition carries special poignancy in Southern California, a region rich in ecological diversity which is rapidly being paved over and sliced away for development. But, for a moment, set aside such apocalyptic visions. "My contention is that it's psychologically essential for a child to bond to the natural world," says Sobel. He says urbanization makes that difficult, but adds that many educators, with good intentions, are making matters worse.

"Just as ethnobotanists are descending on tropical forests in search of new plants for medical uses, environmental educators, parents and teachers are descending on second- and third-graders to teach them about the rain forests," Sobel writes in his slim but eloquent volume, *Beyond Ecophobia: Reclaiming the Heart in Nature Education.* "From Brattleboro, Vermont, to Berkeley, California, schoolchildren ... watch videos about the plight of indigenous forest people displaced by logging and exploration for oil. They learn that between the end of morning recess and the beginning of lunch, more than 10,000 acres of rain forest will be cut down, making way for fast-food, 'hamburgerable' cattle." In theory, these children "will learn that by recycling their Weekly Readers and milk cartons, they can help save the planet," and they'll grow up to be responsible stewards of the earth, "voting for environmental candidates and buying energy-efficient cars." Or maybe not.

"My fear is that just the opposite is occurring," says Sobel. "In our zest for making them aware of and responsible for the world's problems, we cut our children off from their roots." Lacking direct experience with nature, children begin to associate it with fear and apocalypse, not joy and wonder. "If we fill our classrooms with examples of environmental abuse, we may be engendering a subtle form of dissociation." He offers this analogy: in response to physical and sexual abuse, children learn to cut themselves off from pain. Emotionally,

they turn off. "My fear is that our environmentally correct curriculum similarly ends up distancing children from, rather than connecting them with, the natural world. The natural world is being abused, and they just don't want to have to deal with it."

To many environmentalists and educators, this is contrarian thinking — even blasphemy. But some hunting and fishing organizations make a similar case; they point to the rising average age of hunters and, consequently, falling financial support for conservation through hunting and fishing licenses. Yes, they say, fishing and hunting are messy — morally messy — but removing that experience from childhood will do neither children nor conservation any good. The movement to stop hunting and fishing, they say, is led by people who have little direct contact with nature: anti-fur Hollywood stars, for instance. Perhaps the last weasel they met was a casting director.

"You look at these kids [in the animal rights movement], and you largely see urban, disaffected but still privileged people," says Mike Two Horses, a former San Diegan who now lives in Tucson. Two Horses is the founder of CERTAIN (Coalition to End Racial Targeting of American Indian Nations). His organization supports native people such as the Northwest's Makah tribe, traditionally dependent on whale hunting. "The only animals the young animal rightists have ever known are their pets," he says. "The only ones they've ever seen otherwise are in zoos, Sea World or on whale-watching (now whale-touching) expeditions. They've disconnected from the sources of their food — even from the sources of the soy and other vegetable proteins they consume."

Sobel isn't defending hunters, fishers or Indian groups; he's just concerned about spreading ecophobia. "Children are studying the rain forest, but they're not studying their region's forests, or even just the meadow outside the classroom door," he says. "It is hard enough for children to understand the life cycles of chipmunks and milkweed, organisms they can study close at hand. This is the foundation upon which an eventual understanding of ocelots and orchids can be built." Sobel contends rainforest curriculum is developmentally appropriate in middle or high school, but not in the primary grades.

Some educators won't go that far, but they do agree with Sobel's basic premise — that environmental education is out of balance. "This is also the fundamental crux of the curriculum wars, particularly in the area of science," says Dennis Doyle, assistant superintendent in the Chula Vista Elementary School District, who has worked for years to increase students' direct experience with nature. "The science frameworks bandied about by the state have swung back and forth between the hands-on experiential approach and factoid, textbook learning."

Rasheed Salahuddin also sees wisdom in Sobel's thesis. As principal of the San Diego Unified School District's one-week outdoor education program on Palomar Mountain, he sees ecophobia every day. "Too many kids are associating nature with fear and catastrophe, and not having direct contact with the outdoors," he says. But don't just blame education. "This is also part of the way the media portrays everything, in end-of-the-world terms." Salahuddin brings sixth-graders to the mountain and shows them wonder. "Some of these kids are from Eastern Europe, Africa and the Middle East. They view the outdoors, the woods, as a dangerous place. They associate it with war, with hiding, or they view it in a solely utilitarian way, as a place to gather firewood." Inner-city, Hispanic and African-American kids show similar responses. "Some have never been to the mountains or the beach — or the zoo, even though it's within sight of their homes. Some of them spend their entire childhood inside an apartment, living in fear. They associate nature with the neighborhood park, which is controlled by gangs.

"What does this say about our future? Nature has been taken over by thugs who care absolutely nothing about it. We need to take nature back."

English woodlands

CAROLINA READ

(Editors' note: This article was originally published in the *San Diego Union-Tribune*, Sunday, May 14, 2000, Page A-3. Some of it was adapted from Louv's book *Fly-Fishing for Sharks*.)

The Powerful Link Between Conserving Land and Preserving Health

Howard Frumkin and Richard Louv

Public health professionals know that protecting watersheds is one of the best ways to assure clean, safe drinking water — so protecting the sources of clean water protects public health. Clean air is also part of a healthy, wholesome environment. Air pollutants contribute to cardiovascular disease, respiratory disease and allergies. Therefore, protecting air quality is protecting public health.

What about land? Do people benefit from parks and green spaces? When we protect land, do we protect public health? Intuition, experience and theory suggest the answer is yes.

People are drawn to gardens, forests and other natural spots for recreation and for vacations. Homes near parks typically gain in value. The designers and operators of hotels, spas and golf courses know that beautiful grounds attract customers. In the words of University of Michigan psychologist Rachel Kaplan, "Nature matters to people. Big trees and small trees, glistening water, chirping birds, budding bushes, colorful flowers — these are important ingredients in a good life" (Kaplan 1983, p. 155).

This intuition is not new. Henry David Thoreau wrote of the "tonic of wilderness." A century ago, John Muir observed that "Thousands of tired, nerve-shaken, over-civilized people are beginning to find out that going to the mountains is going home; that wilderness is a necessity; and that mountain parks and reservations are useful not only as fountains of timber and irrigating rivers, but as fountains of life" (Fox 1981, p. 116).

A theoretical basis for the notion that nature contact is good for health has been expanding. In 1984, Harvard biologist E.O. Wilson introduced the concept of biophilia, "the innately emotional affiliation of human beings to other living organisms" (Wilson 1993, p. 31). Wilson pointed to the millennia of human and prehuman history, all embedded in natural settings, and suggested that we still carry affinities and preferences from that past. Building on this theory, others have suggested an affinity for nature that goes beyond living things to include streams, ocean waves and wind (Heerwagen and Orians 1993, pp. 138-172).

More recently, environmental psychologists Rachel and Stephen Kaplan have demonstrated that contact with nature restores attention, and promotes recovery from mental fatigue and the restoration of mental focus (Kaplan & Kaplan 1989; Kaplan 1995). They attribute these beneficial qualities to the sense of fascination, of being immersed "in a whole other world" and to other influences of the natural world.

From theory to evidence

In addition to intuition and theory, we now have evidence. And increasingly the evidence suggests that people benefit so much from contact with nature that land conservation can now be viewed as a public health strategy. What does the evidence show?

Some of the most recent studies and reports pertain to children at play. Playtime — especially unstructured, imaginative, exploratory play — is increasingly recognized as an essential component of wholesome child development (Burdette and Whitaker 2005; Ginsburg et al. 2007). Play in natural settings seems to offer special benefits. For one, children are more physically active when they are outside — a boon at a time of sedentary lifestyles and epidemic overweight (Klesges et al. 1990; Baranowski et al. 1993; Sallis et al. 1993). And studies at the University of Illinois show that children with Attention-Deficit Disorder have fewer symptoms and enhanced ability to focus after outdoor activities such as camping and fishing — when compared to indoor activities

University students in nature

ASHLEY AKINS

such as doing homework and playing video games (Faber Taylor et al. 2001; Kuo and Faber Taylor 2004). Anthropologists, psychologists and others have described the special role of nature in children's developing imagination and sense of place (Manuel 2003; Louv 2005).

Adults, too, seem to benefit from recess in natural settings. Researchers in England (Pretty et al. 2005) and Sweden (Bodin and Hartig 2003) have found that joggers who exercise in a natural green setting with trees, foliage and landscape views feel more restored and less anxious, angry and depressed than people who burn the same amount of calories in gyms or other built settings. Research is continuing into what is called *green exercise.*

Fascinating evidence also comes from studies of medical treatment. An often-quoted 1984 study took advantage of an inadvertent architectural experiment. On the surgical floors of a 200-bed suburban Pennsylvania hospital, some rooms faced a stand of deciduous trees, while others faced a brown brick wall, and patients were essentially randomly assigned to one or the other kind of room after their surgery. Patients in rooms with tree views had shorter hospitalizations (on average, by almost one full day), less need for pain medications and fewer negative comments in the nurses' notes, compared to patients with brick views (Ulrich 1984). In another study, patients undergoing bronchoscopy (a procedure that involves inserting a fiber-optic tube into the lungs) were randomly assigned to receive either sedation, or sedation plus nature contact — in this case a mural of a mountain stream in a spring meadow and a continuous tape of complementary nature sounds (e.g., water in a stream or birds chirping). The patients with nature contact had substantially better pain control (Diette et al., 2003).

In fact, the idea of *healing gardens* in hospitals — which dates back many centuries — may reflect longstanding knowledge that contact with nature is therapeutic, not only for patients but also for family, friends and health professionals (Marcus and Barnes 1999; Söderback et al. 2004). Horticultural therapy offers patients the chance to work with plants (Pastor and Straus 1997; Haller and Kramer 2007), and research is beginning to show benefits for heart disease patients (Wichrowski et al. 2005), dementia patients (Gigliotti et al. 2004) and others.

Another line of evidence comes from wilderness experiences — from organized programs such as the National Outdoor Leadership School and Outward Bound and from less formal hiking and camping trips. Sometimes these are used therapeutically for psychological disorders (Eikenaes et al. 2006; Bettman 2007), developmental and cognitive disabilities (Berger 2006), cancer (Epstein 2004) and other conditions (Easley et al. 1990). But healthy people seem to benefit as well. For example, inner city children show increases in self-esteem and well-being after spending the summer in rural camps (Readdick and Schaller 2005). Adults who participate in wilderness excursions describe "an increased sense of aliveness, well-being and energy," and note that the experience helps them make healthier lifestyle choices afterwards (Greenway 1995, pp. 122-135).

New strategies for promoting public health

Nature contact yields surprisingly broad benefits. This contact may occur on a very small scale — plants in the workplace (Heerwagen et al. 1995) or trees outside the apartment building — or it may occur on a larger scale

— a nearby park, a riparian corridor in a city or a wilderness area. In a remarkable body of research in inner city housing projects in Chicago, investigators found that the presence of trees outside apartment buildings predicted less procrastination, better coping skills and less severe assessment of their problems among women (Kuo 2001), greater self-discipline among girls (Taylor et al. 2002), less crime (Kuo and Sullivan 2001a) and less violence and better social relationships (Kuo and Sullivan 2001b). In two recent nationwide surveys in Holland, people who lived within one to two miles of green space reported significantly better health than those without such access, after researchers controlled for socioeconomic status, age and other factors (de Vries et al. 2003; Maas et al. 2006). Overall, contact with nature seems an important component of a healthy, wholesome life.

For these reasons, in the same way that protecting water and protecting air are strategies for promoting public health, protecting natural landscapes can be seen as a powerful form of preventive medicine. Of course, there is still much we need to learn, such as what kinds of nature contact are most beneficial to health, how much contact is needed and how to measure that and what groups of people benefit most (Frumkin 2003).

But we know enough to act. We need to promote land conservation as a way to promote public health, both for people today and for future generations. In an increasingly urbanized society, we need to envision, design and create *green cities* where urban dwellers have nearby access to parks and green spaces (Beatley 1999; van den Berg et al. 2007).

We need to promote dialogue among people from different ethnic cultures, as well as those individuals who work separately and speak different professional languages, such as pediatricians and landscape architects; public health professionals and park and recreation officials; bike and pedestrian advocates and arborists; hunters, anglers, residential developers and environmentalists. We need imaginative social policy, such as the initiative recently announced by New Mexico's Parks Division and Public Education Department that will bring most of the state's fifth-graders to a state or national park or wilderness area during the 2007-08 school year.[1] In advancing all these efforts, we need to be especially mindful of the neediest among us — poor people, people of color, people with disabilities and others who may have the least access to natural settings and who may need it the most.

More than anything, we need a vision of healthy, wholesome places, a vision that extends from densely settled cities to remote rural spreads, from the present to the future, from the most fortunate among us to the least fortunate, from the youngest child to the oldest adult. Conservation of land is central to this vision. Such places will promote our health, enhance our well-being, nourish our spirits and steward the beauty and resources of the natural world.

(Editor's Note: This article originally appeared in a Land Trust Alliance Special Anniversary Report, 2007.)

GUS DIZEREGA

28

Creating a New Land Movement with Children

Peter Forbes

Sit back and listen to these words: Bull Run Farm, Devil's Den, Sages Ravine, Spruce Knob, Dickinson's Reach, Moosilauke, Arun River Valley, Central Harlem, Cedar Mesa, Chama River, Arch Rock, Drake's Beach, Knoll Farm. That's my biography. These words speak of the places and relationships that have created me. These are the waters, the mountains, the forests, the food, the dreams and the memories that literally make up my body. And each of you has your own biography of place.

Some of our biographies of place are powerfully deep, like those of the people honored at this institution: Rachel Carson, Aldo Leopold and Olaus and Mardy Murie. And there are other biographies of place, like those of a whole generation of children in America that are unfulfilled and stunted. Your biography of place is as important to your health and your success and the health and success of our nation as the more typical biography about where you went to school and the titles you have held.

I bring to this gathering the strong and unequivocal belief that our relationship to land,

good, bad, and indifferent, is *still the enduring story of our lives* whether we accept it or not. Even in 2006, no matter where you live, few forces will have as much effect on the course of your life, your family, your community as the quality of that relationship between soul and soil.

Pause for a second. Think back to when you were 8, 10 and 12 years old. Reconnect with that place that most inspired you as a young person. Perhaps it was your grandparent's farm, or a park, an urban garden, or a pond where you grew up or a place that you visited just once. Now, show of hands, for how many of you would that place be impossible to go to today simply because it no longer exists? Twice, now, I've returned as an adult to the childhood landscapes that most inspired me only to find them obliterated.

I remember a magical pond deep in the woods of southwestern Connecticut that I camped alongside many times as a 13-year-old. I can still find inside of me the sense of awe and excitement of coming upon this hidden spot and realizing that human hands had created it perhaps 100 years before. There were giant oaks on either side of a stone dam wide enough, perhaps, to drive a mule and wagon across. There was a gentle rise of land overlooking this half-acre pond, and here my friends and I must have camped a dozen times in the summer of 1974. The spot was so special to us that we did what young teenagers will do; we carved our names in the beech trees and called the place *The Kingdom*.

I returned on a Thanksgiving day 25 years later and wandered silently with my daughter for more than an hour through a sub-division, crossing cul-de-sacs back and forth, looking to find my pond. I was sure I was in the right place, but nothing around me was the same. The stream was gone, and the gentle ravine was gone. When I was about to give up and accept that this was no longer a place but now only a memory, I found myself oriented in just the right way so that everything clicked in place and even though the land had been transformed beyond recognition by bulldozers, my body remembered. I reconnected with a place that had died. Across a stretch of pavement and immediately adjacent to a two-car garage was an old beech tree with *The Kingdom* carved in it.

The woods behind Bull Run Farm did not contain any known threatened species of plant or animal, but they did have a profound impact on one little boy's experience of growing up. I was that little boy. I can only remember how that land had helped me explore, learn and use my imagination. What will it mean for the children who now live where I once grew up, who don't have these natural places?

Thanks to Richard Louv, there's a name for this situation today: *nature-deficit disorder*. And here's the result: today, our culture produces more malls than high schools, more

prisoners than farmers and eats up the land with a similar appetite — 250 acres per hour. The businessman Paul Hawken tells us that the average American child today can recognize 1,000 corporate logos but can't identify 10 plants or animals native to his or her own region.

Tell me, what's the spell we have fallen under to create this world we live in? It's a powerful spell, woven into the 30,000 advertisements that reach our children each year, and that turns our hearts away from the land and away from one another. This spell says that the earth is a warehouse for our use, that nothing that can't be converted into money has value. This spell whispers to us hourly that the point of forests is board feet, the point of farms is money and the point of people is to be consumers.

This spell has fattened our pocketbooks and lengthened our lives, but it has also created a dangerous and deeply unfair world of haves and have-nots, and a culture of isolation, destruction and narcissism. One evidence of this disconnection is that 25% of all Americans now experience serious clinical depression during their lifetime. And if your family income is over $150,000 a year, the incidence of anxiety and depression is even higher. That's what wealth and technology tastes like today without some sense of shared humanity and shared relationship to the land.

Let me go further. Many of the exact things that define the healthy human experience are threatened today.

- Our ability to judge between what is real and what is artificial
- Our sense of our spiritual or metaphysical place in the *big picture*
- Our sense of belonging

- Our sense of tolerance/ acceptance of other life.

The writer and ecologist, Robert Michael Pyle, coined the phrase "extinction of human experience" in his important book *The Thunder Tree*. He wrote:

> So it goes, on and on, the extinction of experience sucking the life from the land, the intimacy from our connection. This is how the passing of otherwise common species from our immediate vicinities can be as significant as the total loss of rarities. People who care conserve; people who don't know don't care. *What is the extinction of the condor to a child who has never known the wren?*[1]

The child who doesn't know the wren is the child who is afraid of walking to school, the child who has already begun to feel boundaries surround her. And, of course, this child is a symbol of the disconnection that many of us feel which is why the topic of children in nature is such an important Trojan horse for talking with America about a set of modern pathologies that are increasingly felt by nearly all of us. Children are not the only way to initiate this dialogue in America's homes about our failed relationships with the land. There's a powerful three-legged stool on which our hopes for transformation rest: children, food and fairness or equity. These three issues are the foundation of a new way to speak to urban and rural America alike about what matters most in their lives.

What we are witnessing today is a spectacular failure of the human imagination to recognize where we are. Where we are is facing the death of real human experience, and we have been blind to it most profoundly in our children. And, frankly, my beloved conservation movement has been blind as well.

What's the role of conservation, then, in turning around this situation?

Conservation can be powerful medicine for what most ails our nation because within our experience and relationship to the land are the essential clues for how to live joyfully

Heiltsuk boy in nature

DUNCAN M. TAYLOR

and responsibly. Our healthy relationship to land is the means by which we humans generate and renew big transcendent values such as community, meaning, beauty, love and the sacred on which both ethics and morality depend. Our healthy relationship to land, therefore, is deeply and directly connected to our sense of patriotism, citizenship, egalitarianism and fairness and our sense of limits. In other words, our relationship to land is a source of our wholeness.

Here's the rub. It's hard to say these words but I must: conservationists have been very good at protecting places and pretty lousy at protecting relationships. For example, a bit more than one-third (42%) of all the privately owned land in America is posted *No Trespassing*, but 78% of all the privately protected land in America is posted *No Trespassing*. Conservationists are almost twice as likely to post their land. I know there are many good reasons to keep people off conserved land, but as we put up harder and harder boundaries between ourselves, eventually we show both our love and our fear only by what we fence out. That is not, nor ever can be, the basis for a broad social movement.

Here's an even larger example. Conservationists have been enormously successful in protecting land, marshalling the money and skills to purchase more than 14 million acres over the last decade, but are Americans, by and large, closer to that land or to the values that the land teaches? *To what degree have our conservation efforts brought people and the land closer together? To what degree have our conservation efforts created a balanced and healthy American culture?*

I would answer, *not enough*. And we conservationists aren't going to positively influence more of our culture until we shift our attention from protecting places to nurturing human relationships with those places. We must change our basic motivating question from "how much land can we protect for how many bucks?" to "what is a healthy, whole community and how do we get there together?"

Numbers don't reflect our values, but they control much of our lives. *Bucks and acres* don't effectively tell our story of reuniting children and nature. They are the old story. The new story has to be more about our highest values, what we care about most, our desire to bring people closer to nature. But it's hard to lead with our values because that's often leading with our chin. And, yet, didn't Rachel Carson lead with her chin? And didn't David Brower and Aldo Leopold lead with their chins? This is not a time to play it safe.

A healthy, whole community is many things, but it starts with people in relationship to each other and to the land. I bring to this gathering the concept that our *relationship to place is as important as the place itself*, and I bring the challenge of making the restoration of our relationships to land the defining goal of a new land movement in America. Are we ready to rise to this challenge? Do we accept that stopping the death of human experience is as important as stopping the death of an endangered species? The child in nature is the symbol of this moment in time, the time of our becoming. In this mature place in the history of conservation a gap has opened between what we practice and what we imagine we can be. We are too often cavalier about the power we have and ethically unprepared to use it responsibly.

The work of conservation is bigger and more important than our smaller interests in easements, acres, plans, dollars and tax benefits. What was once a movement guided by passion, vision and values is in the process of being reduced to a technology and even merely to a commercial enterprise. The true success of land conservation is our ability to remind every American of what is healthy, of what is fair opportunity, what is beautiful and meaningful and what it means to be in relationship. Our challenge is to put the child and ourselves back into nature.

The work of Center for Whole Communities is to make these ideas real in the bone and muscle of today's conservation movement. Our experience of land, community and changing demographics has forged a mission based on three principles.

Relationship is as fundamental as places and things

Conservationists have made an error in assuming that our work is more a legal act than a cultural act. By that I mean assuming one can protect land *from people through laws as opposed to with people through relationships.* Laws exist for when relationships fail.

But what happens when people and communities lose that relationship with the land? Do the values stay? Can laws protect what's already left the heart? I think not. And that's the great misunderstanding of the conservation movement. *Laws cannot protect what's already left the heart.* And the political proof of this is that the protections placed on Arctic National Wildlife Refuge in 1976 have been challenged repeatedly by a different and competing set of values. Laws will not hold what has left the heart.

And so conservationists must focus on the human heart as much as the land itself. And what the human heart needs and craves today, and has through all through the ages, is relationship and connection to the larger, more

ANNA DRENGSON

Montane forest stream

meaningful diversity of life. With relationships in mind, our language changes quickly for the better. First, we realize how strange and even humorous our selection of words has become over the years. For example, environmentalists use a word like *sustainable* to reflect our highest aspirations, but in terms of relationship it quite clearly means the lowest bearable standard. For example, would calling your marriage sustainable be a positive and inspiring description? When we view our work in terms of building relationships, we instead choose words like health, fairness, joy, resilience and respect.

In keeping relationship in mind, we would see how our words can create hard boundaries and soft boundaries between people and the land. To protect or to save begs many people to ask of us, save and protect *from whom*? With relationships in mind, we would shy away from saving and preserving because we're not trying to pickle anything or anyone. We would use instead words like *nurturing* and *cultivating*. And all the words associated with restoration: renew, heal, revive, the one I like the most is repair. We *repair* the land by bringing ourselves whole again with it.

Build bridges and understanding between organizations and movements

Our work at Whole Communities is to help very different groups — from community development to public health to human rights to land conservation — find shared meaning and to learn how to collaborate together in very powerful ways. In a world filled with divides, we help groups to look across those canyons and to recognize new allies. We are creating a powerful new tool, called *Measures of Health*, designed to help all of us who care about children, place and community to better describe, fulfill and measure our different roles in creating healthy, whole communities.

Ground our collective work for whole communities in the power of story

The world is made up of molecules held together by story. Stories change the way we act in the world. They help us imagine the future differently. Stories entertain us, create community and help us see through the eyes of other people. Stories help us dwell in time and help us to deal with suffering, loss and death. Stories teach us empathy and how to be human. We tell stories to cross the borders that separate us from one another. Stories open us to the claims of others. Story is ultimately about relationship. The soul of the land becomes the soul of our culture not through information or data alone, but through the metaphor and analogy of story.

Martin Luther King did not say, "I have a plan." He said "I have a *dream*," and he told a series of stories that many Americans easily understood and could identify with. What is today's "I Have a Dream Speech" for land conservationists? It's a story certainly about children, and it's a story about where our food comes from and it's a story about healing the divides spoken about earlier in this conference.

The people of India who have been trying to protect the Narmada River have a saying that goes "You can wake someone who is asleep, but you can not wake someone who is pretending to be asleep." Our stories must wake the people who are afraid and pretending to be asleep. And we can best do that through empathy, compassion and love … not fear and pessimism or even logic. We wake people through positive stories of the possibility of living in a different way.

Let me go further with this idea by introducing you to Classie Parker.

Classie's a third generation resident of 121st Street in Central Harlem, New York City. She grew up in the same building off Frederick Douglas Boulevard where her mother was born. Classie didn't aspire to be an activist and didn't have a grand vision about running a community program. She was flipping hamburgers at White Castle and thinking about her mom and dad who were growing old and needed a way to work and be outside. Classie got the radical idea to turn the vacant lot alongside her apartment building into a garden. That was almost ten years ago, and today Classie produces food, beauty, tolerance and a relationship to land for more than 500 families in central Harlem. Five Star Garden is almost absurdly small, just a quarter acre, but for the people of 121st Street the garden is their own piece of land to which they have developed a very deep personal attachment. These are Classie's words:

> We think of ourselves as farmers, city farmers. Never environmentalists. Don't call me an environmentalist. We love people and plants; we love being with the earth, working with the earth. There is something here in this garden for everyone. And any race, creed or color ... now, can you explain that? This is one of the few places in Harlem where they can be free to be themselves. It's hard to put into words what moves people to come in this garden and tell us their life stories, but it happens every day. There's love here. People gonna go where they feel the flow of love.
>
> There is a difference. You come in here and sit down, Peter — don't you feel comfortable with us? Don't you feel you're free to be you? That we're not going to judge you because you're a different color or because you're a male? Do you feel happy here? Do you feel intimidated? Don't you feel like my dad's your dad?

Classie boiled it all down: "Don't you feel like my dad's your dad?" I remember laughing a bit nervously as Classie said this because I wasn't prepared for her candor and hopefulness. I paused just a moment, and then looked up at her father sitting 10 feet across from me with his feet firmly planted on the earth, both hands resting on canes, 87 years old, garden dirt on his face. "Don't you feel like my dad's your dad?" Passing one another on the street, our eyes might not have met long enough to see one another's humanity. But there on that patch of earth, what we had in common at that moment was profound: it was the soil, that place, the love and hope that Classie held for us, and the awareness that my own pulse beat in his throat.

That's the soul of the land. It's the generosity, patience, respect and inclusiveness that comes naturally to many Americans. It's also the soul of our country; the empathetic soul that I believe is there waiting to be spoken to by us. It's what we all want our children to taste and to know.

Editors' Note: These comments were made at the Children in Nature Conference, held at the National Conservation Training Center September 8, 2006.)

29

Fairies, Forests and Childhood Education

Briony Penn

The winter holidays always remind me how much I float between three distinct worlds: a wooded Euro-pagan world full of holly and ivy, dark castles, quaint elves and brooding goblins; a desert-Christian world full of camels, palm trees, wise men and angels and a damp Salish-animistic world full of cedar and snowberries, salmon and magical transformers. It is an easy enough passage between the worlds with an adult mind that's dabbled in anthropology and geography. You just substitute one creation myth for another, a flower faery for a raven trickster or horned devil, a desert tree of life for a rainforest tree of life, a castle for a mosque or longhouse. Comparative anthropology at its finest, until you come to explain all these events to a six year old — and then you remember the confusion of childhood. You don't float in your mind at six as much as live in a small, vulnerable body that is trying to synthesize one composite world out of cultural mishmash.

For my six year old, the Euro-pagan part is largely presented in celluloid with vast amounts of money to make it all come alive,

including the battles and the simplistic defenders of good; the desert part is the same except there are desert landscapes, mosques and more machine guns than arrows; the third world is just home and lacking in magic beside the other two contenders. The implications for not being enchanted by your physical world at six are dire; according to Wade Davis, ethnobotanist and author, the extinction of landscapes and species can be attributed to the death of good stories about our place. Stories are the glue that bonds humanity to the natural world. So I started thinking about my enchantment of landscape and species through stories as it all started for me around this time of year when I was six.

I grew up on Christmas Hill in Saanich, British Columbia. My great grandfather named it after a cross-cultural myth no doubt invented by his Christianizing fellow colonists. The story goes that a Songhees chief's baby was snatched away by a huge eagle as he lay in swaddling clothes by the Inner Harbor of Victoria. The families searched the swamps and savannahs for the child before finding him on Christmas Day on top of Christmas Hill. Because of this story, I believed the hill was enchanted. The gnarled oaks and wild-flowers were somehow part of that enchantment in protecting a defenseless child; magic took place there. Mushroom rings encircled faeries and they, with the little Euro-elves, took care of Salish babies. Christmas Hill became as powerful a place as Bethlehem and, when its partial destruction came, I understood the desire to fling oneself into the twin towers of commerce rising there now.

Thirty years later, I had the opportunity to ask an elder with Songhees lineage what his name for Christmas Hill was and what stories there were of the hill. He didn't have a name or a story. He said they had all been lost with the first pass of smallpox — a part of the story that never got told when I was growing up. In his latest book *Light at the Edge of the World*, Wade Davis, who was educated on Vancouver Island as a teenager, warns that the death of storytelling steeped in place is only one generation away. So what role as neo-storytellers does this generation play in these rather critical times? How do we compete with sophisticated Euro-celluloid fantasies that bind kids to places they will never see except on expensive European holidays? Ten thousand year old stories of this place have virtually gone, and all we have is a few shallow tales of big eagles and babies.

So this week I went walkabout in Hwaaqw (Mount Maxwell/Burgoyne Bay) the new protected area on Saltspring Island, British Columbia and thought about the role of magical stories binding islanders to this place. Magic to me is the art of influencing events by working with nature. Agents of magic from faeries to transformers in every ancient culture are really mysterious life forces of creation. They are capricious, inspirational, terrifying, tragic and loving. They are powerful because they bring on the high emotion that comes with that creativity. They are the muses for stories that poets call upon. They summon the possibility of death and life. In the last few years, many of us have been swept into a whirlwind of stories past and present, starting with a renaissance of the Saanich and Cowichan traditional stories: powerful sea creatures were subdued by transformers hurling stones at them, and greedy men with lightning eyes were brought down by the southeast winter storms. The stories became richer and richer as we reenacted age-old battles for place, and elements of other worlds flew into the stories: evil princesses counted money in castles, brooding goblins battled with tortuous machines in the forest, wise men and angels arrived at critical times bearing gifts and good tidings, little elves quietly working magic behind the scene got thrown into dungeons, cedars transformed into magic through celluloid. This cultural mishmash became the story, and to my six year old it makes perfect sense. It is the story of his place. When we go walking in Burgoyne today, faeries are every-where and the art of storytelling steeped in this place is alive for one more generation at least.

The education of the young

Have you ever noticed that discussions about the protection of our forests and natural areas invariably end with the remark that the only solution is to educate the young? My response is usually silence so that I'm not rude. Threatened species and spaces will not wait around for yet another generation. I once had to endure a local politician pontificating at a conference about how nature education kits were going to save our local endangered ecosystem. I had this strong desire to point out that the only possible successful use of those kits was for children to use them as small missile weapons to knock out approaching bulldozer drivers, financiers and politicians that continued to absolve themselves of any responsibility in mowing down the last few remaining acres of Garry oak meadows.

But I am a peace loving person and have continued to support the role of education. There is comfort in the idea, and it can certainly

Big leaf maple

do no harm. With this warm and woolly feeling I decided to conduct a sporadic survey of some of our educational institutions to gauge how they were going to lead our stalwart young down the path to ecological virtue and environmentally ethical behavior or vice versa.

The first thing I did was go to look at a brand new school in north Nanaimo to see if the planners considered retaining the natural landscape as an example to the young. I approached the school with anticipation. The area as I knew it had been classic coastal Douglas fir forest, with maples and arbutus circling a hill that was covered with oak. I envisioned a school nestled into the trees with dense thickets of salal to create forts and tunnels for play and solitude. I imagined big trees and old snags under which teachers would lead discussions as to how woodpeckers create nest cavities for squirrels or how gravity was first conceived or what volume of water a tree can absorb. There would be the pond to do water life studies and old nurse logs to sit upon and recount aboriginal stories of life hundreds of years ago. The values of indigenous species like yew to cancer research would be pointed out in the forest as students explored their surroundings, each other and learned the importance of biological diversity.

I have been known to suffer delusions so it is probably not a surprise that the scenario that greeted my eyes was rather contrary to expectations. Sir Isaac Newton, for example, would not have theorized on the law of gravity at this school for there is nothing within a radius of 7 acres that could even be loosely described as living vegetation, let alone a tree. It would take a singular act of vision to theorize on any physical law, action or principle in these grounds as there is nothing there but a peculiar green turf. There are no secret places to go. There are no places to tell stories. There are no plants, insects, animals or any trace of what came before to encourage a contemplation of history. The tedium of the site stretched before me, and I felt like committing great acts of juvenile delinquency like hurling education kits at the perpetrators of this massacre. I was told by an official that bushes and trees caused students to commit acts of indecency and illegality so they removed them all hoping that they might commit these acts in the malls instead.

But I am a peace loving person, and I continue to support the role of education so I asked a local elementary school kid what the teachers taught about the local environment. He responded that a man had come into the school and given them a video about some tree called Tommy or was it Dougie that liked to be cut down. The man had then given him a genetically superior seedling in a bag that had a forest company written on it that was to be taken home to mummy or daddy so that they could see what a good corporation he represented. How this eight year old would acquire the necessary skills to lead us out of impending ecological disaster with a corporate training is beyond me. However, this much enlightened child, when questioned about what he did with his genetically superior tree, replied that he traded it for a peanut butter sandwich, which was the only sign of hope that I registered that day.

But I am a peace loving person, and I still believe in the role of education so I attended a university meeting to raise awareness for protecting natural areas on campus. Not one member of the administration attended. When initiatives were launched to start a native plant garden and restore native vegeta-

tion, the barriers erected were maintenance costs and threats to union jobs. I suppose that the swerve the industrial lawn mowers would have to make around a patch of camas flowers, lizard habitat and snowberries might constitute lost time or pose a potential safety hazard, but this point could certainly be discussed. I spent the rest of the meeting, dressed in dark clothes, subversively planting native vegetation with students in places that the administration wouldn't spot.

But I am a peace loving person etc., so I went to visit one last school. It is called Sundance, and it seems to be a school with a difference. The kids, the parents and the teachers struggle like all others to juggle the demands of this complicated world and in one small way they have achieved a victory. Pushing up amongst the blades of grass under a canopy of oaks are the buds of a patch of native wildflowers, collected and grown by the students from a site that was bulldozed. The patch is surrounded by a little fence constructed by the kids woven in and out with wools and ribbons, behind a patch of snowberries where they have their fort and conduct childhood experiments out of the eye of the adults. The industrial lawn mowers have agreed to halt their mowing in this patch for the spring, and the neighborhood has joined in the anticipation of watching them bloom.

This all happened because some parents and the teachers felt their children have enough contradictions in their lives without being preached at about conservation with biological deserts for schoolgrounds. They recognized that without the raw material to experience, no number of nature education kits are going to create a love of the natural world. The solution lies in a little judicious reeducation of ourselves first.

30

GUS DiZEREGA

Beyond Ecophobia

David Sobel

Just as ethnobotanists are descending on tropical forests in search of new plants for medical uses, environmental educators, parents and teachers are descending on second and third graders to teach them about the rainforests. From Brattleboro, Vermont, to Berkeley, California, school children hear the story of the murder of activist Chico Mendez and watch videos about the plight of indigenous forest people displaced by logging and exploration for oil. The motive for all this is honorable and just, but what's emerging is a strange kind of schizophrenia. Children are disconnected from the world outside their doors and connected with endangered ecosystems around the globe through electronic media.

One problem we have in schools is premature abstraction — we teach too abstractly, too early. Mathematics educators realized that premature abstraction was one of the major causes of math phobia among children in the primary grades. Unable to connect the signs and symbols on the paper with the real world, many children were turning off math. Mathematics instruction has been reinvigorated in the last two decades through the use of concrete materials (such as Cuisenaire rods, fraction bars and Unifix cubes) and the grounding of math instruction in the stuff and problems of everyday life. The result has been the turning of the tide against math phobia.

Perhaps we have replaced math phobia with ecophobia — a fear of ecological problems and the natural world. Fear of oil spills, rainforest destruction, whale hunting, acid rain, the ozone hole and Lyme disease. Fear of just being outside. If we prematurely ask children to deal with problems beyond their understanding and control, then I think we cut them off from the possible sources of their strength. I propose that there are healthy ways to foster environmentally aware, empowered students. We can cure the malaise of ecophobia with ecophilia — supporting children's biological tendency to bond with the natural world.

Beyond cardboard rainforests

If curricula focused on saving the Earth don't work, what does? One way to find the answer is to figure out what contributes to the development of environmental values in adults. What happened in the childhoods of environmentalists to make them grow up with strong ecological values? A handful of studies like this have been conducted, and when Louise Chawla of Kentucky State University reviewed them for her article, "Children's Concern for the Natural Environment" in *Children's Environment Quarterly*, she found a striking pattern. Most environmentalists attributed their commitment to a combination of two sources: "many hours spent outdoors in a keenly remembered wild or semi-wild place in childhood or adolescence, and an adult who taught respect for nature." Not one of the conservationists surveyed explained his or her dedication as a reaction against exposure to an ugly environment.

What a simple solution. No rainforest curriculum, no environmental action, just opportunities to be in the natural world with modeling by a responsible adult.

The child's expanding world

The formative years of bonding with the Earth include three stages of development that should be of primary concern to parents and teachers: early childhood from ages 4 to 7, the elementary years from 8 to 11, and early adolescence from 12 to 15. Though these age frames need to be considered flexibly, my belief is that environmental education should have a different tenor and style during each of these stages.

Over the past ten years, I have collected neighborhood maps from hundreds of children in the US, England and the Caribbean. Through analyzing these maps and doing interviews and field trips with these same children, I have found clear patterns of development in the relationship between the child and his or her expanding world.

From ages four to seven, children's homes fill the center of their maps, and much of their play is within sight or earshot of the home. Children often describe the worms, chipmunks and pigeons that live in their yards or on their blocks, and they feel protective of these creatures.

From 8 to 11, children's geographical ranges expand rapidly. Their maps push off the edge of the page, and they often need to attach extra pieces of paper to map the new terrain they are investigating. Children's homes become small, inconsequential and often move to the periphery of the map. The central focus in their maps is the *explorable landscape*.

From 12 to 15, the maps continue to expand in scope and become more abstract, but the favored places often move out of the woods and into town. Social gathering places such as the mall, the downtown luncheonette and the town park take on new significance.

At each of these stages, children desire immersion, solitude and interaction in a close, knowable world. We take children away from these strength-giving landscapes when we ask them to deal with distant ecosystems and environmental problems. Rather, we should be attempting to engage children more deeply in knowing the flora, fauna and character of their own local places. The woods behind the school and the neighborhood streets and stores are the places to start.

How do we translate these notions into guidelines for environmental education? I propose three phases of environmental curricula during the elementary and middle school years. In early childhood, activities should center on enhancing the developmental tendency toward empathy with the natural world. In middle childhood, exploration should take precedence. And in early adolescence, social action should assume a more central role.

Empathy: Finding animal allies

Empathy between the child and the natural world should be a main objective for children ages four through seven. As children begin their forays into the natural world, we can encourage feelings for the creatures living there. Early childhood is characterized by a lack of differentiation between the self and the other. Children feel implicitly drawn to baby animals; a child feels pain when someone else scrapes her knee. Rather than force separateness, we want to cultivate that sense of connectedness so that it can become the emotional foundation for the more abstract ecological concept that everything is connected to everything else. Stories, songs, moving like animals, celebrating seasons, and fostering Rachel Carson's *sense of wonder* should be primary activities during this stage. With this conviction in mind, a group of colleagues and I conducted

Shinto Gates in Japan

ARIYOSHI ICHIRO

the following activities with preschool children in Peterborough, New Hampshire, and with second graders at Camp Waubenong in Brattleboro, Vermont.

We initiated our bird curriculum planning at Camp Waubenong by agreeing that we wouldn't have the children identify birds from fleeting glimpses and then look them up in books to start. Boring! Rather, we speculated on what it is about birds that appeals to children. The answer was obvious: they fly, and they make nests. Applying the developmental principle that children like to become things rather than objectify them in early childhood, we came up with our plan.

We gathered a bunch of large refrigerator boxes, cut them into sheets and had the children lie down on top of them, on their backs with arms outstretched. Starting at the neck, we traced around the children, but instead of following along the underside of the arm, we drew a straight line from their wrists to their waists, then down on both sides to about the knees. The children then stood up, we cut out the shape, and voila! Each child had an individualized set of wings. We strapped them on, made it clear that the children were not to try the wings out by jumping off roofs, and away they went. A flock of birds leaped into action, flying through the forests, exploring life as birds.

We made it to the meadow where hay had recently been cut and said, "If we're birds, we need nests." And so we made child-sized nests. Many hours of dramatic play followed.

A few days later, we said, "You all make great birds, but we noticed that you're all brown, and only some of the birds we see around here are brown, but some of them have lots of colors. What are some of the color patterns on the birds?"

Children described some birds they had seen, but we didn't make a point of teaching names. Instead, we pulled out the paints so they could paint their wings. More bird games followed. By the next day, children started to notice the birds around camp. "Hey, that's the same bird as me. That's the color pattern on my wings." Then the bird books came out. Soon, we had children poring over bird books trying to identify what kinds of birds they were and learn what they ate. Because we had started at their level of developmental fascination, had facilitated empathy through their participation in bird consciousness, we prepared them to objectify and enter the more cognitive realm of bird knowledge.

Exploration:
Teaching the landscape

Exploring the nearby world and knowing your place should be a primary objective for the *bonding with the Earth* stage, from ages 8 to 11. The curriculum can mirror the expanding scope of the child's significant world, focusing first on the surroundings of the home and school, then the neighborhood, the community, the region and beyond. Making forts, creating small imaginary worlds, hunting and gathering, searching for treasures, following streams and pathways, exploring the landscape, taking care of animals, gardening and shaping the Earth can be primary activities during this stage. Forts and dens, these special places of childhood that are both found and built, appear to be crucially important for many children from ages 8 to 11. Children in urban, suburban and rural landscapes find and create hidden places, even in daunting circumstances.

David Millstone, a fifth grade teacher in Norwich, Vermont, organized an expedition with his class in which they would follow a stream not knowing where the stream would lead them. In a student-produced newspaper about this expedition, one child wrote:

The Deep, Dark Dungeon

"I can't see five feet," I thought to myself. We were walking through a giant culvert following this stream that runs behind the school and through the Nature Area.

"Watch out, dripping water," Mr. Millstone warned us. I finally realized what is beyond the steel grates that you see along the street. I looked up it and saw the grate 20 feet above me. The culvert seemed to be moving. I think we took a turn somewhere.

"The end," someone shouted. ... I had to walk with my feet widely apart. We got out alive, had a snack, and continued on our adventure."

The children's writing for the class newsletter crackles with excitement over discovering something literally in their backyard. And notice that the project doesn't touch directly on acid rain or groundwater pollution or drinking water quality or evaporation and condensation. It does, however, immerse children in the primary experience of exploring streams and understanding where they go. Wet sneakers and muddy clothes are prerequisites for understanding the water cycle.

Social Action:
Saving the neighborhood

Social action appropriately begins around age 12 and certainly extends beyond age 15. While woods, parks and playgrounds are the landscapes of middle childhood, adolescents want to be downtown. As children start to discover the self of adolescence and feel their connectedness to society, they naturally incline toward wanting to save the world. Managing school recycling programs, passing town ordinances, testifying at hearings, planning and going on school expeditions are all appropriate activities at this point.

An article in the March/April 1989 issue of *Sierra* relates how a group of sixth graders in Salt Lake City, Utah, became concerned when they noticed that a map of hazardous waste sites in the city included a location just three blocks from their school.

"That old barrel yard?" 11 year-old Maxine asked. "Kids climb all over those barrels."

When classroom teacher Barbara Lewis contacted the Department of Health, she was told that "there's nothing children can do; they'll be in high school before they see any results." The students were compelled to act. They contacted the EPA, the owner of the barrel yard and the mayor. They studied literature on hazardous waste and the problems involved in cleaning it up. They attracted reporters intrigued with the children's persistence. And, after a year and a half, they not only witnessed the removal of the 50,000 barrels and the beginnings of the EPA clean up, but they wrote legislation, lobbied legislators and saw the passage of a Utah state law that set up a hazardous waste clean-up fund.

Allowing time for nature

Suffering from the timesickness of trying to do too much too quickly, we infect our children with our impatience. Most nature study or environmental education in American elementary schools lasts a matter of weeks, maybe a month. As a result, depth is sacrificed for breadth, and there's little opportunity for immersion in the landscape. Instead, we make children do workbooks in kindergarten, we let seven year-olds watch Jurassic Park and we bombard them with tragic anxiety.

Jo Anne Kruschak, a first and second grade teacher in Vermont spent all of last year doing a project on a local beaver pond and marsh. These first and second graders visited the pond, about a quarter mile from the school, once a week through all kinds of weather.

"In the beginning," Kruschak recalls, "I thought we'd run out of things to do and study by Thanksgiving. By March I realized that there was no way we could follow up on all the neat opportunities by the end of the year."

If we want children to flourish, to become truly empowered, then let us allow them to love the Earth before we ask them to save it. Perhaps this is what Thoreau had in mind when he said, "the more slowly trees grow at first, the sounder they are at the core, and I think the same is true of human beings."

(Editors' note: This article is adapted from volume one of the Orion Society Nature Literacy Series, *Beyond Ecophobia: Reclaiming the Heart in Nature Education*. To obtain a copy, contact the Orion Society at 195 Main St., Great Barrington, MA 01230 USA; 413/528-4422; e-mail: orion@orionsociety.org; web: orionsociety.org.)

31

The Longest Journey and
Role of an Enlightened Witness

Alice Miller

The longest journey of my life was the journey to my own self. I do not know whether I am an exception in this matter, or whether there are other people who have experienced the same thing. It is certainly not a universal experience: fortunately, there are people who from the moment of their birth were lucky enough to be accepted by their parents for what they were, with all their feelings and needs. Right from the outset these people had unrestricted access to those feelings and needs. They did not have to deny them, nor did they have to embark on long journeys to find something withheld from them when they needed it most.

My experience was different. It has taken me all my life to allow myself to be what I am and to listen to what my inner self is telling me, more and more directly, without waiting for permission from others or currying approval from people symbolizing my parents.

I am frequently asked what I understand by successful therapy. I have in fact answered this question indirectly in many of my books. But after this brief introduction perhaps I can put it more simply: successful therapy should shorten this long journey. It should liberate us from our ingrained adaptation strategies and help us learn to trust our own feelings — something our parents might have made difficult, if not impossible. Because it was prohibited, and hence feared, right from the beginning, many people find it impossible to embark on such a journey. Later, the role played initially by our parents is taken over by teachers, priests, society and morality — all of them conspiring to cement this fear. And cement, as we know, is very difficult to soften.

The wide range of self-help books on non-violent communication, including the valuable and wise advice given by Thomas Gordon and Marshall Rosenberg, are undoubtedly effective if they are consulted by people who, in their childhood, were able to display their feelings without fear of rebuke and grew up in the company of adults who served them as a model for being at one with themselves. But at a later stage children with serious impairments to their identity do not know what they feel and what they really need. They have to find this out in therapy, repeatedly applying what they have learned to new experiences and thus achieving the security that tells them they are not mistaken. As children of emotionally immature or confused parents they were forced to believe that their feelings and needs were wrong. If they had been right, so they believe, then their parents would not have refused to communicate with them.

My belief is that no therapy can fulfill the wish that many people probably harbor: the wish to be able, at long last, to solve all the problems they have painfully confronted so far. This is impossible because life repeatedly confronts us with new problems that can reawaken the painful memories stored up in our bodies. But therapy should open up access to our own feelings: the wounded child must be allowed to speak, and the adult must learn to

understand and engage with what that child is trying to say. If the therapist is a genuine Enlightened Witness, as opposed to an educator, then the client will have learned to admit his/her emotions, to understand their intensity and to transform them into conscious feelings leaving new traces of memory. Of course, like any other individual, the former client will need friends with whom to share worries, problems and questions. But here communication will take on a more mature form, free of any kind of exploitation, because both sides have seen through the exploitation experienced in childhood.

The emotional understanding of the child I once was gives me a clearer conception of the biography of that child. Accordingly, it will give me a different kind of access to my own self. It will also give me the strength to deal

Ancient tree in Japan

ARIYOSHI ICHIRO

with present-day problems more rationally and effectively than before. We can hardly expect to be spared any kind of encounter with pain or distressing experience. That is something that only happens in fairy tales. But if I am no longer a mystery to myself, then I can act and reflect consciously, I can give my feelings the room they need to develop. This is because I understand them. And once I understand them, they will no longer cause so much fear as they once did. This sets things in motion, it gives us a kind of resource that we can draw upon if and when depression or physical symptoms reassert themselves. We know that these physical or mental states are an announcement of something, that they are perhaps trying to bring a suppressed feeling to the surface. And then we can try to admit to that feeling.

As the journey to ourselves is a life-long journey, its end will not coincide with the end of therapy. But successful therapy should have helped us to discover and perceive our own genuine needs and to learn to satisfy them. This is precisely what individuals wounded in early childhood have never been able to do. So after therapy the point at issue is still that of satisfying needs, needs that now assert themselves much more strongly and clearly than they did before. The satisfaction of those needs can then take place in a way that accords with the individual in question and does no one else any harm.

We may not always be able to obliterate the traces left by our early upbringing. But once they have been consciously perceived for what they are, they can be used constructively, actively, and creatively, instead of being merely suffered in a passive and self-destructive manner. These people can then become Enlightened Witnesses, assisting others by taking their part and siding with them.

The essential role of an enlightened witness in society

Since adolescence I have always wondered why people take pleasure in humiliating others. Clearly the fact that some people are sensitive to the suffering of others proves that the destructive urge is not a universal aspect of human nature. So why do some tend to solve their problems by violence while others don't?

Philosophy failed to answer my question, and the Freudian theory of the death wish has never convinced me. It was only by closely examining the childhood histories of murderers, especially mass murderers, that I began to comprehend the roots of good and evil: not in the genes, as commonly believed, but often in the earliest days of life. Today, it is inconceivable to me that a child who comes into the world among attentive, loving and protective parents could become a predatory monster. And in the childhood of the murderers who later became dictators, I have always found a nightmarish horror, a record of continual lies and humiliation which, upon the attainment of adulthood, impelled them to acts of merciless revenge on society. These vengeful acts were always garbed in hypocritical ideologies, purporting that the dictator's exclusive and overriding wish was the happiness of his people. In this way, he unconsciously emulated his own parents who, in earlier days, had also insisted that their blows were inflicted on the child for his own good. This belief was extremely widespread a century ago, particularly in Germany.

I found it logical that a child beaten often would quickly pick up the language of violence. For him, this language became the only effective means of communication available. Yet what I found to be logical was apparently not so to most people.

When I began to illustrate my thesis by drawing on the examples of Hitler and Stalin, when I tried to expose the social consequences of child abuse, I encountered fierce resistance. Repeatedly I was told, "I, too, was a battered child, but that didn't make me a criminal." When I asked for details about their childhood, I was always told of a person who loved them, but was unable to protect them. Yet through his or her presence, this person gave them a notion of trust and of love.

I call these persons helping witnesses. Dostoyevsky, for instance, had a brutal father, but a loving mother. She wasn't strong enough to protect him from his father, but she gave him a powerful conception of love without which his novels would have been unimaginable. Many have also been lucky enough to find later both enlightened and courageous witnesses, people who helped them to recognize the injustices they suffered, to give vent to their feelings of rage, pain and indignation at what happened to them. People who found such witnesses never became criminals.

Anyone addressing the problem of child abuse is likely to be faced with a very strange finding: it has frequently been observed that parents who abuse their children tend to mistreat and neglect them in ways resembling their own treatment as children, without any conscious memory of their own experiences. It is well known that fathers who bully their children through sexual abuse are usually unaware that they had themselves suffered the same abuse. It is mostly in therapy, even if ordered by the courts, that they discover, stupefied, their own history and realize thereby that for years they have attempted to act out their own scenario just to get rid of it.

How can this be explained? After studying the matter for years, it seems clear to me that information about abuse inflicted during childhood is recorded in our body cells as a sort of memory, linked to repressed anxiety. If, lacking the aid of an enlightened witness, these memories fail to break through to consciousness they often compel the person to violent acts that reproduce the abuse suffered in childhood which was repressed in order to survive. The aim is to avoid the fear of powerlessness before a cruel adult. This fear can be eluded momentarily by creating situations in which one plays the active role, the role of the powerful, towards a powerless person.

But this is not an easy path to rid oneself of unconscious fears. And this is why the offence is ceaselessly repeated. A steady stream of new victims must be found, as recently demonstrated by the pedophile scandals in Belgium. To his dying day, Hitler was convinced that only the death of every single Jew could shield him from the fearful and daily memory of his brutal father. Since his father was half Jewish, the whole Jewish people had to be exterminated. I know how easy it is to dismiss this interpretation of the Holocaust, but I honestly haven't yet found a better one. Besides, the case of Hitler shows that hatred and fear cannot be resolved through power, even absolute power, as long as the hatred is transferred to scapegoats. On the contrary, if the true cause of the hatred is identified, is experienced with the feelings that accompany this recognition, blind hatred of innocent victims can be dispelled. Sex criminals stop their depredations if they manage to overcome their amnesia and mourn their tragic fate, thanks to the empathy of an enlightened witness. Old wounds can be healed if exposed to the light of day. But they cannot be repudiated by revenge.

A Japanese crew shot a film of therapeutic work in a prison in Arizona, where the method was based, *inter alia*, on my books. I was sent the video cassette and found the results very revealing. The inmates worked in groups, talked a lot about their childhood, and some of them said, "I've been all over the place, and killed innocent people to avoid the feelings I have today. But I know that I can bear these feelings in the group, where I feel safe. I no longer need to run around and kill, I'm at home here, and I recognize what happened. The past recedes, and my anger along with it."

For this process to succeed, the adult who has grown up without helping witnesses in his childhood needs the support of enlightened witnesses, people who have understood and recognized the consequences of child abuse. In an informed society, adolescents can learn to verbalize their truth and to discover themselves in their own story. They will not need to avenge themselves violently for their wounds or to poison their systems with drugs, if they have the luck to talk to others about their early experiences and succeed in grasping the naked truth of their own tragedy. To do this, they need assistance from persons aware of the dynamics of child abuse, who can help them address their feelings seriously, understand them and integrate them as part of their own story, instead of avenging themselves on the innocent.

I have wrongly been attributed the thesis according to which every victim inevitably becomes a persecutor, a thesis that I find totally false, indeed absurd. It has been proved that many adults have had the good fortune to break the cycle of abuse through knowledge of their past. Yet I can certainly aver that I have never come across persecutors who weren't victims in their childhood, though most of them don't know it because their feelings are repressed. The less these criminals know about themselves, the more dangerous they are to society. So I think it is crucial for the therapist to grasp the difference between the statement, "every victim ultimately becomes a persecutor," which is false, and "every persecutor was a victim in his childhood," which I consider true. The problem is that, feeling nothing, she remembers nothing, realizes nothing, and this is why surveys don't always reveal the truth. Yet the presence of a warm, enlightened witness — therapist, social aid worker, lawyer, judge — can help the criminal unlock repressed feelings and restore the unrestricted flow of consciousness. This can initiate the process of escape from the vicious circle of amnesia and violence.

(Editors' Note: The first half of this article was written in 2005 while the second half was written in 1997. Both of these articles are posted on Alice Miller's website (Alice-Miller.com) and are reprinted with permission.)

32

GUS DIZEREGA

Access to Free Nature

Arne Naess

In the cities a generation ago — at least in Scandinavia — small children had areas where they were permitted to do everything they wanted except make random fires. In winter they made small ski jumps. No artificial structures whatsoever. But they occasionally would build things. The free areas were big enough so that the children did not ruin the vegetation. Very gradually these areas of free nature were ruined because the pieces of the land, by an evil misconception of a fatal sort called the value of the property, we're deemed too high to allow them to remain undeveloped.

In the absence of such areas and considering the increasing population pressures, we may have to limit space available for all children of the next generation. Therefore I propose to speak of safe access to patches of free nature rather than to areas. Based on what older people recount about their happy days as small children in areas of free nature, it is a duty at least in the rich countries to protect every existing such patch of free nature. Parents should be responsible for the behavior of wanton destruction which did not endanger free areas a generation ago! The situation is grave: if there are rules of behavior laid down by the neighborhood or the parents, the feeling of freedom may be reduced. If there are no rules introduced today, some children less than ten years old may destroy for the sheer joy of destruction.

The ready access to large areas of non-human dominated nature is yearly diminished at a catastrophic rate through thoughtless concentric widening of cities, suburbs and towns. A birthday cake, for example, is traditionally cut into moderate pieces with a core remaining. If every other piece is eaten there remains the core and free space between each piece. If the result of development is symbolized by the pieces eaten, there still remains wide access to the core, the markets and the institutions. Wide access guarantees that, if you live or work in the core area of human domination, the distance to large free areas is relatively short. How short? Here there is room for visions and utopias. The extremes of decentralization, the vision of global anarchy, picture cores as mere local community centers. According to the

Tim Quick

Gandhian vision of panchayats, the greatest units of administration and other institutions are community centers of five villages. There have been attempts to realize this on a small scale in India. The Sami people (they don't like being called Laplanders) made up the only non-violent anarchy of great expansion I know of, covering large areas of Northern Norway, Sweden, Finland and Russia. A strong feeling of solidarity bound them together. They were completely helpless facing expanding nation states based on violent defense institutions.

Enough about political and social conditions! The easy access to free nature has been a cornerstone of decentralized societies — that is, regional aggregates of communities. Easy access to free nature is only one factor which in the early childhood and formative years moderate the asocial tendencies and the quest for ever higher level of consumption. To lose this access may have a deep influence on human character, and as I see it, every continued destruction of such access, especially in the formative years of human personality, should be looked upon as a calamity.

Arne Naess in Norway

33

Ecointelligence and Hope

Norah Trace

Alarm beeps. My head happens to be facing the window, and as I open my eyes I look out onto a soft, West Coast autumn sunrise over the forested mountains; a slight mist over the forest is still almost-black green, the light imminent. Forty-five minutes later I am walking my bike up my driveway to the road, ready to ride out into this world. The air is crisp, and there remain some maple leaves to fall, though right now the trees are holding their frosted leaves to the early light. I click into my pedals and am off onto winding, hilly back roads through the park, to the first highway which edges the forest. I have seen many forms of life on my rides through here — owls, eagles, hawks and many songbirds and woodpeckers; ermine, raccoons, deer — and deep in the woods I have seen cougar and signs of bear. Turning down the hill now, I pick up speed, exhilarated by the air, chill and sharp with scents of autumn from the forest. I crest the last rise before developed areas focus the view. From the bottom of the mountain I note traffic approaching, a three-quarter ton truck behind a small economy car. I can hear

an SUV coming down behind me as I aim into the mist floating in the valley. An antlered buck at the side of the road waits patiently for the car to pass and then leaps gracefully in front of the truck. I am off of my bike, walking slowly toward him. I stand in the middle of the road and see that mercifully his death was instant; he is already gone. That fast. Mist still hangs around his nostrils, heat still emanates from his body, but his eyes are emptying. Peripherally I become aware that I am standing in the middle of the highway alone with a dying deer. I realize that none of those three vehicles stopped. Not the economy car, not the SUV and most especially not the offending hit-and-run driver of the truck. Later I will realize that this is what hurts me the most. At this moment, however, I help the deer's body finish crossing the road. I hold his four hooves in my two hands and pull him to the side. I straighten his head, stroke his antlers and nose. I send a wish with his spirit that he will be reborn somewhere with no highways, lots of healthy wild food, safe wild spaces to roam and forage, pure creeks and lakes and lots of his kind, happy and hale. I realize I am probably sending him into the past, because it is hard to think of very many remaining wild forests that fit the needs of this type of deer. I climb back onto my bike and continue floating down the mountain, into the city, into the evolution of my species and its effect on Life in all forms as we know it; into the world of which we are all a part, all influencing its destruction or its betterment.

Now, I am no saint myself. I feel like I am doing well if I ride my bike into the city two days a week. And because I have heard real life stories of cougars jumping cyclists in the night and human predators disappearing women who are out at night, I often ask my partner to pick me up somewhere on the edge of the city so I am not riding back up the mountain into the forest, in the dark. I do love the workout climbing the mountain on a summer evening, but I have to weigh that out with my fears. I will happily give the night over to the cougar — let them have the wild dark forest. I live here and pay high taxes so I can vote for stewardship instead of uncontained development. Others work much harder than me on that directly. Even others spend their lives *developing* the forest — scraping it down, blowing it up, re-shaping it for houses, golf courses and big box stores. Thinking of the stores my mind follows the map to the various producers of goods sold in those stores — the full continuum from local organic farmers to slaves in some developing country. From there to refugees in fourth world countries and should I send money to the UN Refugee agency like a flyer in my mailbox asks me too — for a few dollars I can buy either a plastic tarp or, for a few dollars more, a canvas tent for a family stuck in desertified landscapes in the Sudan or Chad, where long, long ago it was forest? I

hold that reality for a few moments as I dig into a hill. I recommit to doing more of what I can do about it all, this destruction and misery that we create, when we could be creating peace and connection instead. All I can do is practice the eightfold path as best I can. All things are connected.

I gave the description of that morning on my bike to a few people. Some of them kindly said people don't want to read stuff like that. Instead, I should tell the story differently:

The deer leaps to safety instead of dying (I wish!); that will be more inspirational. It would be so nice if polar bears could adapt quickly enough to survive the thaw, or if deer could learn when to cross the road. That people drive through the park at the speed limit, watching for deer as the signs say (I wish again!) would be more inspirational. Someone else suggested I just talk theory and skip the emotionally evocative stories because they are unpleasant for people, and if you must drag dead animals off of the road then have the courtesy to spare the rest of us the details (well, quite frankly, I have). A few other people said thanks for the story and told me stories of their own. I wonder, instead of needing protection from the truth or minimizing its emotional impact, why not be inspired? To witness the losses and suffering and yet work to remain optimistic is sometimes a difficult place, and it is harder when doing it alone. I can't see these things without needing, after a while, to reach for hope. Gratefully, I easily find lots of reading material, documentaries and people to converse and hike through wild forests with to share in sustaining our hope for, and action toward, a wilder future.

Complexity theory, cognitive, emotional and social psychologies and ecopsychology give a basis for addressing the dangerous conflict arising from the alienation between our urban psyche and our sense of interwovenness with nature. Healing this estrangement is our most important developmental task. Systems disintegrate in order to reorganize into more complex forms, becoming increasingly capable of adapting to and influencing the environment in which they live. Intelligent evolution is in the coevolution of system and environment. Change occurs at bifurcation points, proceeds through chaos or transitions and completes with reorganization. Mutation and innovation happen in the free zone at the edge of chaos where a new form of organization can occur. Perhaps this is on the road where forest and city meet.

We need to make use of all forms of intelligence to have ecological intelligence. Cognitive intelligence is our ability to logically reason, remember, understand, inquire, critique, create and choose actions. Emotional intelligence is awareness and use of our emotional experience as information about what is important; it includes equanimity. People who are generally considered to be wise (e.g., the Dalai Lama, Pema Chodrin, Thich Nhat Hanh, Joanna Macy, Ken Wilber) say that we are not supposed to decrease our emotional experience, but to strengthen our capacity to live on the edge of emotional chaos and to stay calm and present. We cannot separate the experience of an emotion from the world in which we live. Social intelligence models have recently been re-refined. Older versions of social intelligence referred to reading the interpersonal situation to facilitate direction (on a continuum from best outcome for all through narcissism to sociopathy). Social intelligence now means to create a scenario that includes individual value, diversity, healthier connectedness and shared valuing of life.

The essence of the four noble truths of Buddhist philosophy is that as soon as we see and feel deeply we open ourselves to suffering; we can see what we do that causes suffering; we can cease to do it and instead we can do something that promotes well-being. I've seen this work in individual lives every day, over and over. Small change in sense of connectedness can lead to big changes in behavior, and the changes will manifest in non-linear, unpredictable ways. Each moment offers fresh possibility.

It is important to tell and to feel the story of the deer on the road between city and forest. Whenever we draw a line and say we are separate from the deer we miss a chance to feel a connection. That path has led to a world where deer and their forests are expendable.

It seems to be a Life Wish or Death Wish kind of choice. We often say that people who commit suicide are really trying to kill off a painful part, usually the most emotionally sensitive part that has been wounded and alienated. Why as a species are we suiciding by killing the most beautiful and sensitive parts of our selves and our world? What does it mean if this goes unnoticed, unacknowledged, unfelt? What if we take it all in and intentionally encourage a Wish for Life?

Now I want to go back and actively imagine that someday I get to write a true story with one of the following endings.

- The Hart doesn't die because cars aren't going through the wild forest to begin with. He is in a meadow beside a stream bed that has not been turned into a road.
- The road is there but the stag doesn't die because people drive slowly while enjoying their drive through the forest.

They watch for wild creatures and make it a pleasant part of their day, knowing they are in one of the precious remaining forests on the planet.

What is true is that at the end of that work day I chose to ride home through the park at least halfway up the mountain. I like this ride home; it's a chance to integrate my day and rejuvenate my body. Today I sat with a mother struggling with depression after the death of her son; a teenage girl survivor of sexual abuse; a young man with a head injury from a car accident; a marriage hard at work; a soldier back from Kandahar; a meeting about refugees; a refugee mother grieving her losses while raising two children brimming with hope and possibility. Every day I sit with a sampling of people wounded by our world and in each one of them it is possible, not even difficult, to access the spark of caring, appreciation for beauty, love of life and hope. All have the seeds of rejuvenation in them; with time and right conditions they come back toward the Wish for Life. They are not yet desert.

As I turn to head up the mountain on this night the moon is now behind me. Almost full, it is brighter than my three top-of-the-line bike lights put together. Just at the steepest part a male deer steps out, about 20 feet in front of me. Close to where I took his brother off of the road this morning. He is Beauty in a Body — his eyes spark, he snorts out mist, his coat almost glows in this light. He pauses. Then, in what seems like one move he is through the ditch and over the fence and into the depths of the forest.

Adventure therapy

DUNCAN M. TAYLOR

34

Students Becoming Teachers
through Place-Based Education

Alan Drengson

Reading stories about the many successes of place-based education reminds me of a deeply transforming experience I enjoyed when in my mid teens. An older man in our community was a leader and mentor able to help children find our own power to learn and change. For a variety of reasons, our neighborhood-based informal hiking club decided to become a Boy Scout Troop. After the troop was officially recognized, our leader suggested that we should go to Scouting events and competitions coming up during the year. We discussed this and agreed that we wanted to do well in those events. He pointed out that the other troops had been organized a long time and that many of the scouts in them were more advanced in scout training. If we were to compete, he said, we would each have to become a teacher to the other boys in our group. Each of us could volunteer to take one area of Scout skills and knowledge, learn it and then teach it to the other boys. One boy did first aid, another did knots, another taught map and compass — and so on it went, until all areas were covered. Our mentor also

provided us with places to play where we had great freedom. He gave us confidence in ourselves to be self-directed learners and teachers. We did exceptionally well in the Scouting events, which also included camping and hiking skills. *Place-Based Education* describes the same approach to student initiative I have just described.

Becoming teachers to ourselves and co-learners with one another in our home place is a profound learning experience. We can learn all manner of things on our own and then share and help others to learn them. What we find out in the process is that we each have far more ability and know-how than we usually think. As Arne Naess loves to say, "We tend to greatly underestimate ourselves." Each of us is capable of *beautiful actions*. In some ways this is the essence of Buddha's teachings when he said, "Be a light unto yourselves." When we broaden our experience to include the natural world, the beings of nature become our teachers. We gain deep insight from our home places, ignite our passions and turn on our own natural intelligence.

If young people are given responsibility to describe problems, issues and challenges facing a community and themselves, they find ways to understand the situation, ways to solve problems and ways to create new possibilities that most of our current methods and top down approaches cannot begin to realize. Whether it is addressing problems of resource use, lack of organization or local economic issues, we have the answers to our problems within our own local resources and human communities. Instead of searching abroad, we should look to our own relationships and ways of interacting to see how to free and unify the spiritual, intellectual, emotional and physical energies of ourselves and our own people. The quality of our lives depends ultimately on the quality of our relationships to ourselves, to each other and to the natural world in which we live. My own daily practices involve walking in nature in my home place, returning to the same places in my area over and over throughout the year. Each time I learn a little more and can communicate a little bit more with the many beings that are part of this ecological community.

Wherever we lived when I was younger, there were always places to play in nature and to be in nature, alone and with other youngsters. We were not supervised or told what to do much of the time. We built camps, huts and cabins and little trails. We had many secret hideouts and places we thought of as our own. It became clear to me as I grew older what a fantastic gift this had been. So much of our development and self reliance came out of this background. Our neighborhood group had access to lots of free nature in the surrounding area where we could play in unsupervised ways and we built tree houses and cabins. Our mentor had a house and yard that was filled

with places for us to undertake similar adventures indoors. These opportunities helped us to further develop our own sense of independence from the more structured worlds of school and work. An extension of these neighborhood resources was found in the more distant wilderness areas where we went on hikes, and later mountain climbing trips, to spend time in the wild. Looking back I now appreciate how rich this environment was for us and how impoverished many of the technological systems are by comparison.

It is a serious problem we face — that so much of our time and of our children's experiences are submerged in a technological system that is always feeding us stories made up by others, usually with a commercial message. This is not a good source for self-directed learning and competence to be in the natural world. In many countries and cultures there is still emphasis on the importance of journeying in the natural world. In Norway and other Scandinavian countries, regular activities in free nature are part of a tradition called *friluftsliv*

Camp on Sunshine Coast

(free air life). It is widely valued and recognized as important for children and adults to have this kind of outdoor activity on a regular basis. Oslo, one of the most urbanized areas in Norway, has an extensive city forest, with walking and hiking trails and parks all over the city, as well as lakes, extensive inland marine waterways and shorelines.

In the city of Victoria, British Columbia where I live, we have well developed plans for preserving and setting aside more, small and extensive green spaces and designing and building trails for walking and biking. Despite increasing urbanization related to continuing population growth in our area, there are increasing numbers of groups focusing efforts on local places, from marshes to extensive wooded parklands and rocky tops, within our larger region. More and more of us realize that this is not just a luxury — but a necessity that raises our quality of life to higher levels. These undertakings fit into the larger efforts to green our cities and make them examples of sustainable, livable places that solve rather than create problems. These are all part of a larger pattern of change going on in our society and around the world. This greening is a transition to societies that are growing *ecosophies*. *Wild Foresting* is an invitation to take our own regular journeys outdoors and especially to nearby forests and to get involved in the many restoration, conservation, preservation and other efforts that are discussed in this book and referred to in Appendix 2.

Part VI

Wild Forests and the Fate of the World

Thunderstorm

35

Earth's Greatest Crisis

Guy Dauncey

This is a tale of trees that lived hundreds of millions of years ago. Their ghosts have returned to threaten the very existence of their ancestors today. It is the biggest blockbuster of all time, with an ending that could be either catastrophic or glorious, depending on how we respond.

It is a story of Earth's forests and the legacy they left that could destroy us all.

When Earth's forests first appeared four hundred million years ago, during the Devonian period, life was emerging from the oceans and beginning to colonize the land with seed-bearing plants. The trees lived then, as they do today, off sunshine, water and minerals from the soil, using photosynthesis to obtain their energy and storing carbon in their roots and branches.

From 360 to 286 million years ago, during the period we call Carboniferous, magnificent trees and gigantic ferns lived in lush swamp forests. Sometimes, when they fell into water or mud, instead of rotting on the land their carbon was preserved and locked away underground. Over millions of years, the ground

bent and twisted as entire continents moved across the world, exerting heat and pressure, slowly converting the fallen trees and ferns into the sedimentary rock we call coal.

Millions of years later we humans evolved, walking upright on the plains of Africa. After a while we started using fire, burning wood to make heat. It was wood from the forests that gave us warmth through the ice age, enabling us to walk to the far corners of the Earth. It was wood that enabled us to build our first cities and civilizations; we grew in self-importance as we marveled at our achievements. It was wood that enabled us to build ocean-going ships, traveling the world to settle in new lands.

The forests' ancient carbon, that we call coal, was first used in China around 1000 BC to smelt copper. Later, in the 12th century AD, it was used in England to make heat, since so much of the forest had been cut down. Being uneducated in the sciences, we had no notion we were releasing ancient sunlight that had been locked away for 200 million years.

Then came the industrial revolution, when we used the coal to make steam, powering the mechanistic transformation that has led to today's world. We burned the coal in total ignorance of what it was. We took Earth's incredible abundance for granted, never pausing to wonder what might happen if we burned all this ancient carbon. The Swedish scientist Svent Arrhenius calculated in 1896 what would happen if we continued burning Earth's store of fossil fuels — predicting a rise in the global temperature of 7-11°F[1] — but we did not pay serious attention until very recently.

Today, using bulldozers, chainsaws and fire, we fell or burn 80,000 acres of the world's tropical rainforest every day, an area the size of Florida.[2] From the Amazon to Indonesia, the Congo to Nigeria, people and businesses cut and burn the forest to raise cattle, to grow soybeans to feed to their cattle, to plant monocultured trees for pulpwood, to plant palm oil plantations for biodiesel to run their cars, to harvest the valuable tropical hardwoods and to make space for human settlements.

Whether in Europe or Siberia, Surinam or Ecuador, Earth's forests are filled with magic, and an astonishing wealth of biodiversity. Often still inhabited by the forest people who have lived there for thousands of years, they are a source of wonder to anyone who has spent time in them.

They are also immensely important for the world's climate balance. Since the start of the human adventure, we have cut down 80% of the Earth's forests, but 20% still remain. They cover 12% of the Earth's land area and store 40% of the world's terrestrial carbon.[3]

As we enter the ancient forest and feel its cool, dark shade, we enter a primeval ecosystem. The relationship between trees and climate change is critical, because forests sequester carbon. They do it as part of the natural cycling of carbon that has been occurring on Earth for millions of years. All living plants on this planet — whether in the ocean, soil or forest — are carbon-based organisms that take in carbon dioxide to build their tissue. While alive, they store it as carbon. When they die, they release it as carbon dioxide.

The rainforests host more than half of Earth's known plant and animal species, but at the current rate of loss, leaving climate change out of the picture, most will no longer be functioning ecosystems in 100 years time. Add climate change, and the future becomes even more alarming.

The trouble also affects temperate forests. In 2003, Siberia's boreal forest lost 9.8 million acres to forest fires. In Canada, 6.4 million acres are being lost to fire each year as the heat increases, compared to 2.5 million acres a year in the 1970s.[4] Researchers at the Russian Academy of Sciences Forest Research Institute fear that Russia's boreal forests will be so dry by 2090 that they will turn into grassland.[5] As the temperature rises, a new kind of megafire has been appearing that cannot be controlled by the known methods of fire suppression.[6]

As the world's temperature rises, forests are being stressed by heat, attacked by new insects and suffer an increase in forest fires. Between 1980 and 1997, Canadian forests experienced five of the seven worst fire seasons in recorded history — coincidental with the warmest years. Due to the increased fires, logging and insect attack, Canadian forests are no longer a net carbon sink of greenhouse gases. Prior to 1970, they sequestered 188 million tons of carbon per year. By 2001, they were releasing 57 million tons.[7]

The Amazon rainforest, storing 132 billion tons of carbon in its trees and soil, is particularly affected. It is sustained by rainfall from the Atlantic, but the warming ocean is bringing droughts, and research by staff at the Woods Hole Center shows the Amazon can only survive two consecutive years of drought. In the third year the trees fall over and die. In 2005 and 2006 parts of the Amazon suffered extreme drought, causing major tributaries to dry up, but luckily the rains returned, enabling it to dodge the bullet. With drought comes fire. After a point, the forest can no longer recover from the fires, and a process of rapid drying begins that leads to savannah, then desert. At the Hadley Centre for Climate Prediction in Britain, researchers who have looked closely at the future of the Amazon warn that if the world's temperature continues to rise as predicted, the Amazon will cease being a net store of carbon by 2040. As the temperature rises it will be subject to repeated droughts and fires, and by 2100 it will be dead. "The region will be able to support only shrubs or grasses at most."[8] In dying, it will release its store of carbon, increasing the expected rate of global warming by 50%.

As an ecosystem type, forests can adapt in response to gradual climate change. When the planet warmed up after the last ice age the forests moved north into what used to be tundra, and the tundra moved north into what used to be ice. Most trees only migrate by a few yards a century, but with rising temperatures they will need to move several hundred miles north or south to get away from the heat. The trees that cannot take the heat are dying and releasing their carbon. As a result of these forces, the world's forests are losing 2.2 billion tons of carbon a year, 20% of our total CO_2 emissions.[9] Since forest fires also produce black carbon and contribute to the formation of tropospheric ozone, their contribution to global warming is significant. It is

their ancient carbon, however, dug from its resting place and burned to power 85% of the energy that our civilization uses, that is the killer.

So here we have the terrible consequence, the legacy of carbon from those ancient forests, which, if we do not make a sudden and dramatic turn in the way our civilization is organized, will destroy us all — forests, bears, butterflies and humans alike. In his book *Six Degrees* the British author Mark Lynas shows with frightening detail the future that awaits us as the temperature rises by each successive degree. When it reaches +10°F, which is within the range of the increase forecast for this century — it is game over for virtually every living species on the planet.[10]

So what must we do?

When Al Gore responded to being honored with the Nobel Peace Prize in October 2007, he said: "We face a true planetary emergency. The climate crisis is not a political issue, it is a moral and spiritual challenge to all of humanity. It is also our greatest opportunity to lift global consciousness to a higher level."[11]

If we assume that Earth's people respond to the challenge and lessen the risk of disaster from global climate change, we will still need to protect Earth's forests. How can we do so? Here are five measures, all of which are needed urgently.

Protect the tropical rainforests

In the last 50 years, almost half of the world's tropical rainforests have been cleared, producing nearly 20% of the greenhouse gas emissions from human activities. For every mahogany tree in the tropics that is found and cut down, a bulldozer smashes its way through 60 other trees.[12] We need to establish a large global forest protection fund that can be used to purchase threatened forests and hold them in trust for their indigenous forest peoples, giving them permanent protection. This could be financed either by a global carbon tax or by the sale of carbon offsets under a system of *avoided deforestation* which countries could trade as an incentive to protect their forests. Whichever method we choose, we need it urgently. As Andrew Mitchell of the Global Canopy Program says, "Tropical forests are the elephant in the living room of climate change" because we have not given this aspect of the problem anything like the attention it needs.[13]

We should also ban the import of mahogany and other threatened tropical woods. We should write legislation to prevent US and Canadian corporations from logging outside North America in forests that have not been certified, or tax such forest products so heavily that consumers cease buying them. We should rewrite the world's trade rules so that laws of this kind are not ruled illegal by the World Trade Organization. We should assist the countries of the South to pursue development paths that preserve their forests, instead of subsidizing their destruction with export credit loan guarantees. We must do all that we can to protect what remains of the world's forest carbon store.

Place a moratorium on deforestation

Costa Rica has made it illegal to convert forest into farmland. In Paraguay, the government placed a moratorium on deforestation in the eastern half of the country in 2004, using satellites to keep a check and sending in forestry officials and police when they spotted a problem, reducing deforestation by 85%.[14] Where

the political will is strong, deforestation can be stopped.

In Peru, the government has reduced the loss of forest in protected areas to less than 0.2% a year using a combination of protected parks and indigenous reserves, the titling of native territories to the forest people who live there, the sanctioning of long-term commercial timber production in chosen areas and satellite monitoring.[15]

Providing locally enforceable rights over forest management to local forest communities is an important part of the solution. India, which recently brought in a law returning the bulk of its forests to local communities for management, is one of the few countries (along with China and the US) where there is a net increase in forest cover.[16]

Expand FSC certification

One solution lies in forestry practices certified by the Forest Stewardship Council that seek to maintain the ecological integrity of the forest while still harvesting its timber. Ecoforestry methods never allow a clearcut, and rarely a patch-cut, relying instead on individual tree selection. Over 60 years, an ecologically managed temperate forest will yield more timber of higher quality than one that has been clearcut. The roots and soil are left undisturbed, along with their carbon; the seedlings take root from the genetic stock of the best old trees; the diversity of insect and bird life controls the pests and because the trees grow more steadily in a semi-canopy, their fiber is tighter. Each year, the annual growth of the forest is carefully removed; over 60 years, the overall yield is higher than if the forest had been clearcut and left to grow for 60 years before being cut again. Because of its methods, it is almost certain that an eco-certified

VICTORIA STEVENS

Surprise Lake and Montane Forest

disturbance to the forest floor during harvesting, while maximizing the accumulation of carbon in the forest.

A typical coastal Douglas fir forest in Canada's Pacific Northwest grows by 2 - 4% per year until it reaches an old growth condition.[18] Industrial forestry clearcuts the timber in one area and leaves the forest to regrow from scratch. Clearcutting has been banned in Switzerland and parts of Germany because soil is lost along with its carbon, and the sustainability of the forest cannot be guaranteed beyond two or three cuts.

Ecoforestry, by contrast, views the forest as an integrated ecosystem and uses single tree selection to harvest the annual growth, leaving the forest standing. In the 94,000 acre Almanor forest in Northern California, the Collins Companies have been following this method since 1943, keeping careful records. The forest has been logged continuously for five decades, and in 2001 it had yielded more than 1.7 billion board feet of timber, yet with a higher inventory of timber than in 1943, much of it in mature trees.[19]

Ecoforestry protects a forest's principal while harvesting the interest; industrial forestry takes the principal and hopes it will regrow. The loss of carbon in the soil during clearcutting results in reduced carbon in the new trees and causes overall yields to be lower. Industrial forestry may maximize short-term profits, but it minimizes sequestered carbon and weakens long-term profits while undermining the ecological integrity of the forest along with its habitat and recreational values.

A national Sustainable Forestry Act might require Forest Stewardship Council certification as a condition of all timber operations, whether on private or publicly owned land, and place a carbon tax on all non-certified

forest will store more carbon and minimize carbon-loss during harvesting than a clearcut forest, although sufficient research has not yet been done to test this.

As of October 2007, around the world, 222 million acres of the world's forests have been certified in 77 countries, including 11.8 million acres in Brazil, 1.7 million acres in Indonesia, 27 million acres in Sweden, 12 million acres in Poland, 22 million acres in the US and 44 million acres in Canada.[17] Timber from certified forests is in strong demand, especially in Europe, thanks to consumer awareness and campaigns by the Rainforest Action Network and the Natural Resources Defense Council.

Encourage sustainable forestry

A climate-friendly forest policy, adopted by a nation's government, would seek to maximize the carbon content in the forest by encouraging harvesting methods that cause minimum imported forest products to account for the loss of carbon that occurs during harvesting.

Reduce our demand

We must also take action to reduce our personal and cultural demand, providing less reason to interfere with the forests. If all of the world's people were to live like most North Americans we would need three additional planets to provide the resources needed. It is impossible for the world's forests to satisfy all our wants, as opposed to our needs.

We need legislation that requires all newsprint to use 50% recycled content, for instance. We also need legislation to phase out the use of wooden pallets, which represent an extraordinary waste of resources. In the US, 11% of the harvested timber and 40% of the hardwood is used to make 400 million new pallets a year, and 300,000 houses could be built each year from the discarded pallets alone.[20] A global phase-out would allow for their substitution with durable pallets made from recycled plastic. In Germany, some pallets are bar-coded, with the original owner receiving a royalty each time a pallet is used and being charged each time it needs fixing.[21]

Simply changing the way we frame our houses could save large quantities of timber. 27% of the world's timber harvest is consumed in the US, and 72% of US lumber is used in house-building, averaging 35 trees per house (16,000 board feet). More efficient framing methods could reduce this by 20%, while the use of engineered wood products could achieve a 50% saving.[22]

In Conclusion

We face a planetary emergency. The absolute urgency of the climate change warnings tell us conclusively that we *must* adopt these changes, if we want our civilization and the planet's ecology to survive. We are on the threshold of a terrible catastrophe — or a remarkable breakthrough to global consciousness, global treaties and the globally responsible management of the world's forest according to sustainable, ecological principles.

The forests of the Earth were here 400 million years before we were. As a species, we have a deep genetic memory with its roots in the forest. Our closest relatives, the apes and chimpanzees with whom we share most of our genes and who knows what else, live immersed in the forest. The Japanese have a cultural recognition that walking in the forest does something important to both the spirit and the body. They call it *shinrin-yoku* or *wood-air bathing*, and they have learnt, for instance, that when diabetic patients walk through the forest, their blood sugar drops to healthier levels.[23]

We live at a critical moment in the evolution of our civilization. On this side of the danger there is fear and alarm. On the far side of the danger there lies the awe-inspiring prospect of a planet whose people have learned how to live in harmony with their forests, instead of trying to conquer and fell them.

We *must* negotiate this stage in our development on planet Earth — and when we have done so, when wood-air bathing is as natural to Earth's people as ecological forest management is to its foresters — we shall be able to look back and wonder in disbelief that we could ever have acted so stupidly as to destroy the forests.

The Future of British Columbia Forests Requires Resilience Management

Richard J. Hebda

Forests still rule in British Columbia. Magnificent coniferous giants stand sentry on our Pacific coast, gnarled caricatures of trees hug our mountain tops, and rank upon rank of evergreens marches through our cool and dry interior landscape. Yet all is not well. Tens of thousands of square miles of pine species have succumbed to the attacks of the mountain pine beetle (Carroll et al. 2006); the iconic western red cedar excessively sheds bright orange branchlets in profusion in the fall; outlander species invade the understorey undermining the very core of ecological integrity. Human demand on forest resources and forest space and alterations in the composition of the atmosphere threaten forest ecosystems globally. At the same time, we recognize as never before that without healthy functioning forests, humanity — never mind countless other species — can contemplate only a bleak future.

The economic future of forests under climate change remains uncertain with some predicting little over-all impact, others increased yields, whereas others decreased yields (Easterling et al. 2007). Regional variation, inadequate models and the complexity of interactions all contribute to this uncertainty. On one front however the key role of forests is clear. Forests and oceans are the two macro-systems which remove large amounts of carbon dioxide naturally through photosynthesis. Forest ecosystems, including their soils, also store huge amounts of carbon (ca 1,1442,214 tons of CO_2 living biomass globally in 2005) (Nabuurs et al. 2007). The use of forest for scrubbing and sequestering carbon and as a source of biofuels is widely touted as a key strategy to mitigate climate change. Forest ecosystems are central to effective carbon stewardship on the globe.

In this contribution I explore the past history of British Columbia forests and look at models of future conditions to demonstrate the potential impacts of climate change. I then contemplate management strategies with an eye to ensuring that forests fulfill their many potential roles. Whatever we may think about what climate change means to the city dweller, there is little question that it will transform the living landscape and impact forest ecosystems, forest values and management. Forestry is ecology, and ecology depends on climate. Without forest ecology there is no forest economy. At the primary level, human communities depend on plant communities in the forestry sector.

The past is a key to the future

In British Columbia the record of fossil pollen, cone and needles from the last 10,000 years reveals major changes in the forests. Cyclically high solar radiation 7,000-10,000 years ago fostered a warmer (4 - 7°F) and drier summer climate than today (Hebda 1995), much as expected in the next decades. Grassland and parkland stretched far beyond their modern limits. Forest ecosystems without modern equivalents occurred in BC and may have been widespread. Charcoal in sediments reveals that fires burned widely. Tree lines reached about 300 feet higher into today's alpine realms. Where damp spruce forests occur today in the central parts of the province, pine-dominated ecosystems predominated. A 4,000 year-old tree ring record from Vancouver Island shows dramatic decline in tree growth over 10 years about 3,900 years ago, an indication that climatic shifts can occur rapidly with major impact on growth increment (Zhang and Hebda 2005).

The fossil record of the last 4,000 years indicates a relatively stable climate, compared with preceding millennia. Forest ecosystems and species distributions achieved a relative equilibrium with the climate. The rich thriving western hemlock and western red cedar ecosystems so widely treasured by British Columbians became established in place only at this time (Brown and Hebda 2002). Grasslands shrank to occupy their modern range.

In general, considering the past 10,000 years, we can expect future climate change to be rapid, of large amplitude and occur as variations between extremes. But unlike the case in earlier millennia, the change will play out on a disturbed and fragmented landscape, one with markedly reduced ecological resilience.

Models of the future

Global climate change models use principles of mathematics and physics to estimate climates for different concentrations of atmospheric greenhouse gases. Climate impact models combine the output from climate change models with data defining the climatic envelope or limits of species, ecosystems or processes to anticipate where, geographically, species and ecosystems of interest might be distributed in the future (Hamann and Wang 2006).

Several climate models are available for a range of future greenhouse gas concentrations, and new models and runs continue to appear. Their outcomes vary, but on average for western Canada a mean annual temperature increase of about 9°F is indicated, with about a 10% risk of as much as 18°F change by the end of this century.[1] Precipitation is expected to increase slightly but with stronger summer droughts. These climatic conditions will be without precedent for the last tens of millions of years, taking us back geologically to a time when forests grew in Canada's high Arctic. Current measured trends for British Columbia are consistent with and even greater than forecasts from models (Austin et al. 2008).

The impacts models reveal an ecological transformation ahead. For example, Hamann and Wang (2006) used a Canadian climate model to show that the climate of BC's Ponderosa pine Biogeoclimatic zone (representative of the dry climates of the Okanagan valley of southern interior British Columbia) might occur in the Peace River region and reach into the Northwest Territories by 2080. Royal British Columbia Museum models for western red cedar reveal the disappearance of suitable climate in much of lowland southern BC and its spread into northern BC by 2080.[2] Major shifts in the region of suitable climate for this iconic species will be underway by 2050. Western red cedar is a good proxy species or indicator for the highly productive coastal temperate rainforests of northwestern North America. Potential shifts in its distribution signal major changes in the character and distribution of this globally important biome in the near future.

In contrast to the situation for western red cedar, the climatically suitable region for warmth-loving Garry oak is likely to expand dramatically in southern British Columbia. Areas of suitable climate could appear in the Alaska panhandle and on the adjacent mainland coast by mid century. Especially notable is the enormous increase in area of suitable climate inland of the coastal mountain ranges by 2080.[3]

Elements of carbon stewardship, their characteristics and values

MODIFIED FROM R.J. HEBDA (2007)

Carbon Stewardship
Adaptation and Mitigation:
Balanced values for the future

- *Living carbon:* organisms and ecosystems; sustains humans, ecological process; provides resilience and raw material for future ecosystems and uses; removes CO_2
- *Dead carbon:* organic matter in soils, wastes; sustains living carbon, stored carbon; bioenergy source
- *Ancient carbon:* fossil fuels; ready and reliable energy source; predominant cause of climate change

It should be noted that climate impact models only address the question of where suitable climate may occur. At the predicted rate of change, the range loss of some tree species such as cedar will be much more rapid than any range expansion into newly suitable regions. Long-lived species, such as dominant trees, are relatively slow to reach reproductive maturity, and their seeds typically have limited capacity to disperse (hundreds of yards per reproductive cycle). This *big squeeze* of the geographic range means that it will be many centuries before any sort of natural ecological equilibrium is achieved in our forest ecosystems. Furthermore, stable forest ecosystems also require the development of appropriate soils with characteristic organic matter, a process requiring centuries of time.

A special role for forests

The challenge of climate change is all about carbon stewardship. We use too much Ancient Carbon (oil, gas, coal) releasing carbon dioxide to the atmosphere. The anticipated climatic changes threaten the Living Carbon of ecosystems, biodiversity, agriculture and human communities. The Living Carbon depends on conserving the recently Dead Carbon of soils and peatlands. *Forests are the central element of Living and Dead Carbon on the land, and thus will have to play a huge role in good Carbon Stewardship.*

The effort to meet the challenges of climate change is focused on reducing emissions from Ancient Carbon, a wise strategy for sure, but it pays inadequate attention to the importance of Living Carbon as part of appropriate carbon stewardship. We contemplate removing huge amounts of organic matter for bio-energy from the forest landscape of central British Columbia devastated by the mountain pine beetle. The bioenergy thus generated offsets our demand on Ancient Carbon. Yet by removing this Dead Carbon do we not jeopardize, and potentially starve the Living Carbon of the forests? We may potentially increase the risk of that Living Carbon (the ecosystem) being transformed rapidly into a different and non-forest ecosystem. With the tree canopy removed the soils warm leading to the conversion of organic matter to CO_2 and its release to the atmosphere. In some parts of the world forest ecosystems may be converted to the cultivation of plants to generate ethanol for biofuels. Again the focus is on Ancient Carbon replacement. What about the role of the Living Carbon of the forest as a source of food, materials and employment? What about its role in moderating local climate and hydrology, preventing erosion and scrubbing carbon dioxide from the atmosphere, never mind the loss of biodiversity? Appropriate stewardship of Living Carbon is at least as important as reducing dependence on Ancient Carbon, and forests have a particular role in both mitigating climate change and especially in adapting to it.

The range of values of forest ecosystems is well documented, particularly so with respect to human needs (Scientific Panel for Sustainable Forest Practices in Clayoquot Sound 1995: Table 1 for a thorough summary). The importance to and role of forests in the global carbon equation (See Kurz and Apps 1999 as an example) however has not been well articulated and is poorly understood by the public and policy makers. By and large the focus seems to be on planting trees as a mechanism to mitigate climate change by removing CO_2 from the atmosphere in the future. This mechanism is widely recognized as a way of off-setting carbon emissions and gaining carbon credits (Wilson

and Hebda 2008). Yet concerning atmospheric CO_2, a more effective approach with immediate return, is to *avoid converting any more forests to alternate uses.* This effect is particularly obvious in the conifer forests of British Columbia which contain huge amounts of Living and Dead Carbon, in the order of 357 tons of carbon per 2.5 acres (Kurz and Apps 1999).

Converting a forest to a field or urban use disturbs the natural vegetation and soil and releases carbon dioxide rapidly to the atmosphere as bacteria, fungi and other organisms decompose organic matter. Carbon dioxide release continues for many decades until decomposable organic matter is used up or plants reoccupy the site and contribute abundant Dead Carbon to the soil. Reforestation of a field or severely degraded forest does not reverse the CO_2 loss for decades because the original organic material continues to decompose until the new trees begin accumulating large amounts of biomass (Living Carbon) and producing litter that is stored in the soil. In comparison, undisturbed old-growth forests continue to remove carbon from the atmosphere and contribute it to the soil at a slow but steady pace and certainly do not rapidly emit large amounts of CO_2 (Wilson and Hebda 2008).

Much is yet to be learned about forest ecosystems and their carbon balance, particularly how the rate of release and scrubbing of CO_2 varies in different regions with different ecosystem types, degree of disturbance and stage of succession (Nabuurs et al. 2007). Nevertheless, a forest left is much better than a forest taken by many measures including those of climate change, a point explicitly made by the IPCC (Nabuurs et al. 2007:543.)

A forest left, however, is not a forest preserved as if in a museum case. As I have already

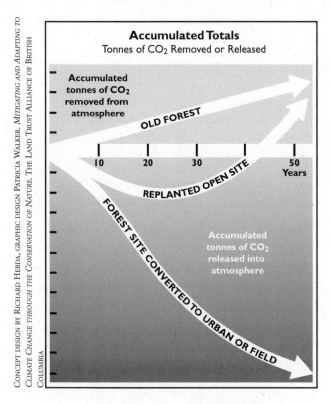

CONCEPT DESIGN BY RICHARD HEBDA, GRAPHIC DESIGN PATRICIA WALKER. *MITIGATING AND ADAPTING TO CLIMATE CHANGE THROUGH THE CONSERVATION OF NATURE*. THE LAND TRUST ALLIANCE OF BRITISH COLUMBIA

Accumulated Totals
Tonnes of CO_2 Removed or Released

Accumulated tonnes of CO_2 removed from atmosphere

OLD FOREST

REPLANTED OPEN SITE

10   20   30   50 Years

FOREST SITE CONVERTED TO URBAN OR FIELD

Accumulated tonnes of CO_2 released into atmosphere

Release vs removal of CO_2 from coast forests: Management options

ensure that they contribute their key carbon functions, and *third* to foster the many values forests provide. In British Columbia the Ministry of Forests and Range (2006) specifically has identified resilience as the focal attribute in preparing for climate change.

Ecological management strategies

Forest management is an ecological exercise. It involves the manipulation of stand structure and composition, of individual species to reap timber, of non-timber forest products and other values all of which demand an appreciation and understanding of ecology. Planting, thinning, fertilizing, sheep grazing, selecting seed stocks and insect pest management are all ecological experiments designed to enhance varied and often specific values. The decades of knowledge gained through repeated experimentation by forest practitioners has allowed us to manage forest ecosystems and produce more and better timber while still, in places, sustaining a variety of other values.

However, the ecological framework within which we have gained our management experience is undergoing a transformation such that our empirical and experimental knowledge may no longer apply fully, or at least apply on a limited scale or in different places. The ecological changes ahead pose enormous challenges because they require thinking about shifting targets. For example consideration of secondary interactions such as those involving pest-host relationships must be included; these may control what can grow, how well and where. In the overall context, fine-scale tinkering and manipulation with genetic stocks and adjustments in silviculture or wildlife prescriptions will not suffice. Strategies based on broad ecological principles are

outlined, our forests will change no matter what we do because some climate change is unavoidable. Furthermore forests contribute to our well-being and sustenance in many critical ways and are the cultural and economic lifeblood of so many communities around the globe. Particularly with respect to the potential of removing and storing carbon from the atmosphere, *collaborating* with forest ecosystems has considerable mitigation potential (Nabuurs et al. 2007).

From the perspective of climate change and fostering of key forest values, we need to engage in a wide range of forest management strategies, *first* and foremost among them to ensure that forest ecosystems remain resilient to survive climate driven changes, *second* to needed, especially those involved during times of instability.

First we need to develop climate-change sensitivity maps in anticipation of species range shifts and ecosystem transformations. These maps will serve to alert us to geographic areas and ecosystems of particular concern and help to devise appropriate and admittedly experimental management approaches. For silviculture this may involve trialing new species planting mixes and management measures. In some cases, such as in parts of southern interior British Columbia, the future climate may support no forest at all (Hebda 2007), the consequences of which need to be considered.

Second we must understand better how forests work. In British Columbia we have an excellent grasp of forest types, their distribution and climatic boundaries (Meidinger and Pojar 1991). However our knowledge of key ecological drivers such as soil formation, the role of mycorrhizae and many others is rudimentary. Once we understand what the essential ecosystem characteristics (Harewell et al. 1999) of each forest type are, then we can foster and conserve them, or at least appreciate which ones we cannot affect. Today many of our forest management strategies are highly reductionist, focused on elements such as timber, endangered species and wildlife trees rather than on the forest as a whole. These are biological and ecological elements that we often try to enhance without a full understanding of the functioning of the entire system. A return to system rather than element appreciation and management is central in fostering resilience, which represents the capacity of the system to withstand stress.

Third, we have to approach our forests from the perspective of the landscape scale (Hebda 1994). Species shifts are expected to extend over hundreds of miles and hundreds of yards in elevation (Hebda 1997). The requirement for maintaining and re-establishing landscape scale connections for natural migration to take place is well understood. Maintaining a diversity of habitat types on the landscape is also an important strategy for providing a diversity of opportunities for species to exploit as they adjust to new conditions. Species move, forest ecosystems do not. We cannot possibly anticipate how each species may find its way to a new ecological and geographic space, and practically we cannot intervene on the scale required in the adjustment processes that will take place. Strategies that focus on specific sites are at considerable risk of failure because local effects of climate change are impossible to foresee. Essentially landscape scale management distributes the risk of failure over a large area increasing the likelihood of success.

Fourth, now is a time for wide scale experimentation with adaptation strategies — thinking and practicing outside the box. The establishment of a network of experimental seed testing nurseries and plots having a wide range of genetic diversity can provide information on pre-adapted stock. By monitoring growth over a wide range of climates we can detect positive and negative responses to climate change and anticipate locations where facilitated migration (moving species beyond their natural range) can be attempted. In a similar manner there is a need to try a wide range of forest management techniques, from leaving the forest ecosystem alone to intervening intensively. In some cases, raising timber trees may best be carried out by intensive management of ecologically intelligent plantations as a way of reducing risk and countering uncertainty. Similarly, specific forest values might be enhanced and exploited in limited areas while letting the rest of the forest landscape function more holistically. The experimentation needs to include different types of land tenure, such as small woodlots, too, where more people interact with the forest in a more diffuse and diverse manner, a strategy that has potential to generate a wide range of much needed knowledge.

Fifth, to as wide an extent as possible, we have to limit major disturbance in forested ecosystems. Fischlin et al. (2007) point out that the acute threat to global ecosystems and their processes is not just climate change, but the combination of climate change and continuing overexploitation, conversion and degradation by people. Human disturbance and degradation usually weakens ecosystems, has negative impacts on species and alters key processes. All of these contribute to loss of resilience and predispose forests to catastrophic conversion to alternate states. Furthermore many non-natural types of disturbance (fragmentation by conversion for example) deplete native biodiversity, reducing options for the future. In the high risk situation of climate change, keeping as many of the biological pieces for the future, fostering and supporting complexity are vital strategies. Complexity and connections allow for internal functional replacements as some species are affected by climate change more than others.

Restoring forest health and integrity is part of the strategy of limiting and reversing disturbance. The field of restoration ecology has advanced widely in the past two decades. It includes not only the return of forest structure, composition and function but acknowledges the importance of human needs. We are going to need every bit of forest functioning to its capacity. Initiatives to replant native species, restore wildlife trees, reduce local atmospheric pollution, rehabilitate streams and their riparian zones are key especially in urban and agricultural zones.

Sixth, the threat of invasive species requires special attention. Invasive plants and animals are mostly well-adapted to disturbance. They have the capacity to increase their number and disperse widely. In so doing they alter the natural paths of succession and even invade apparently intact ecosystems weakened or challenged by insects, drought or over-harvesting. Often, uncommon species may linger for decades until some minor evolutionary event gives them a competitive advantage. Furthermore a non-native species may harbor genetic pre-adaptations to new conditions that arise with climate change. In the last decade on Vancouver Island, a relatively innocuous evergreen shrub, laurel-leaved daphne, has spread explosively invading and overtaking the apparently natural understorey of intact conifer forests. We also need to resist introducing foreign species with what may appear at first to be sound intentions such as restoring eroding surfaces, improving the rate of carbon uptake or increasing timber production. Our responsibility must first be our native forest ecosystems and their biodiversity. Introduction of other species from distant continents should be viewed only as last resort. Monitoring for and control of vigorous invasive species is an imperative adaptive strategy for climate change (Fraser Basin Council 2004).

Seventh, where widespread direct human use of the forest is involved, we must strive to achieve multiple benefits over as long an interval as practical. The degradation or conversion of forested land for single-use, short-term purposes delays, reduces or sometimes eliminates a wide range of future values. In the context of

THE LAND CONSERVANCY

Big leaf maple

climate change some of these values will undoubtedly be vital to mitigation and adaptation. Ensuring water supply and preventing catastrophic floods must certainly be more important than clearcut logging. Preventing loss of Living and Dead Carbon and the diversity it supports by clearing forests must certainly be more important than growing crops to produce biofuels.

Eight, to meet the challenges and opportunities posed by imminent forest transformation we need skilled and informed people. Training at both the conceptual and practical level is imperative as is the education of individuals and communities. Our globalized society has become disconnected from the reality and function of our forests. We need people informed and practiced at all levels of knowledge, from academic scholars who probe the principles of primary processes to local forest managers who know each tree in its place. Local forest stewards understand their forest ecology and

people's use of resources. They need to be well connected to their local community and other practitioners in order to contribute and integrate local ecological knowledge and feed it up to the broader regional scale and to theoreticians and policy makers. Only in this way will we know what worked and what did not, what changes are evident in the forest and what implications they may have for forest integrity.

Our forests will be transformed within the next human lifetime. Our relationship with these globally pivotal entities will have to shift from a focus largely on exploitation to one of stewardship and support. Future forests will not only have to support traditional values but will have to retain and accumulate even more carbon to reduce global warming. By shifting our focus we can foster and sustain biodiversity for an uncertain future. Forests for people, yes, and for the planet too!

Aboriginal Forests, Innu Culture
and New Sustainable Economics

Tom Green

Clyde Wells, then Premier of Newfoundland and Labrador (a province in the Northeastern corner of Canada), was the only person in the large canvas tent not seated on fragrant balsam boughs. Too dignified to sit at ground level, the premier was given a five gallon bucket of pork-in-brine from which to hold audience. It was the summer of 1991, and this was the first meeting between a Newfoundland premier and the Innu to be held within Nitassinan, their traditional territory. The meeting was the culmination of an Innu blockade days earlier. The blockade went up after the province's Forestry department began extending a logging road further through a scrawny boreal forest into the heart of Innu hunting territory. The Innu refused to take down the blockade until the premier came in person to their territory to hear their grievances.

For over two hours as the tin woodstove crackled away and as endless kettles of tea were passed through the tightly packed crowd, speakers told of the Innu's communal ownership of the forest since time immemorial and their rejection of Newfoundland's claim to this same land. With great passion, they told of the Innu relationship with the forest; how hunting was deteriorating as trees were carted away on the growing network of roads, roads which also provided non-Innu hunters easy access to game. They also attacked the province's approach to forestry, the assumption that stands could be clearcut every 140 years in this cold, harsh climate, and that wildlife would not suffer. They were steadfast in their refusal to see the forest liquidated for a few short-term jobs in far away communities.

The premier appeared to be listening carefully and respectfully; I had hope. Might a new relationship between Innu and the province, and between the province and these northern forests emerge from this historic meeting? Might the province see the wisdom of leaving most of these forests unroaded, might stands of diminutive spruce, balsam and larch be left to go through their cycle of growth, fire and rebirth?

At last the premier spoke, and my hope evaporated. The premier explained that the province had to manage resources for the economic benefit of all Newfoundlanders, and that both fiber and jobs were central to the Newfoundland economy. The Innu's complex portrait of the relationship between forests and themselves, their advocacy for a more ecologically grounded basis for forestry decisions was unable to penetrate the premier's vision of progress, of what a healthy economy looked like.

The premier's reliance on economic rationale for proceeding with status quo industrial forestry was quite unremarkable. Variations on this story have been repeated countless times in different locales around the world. Mainstream economic reasoning is used to sanction decisions that have social and ecological implications, often of great consequence to a less powerful party such as the Innu. It is the trump card that is played to justify or sway decisions. This economic trump card can be beaten only by another trump card from the same suit of economic reasoning.

I owe it to the premier of Newfoundland, sitting on a bucket of pickled pork, to make blatantly apparent the inadequacies of mainstream economics when it came to issues of human rights, of complex ecosystems, of the relationships between humans and their environment and of human well-being. The premier's economic rationalization of resource liquidation policies eventually pushed me to become an *ecological economist*, and for this I thank him. Ecological economics gives me hope that wiser decisions that sustain both humans and ecosystems are possible. Nonetheless, the mainstream carries on as before. A revolution in economic thinking is needed.

Economic assumptions

It is the metaphysics of mainstream economics that most erodes prospects for the world's forests. Every society needs a belief system which helps explain societal arrangements and thereby diminishes social tensions. Such belief systems bless certain activities and condemn others. Industrial market societies are no different, and with the declining influence of organized religion under scientific progress and secularization, economics has admirably evolved to serve this function.[1]

There are four metaphysical assumptions underlying virtually all economic analysis. The *first* is that economists assume that progress will improve the human condition. The *second* assumption is that economic efficiency is desirable. The *third*, which is closely related to the first two assumptions, is that economic growth is beneficial and necessary. The *fourth* is that markets are, by and large, the best institution for allocating society's resources and that they emerge spontaneously and must be left to self-regulate rather than being shaped by society.

Assumption one: Progress improves the human condition

Economic progress is increased availability of resources for productive and consumptive uses. This emphasis on material progress originates with the economist's perspective that humans were born into scarcity, where the threat of starvation and insufficient food and shelter was ever present. As economists see it, humans react to this scarcity by being selfish and having insatiable desires. These reactions can lead to conflict and vice, but if an era of abundance can be brought about, humans will experience less strife and greater harmony. Heaven can be established on earth. Once a state of plenty is reached, there will be no need to ask about distribution of wealth. This economic progress must harness those very selfish, greedy qualities and motivate each individual to do their part to maximize total output.

Present day economists fail to recognize that for their beloved markets to function, certain shared values, norms and institutions (laws, judges, courtrooms, police) must exist. They also neglect to examine how property owners came to hold title; was the process just and based on effort or was common property privatized at the expense of the broader community? Or worse, were some indigenous people dispossessed of their land and resources? Economists fail to recognize how Adam Smith's invisible hand, by motivating each to do their part in maximizing total output, now threatens global society as production and consumption exceed ecological limits. Nor do economists see how progress and expanding markets imply that all cultures and regions are subject to profound transformation under the forces of competition and technological progress — the lament we hear in "pave paradise, put up a parking lot."[2] People affected may not welcome the transformation of their society and culture entailed by the need to adapt to the market's competitive drive and the need to produce that which sells. Finally, economists by and large neglect how the invisible hand comes with an invisible foot: parties to market transactions neglect those costs which accrue to those beyond their handshake.

Assumption two:
Economic efficiency is desirable

Economists have an understanding of efficiency that is very different from that commonly understood. To an economist an efficient outcome is one where total output and consumption is maximized and where the winners from a decision could compensate the losers (but in effect, almost never compensate the losers). So a decision to log an indigenous people's territory and plant soybeans can be efficient if the value of the additional wealth created by liquidating the forest and growing soybeans is greater than the value of the resources used up logging the land and growing crops and the hypothetical cost of compensating the indigenous people.

Ecologically speaking, it would be hard to conclude the decision to log the forest could be deemed *efficient*: a diverse forest that likely coevolved with its indigenous inhabitants has been replaced with a soybean monoculture. From the indigenous people's perspective (assuming they have not consented to the wholesale transformation of their forests) they have likely suffered a violation of human rights. From a social justice perspective, the decision may be undemocratic and unfair. Although the decision adds to society's total wealth, if all that incremental wealth ends up in the hands of a few millionaires while the rest of society is no better off (or indeed, ends up burdened with higher taxes to cover welfare payments for the now impoverished indigenous tribe), the average person would not tend to see the outcome as efficient.[3]

However, economists have trained themselves to be silent on such matters. In the quest to be scientific, the mainstream economist has had little to say about distribution or fairness. Many economists go into economics because they want to contribute to alleviating poverty — and yet, tragically, by the time they finish their training they confuse increasing total output with improving the lot of the poor. And as standard theory recognizes, public goods — such as clean air and water, national parks — are not supplied by markets and are hence without market value. This makes public goods very difficult to incorporate into economic analysis. For all these reasons and more, market values are inevitably and pervasively distorted, mostly against sustainability.

Assumption three: Economic growth is desirable

A couple of generations of economists have been working away on economic growth theory — trying to understand when it occurs and how it can be brought about. Much of their work takes off from equations that have the following form, where income or output is modeled as a function of capital and labor.

VICTORIA STEVENS

$$Y = F(K,L) = A \; Ka \; Lb$$
Y = Income or output
K = Capital
L = Labor
A = Technology
a and b are positive parameters

Note here that there are only two variables — capital and labor — and that by increasing the input of either, economic growth results. Now naïve folks who have actually stood beside a standing tree, taken a blade to it, watched it fall and seen it carted off to the mill, might wonder why natural resources do not enter the equation. After all, economies seem to need wood, cement, steel, energy and the like — and especially so when they are growing. With growth, increasing affluence tends to result in increased consumption which draws on natural resources and has environmental impact.[4]

It turns out that back when populations were small and resources seemed unlimited, economists decided that resources could be

Pollinators

omitted from their growth models without much loss in explanatory power. This intellectual laziness has had dire results. A couple of generations of economists, the high priests of industrial society, have learned that resource exhaustion is a non-issue that worries only those who are economically ignorant. They have passed this falsehood onto broader society through introductory economics courses and their role as advisors and pundits.

Also missing from the mainstream model of economic growth is the waste side of the equation. Human prospects are increasingly undermined from overuse of *sinks*, such as the accumulating levels of carbon dioxide in the atmosphere and accumulating amounts of heavy metals and persistent organic pollutants in the biosphere. As well, this mainstream growth model is totally ignorant of issues such as habitat fragmentation and the disruption of natural processes and how this can compromise ecosystem integrity and thereby the benefits that humans derive from ecosystems.

Assumption four: Markets regulate themselves and benefit all

Adam Smith thought that because humans had a propensity to *truck and barter,* markets emerged and spread spontaneously and inevitably to fulfill this need. The evidence is quite the contrary. Markets are the results of frequent and forceful government intervention through legislation, force and other institutions. For instance, markets became increasingly important in England as a result of the enclosure laws, the strengthening of property rights and the use of courts to enforce contracts. We can see the phenomenon of markets being forcibly expanded in our own era as well: governments have granted patents over life forms such that seeds, formerly the common property of farmers, increasingly become the private property of corporations.

Unless social safety nets are put into place, there is no limit to the potential exploitation of workers, and they are left highly vulnerable to the turbulent path implied by capitalism's *creative destruction* as new firms and new technologies displace old ones. Rather than markets being a useful human invention that, under certain constraints implemented democratically, can serve human needs, humans and society have become subservient to ensuring that markets are efficient and expanding whatever the cost.

With economists mesmerized by markets, it is natural that they should also have fallen in love with private property and are dismissive of collective and common property. When it comes to forestry, they have encouraged the privatization of forests in order to ensure that the forest owner has the incentive to replant and manage the forest for the long term. What this fails to understand is that the property owner's interests are to maximize

revenues from timber production. The broader ecosystem services and cultural values supported by forests do not affect the property owner's bottom line, so the manager will have an incentive to grow fiber rather than to be a steward of a functioning forest.[5]

If private property were indeed the answer to stewardship, one would expect a visit to the extensive tracts of private land managed by big companies on Vancouver Island to be a model worth replicating. Instead, one finds stands that are aggressively clearcut on short rotations — this on land where stand replacing events were rare, old growth conditions were the norm and trees often lived 500 or more years. These private forest lands are not forests, but ecologically impoverished fiber plantations devoid of much of their original inhabitants.

Much economic theory has sloppily confused open access resources (which are unmanaged and where a free-for-all exists) with common property resources (where various institutions, norms and sanctions act to constrain resource exploitation by users). There are many instances where forests have been managed as common property resources or have been retained as public property while maintaining a broader set of values and where ecosystem health over time. I saw this first hand when I worked with the Harrop Proctor community in BC as they developed a business plan to manage the forests that made up their watershed. The community prioritized ecosystem integrity and the health of their water supply over timber production. And timber production was but one of several economic opportunities they saw their forests supporting. The objective was not to maximize the net present value of income over expenses, but rather to manage prudently so as to achieve economic viability while ensuring jobs and a range of other benefits flowing to the local community in perpetuity. In the developing world, forests formerly successfully managed as common property by communities were forcibly brought into state and/or private ownership. The subsequent focus on fiber production to the neglect of fuel, fodder and other resources for local use resulted in both local impoverishment and ecosystem degradation.[6]

The supposed virtue of markets has also allowed economists to avoid asking awkward questions about the end uses of the various goods and services that an economy produces. Well functioning markets are seen to ensure that each good or service goes to its best and highest use. If the millionaire is going to pay more for a bundle of lumber to add a deck to his mansion than a nonprofit can pay for it to build basic shelter for the homeless, it would be inefficient, from the economist's perspective, to divert the lumber from the higher-paying millionaire. Perhaps a dozen people will die of cold because the shelter is not built, but still, since the millionaire is willing to pay more, it must be the higher end use. Economists have disqualified themselves from incorporating into their analysis any differentiation between wants and needs — and in a limited, highly populated world, an important distinction needs to be made between the two.

Valuation to the rescue?

The values and analytical framework presumed by mainstream economics is largely hostile to a prudent relationship between humanity and forests. As the extent of deforestation and degradation of forest ecosystems has become increasingly apparent, some economists and activists have sought to use economic analysis to further forest conservation and stewardship. It is true that economists can help design effective eco-levies and to help green the tax system. Such measures are indeed needed, urgently needed. They provide the price signals that influence consumption and investment decisions, shifting for instance whether individual forest owners can earn their livelihood as a wise steward of their forest or whether they must log aggressively to pay their taxes.

Economists have also offered their skills to assign values to ecosystem services. By incorporating the value of these ecosystem services into the economic calculus, it is argued, greater protection of ecosystems will result as decision makers consider these missing values. Based on both theoretical considerations and my involvement in valuation exercises, I am not so optimistic. I've provided technical advice to both the British Columbia government and NGOs on ecosystem valuation, in both instances reluctantly in default of a willingness to use an ecological economics approach. The results of such studies do not necessarily help forest conservation. For instance, one relatively recent study evaluated the optimum amount of old-growth preservation in British Columbia and concluded that under certain *conservative* assumptions, too much primary forest was being protected.[7]

Real sustainability requires deeper change

I'd much rather see economists being forthright about the modest capabilities of their craft and being explicit about the values underlying their analysis. Instead of engaging in costly valuation exercises that may do little to influence what happens in the forest, they should be focused on two things. The *first* is revisiting the implicit assumptions of mainstream economics around progress, efficiency, growth and self-regulating markets. The *second* is helping communities and enterprises find opportunities to support well-being over the long term within sustainability constraints. *In other words, in a wild forestry context, how does one make a living and sustain fully functioning forests that probably benefit society?*

An ecological economics approach[8] requires studying the ecosystem, deliberation over end goals and the values at stake, and transparent, democratic decision making. Also, attention is required to issues of fairness. Forest management issues are at their heart ecological, political and ethical in nature. Then, within these constraints designed to protect both ecosystems and society, the market mechanism can play its useful role. Economists can help community forests explore alternative business plans.

If means were found to help neighbors learn to share decks (or even better, houses) total well-being could increase while pressure on forests could be reduced as resources were used more efficiently (one deck serving two or three families). But the mainstream economists of today would in a world of such sharing detect a diminishment in economic activity and might incorrectly conclude that society was worse off. This illustrates why economic development in the industrialized nations in particular should be reconceptualized as including anything that allows for doing more with less — and also expecting less. Lord Layard, a respected British economist, notes the increased well-being that results when people learn to be happy with what they have.[9] Encouraging people to resist expanding expectations is not an argument to convince poor people to accept their lot in life, but a warning of the futility built into the consumer economy. That economy requires ever increasing consumption and thereby needs to generate ever expanding desires or needs. People were once happy sitting on picnic blankets — perhaps the deck and the wood to build it are not needed at all.

Bringing values back into the market

Key to sustaining forests is recognizing that norms and values must factor into markets. There are two main ways values can influence market transactions. First, and most effective because of its binding nature, society should draw on values to shape the marketplace — setting rules on what can be exchanged and how. Second, producers and consumers bring values into their individual marketplace transactions, and these values change the markets.

Customers of wood products, from the individual furniture maker to the large-scale housing developer, need to be interested in how timber was produced, both ecologically and socially. The house buyer should be concerned about how the developer sourced raw materials. Within reason, community forest enterprises (and ideally, enterprises more generally) should prioritize selling their output towards users who address needs rather than wants (or per the Lorax thneeds[10]), even if this diminishes profitability. Investors should tone down their expectations for high rates of return on investment and focus on enabling enterprises that are diligently working to be sustainable and whose output meets human needs.

However, it would be naïve to think that one could solve the world's problems by depending on consumers, producers and investors to voluntarily bring ecological and social considerations into their marketplace decisions. In most buying and selling, particularly as economies have globalized, we know little about the history of a product: how it was produced, where the raw materials came from, how labor was treated and the consequences of disposing of it once it is used up. Reliable information is hard to come by, and we don't have the time to assess each product individually. Many people, out of necessity, lack information or concern — and because it is what we have been socialized to do — default to whatever is cheapest. Therefore, society needs to put constraints on markets. Certain types of market exchanges must be blocked. Just as society deemed the selling and buying of humans to be unacceptable and thus made slavery illegal, so society can decide that logging the last remnants of an endangered species' habitat is unacceptable.

Unfortunately, at present governments are so beholden to corporate interests and blinded by the progress myth and free market ideology, that they are unwilling to set sustainability and ethical constraints on market transactions. Civil society has responded to this vacuum in leadership in various ways to constrain the corrosive potential of the market and to ensure more desirable outcomes.[11] A prime example of this is the Forest Stewardship Council certification scheme, which although imperfect, generally asks the right questions for buyers and sellers: how was this forest managed for ecological values, how were rights of indigenous peoples and workers respected, can the output be sustained over time? Organizations such as Greenpeace and ForestEthics have engaged in marketplace campaigns to pressure corporations to shun wood from endangered forests.

To sustain the world's forests we must build on the recognition that forests — however owned — are the common heritage of humankind upon which we are all ultimately dependent. Governments must be pressured incessantly to take up their responsibilities to ensure forest stewardship both at home and by ensuring that imports meet sustainability requirements. Rich countries must also find ways to help poor nations sustain their forests and must avoid activities that degrade forests (hence, climate change-inducing economic activities must be brought under control). International trade and financial institutions need to have policies and financing that enable investments in forest ecosystem conservation and community forestry while making life difficult for rogue loggers.

Ultimately, sustaining the world's forests will require many higher level economic changes that appear radical given the recent triumph of neoliberal economic theory and policy.[12] To avoid deck versus shelter trade-offs, a much more equitable distribution of income is needed both within and between nations. Guaranteed minimum incomes are required to avoid the poor despoiling forests out of necessity. Likewise, maximum income levels are needed to avoid the rich having excessive ecological footprints. Ecologically harmful production and consumption needs to be reduced through regulations and taxes, while societies must put in place incentives and find the funds to ensure ecosystem restoration and stewardship. More emphasis must be placed on designing policies and institutions to augment and sustain common property resources.[13]

Hopeful trends in economics

The policy changes advocated in this chapter face resistance from conventional wisdom as informed by economic theory. There are signs that, at last, there is some relevant intellectual debate within the tent of mainstream economics, and some of its most respected members are increasingly critical of the discipline's core assumptions and beliefs. For instance, Joseph Stiglitz, Nobel laureate and former Chief Economist of the World Bank, has written critically about globalization. He is deeply concerned about global environmental prospects. He is clear that there is no valid intellectual defense for market fundamentalism and writes "the reason that the invisible hand seems invisible is that it is not there. Without appropriate government regulation and intervention, markets do not lead to economic efficiency."[14]

Economists are at last beginning to pay more attention to other fields such as psychology and recognizing that consumption does not equate to well-being. By actually delving into what enables happiness, the futility of much of what was conventionally labeled as progress becomes apparent. For instance, beyond a certain threshold increased income and consumption does little to improve well-being. Much more important to happiness is whether we have meaningful work, time with friends and family, good health. Happiness research also points to the well-being enhancing possibilities enabled by income redistribution, since additional income for the rich doesn't do much to their happiness but greatly improves the lot of the impoverished. This allows a shift from a *survival of the fittest* society to one able to show solidarity for those who are less fortunate or able. At last, economics will come around to recognizing that society is not just an agglomeration of atomic individuals, but that we are members of families and communities, nations and ultimately one planet. If human well-being is a key measure of success, economists can no longer sanctify a policy or project merely because it enhances output or is economically efficient. A collaborative, transdisciplinary exploration of ecological limits, of society's desired ends and values, of

Shinto shrine, Japan

ARIYOSHI ICHIRO

different options and their fairness become essential.

There are further encouraging trends in the field of development economics. The harsh realities faced by so much of the world's population have forced development economists to focus more on ensuring actual improvements of the conditions of the poor rather than assuming improvements in macroeconomic indicators such as GDP will automatically improve the lot of the poor. The concept of development has broadened to be "about the fulfillment of human potential, in all its dimensions — for each and every one. It's about economic as well as political democracy."[15] Furthermore, development economists increasingly recognize the importance of a healthy environment in supporting human well-being.

Finally, ecological economics is likely to have considerable effect on mainstream economics over than next couple of decades. The evidence is now clear for all to see: humanity is overstepping nature's limits; we have a collective ecological footprint that overshoots our one planet's biocapacity. The specter of resource depletion is clear to see with examples like the ocean's commercial fish stocks predicted to be wiped out by 2048.[16] Economic analyses must be based on a solid model of ecosystem and economy linkages.

Taken together, the likely evolution of economic theory to a more realistic, interdisciplinary, gendered and ecologically savvy theory should help undermine the use of economics and economic analysis as a means of sanctioning forest liquidating activities and policies which pursue economic growth for its own sake. Sustainable economics will support wild forestry, community forestry, public ownership of forests and their management for human well-being.

Back to the Innu forests

It has been almost two decades since the Innu blockade on the forest access road. Through their persistent efforts, the Innu Nation was able in 2001 to get the Province of Newfoundland to agree to a process whereby an ecosystem-based plan would be jointly developed for the area in question. The planning team adopted the following guiding vision:

> To create an ecosystem-based forest management plan ... that protects ecological and cultural integrity, productive capacity, resiliency and biodiversity while advancing economic opportunities for the sustainable development of forest-based industries.[17]

It's perhaps not the perfect vision statement — note the lack of emphasis on human well-being, the emphasis on industries rather than conceiving of the economy as including both commercial activities and other forms of sustenance and human activities. Yet it is a hopeful sign of how much can and has changed. Under the resulting ecosystem-based plan, the likelihood that the Innu's relationship with the forest can be sustained over time and that future generations visiting these forests will indeed see forests is much improved.

Creating Institutions of Care —
The Case for Democratic Forest Trusts

Gus diZerega

In a 1999 survey for the EPA and the President's Council on Sustainable Development between 60 and 70% of Americans indicated agreement with strongly pro-environmental values and beliefs (Ray and Anderson, 139-67). Most Americans also consider other political issues more important than environmental concerns, enabling politicians unsympathetic to environmental issues to wage and win campaigns on other grounds. Environmentally concerned citizens exist as fragmented and dispersed publics submerged within larger groups of usually friendly but uninvolved citizens. On environmental issues many concerned citizens are intermingled geographically with those for whom these issues are not important. Often a public concerned about a geographical area is dispersed beyond that area's boundaries. No democratic institutions exist that focus on environmental concerns alone. National Forests are one of the major casualties of this lack of institutional fit.

On the other hand, Native Americans such as Wisconsin's Menominee in governing their commons have managed a forest for 146 years, and it is more healthy and diverse than any other forest in the state, including national forests (Davis 2000). This is so even when they also engage in the market economy. This is because their institutions are responsive to deeper and more complex values than are contemporary, impersonal, modern ones. Traditional forms of organization can teach us but cannot be copied. However, the National Trust of England, Wales and Northern Ireland suggests a way similar values can be applied in a modern context. These insights build a case for democratic national forest trusts to govern American National Forests.

Forest preservation and most other environmental values based on particular areas of land and water are inadequately served by traditional democratic institutions in such countries as Canada and the US. We need to devise institutions of care for the natural world. Such institutions can help harmonize ethical and instrumental relationships in the world. Here I will make the case that institutions which preserve ecosystems are best rooted in civil society rather than in government or the economy. Richard Cornuelle termed this social realm the *independent sector*, a "third sector in our national life, the one which is neither governmental nor commercial" (Cornuelle, 26). His term is a good one.

National forests and public values

Our 147 National Forests represent public values for many — probably most — citizens. Within this context of support, the forests are sites of serious contention among citizens concerned with their well-being, but motivated by often conflicting priorities. These concerned citizens are immersed within a larger sea of citizens for whom these values are unimportant.

Usually those elected to serve the more inclusive community owe little in their victory to their views on national forests. Most elected representatives find forest well-being of little importance unless they have a personal commitment. The dispersed publics that do care for them have often been unable to protect these forests against assault by private interests or malfeasance by public agencies charged with protecting them, except through the courts. But policy by lawsuit is a poor way to administer anything.

The Mountain Maidu are a small group of Native Americans presently involved in implementing a tribal approach to forest management on 2,100 acres of Plumas National Forest. The Mountain Maidu are restoring the oak and pine woodlands that predominate in the lower elevations of that region of the Sierra Nevada. Loreena Gorbet, a tribal member, is coordinating activities with the US Forest Service.

In an account of their activities, Gorbet was quoted as saying the Mountain Maidu view themselves as deeply enmeshed within their natural landscape. "The plants and animals — they're our relatives. We talk to them to find out what they need." This is the language of relationship and ethical involvement. It is not the language of the US Forest Service. In Gorbet's words, to do her job she has had to learn to speak *Forest Service* (Little, 7). There is also a larger problem here. The Mountain Maidu are native to the place, the Forest Service to Washington, DC. Each is adapted to its own very different niche. This is why, as Jane Little writes, "the stewardship partners also approach forest management with diametrically different concepts of time. The Maidu's initial proposal involved a 99 year demonstration — an eternity to an agency that gets its funding on a year-by-year basis. The Forest Service eventually agreed to a ten year project" (Little, 7).

The Forest Service itself is about 100 years old; it was created largely through legislation passed between 1905 and 1911. It possesses a great deal of knowledge about the political ecosystem on which it depends. However, the Forest Service rotates its rangers on a regular basis, mostly to keep them loyal to the service rather than *going Native*. As a consequence, while rangers have considerable local knowledge about the Service and its traditions, they do not have nearly so much about the particular locality where they happen for the moment to be stationed (Kaufman, 155-6, 175-97). Like any large organization, the United States Forest Service's primary loyalty is to itself. Randal O'Toole emphasizes budgetary incentives as primary motivations behind USFS decisions; Nancy Langston emphasizes agency autonomy (O'Toole 1988; Langston 1995). The career and budgetary incentives facing the Service and its employees are dependent on political and economic processes long before they are dependent on scientific and ecological ones. Government agencies are focused on the budgetary year, and subordinate other values to it. There is a deep disconnect between the political feedback most important to the Service and ecological feedback helping it attend better to the health of our forests.

In addition, Congress is institutionally incapable of providing long-term oversight for our national forests. Occasionally it can adopt reforms and make wise decisions, but once made, the public pressure encouraging these reforms dissipates. Those who would undermine the reforms' intentions for financial gain patiently remain, to subvert the legislation as the opportunity arises and the public's attention wanes. Sometimes such approaches cannot be avoided, and these problems are simply the inevitable costs of getting things done that need doing. But if public values can be adequately served by institutions lacking both the power to tax and the capacity to pass laws, they will be freed from major sources of corruption and distortion.

The Progressive Era ideal of dispassionate scientific administration of our national resources never really existed in practice. The Bush administration should prove to even the most idealistic advocate of traditional political solutions that government is a poor protector of such values. Government agencies can successfully serve well-defined values with clear standards for success, such as landing a man on the moon or delivering social security checks. Performance plummets as the values they are to serve multiply and standards of attainment become vague (Wilson 1989, 113-136, 154-75). Multiple values and vague standards are characteristic of the complexities of our relationships with the natural world.

However, people have repeatedly devised institutions taking truly long run perspectives on our interactions with the natural world. The Menominee forest contains a varied forest community with many trees of old growth size and age. While only about twice the size of neighboring Nicolet National Forest, the Menominee cut twice the timber, with a saw timber cut thirty times greater. What we can learn from them is very important. First, it is possible for people to develop institutions able to sustain long-term human interactions with their environment. Second, their institutions are self-governing, their decisions not normally subordinated to any other body whose members were less concerned with the health of their lands. Third, these people do not manage their land to maximize their financial income. While their lands serve economic needs (and most people in any society would prefer more wealth to less), they also honor non-financial values in their decision making. Fourth, they know their lands personally and intimately and act accordingly. For us, the critical question is whether these enabling elements are robust enough to provide long-term protection and management even when people are mobile, individualistic and, despite good intentions, usually ignorant of the needs of any particular forest, let alone forest ecosystems in all their variety and complexity.

A way forward

Gary Snyder has written that the public domain in North America constitutes a kind of national commons "we are all enfranchised to work on" (Hardin 1968; Snyder 1990, 29). Unlike Garret Hardin's misleading use of the term, the village commons of the Middle Ages and of many other places and times were managed by the community in order to preserve the land from exploiters (Snyder 1990, 35-6; Ostrom 1990). But there is more to a commons than this. Snyder emphasized "the commons is both specific land and the traditional community institution that determines the carrying capacity for its subunits and defines the rights and obligations of those who use it, with penalties for lapses ... it is traditional and local" (Snyder 1990, 30).

Public lands are not governed by communities that care about them. Most politicians are uninterested in their fate, at least compared to other values, and their votes are up for grabs. So the basic requirement for a successful commons does not exist at the level of national administration. Consequently, Snyder advocated returning these public lands to regional control (Snyder 1990, 31). But what defines the region? The small Sierra Nevada watershed where he lived for many years was well suited to his vision. But many areas are larger and less well defined.

Some US political conservatives and advocates of western autonomy want to turn the public lands, including the National Forests, over to the states. But these are genuinely public lands, of great concern to millions of Americans who do not necessarily live in the states where they are located and whose taxes have long helped support these states and nearby communities. Simply living in a western state does not mean a person cares about these lands. More than one Westerner sees the land primarily through an accountant's eyes. No necessary connection exists between existing political boundaries and concerned publics.

State governments can be as open to other interests and little focused on their public lands as are the national governments. An early study comparing state to federal salmon protection observed "the greater vulnerability of the state conservation policies to pressure from groups whose interests may be injured by regulatory action and whose influence counts more in state capitals than it does in the larger arena of national politics" (Gregory and Barnes 1939, 39; quoted in Montgomery 2003, 143). This is as Founding Father James Madison would have expected: smaller polities are more vulnerable to influence by well organized factions pursuing private interests at the expense of the community as a whole.

Another strategy mentioned for forest reform is increasing local control over national forest policy via *collaborative conservation* that focuses on local solutions to local environmental problems by local stakeholders. It has been identified by many Americans as a promising solution to establishing viable environmental policies (Kemmis, 127-49; Brick et al. 2001). Daniel Kemmis, for example, emphasizes that due to the enormous amount of publicly owned land in most Western states, local citizens feel essentially colonized by a faraway power over which they have no influence, and towards which they have considerable resentment. He writes when Westerners "balance their experience of joining with old enemies to solve hard problems together against the hidebound procedures of a national government and a national democracy that no longer seem to work, they feel they are the real democrat" (Kemmis 2001, 226). Ideas such as Kemmis's are not simply theoretical. The Quincy Library group, consisting of people in extractive industries and environmentalists, devised by consensus a governing plan to cover three National Forests which won endorsement by 434 members of the House of Representatives.

There is much to recommend in collaborative models. However, with respect to National

Forests there is a basic weakness to purely local approaches to environmental management. Many, perhaps all, National Forests have a genuinely national constituency. Local control would freeze out from policy discussions many citizens with a strong interest in their well-being in favor of some who may care a great deal less. The political power that ended the Forest Service's rapid liquidation of all old growth forests came from aroused citizens at the national level, particularly in cities. Local communities were often deeply tied to business as usual even when that business threatened their long-term viability. Once issues become more complex than what can be addressed by local knowledge, many small communities are all but powerless in confrontations with ruthless large corporations, as the citizens of Libby, Montana, learned to their sorrow (Matthews 2000; Nijhuis 2003). Even with Quincy, the political strength possessed by local citizens proposing alternatives to logging came from being part of a national movement.

Yet local interests are disproportionately impacted by forest policies over which they exercise little to no control. Further, in many cases local knowledge and support will be vital components in developing effective policies able to be implemented successfully in a democratic system. Collaborative arguments focus on a key part of an effective solution to forest preservation, but define themselves too narrowly because they ignore the larger context of public values. They inappropriately apply a geographical conception of citizenship to an instance where it often does not fit. These interests deserve an important seat at the table, but they do not deserve all the seats.

The democratic forest trust

Institutions are needed that are responsive to Americans who care about the environment while circumventing interference by politicians who don't. In the case of our national forests these institutions also need to be open to all Americans, for they are public lands. Gary Snyder's focus on local inhabitants is politically impossible to implement in this case, and probably not altogether wise if it were, but his model of a commons remains perhaps

Russian River Morning, California

GUS DIZEREGA

the only viable alternative to the failures of corporate forestry or political management.

A democratic land trust suggests a practical solution to this challenge. The land trust concept offers an alternative institutional framework for managing forests that is also harmonious with the political realities of American democracy. Trusts are a time honored means by which a person or institution is charged with protecting and managing the property of another in trust. They are widely used in many areas of private life and are becoming increasingly important in private conservation efforts. Trusts have also been used by many Western states to manage their forests, primarily for the benefit of schools. However, these state trusts serve financial rather than broader public values. Their financial orientation makes them inadequate models for preserving our National Forests (Souder and Fairfax 1995, 44-53).

Land stewardship trusts remove land from the real estate market, enabling it to be managed — *stewarded* — on behalf of future generations (Banighan 1990; 1997). Land trusts are traditionally non-governmental, non-profit organizations created to preserve the ecological, historical, agricultural or wilderness value of the land. Land stewardship trusts focus on preserving and fostering sustainable forestry and agricultural practices, wildlife habitat and recreation. Because key property rights to the land are removed from the market *in perpetuity* or for an extended period, their economic value cannot be used as collateral for obtaining loans. Operating funds must come from other sources, such as fees, membership dues and donations. A firewall is erected between the land and domination by market forces. The price system guides but cannot command. Similarly, the law enables but does not control.

In the US, land trusts are increasingly relied upon to serve environmental values (Forbes 2001; Brewer 2003). However, the history of US land trusts is brief — usually under 25 years — and most American trusts are small. Most are also not internally democratic. These limitations give reasonable pause to anyone trying to adapt land trusts to the care and protection of our National Forests.

The National Trust of England, Wales and Northern Ireland is another matter; it celebrated its centenary in 1995. The National Trust's properties now extend to 612,000 acres (about 1000 square miles) in the UK, including almost 600 miles of coastline, about 18% of the total coastline of England, Wales and Northern Ireland. After the Crown, the National Trust is the largest landowner in the UK. It has over 3 million members, and unlike the US Forest Service is very popular. A similar trust also exists in Scotland. The National Trust's ability to incorporate ecological as well as historical values and its consistent acquisition of new land even in densely settled lands is impressive evidence of the concept's promise.

The National Trust has a substantial democratic component. Anyone can join and thereby obtains voting rights. As of 2005, The National Trust has a Council consisting of 52 members, 26 elected by its membership, another 26 appointed by outside bodies. Direct management of the National Trust is through an Executive Committee, under which are a number of decentralized Regional Committees. Far from lacking political debate, the National Trust is frequently the site of vigorous campaigns by members seeking changes in policies regarding hunting, recreational use and similar issues (Dwyer and Hodge 1996, 84).

Enabling legislation could be passed so that US National Forest Trusts could be established with primary responsibility for governing our National Forests; one trust for each forest. Membership in each Forest Trust would require only that members pay a fee covering their membership expenses in order to join. Judging from the dues of modern mass membership organizations, such expenses would not be high. However, the hurdle of having to pay to join a Trust would ensure that only people genuinely interested in the forest and its fate would usually take the time to join. Perhaps, as Karl Hess, Jr. suggested, work-trade arrangements could be made for people lacking the means to pay even these modest fees. Work would also likely commit the laborer far more strongly to the forest's well-being than simply writing a check.

Enabling legislation should make it possible for Forest Trusts to be formed only if there is substantial popular interest. Open procedures and membership and a means for ensuring a diversity of member perspectives would be required, but little more. Like a natural ecology, human communities are too complex for one-size-fits-all approaches. Organizational details would be up to the membership and its Governing Board. Apparently the very act of organizing a self-governing body helps to create the trust, skills and infusion of local knowledge that enables an organization to survive (Blomquist 1992; Ostrom 1990; Tang 1992, 32-3).

The number of citizens needed to create a Forest Trust should vary because National Forests themselves vary in size, proximity to citizens and public interest. Probably some formula reflecting both the number of annual visitors and the immediate population in the region would be best. Clearly different numbers should apply to Umatilla National Forest in eastern Washington and Oregon compared to Wenatchee National Forest near Seattle. In all cases numbers should be high enough to require sustained organizing and trust building to succeed, but low enough that such efforts have a reasonable chance of success.

The potential for a large American membership is high. The UK National Trust has 3 million members for a much smaller national population. Even when distributed among approximately 150 National Forests, each US Forest Trust would probably have many tens of thousands of members, some far more than that. Some members would be nearby residents, often involved in extractive or recreational industries using forest resources. Many more locals and non-locals alike would be people making personal recreational use of the forest, and some would likely be people simply concerned with its well-being.

A pilot project developed in California's Trinity County suggests the kind of alternative arrangements democratic Forest Trusts could institute. In 1997 a group of loggers, environmentalists, local contractors, Forest Service employees and concerned citizens met after the county's largest remaining employer, a sawmill in Hayfork, closed down. They sought to find a way to recover from the loss in jobs and the crisis the county was undergoing. Cecilia Danks writes "The group determined that a properly scaled, multiyear, multitask contract that addressed all the stewardship needs of a given tract could provide steady, long-season work that would improve both the biological health of the forest and the economic health of the community" (Danks 2003, 253).

As a result of these discussions, the Forest Service developed a contract oriented to the needs of the local communities and the needs

Victoria Stevens

Subalpine forest

of the forest. Local businesses won the bid, only to have it withdrawn later for lack of funding. Two more contracts along similar lines are currently being put together (Phone conversation with Lynn Jungwirth, Executive Director, Watershed Research and Training Center, Hayfork, CA). A democratic trust with considerable local membership would prove more compatible to following through with such opportunities to the benefit of both the forest and neighboring communities. The Menominee example of creating their own sawmill to handle cuts from their forest is an instructive example (Davis 2000).

Governance and funding

A US National Forest Trust would be established once enough would-be members have created an organization meeting legal requirements. To prevent one group from grabbing control of a board from the beginning, once created and certified, membership opportunities should be widely publicized for a year, after which election of the first Forest Trust Governing Board would occur. The Board would take over policy management after sufficient time has passed for consultation with the Forest Service during the transition.

Several possibilities for Board structure exist, and the one selected should be the choice of those joining the Trust. A board might be entirely democratically elected. Another might have a mix of elected and appointed members, such as from local university Departments of Forestry and Biology (Hess 1993). However, any less than fully elected Boards should be subject to periodic membership approval to guarantee their democratic character.

The Board would decide basic policy and select subcontracting agencies for their implementation. The USFS would probably subcontract its services to the Board. However, to ensure the Service's responsiveness, the Board must be able to contract with other agencies such as state departments of forestry. The option to choose another agency would keep the Forest Service responsive to the Board's priorities. It would have to adapt to them as well as it currently adapts to Washington, DC's political environment. Existing environmental laws such as the ESA, NEPA and other statutes would remain in force.

The trust would be responsible for raising enough money to meet its normal costs. User fees of many kinds would probably be major income sources but, unlike the USFS, policy decisions would be determined by citizen members, most with no personally significant financial stake in the trust's income. There are other potentially important resource sources. In many contemporary land trusts and even National Forests, volunteers provide considerable assistance. Additionally, private and foundation donations and grants could fund specific projects or, most importantly, help create a forest endowment that would grow over time. Given people's love for forests, it seems probable that in time endowments could become an important source of long-term financial viability. Unlike market-oriented models of reform or state forest trusts as they presently exist, National Forests would be under no institutional incentive to maximize profits. My emphasis differs here from Randal O'Toole's pioneering work. O'Toole proposed to fund trusts from net revenues, creating a powerful incentive to respond to market values

(O'Toole 1995). However, to serve public values, trusts should be institutions of civil society, and therefore partially independent from both government and market, and able to use any mix of revenue, donations and volunteer labor they can acquire. Lack of access to tax monies eliminates any incentives to subsidize extractive industries or other private interests. It also prevents Congress from using financial threats to interfere with forest policies. The forests would become much freer from political intervention by parties unconcerned with their long-term well-being.

One major problem would be the cost of fire suppression. While Congress will probably be willing to supply funding for such measures because they constitute considerable pork for local districts throughout the west, in the long run such an arrangement is undesirable. One alternative is for forests to take out insurance policies (Williamson, forthcoming). One advantage is that as the forest becomes less vulnerable to catastrophic wild fire premiums will go down; this should provide an additional incentive for wise management, the opposite of current circumstances.

In addition, forest trusts will be able to learn, adapt and resist institutional sclerosis. The trusts' internal and external polycentricity encourages openness and adaptability. Because there would be many trusts, each with responsibility for only one forest, membership would be focused on the needs of particular forests. With local members local knowledge would be as accessible as more general and abstract principles of forestry and ecosystem stewardship when determining policy options and value choices. The Internet easily allows every trust to have a website where a wide variety of information can easily be made accessible to members at a minimal cost, encouraging the exposure and correction of errors and dissemination of successes as they are discovered (Polanyi 1951, 71-84; Ostrom 1991, 223- 44).

Finally, compared to the needs of the electoral cycle, rate of interest, politics of the budget and even individual financial concerns, democratic forest trusts will have long time horizons. In the United States short term factors constitute legitimate elements of our social and political environment. But if they are the dominant institutional influences on environmental decision making, we can be sure that many shortsighted decisions will be made, with bad consequences for the forests themselves.

Most Americans already support environmental values. The trusts' independent status would be buttressed by millions of motivated citizen members opposing legislative overruling of trust self-governance in favor of private interests. They will already be organized and have close ties with the rest of society, protecting forests from Congressional and corporate intervention in their affairs. Further, they will have many non-member connections, as with sympathetic friends and family members. People who use the forest will observe for themselves the impact of managerial decisions. Renewal of directors through public debate and elections, where contrasting visions compete for the allegiance of voters deeply concerned with the forest's fate, would inhibit the rise of self-serving elites and in-grown administrations. Karyn Moskowitz and Randal O'Toole have written a suggestive discussion of how small communities and ranches can cope with today's changing rural environment (Moskowitz and O'Toole 1993; see also Best 2003 and Brighton 2003). However, unlike Moskowitz

and O'Toole, I think their proposal for a development trust should remain in the hands of the people with a personal more-than-financial interest in the region (diZerega 1998).

Conclusion

Environmental thinkers as different as bioregionalist Gary Snyder and free market economist Randal O'Toole have independently arrived at the insight that the commons model, where land is governed by a small number of people personally concerned with the land itself, is superior to both traditional private and traditional government management. The model creates an institution of care that does not fit into the sterile ideological boxes currently afflicting our society. It offers a practical framework buttressed by one hundred years of experience in England, suggesting that given appropriate institutional contexts, modern westerners can practice a wise and sustainable approach to the land. We, too, can plan in 99-year scale, like the Mountain Maidu.

(Editors' Note: This chapter was originally pubished in Alan Watson, Liese Dean, *Janet Sproull*, eds. 2005. *Science and stewardship to protect and sustain wilderness values: Eighth World Wilderness Congress symposium; 2005 September 30–October 6; Anchorage, AK.* Proceedings RMRS-P-000. US Department of Agriculture, Forest Service, Rocky Mountain Research Station.)

Transforming Ourselves, Renewing the Earth

Duncan M. Taylor and Graeme M. Taylor

Wild foresting practices exemplify the ability of both communities and forest ecosystems to remain sustainable over long periods of time. Living biological and social systems are sustainable as long as they are able to manage and adapt to change. Sustainability is a function of a system's ability to meet its needs and maintain health, wholeness and resilience. The global economic system is based on destructive views and values that promote competition, exploitation, inequality, fear, violence and waste. For a global system to be sustainable, it must be based on constructive values that enable environmental, social and individual needs to be fully met.

Global events are being shaped by two trends: the dominant trend towards collapse (due to biophysical limits on growth) and the emerging trend towards societal transformation. While the key elements of a sustainable system have begun to emerge, they are still very fragmented. We need to support their development through local initiatives such as those that are embraced in wild foresting. In turn, the Earth Charter is a cornerstone in this vision. The Earth Charter was mandated by the UN as a set of fundamental guiding principles for the 21st century based on the values of social justice and environmental sustainability and protection.

Our current civilization may very well destroy itself

The world as we know it is coming to an end. Industrial civilization will soon collapse because of a fatal flaw: it is designed to grow constantly within a finite planet. On every continent water tables are dropping, forests are disappearing, major fisheries are degrading, topsoil is eroding, oil and mineral discoveries are becoming rarer and more expensive to mine and the air is being polluted. Humanity is currently using 25% more renewable resources each year than the biosphere is producing (World Wildlife Fund 2006). This is deficit spending, which means that we are now consuming the biophysical foundations of our civilization.

The pace of environmental destruction is likely to accelerate: between the year 2006 and 2050 the world population is projected to increase from 6 billion to 8.9 billion (United Nations 2006), while world consumption is projected to almost quadruple (Poncet 2006). If present trends continue, global warming alone may cause the extinction of 25% of all existing animal and plant species within 50 years (Tidwell 2006).

Environmental and demographic trends alone indicate that the frequency, severity and scale of crises will escalate over the next two decades. These regional crises will progressively interact with each other to create global crises. A failing world economy will affect increasing numbers of people, who will begin to question the values and institutions of the current world order. At this point humanity will reach a bifurcation point: our unsustainable global civilization will either transform itself into a sustainable planetary system, or it will enter a prolonged period of escalating

Globalization marks the end of unexplored terrestrial frontiers. An economic system based on limitless growth is no longer viable.

Globalization: the end of unexplored terrestrial frontiers

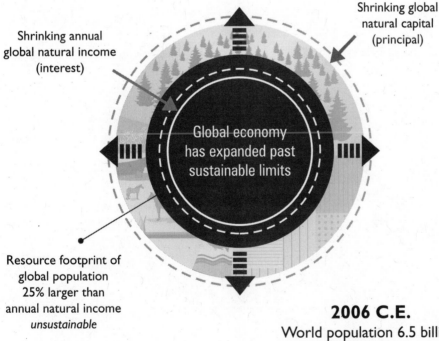

Shrinking annual
global natural income
(interest)

Shrinking global
natural capital
(principal)

Global economy
has expanded past
sustainable limits

Resource footprint of
global population
25% larger than
annual natural income
unsustainable

2006 C.E.
World population 6.5 billion
Global industrial economy
Consumer culture

Diagram not to scale

crises marked by the collapse of vital ecosystems, conflicts over disappearing resources, population decline, political fragmentation, economic and social regression. One way or the other the world as we know it will soon end.

Social systems are dependent on biophysical systems

The long-term viability of human societies is utterly dependent on the long-term viability of the biophysical systems that support them. Consequently, the long-term sustainability of human systems requires the maintenance and restoration of ecosystem integrity, resilience and biodiversity. Industrial economies are based on a mechanistic worldview: reality is made up of discrete objects rather than interrelated systems. As a result they convert *natural capital* into manufactured and financial capital without taking into account environmental costs.

Driving our unsustainable global economy is an unsustainable culture. The consumer culture creates false needs for power, status

Will economists realize that fresh air and water have value?

Orthodox economics dismisses social and environmental costs as *externalities*. This means that values such as health and well-being are not included in economic modeling, planning or accounting.

BEST FUTURES

Will Economists Realize that Fresh Air and Water have Value?

Money is not the real bottom line.

and wealth instead of satisfying real needs for meaning, community and survival. Consumer society creates the illusion of scarcity in the rich world, where people try to satisfy their emotional and spiritual needs through consuming things, and real scarcity in the poor world, where the resources do not exist to meet basic human needs for food, shelter, health and education.

Because real human needs cannot be satisfied by a consumer culture, people will never feel that they have enough, and there will never be an end to the destruction of the environment. However, our most basic need is to survive, and without a livable environment we will not survive. A culture based on greed is not just morally wrong, it is unsustainable.

Technological solutions can't fix social problems

Every developing country in the world is counting on technological breakthroughs and

 = **4.5** acres   Each person's fair **earthshare** in 2003.

Average footprints increase each year

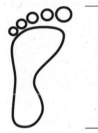 = **23.5** acres   The average footprint* of **US citizens** in 2003.

 +

Human economies will only survive over the long term if they are able to function within the carrying capacity of planet Earth.

The resources of 4 more planets would be needed for everyone in the world to live like Americans. The globalization of the American consumer society is not possible.

* The per capita ecological footprint is a tool for measuring the average annual resource consumption and waste output of individuals.

Estimates based on 2003 data. From: WWF *Living Planet Report 2006*.

BEST FUTURES

increased production to provide them with the standards of living of industrialized countries. It can't be done. Despite this fact, in almost every country advertising is urging people to live like Americans. The people of the world are being sold an impossible dream.

Although modern industrial development has improved the living standards of much of the world's population, all further plans for meeting the needs of humanity through increasing the consumption of natural resources are unrealistic, given that the carrying capacity of the biosphere is already in decline. In the coming decades the global economy will have not more but fewer resources at its disposal. It will not be enough to reduce the rate of destructive growth if we wish to avoid the total collapse of human civilization: the process of destruction has to be reversed and the environment restored.

Moreover, in order to meet the minimal needs of a growing global population, resources will have to be redistributed. At present global inequality is steadily increasing (Milanovic 2005). Ecosystems will only be preserved when humans enjoy peace and basic prosperity, since desperately poor people are often compelled to scavenge their environments and fight over scarce resources in their efforts to survive.

Many people hoped that the introduction of information technologies would reduce the need for natural resources and human labor. Instead profits have been increased through increasing the intensity of production. Smokestack industries have not disappeared; they have simply been transferred from high-wage to low-wage countries. New technologies may delay the collapse of industrial civilization, but they will not prevent it. While technological advances will reduce waste and improve efficiencies, they will not change the values and social structures that promote unsustainable exploitation, inequality, greed and war.

Our unsustainable global civilization cannot be made sustainable

It will be argued that the collapse of contemporary civilization will not happen because governments and businesses will eventually act to avert the developing crises. The reality is that the politicians and business leaders that govern our world will not and cannot reallocate the resources of their countries and corporations in order to develop a peaceful, equitable and sustainable global system. All the material resources and scientific knowledge needed to resolve the major problems on the planet have been available for decades, but the will to change the political and economic priorities of society has not.

We can be certain that politicians and business leaders will increasingly respond to the collapse of vital ecosystems and the rising cost of scarce resources through implementing policies for *sustainable development*. However, to date most of these policies have been designed to sustain growth (quantitative expansion) rather than to develop sustainability (qualitative transformation). Attempts to adjust the existing system without making fundamental changes will not work because all growth-based development is ultimately unsustainable (Daly 2005).

A civilization will only be sustainable if it can satisfy humanity's real needs

The sustainability of a living biological and social system is determined by its ability to have its essential needs met on an ongoing basis.

Meeting these needs enables the system to maintain itself over a relative time period with sufficient resilience to withstand normal environmental perturbations and stresses and to reorganize in healthy ways in response to changing conditions. Open living systems are sustainable as long as they can adjust in order to continue functioning within existing parameters, or evolve in order to function within new parameters.

In the 1987 *Brundtland Report*, sustainability was defined as "meeting the needs of the present without compromising the ability of future generations to meet their own needs" (World Commission on Environment and Development 1987). Sustainable development has also been defined as "improving the quality of human life while living within the carrying capacity of supporting ecosystems" (World Conservation Union et al. 1991). Human needs are more than simply material needs for food, shelter and safety: they are also emotional, intellectual and spiritual needs — for meaning and belonging, for relationship to both community and nature. Since living systems can only survive if they are individually healthy and members of healthy communities and ecosystems, it is more accurate to say that the essential needs of all biological and social systems are for health and wholeness.

The self-destructive behaviors of industrial civilization prevent it from meeting real needs. Complex human societies will only survive if the current unhealthy and unsustainable global economy is replaced with a sustainable economy based on the maintenance of social, physical and biophysical health and wholeness. Human society will only be able to end scarcity, and international competition over limited resources, when it is able to satisfy the minimal physical, emotional, mental and spiritual needs of all the humans on the planet. This means that we need to replace an unsustainable system that is designed to increase the quantity of things, with a sustainable system that is designed to improve the quality of people's lives. And, in turn, because basic human rights and a quality of life cannot be achieved in a degraded and toxic environment, these goals will only be met by also meeting the needs of the planet's biophysical systems.

Human needs include needs for community, meaning, identity and justice

As industrial civilization expands, it consumes and degrades not only natural resources but also other civilizations and cultures. When it comes in contact with traditional agrarian or tribal societies, the force and attraction of its superior power and wealth begin to break down the economies, values and social institutions of the older societies.

Rapid urbanization has been accompanied by soaring rates of poverty, crime and addiction. People compete and fight over material goods when they fear material scarcity, and people compete and fight over religious, ethnic and national issues when they fear the loss of cultural identities.

Industrial civilization perpetuates conflict by perpetuating fear and alienation: it pits the individual good against the common good and material needs against emotional needs. In order to eliminate war and preserve the environment, a sustainable global system will have to meet our needs for meaning, identity and justice. While current social structures facilitate competition, inequality, injustice and conflict, sustainable structures will need to facilitate cooperation, equality, justice and peaceful conflict resolution.

A sustainable global civilization must value interdependence and diversity

Two mass extinctions are taking place on our planet. Our current civilization is not only destroying species, it is also destroying cultures. There were 6000 languages spoken on Earth in the year 2000. If trend continues, half of these will have disappeared by 2050 (Davis 2001). With the extinction of each ancient culture, humanity will lose a unique perspective along with knowledge accumulated over thousands of years. Since human knowledge and behaviors are primarily transmitted through culture, the loss of cultural diversity threatens the survival of complex societies.

Systemic resilience is lost with the destruction of both human cultural diversity as well as ecosystem biodiversity, increasing the likelihood of widespread social and biophysical collapse (Berkes et al. 2003). As the many varieties of human civilizations and societies become undifferentiated parts of an expanding societal monoculture, the system loses checks and balances. The result is an increasingly closely connected but unstable world system: new crises can rapidly spread throughout the system's political and economic structures.

Viable societies will require more efficient and less bureaucratic social structures

In the past many successful societies have expanded to the point where their resources could no longer maintain their increasingly complex social structures. When easily accessed resources were exhausted, they were forced to seek out ever more distant and expensive resources. Eventually the political, economic and military cost of acquiring new resources reached an unsustainable point and the societies collapsed. Our industrial civilization, with its bureaucratic structures and expansionist economy, is following the same unsustainable trajectory of other great civilizations (Tainter 1988).

The majority of industrial countries are democratic and capitalist to varying degrees. The competing nations, institutions and corporations in industrial societies have social structures that distribute power and wealth unevenly within and between countries. Elites in every country and institution collect information, make decisions and then enforce compliance through regulations and sanctions. Because this societal system is based on inequality, it can only be maintained through complex financial and regulatory bureaucracies and repressive military, police and judicial systems.

In order to meet the real needs of humanity in a sustainable fashion, human societies must eliminate unnecessary waste, including the enormous cost of regulation and repression. Currently much of the world's economy is engaged in unproductive activities connected with the control of power and wealth. If complex societies are to survive, humanity must develop new economic structures that utilize energy and resources more efficiently and new political structures that more efficiently process information and allocate tasks and resources.

Sustainable societies must be decentralized and self-regulating

The concentration of information and decision making at a few powerful centers creates bottlenecks in which critical parts of the social network are overloaded while most of the system is underutilized.

The practical alternative to centralized decision making is decentralized decision making. In order to function more efficiently, political and economic structures will have to be transformed from being primarily centralized to being primarily decentralized, and from being primarily focused on the production of quantities of goods for trade to being primarily focused on improving the local quality of life. A decentralized network can improve efficiency by giving all its parts the ability to respond flexibly and autonomously to local conditions. The need for energy and resources can be reduced by having most social and environmental needs met at the local level with local resources (Madron & Jopling 2003).

Although most needs can be met at a local level, not all functions can or should be devolved. Indeed, national and international environmental and human rights standards are necessary as buffers to guard against any infringement of these rights at the local or regional levels. A decentralized network will require a holarchical structure (in a holarchy each successive holon, or system, transcends but includes its predecessors) that supports the appropriate distribution of power and resources and the appropriate self-regulation of each node and level. Although most industrial countries are democracies, most people have little say in the day-to-day decisions made in their workplaces or communities. To the extent that people can participate in the political process, many do not because they are poorly informed and motivated. A major cause of public apathy is that knowledge in industrial civilization is fragmented, specialized and controlled.

In reality we have not yet made the transition from an industrial economy to an information economy. Information technologies will not become an integral part of a new societal system until sustainable holarchical social structures begin to form in the midst of the collapse of industrial civilization.

Sustainable societies require integral worldviews

Life in the consumer society is morally and intellectually contradictory, and this confusion is corrosive and disempowering. Because the consumer worldview represents the commodification of both humans and the natural world, it promotes the illusion of a separate self that exists independently of both the larger human and biophysical communities (Sivaraksa 2002). On the other hand, more local and decentralized communities help to foster a greater sense of caring both for other humans and for the local environment (Norberg-Hodge 2002).

People and communities will need greater access to the theoretical and practical tools required for self-direction, self-regulation, self-organization and constructive action. For this to occur the dominant industrial model must give way to an integral model that recognizes the inextricable interconnectedness of both human and biophysical systems and the environmental limitations placed on human activities. A fragmenting worldview must be replaced with an integrating worldview, since people can only control their lives when their understanding of reality permits them to act effectively in the real world.

A sustainable society will need values and social structures that support the relatively egalitarian distribution of power, information and resources to every part of the system. The shift from a primarily centralized societal system to a primarily decentralized societal system is the shift from partial democracy to partici-patory democracy.

Entering the bifurcation: civilization will either collapse or transform

There are only three possibilities for the future of civilization:

(a) Cascading environmental crises will rapidly escalate, producing uncontrol-lable economic and political crises. At some point these crises will cause the catastrophic collapse of the societal system. This process may produce irreversible damage to social and bio-physical systems.

(b) Political and business leaders will proactively respond to the growing crises through supporting environ-mentally friendly technologies, introducing policies for sustainable development and preventing political unrest. These efforts will slow the rate of environmental destruction and help to extend the life of industrial civilization. However, attempts to improve the system without redesign-ing its unsustainable structure will ultimately fail. Over time efforts to manage crises will consume more and more scarce resources, and industrial civilization will collapse.

(c) As regional and global crises increase and the world economy begins to fail, the ability of existing political and economic structures to influence and control people will weaken. Growing numbers of people will question the values of contemporary civilization and start to organize alternative struc-tures. Maintaining and restoring large areas of the earth's biosphere will become an international priority. At this point a successful transformation to a sustainable societal system is pos-sible if new values and technologies that reflect developed appropriate worldviews — ones capable of organ-izing functional new social structures. Should this happen, the collapse of contemporary civilization will become a springboard for the evolution of a sustainable planetary one.

We believe that we are currently beginning a period of major societal and biophysical transformation. Since World War II there has been a dramatic accumulation and concentra-tion of wealth as well as the rapid conversion of natural capital to manufactured and financial capital. With this has also come the emergence of greater vulnerability, due to the increasing number of interconnections that link that wealth and those that control and maintain it. This growing connectedness leads to increas-ing rigidity and brittleness as the system becomes ever more tightly bound together. This has reduced resilience and the capacity of the system to absorb change, thus increas-ing the threat of abrupt change.

We are entering what panarchy theorists refer to as the *backloop* of reorganization, we shall witness a collapse of existing structures and accumulated connections, and the release of bound-up knowledge and capital (Gunderson & Holling 2002). On the one hand, this col-lapse will inevitably initiate a reversion to *lower* levels of response in the form of *blood-and-belonging* and *us/them* fear-based security reactions. On the other hand, the creative aspect of this backloop releases knowledge and the appearance of new or latent elements which can then be reassociated in novel and unexpected ways to trigger regrowth and reorganization into fundamentally new forms of learning and innovative social patterns.

The emergence of an integral worldview is critical for the creation of a sustainable societal system

Evolution is an unpredictable process that involves the emergence of previously unknown properties that take hold and spread because they are more relevant and functional than previously existing attributes (Laszlo 1987). While we know that industrial civilization is no longer viable, we do not know all the new properties that will evolve during the transformation of the current global system to a sustainable alternative system. We can be sure that the process of transformation cannot be dictated by any center: evolution is an organic process, and a sustainable, decentralized and empowered societal system can only develop in a process of self-creation and self-organization.

New paradigms began to develop over a hundred years ago with the discovery of force fields and relativity theory. Important emerging elements of the new integral society are now everywhere. Some examples are quantum mechanics, computer networks, feminism, ecology, conflict resolution, the peace movement, non-governmental organizations and the International Criminal Court.

However, the emerging property that will be critical for the creation of a sustainable global societal system is an integral worldview, as it will provide the organizing pattern around which sustainable social institutions can be formed. The articulation of this integral worldview will assist with the development

and integration of emerging theories, values and organizations. Many people have contributed to the science behind an integral worldview; we are writing this article in order to help it emerge as a coherent perspective. (We see this integral approach as including great diversity of local and personal worldviews that can meet in various larger regional forums up to the global level.)

Peaceful transformation will only occur if new structures Include and transcend the old

In order to make a successful transformation to a viable global system people must be educated about our common need: if we wish to survive, all human societies must become sustainable. The key to successful conflict resolution is maximizing cooperation around common interests while minimizing competition over scarce resources and differing values (Cloke 2001).

Resistance to change occurs when people believe that they have more to lose than to gain. The expansion of industrial society is still being resisted by many agrarian and pre-agrarian societies because they fear the loss of meaning and community. A successful transformation to a sustainable civilization must include and transcend older societal systems, retaining the positive aspects of the older societies while meeting a wider range of needs. Although ruling elites and societal inertia will inevitably oppose change, much opposition can be avoided through promoting values of diversity and inclusiveness.

The cure for a dying planet cannot be the replacement of one monoculture by another; instead we need to create a global system that promotes and protects both cultural diversity and biodiversity. In order to support resilience, a viable global system should include a variety of sustainable societal systems from simple (e.g. hunter-gatherer economies) to complex (e.g. information-based economies).

Organizing for change

People in every country need to know that while systemic change is inevitable, destructive outcomes are not. Positive change is possible if concerned people unite around a common vision of a peaceful and sustainable planet. The Earth Charter calls for international agreement to "bring forth a sustainable global society founded on respect for nature, universal human rights, economic justice and a culture of peace" (Earth Charter Initiative 2000).

The vision of a sustainable planetary civilization

A global movement needs to be mobilized to secure international agreements on the following points:

(1) Because our planet has finite resources, there are limits to growth. If the global economy continues to exceed sustainable limits it will destroy its biophysical foundations and collapse.

(2) Our collective survival depends on human economies becoming sustainable.

(3) Essential human and biophysical needs must be met in order for human economies to be sustainable.

(4) Resources must be redistributed to meet essential human and biophysical needs.

(5) Cultural and genetic diversity is essential for health and wholeness.

(6) In order for different cultures and societal systems to coexist, their values

Humanity needs to unite around a vision of a sustainable planetary civilization.

Humans belong to thousands of different cultures. Every large geopolitical and cultural formation is ethnopolitically diverse.

SOUTH AMERICA · NORTH AMERICA · CHINA · EUROPE · ISLAMIC WORLD · AFRICA · INDIA

- Meeting Human and Biophysical Needs
- Peaceful Cooperation
- Respect for Diversity

The experience of the European Union shows that increased transnational cooperation can improve cultural diversity and minority rights.

Different cultures and political systems can coexist if their values and structures promote peaceful cooperation and sustainability.

Values based on *The Earth Charter (2000)*

and structures must promote peaceful cooperation and sustainability.

The earth charter – developing a transformative vision

We are at a point in human history when we are witnessing two very different world views and visions for the future of this planet — a dysfunctional expansionist model and an emerging ecological one. Over the past decade, at the same time that proponents of international free trade were arguing that commercial interests should supersede all other interests including regional and community environmental and human rights standards, a global United Nations Earth Charter was being prepared that recognized that the well-being of individual and social systems is utterly dependent upon the well-being of the ecosystems in which they are embedded or depend. Indeed, the Earth Charter challenges humanity to acknowledge both the intrinsic value and sacred nature of the world in which it lives. As such, its advocates argue that it goes a long way to help formalize many of the values that are desperately needed if humanity and the millions of other sentient beings with whom we share this planet are going to have a quality of life and viable future. Indeed, the six points listed above are integral components of the Earth Charter's vision.

With the 1972 United Nations Stockholm Conference on the Human Environment and again with the Brundtland Commission Report in 1987, it was becoming increasingly obvious that individual and collective human rights can only flourish in a biophysical world that is also flourishing. In other words, it is virtually impossible to obtain one's right to basic health and living standards when the environment in which one lives is a toxic waste heap. Consequently, an Earth Charter that set forth the principles and values needed for ecological security was expected to be a major outcome of the 1992 Rio de Janeiro Earth Summit. Agreement among various governments was not reached, and so in 1995 at the Hague a broad multi-constituency process was set up to draft a charter that would reflect cross-cultural values in terms of global interdependence and human and biophysical rights and obligations.

The Earth Charter's Preamble underscores the idea that humanity has reached a critical bifurcation:

> We stand at a critical moment in Earth's history, a time when humanity must choose its future. As the world becomes increasingly interdependent and fragile, the future at once holds great peril and great promise. To move forward we must recognize that in the midst of a magnificent diversity of cultures and life forms we are one human family and one Earth community with a common destiny ... Towards this end, it is imperative that we, the peoples of Earth, declare our responsibility to one another, to the greater community of life, and to future generations (Earth Charter Initiative 2000).

With the beginning of the 21st century it has become increasingly apparent that current economic values and models of development are completely at odds with the sustainability of biophysical systems and, ultimately, with our own and other species' long-term survival. Consequently, in preparing for a sustainable society, we must be clear about one thing: the status quo will not suffice. Moreover, any discussions regarding social and biophysical sustainability must be predicated upon a restructured South-North dialogue as well as upon a very different set of human and environmental values and practices. Meeting essential human and biophysical needs must be given the highest priority, while at the same time articulating a new vision and world view that can give hope and be a viable alternative to the dominant current one. The Earth Charter has been drafted as a guiding set of principles to this end.

The articles in this anthology underscore the depth of commitment on the part of individuals, communities and NGOs from around the world to discover ways to practice viable forms of living while simultaneously supporting the health of the ecosystems within which they reside. In turn, these practitioners of ecoforestry, permaculture, ecoagriculture and other manifestations of *wild foresting* are already demonstrating how various principles contained in the Earth Charter are currently being put into practice. Such examples show us that this new direction is not only possible but that, by helping to maintain the long-term viability of the millions of human and non-human forms with whom we share this planet, we shall be significantly deepening the meaning and quality of our own lives.

Editor's note: Some of the material in this article is also found in the authors' articles "The Collapse and Transformation of Our World," *Journal of Future Studies,* 11(3), 2007, and in "The Requirements of a Sustainable Planetary System," *Social Alternatives,* 26(3), 2007.

Shifting Direction to Local Interdependence

Helena Norberg-Hodge

Reflections today: *I would say that in a material way things have definitely gotten worse worldwide. And in every country I know of governments are working with global capital not only to destroy the natural world but also human rights and also any semblance of democracy. It is quite alarming ...*

On the other hand I also see a tremendous increase in awareness, and I continue to have faith in the power of nature and a basic intelligence and even kindness in human nature.

For me it is all about an ignorance born of specialized knowledge combined with ever larger scale. So I think even in government and big business as well as in the activist world an inability to see connections is the main reason behind our escalating crises. But as I wrote in *Ancient Futures*, more holistic information and vision could be communicated very rapidly with modern communication techniques. There is a possibility that economic growth à la globalization will be recognized for what it is. So things could change very rapidly for the better. At the grass roots when communities turn toward nature and one another for their sustenance we can see the enormous healing and benefits almost instantaneously.

From global to local

If globalization is the root of so many problems, localization — a shift away from the global and towards the local — is an obvious part of the solution. Localization would not mean encouraging every community to be entirely self-reliant; it would simply mean shortening the distance between producers and consumers wherever possible and striking a healthier balance between trade and local production. Localization would not mean that everyone must *go back to the land*, but that the policies now causing rapid urbanization would be changed. Localization would not mean that people in cold climates would be denied oranges or avocados, but that their wheat, rice or milk — in short, their basic food needs — would not travel thousands of miles when they could all be produced within a fifty mile radius. Rather than ending all trade, steps towards localization would aim at reducing unnecessary transport while encouraging changes to strengthen and diversify economies at the community as well as national level. The degree of diversification, the goods produced and the amount of trade would naturally vary from region to region.

Reversing our headlong rush towards globalization would have benefits on a number of levels. Rural economies in both North and South would be revitalized, helping to stem the unhealthy tide of urbanization. Farmers would be growing primarily for local and regional rather than global markets, allowing them to choose varieties in tune with local conditions and local needs, thus allowing agricultural diversity to rebound. Production processes would be far smaller in scale and therefore less stressful to the environment. Transport would be minimized and so the greenhouse gas and pollution toll would decrease, as would both the financial and ecological costs of energy extraction. People would no longer be forced to conform to the impossible ideals of a global consumer monoculture, thereby lessening the psychological pressures that often lead to ethnic conflict and violence. Ending the manic pursuit of trade would reduce the economic and hence political power of transnational corporations (TNCs), and eliminate the need to hand power to such supranational institutions as the WTO, thereby helping to reverse the erosion of democracy.

Countering objections

In these and many other ways, a shift towards the local simply makes sense. Nonetheless, calling for a fundamental shift in direction tends to elicit a chorus of objections. Some claim that the promotion of decentralization is *social engineering*, involving serious dislocations in

the lives of many people. While it is true that some disruption would inevitably accompany a shift toward the local, it is far less than is already resulting from the current rush towards globalization. It is in fact today's *jobless growth society* that entails social and environmental engineering on an unprecedented scale: vast stretches of the planet and entire economies being remade to conform to the needs of global growth, just as people around the world are being encouraged to abandon their languages, their foods and their architectural styles for a standard monoculture.

Another objection is the belief that people in countries of the South need Northern markets in a globalized economy to lift themselves out of poverty, and that a greater degree of self-reliance in the North would therefore undermine the economies of the South. In large measure, this view arises from the erroneous belief that poverty in the South is simply due to a lack of development — that this is how people lived before they had benefited from Western-style modernization. However, an honest appraisal of the historical record beginning in the pre-colonial era reveals that poverty in the South is primarily a *consequence* of development from the colonial period to the present day.

The truth of the matter is that a gradual shift towards smaller scale *and* more local production would benefit both North and South and would facilitate meaningful work and fuller employment everywhere. The globalized economy requires the South to send a large portion of its natural resources to the North as raw material; its best agricultural land must be devoted to growing food, fibers and even flowers for the North; a good deal of the South's labor is employed in the cheap manufacture of goods for Northern markets. Rather than further impoverishing the South, producing more *ourselves* would allow the South to keep more of its own resources, labor and production for *itself*. Globalization means pulling millions of people away from sure subsistence in a land-based economy into urban slums from which they have little hope of ever escaping. Diversifying and localizing economic activity offers the majority, in both North and South, far better prospects.

Modern prejudice

The idea of localization also runs counter to today's general belief that fast-paced urban areas are the locus of *real* culture, while small, local communities are isolated backwaters, relics of a past when small-mindedness and prejudice were the norm. The past is assumed to have been brutish, a time when exploitation was fierce, intolerance rampant and violence commonplace — a situation that the modern world has largely left behind. These assumptions echo the elitist or racist belief that modern people are superior — more highly evolved even — than their *underdeveloped* rural counterparts. It is noteworthy that rural areas are described in development literature as backward, poor and primitive while in tourist literature the very same regions are presented as idyllic, peaceful and beautiful. Millions of wealthy city-dwellers will spend a substantial proportion of their salary to escape for a few weeks to enjoy life in these *primitive backwaters*. It is also perfectly normal for the over-stressed businessperson to seek out, as a place to retire, precisely the kind of simple village that is deemed to be *underdeveloped* — indeed, it is such a widespread desire that small cottages in rural areas now often cost more than city apartments.

Yet the whole process of industrialization has systematically removed political and economic power from rural areas with a concomitant loss of self-respect in rural populations. In small communities today, people are often living on the periphery, while power — and even what we call *culture* — is centralized somewhere else. In order to see what communities are like when people retain real self-respect and economic power at the local level, we would have to look back — in some cases hundreds of years — before the enclosures in England, for example, or before the colonial era in the South. Though such information is not widely publicized, there are numerous accounts that show what life in largely self-reliant communities was like.

The isolated region of Ladakh, or *Little Tibet*, is just one place that can provide some clues about life in largely self-reliant communities. Unaffected by colonialism or (until recently) development, Ladakh's community-based economy provided people with a sense of self-esteem and control over their own lives. But since the early 1970s, in less than a generation, this culture has been dramatically changed by economic development. Development has effectively dismantled the local economy; it has shifted decision making power away from the household and village to bureaucracies in distant urban centers; it has changed the education of children away from a focus on local resources and needs towards a lifestyle completely unrelated to Ladakh and it has implicitly informed them that urban life is glamorous, exciting and easy and that the life of a farmer is backward and dull. Because of these changes, there has been a loss of self-esteem, an increase in pettiness and small-minded gossip and unprecedented levels of divisiveness and friction. If these trends continue, future impressions of village life in Ladakh may soon differ little from unfavorable Western stereotypes of small town life.

Urban or rural?

An equally common myth employed in arguments against localization is that *there are too many people to go back to the land*. Interestingly enough, a similar skepticism does not accompany the notion of *urbanizing* the world's population. What is too easily forgotten is that roughly half the global population today — mostly in the so-called developing world — is currently on the land. Ignoring them — speaking as if people are urbanized as part of the human condition — is a very dangerous misconception, one that is helping to fuel the whole process of urbanization. It is considered *utopian* to suggest a ruralization of America's or Europe's population, while China's plans to move 440 million people *off* the land and into cities in the next few decades is accepted without argument. This *modernization* of China's economy is part of the same process that has led to unmanageable urban explosions all over the South — from Bangkok and Mexico City to Bombay, Jakarta and Lagos. In these cities, unemployment is rampant, millions are homeless or live in slums and the social fabric is unraveling.

Even in the North, an unhealthy urbanization continues. Rural communities are being steadily dismantled, their populations pushed into spreading suburban megalopolises where the vast majority of available jobs are located. In the United States, where only 2% still live on the land, there are now fewer farmers than there are people incarcerated; yet farms continue to disappear rapidly.[1] It is impossible to offer that model to the rest of the world where the majority of people earn their living as farmers.

People rarely observe that we are too many to move to the city because it is implicitly assumed that centralization is somehow more efficient, that urban populations use fewer resources. When we take a close look at the real costs of urbanization in the global economy, however, we can see how the opposite is true. Urban centers around the world are extremely resource intensive. The large-scale, centralized systems they require are almost without exception more stressful to the environment than small-scale, diversified, locally adapted production. Food and water, building materials and energy must all be transported great distances via vast energy-consuming infrastructures; their concentrated wastes must be hauled away in trucks and barges or incinerated at great cost to the environment. In identical glass and steel towers with windows that never open, even air to breathe must be provided by fans, pumps and non-renewable energy. From the most affluent sections of Paris to the slums of Calcutta, urban populations depend on increasing amounts of packaging and transport for their food, so that every pound of food consumed is accompanied by a dramatic increase in petroleum consumption as well as significant amounts of pollution and waste.

Precisely because there *are* so many people, a globalized economic model which can adequately feed, house and clothe only a small minority has to be abandoned. It is essential to support instead knowledge systems and economic models that are based on an intimate understanding of diverse regions and their unique climates, soils and resources.

In the North, where we have for the most part been separated from the land and from each other, we have large steps to take. But even in regions that are highly urbanized, it is possible to nurture a connection to place. By reweaving the fabric of smaller communities within large cities and by redirecting their economic activities toward the natural resources around them, cities can regain their regional character, become more livable and less burdensome to the environment. Our task will be made easier if we support our remaining rural communities and small farmers. They are the key to rebuilding a healthy agricultural base for stronger, more diversified economies.

People power

A final objection to shifting course is that there is already too much momentum towards globalization, with policy-makers the world over wedded to it. But the scope and potential for public pressure to bring about changes in government policy is actually quite significant, as recent history shows.

A very visible example has been the massive public resistance in Europe against the genetic modification of foods. Despite the attempt of the biotechnology industry and the United States government to force GM foods down the throats of European consumers, public pressure to severely restrict or even ban imports of these foods has escalated. As a consequence, it has become impossible for European governments to ignore their voters. In the name of sovereignty and consumers' rights, some of these governments even seem willing to risk a trade war with the US. In 1999 the four major supermarket chains in Britain and several others on the continent publicly stated that they would not allow genetically modified ingredients to be used in their own brands as a result of enough consumers making their opinions known.

Another less publicized victory for citizens was the stalling of the Multilateral Agreement on Investment. The MAI was an international agreement, written mainly by representatives of transnational banks, global corporations and government trade officials, which aimed to force governments to relinquish much of their power, especially their ability to protect their citizens and maintain social, environmental and health standards. A relatively small number of activists and informed citizens put pressure on governments around the world and forced the stalling of the agreement — a feat made even more impressive by the fact that these negotiations were conducted in total secrecy. Most elected officials, including many ministers, were not even aware of the MAI's existence!

A third example is the US Department of Agriculture's (USDA) retreat from its attempt in 1998 to weaken organic standards in order to allow large agribusinesses to take advantage of the increasingly lucrative market for organically grown foods. Among other flaws, the proposed rules would have allowed *organic* foods to be grown from genetically modified seed, fertilized with chemically tainted municipal waste and sterilized by irradiation — techniques considered acceptable within the global food system but consistently repudiated by organic farmers. After USDA offices were flooded with thousands of irate letters, calls and e-mails from consumers and farmers the department backed down.

But undoubtedly the most encouraging and significant expression of resistance was the mass protest in Seattle during the WTO meeting at the end of 1999. The demonstrations there involved an extraordinary array of farmers, businesspeople, mothers with young children, environmentalists, indigenous people and members of labor unions. Protestors numbered in the tens of thousands and brought worldwide attention to a process that has over the years taken place behind closed doors. The message of the people marching in the streets was very clear: globalization is not a natural or evolutionary process — it is about specific trade agreements and government policies, and these must be changed. The atmosphere of resistance created by these protests undoubtedly played a major role in the collapse of the Seattle talks and has certainly ensured that future trade decisions — which so fundamentally affect the well-being of the planet and its citizens — will no longer be made outside the glare of public scrutiny.

These examples show that ordinary citizens can force changes in policy. Even a relatively small group of well-organized and informed people can have a huge impact. Getting governments to shift course is not impossible or even unlikely once enough people understand how disastrous our present course really is.

Signs of renewal

The increasingly globalized economy is not only leading to active resistance; it is also giving rise to a wide range of spontaneous efforts to reweave the social and economic fabric in ways that mesh with the needs of nature — both wild and human. Evidence of such changes are emerging everywhere: increasing numbers of doctors and patients are rejecting the commercial, mechanistic medical mainstream in favor of more preventative and holistic approaches; many architects are finding inspiration in vernacular building styles and are employing more natural materials in their work; awareness of the harmful health and environmental effects of large-scale industrial agriculture is on the rise, and thousands of farmers are switching to organic

practices; dietary preferences among consumers are shifting away from processed foods with artificial colorings, flavor and preservatives towards fresher foods in their natural state.

Positive trends like these are growing stronger and more numerous day by day and point to people's longing to attune themselves and their communities to the natural world and its processes. These and other positive *micro-trends* are evidence that people are ready — even eager — for a fundamental shift in direction. Now let's consider some concrete ways such a shift can occur.

Getting from here to there

For a shift towards the local to occur, steps will be needed on several levels. Already, many individuals and organizations are working from the grassroots to strengthen their communities and local economies. Yet for these efforts to succeed, they need to be accompanied by policy changes at the national and international level. How, for example, can participatory democracy be strengthened if corporations are allowed to control government policy and manipulate public opinion? How can small farmers and locally owned shops flourish if governments continue to champion free trade and subsidize global TNCs? How can cultural diversity be nurtured if monocultural media images continue to bombard children in every corner of the planet? How can small-scale renewable energy projects compete against massive subsidies for huge dams and nuclear power plants?

Clearly, local initiatives need to go hand in hand with policy changes if the globalization process is to be reversed. Rather than just thinking in terms of isolated, scattered grassroots efforts, it is necessary to encourage government policies that would promote *small scale on a large scale*, allowing space for more community-based economies to flourish and spread.

Policy shifts

Changing the direction of the economy means rethinking global economic and financial policies. It means looking at trade agreements, public expenditures, regulatory reform and development policies. Here are some examples of the way shifts in government financial support could lead towards more diversified and localized economies.

Transport

The money currently spent on long-distance ground transport alone offers an idea of how heavily subsidized the global economy is. In the United States, where there are about 3.9 million miles of public roads, another $175 billion was earmarked for ground transportation with the goal of "improving access to markets worldwide."[2] The European Community, not to be outdone, planned to spend $465 to $580 billion on a *Trans-European Network* including new high-speed rail links in and between France, England, Italy, Austria, Germany and Spain; motorways in Greece, Bulgaria, Portugal, Spain, Ireland, Great Britain and all the Scandinavian countries and surface crossings between Denmark and Sweden and between Britain and Ireland.[3] Throughout the South, scarce resources have been similarly spent. The World Bank, for example, loaned $400 million to China for highways to "improve long-distance travel and promote trade."[4]

Rather than continually paying to expand trade-based transport networks, a portion of those funds could instead go towards a range of transport options that favor smaller, more local enterprises. This shift would bring enormous benefits — from the creation of jobs, to a healthier environment, to a more equitable distribution of resources. Depending on the local situation, transport money could be spent on building bike paths, footpaths, boat and rail service and, where appropriate, paths for animal transport. Even in the highly industrialized world where dependence on centralized infrastructures is deeply entrenched, a move in this direction can be made. In Amsterdam, for example, steps have been taken to ban cars from the city's center, thus allowing pavements to be widened and more bicycle lanes to be built.

Markets and public spaces

High-speed motorways built with government funds (or through public and private partnerships) inherently promote the growth of corporate superstores, hyper-markets and sprawling shopping malls. Spending some of that money instead to build or improve spaces for public markets — such as those that were once found in virtually every European town and village — would enable local merchants and artisans with limited capital to sell their wares. This would enliven town centers while reducing car use, fossil fuel burning and pollution. Similarly, support for farmers' markets would not only benefit cities, it would help to revitalize the agricultural economy of surrounding regions while reducing the resources wasted on processing, packaging and transporting food. Creating and improving spaces for public meetings — from town halls to village squares — would encourage face-to-face exchanges between decision makers and the public, serving both to enliven communities and to strengthen participatory democracy.

Energy

From nuclear power stations to big dams, large-scale centralized energy projects are today heavily subsidized, their environmental costs largely ignored. Phasing out these multi-billion dollar investments while offering real support for locally available renewable energy supplies would result in lower pollution levels, reduced greenhouse gas emissions and less dependence on dwindling petroleum supplies and dangerous nuclear technologies. Decentralized energy sources would also help to keep money from leaking out of local economies. (There are many examples in Europe today of small scale local energy production, e.g. in Germany.)

In the South, large-scale energy plants are systematically geared towards the needs of urban areas and export-oriented production — thus promoting both urbanization and globalization. Supporting decentralized renewable energy infrastructures instead would strengthen villages, smaller towns and rural economies in general and thereby help to halt the urbanization process. Since the energy infrastructure in the South is not yet very developed, there is a realistic possibility that this strategy could be implemented in the near future if there were sufficient pressure from the public on banks and funding agencies. Awareness of global warming may help to encourage a rapid shift in this direction.

Agriculture

Farm subsidies in most countries today heavily favor large-scale industrial agribusinesses. In the UK, for example, only 0.2% of the £3.2 billion in direct subsidies for agriculture are used to encourage organic farming practices.[5] It is not only direct payments to farmers that are biased towards large-scale agriculture; funding for agricultural research is heavily skewed in favor of biotechnology and chemical- and energy-intensive monoculture. Shifting these expenditures towards simpler technologies needed for smaller-scale, diversified farming would help to revitalize rural economies in both North and South, while promoting biodiversity, healthier soils, food security, balanced and diverse diets and fresher food.

In countries of the South, colonialism, development and globalization have meant that the best land is devoted to crops for Northern markets. Shifting the emphasis to diversified, low-input production for local consumption would not only improve economic stability; it would reduce the gap between rich and poor while eliminating much of the hunger that is now so endemic in the so-called developing parts of the world.

Global media

Television and other mass media receive massive subsidies in the form of research and development, infrastructure development, educational training and other direct and indirect support. Even national broadcasting companies are threatened with takeover by global media empires. These conglomerates are rapidly homogenizing diverse traditions around the world. Supporting facilities for regional entertainment — from music and drama to dances and festivals — would offer a healthy alternative. Communities and nations should have the right to restrict the bombardment of their children by violent and commercial media images.

Education

Schooling has been increasingly geared towards the needs of corporations, which are presumed to be the future employers of today's children. Curricula are ever more standardized and technology-focused. Shifting course so as to provide training in regional agriculture, architecture and appropriate technology would further a real decentralization of production for basic needs. Rather than encouraging specialization for a competitive, *jobless growth economy*, children would be educated for diverse environments, cultures and economic systems. This does not imply that the flow of information from other cultures would be curtailed; in fact cultural exchange would be an important part of education.

In much of the South, formal education continues to be based on the colonial model —with rote-learning in the language of the colonial power, with cultural, historical and other information coming from abroad and with training in skills relevant to the export economy rather than the local or regional economy. In most countries, this form of education filters out any information from around the world about widespread social and economic problems, leaving idealized myths about *development* and Western urban life intact. The South would benefit enormously from a shift away from this monoculturing model towards diverse forms of education that are related to living and working in specific environments and cultures.

Health care

At present, investments in health care favor huge, centralized hospitals serving urban populations. The inevitable pressure to cut costs means that doctors and nurses have to serve more and more patients, inevitably eroding the quality of attention given to each patient. Spending the same money instead on a greater number of smaller local clinics —

relying less on high technology and more on health practitioners, local health education and preventative medicine — would bring health care to more people while boosting national and local economies.

In the South, local economies and communities would similarly benefit if support for capital- and energy-intensive, centralized health care based on a Western model were shifted towards more local and indigenous alternatives that are affordable to the majority of the population.

Regulatory reforms

In addition to the many direct and indirect subsidies given to them, large-scale, globally oriented businesses also benefit from a range of government regulations — and in many cases, a lack of regulations — at the expense of smaller, more local enterprises. Although big business complains loudly of *red tape*, much of the regulatory bureaucracy could be eliminated if production were smaller in scale and based more locally. In today's climate of unfettered free trade, some regulation is clearly necessary, and citizens need to insist that governments be allowed to protect their interests. This could best come about through international treaties in which governments agree to change the rules of the game to restore real diversity and decentralization in the business world. Here are some areas that need to be examined.

Trade treaties

Free trade policies are leading to greater power and freedom for corporations while leaving national and local economies ever more vulnerable and constrained. Instead, a careful and, ideally, internationally agreed policy of using trade tariffs to regulate the import of goods that could be produced locally would be in the best interests of the majority. Such *protectionism* would not be targeted against fellow citizens in other countries; rather, it would be a way of safeguarding jobs and defending local resources worldwide against the excessive power of transnational corporations.

Many people in the South are aware that they would be far better off if they were allowed to protect and conserve their natural resources, nurture national and local business enterprises and limit the impact of foreign media and advertising on their cultures. In much of the South, even fair trade may not be in people's long-term interest if it pulls them away from a relatively secure local economy.

Capital flows

The unregulated flow of capital has been a prerequisite for the rapid growth of transnational corporations. The ease with which they can shift profits, operating costs and investment capital to and from all of their far-flung enterprises enables them to operate anywhere in the world and even to hold sovereign nations hostage by threatening to leave and take their jobs with them. As a consequence, they can obtain subsidies denied to smaller companies. Limiting the free flow of capital would help to reduce the advantage that huge corporations have over more local enterprises and help to make corporations more accountable to the places where they operate.

Yardsticks of economic health

Decision makers often point to rising levels of Gross Domestic Product (GDP) as proof that their policies are succeeding. GDP considers only the portion of economic activity that involves monetary transactions, thereby leaving out the functions of family, community

and the environment. Thus, paying to send one's children to a day-care center adds to GDP, while care at home by members of the family does not. Similarly, a forest cut down and turned into pulp adds to GDP, but a standing forest — crucial to the health of the biosphere — does not. As a result, policymakers who rely on GDP can easily embrace policies that do irreparable harm.

In the South in particular, policies that focus on elevating GDP systematically lead to the breakdown of economies in which people's needs are provided with little use of cash. Through this process of so-called development, healthy self-reliance is thus replaced by real poverty within the global economy.

More accurate and complete measures of economic health reveal many of the hidden costs of our present globalizing course and make clear how much better off a shift in direction would leave us.[6]

Tax systems

In almost every country, tax regulations systematically discriminate against small and medium-scale businesses. Smaller-scale production is usually more labor-intensive, and heavy taxes are levied on labor through income taxes, social welfare taxes, value-added taxes, payroll taxes and so on. Meanwhile, tax breaks (e.g. accelerated depreciation, investment allowances and tax credits) are afforded to the capital- and energy-intensive technologies used by large corporate producers. Reversing this bias in the tax system would not only help local economies; it would create more jobs by favoring people instead of machines. Similarly, taxes on the energy used in production would encourage businesses that are less dependent on high levels of technological input — which again means smaller, more labor-intensive enterprises. And if gasoline and diesel fuel were taxed so that their price reflected their real costs — including some measure of the environmental damage their consumption causes — there would be a reduction in transport, an increase in regional production for local consumption and a healthy diversification of the economy.

Banking policies

Another area to address is the lending policies of banks, which today discriminate against small businesses by charging them significantly higher interest rates for loans than they charge big firms. They also often require that small business owners personally guarantee their loans — a guarantee not sought from the directors of large businesses. Ending these practices would eliminate one of the unfair advantages large corporations now enjoy.

Banks also encourage dependence on centralized, non-renewable energy sources through their mortgage lending policies. Homes that use wood-burning stoves or solar or wind power to provide electricity are considered *non-conforming*. Mortgage rates for those houses are higher than for homes that are connected to the power grid and are centrally-heated with fossil fuels. Eliminating this hidden penalty for using local energy sources would benefit both the environment and local economies.

Land use regulations

Local and regional land use rules could be amended to protect wild areas, open space and farmland from development. Political and financial support could be given to the various forms of land trusts that have been designed for this purpose. In some cases, local governments have used public money to buy the development rights to farmland, thereby protecting the land from suburban sprawl while simultaneously reducing financial pressure on farmers. Studies have also shown that developed land costs local governments significantly more in services than the extra tax revenues generated — meaning that when land is developed, taxpayers not only lose the benefits of open space, they lose money as well.

In urban areas, zoning regulations usually segregate residential, business and manufacturing areas — a restriction necessitated by the needs and hazards of large-scale production and marketing. These could be changed to enable an integration of homes, small shops and small-scale production. A rethinking of restrictions on community-based ways of living would also be beneficial: zoning and other regulations aimed at limiting high-density developments often end up prohibiting environmentally sound living arrangements like co-housing and eco-villages.

Health and safety regulations

An unfair burden often falls on small-scale enterprises through regulations aimed at problems caused by *large-scale* production. Battery-style chicken farms, for example, clearly need tough environmental and health regulations. The millions of closely confined animals are highly prone to disease; their tons of concentrated effluent need to be safely disposed of and the long-distance transport of eggs and fresh chicken entails the risk of spoilage. Yet a small producer — such as a farmer with a dozen free-range chickens — is subject to essentially the same regulations, often raising costs to levels that can make it impossible for them to remain in business. Large-scale producers can spread the cost of compliance over a far greater volume, making it appear that they enjoy economies of scale over smaller producers. Such discriminatory regulations are widespread and have damaged farm-based cheese production in Europe as well as small-scale apple cider production in the US.

How can regulations on large-scale operators be tightened without placing a killing burden on small operators? One solution is a two-tier system of regulations: stricter controls on large-scale producers and marketers (with strong safeguards against the *revolving door* between regulatory agencies and Big Business) — and a simpler set of locally determined regulations for small-scale, local enterprises. Such a system would acknowledge that communities deserve the right to monitor foods that are produced locally for local consumption and that such enterprises involve far fewer processes likely to damage human health or the environment.

Community-based minimum standards for local production and retailing would likely vary from place to place, influenced by local conditions and community values. Community peer pressure would ensure compliance with agreed-upon standards much more effectively than current systems of national or statewide standards which are largely anonymous and rely upon expensive enforcement mechanisms. Local regulation would allow more flexibility, encourage more accountability and would dramatically reduce the cost of both monitoring and compliance.

Highly local community regulations would co-exist with national and international regulations for goods produced in one region and sold in another. Small-scale businesses oriented towards local markets would not be burdened by inappropriate regulations, but people and the environment would still be protected from the excesses of distant, large-scale enterprises.

Grassroots initiatives

In addition to these policy and regulatory shifts, we need countless smaller, diverse, local initiatives of the kind that are already emerging. Unlike actions to halt the global economic steamroller, these small-scale steps require a slow pace and a deep, intimate understanding of local contexts and are best designed and implemented by local people themselves. If supported by the policy changes discussed above, such initiatives will, over time, inevitably foster a return to cultural and biological diversity and long-term sustainability.

Economic localization implies an adaptation to cultural and biological diversity; therefore, no single blueprint is appropriate everywhere. The range of possibilities for grassroots effort is as diverse as the locales in which they would take place. The following survey is by no means exhaustive, but illustrates steps being taken today.

Community banks and loan funds

In a number of places local funds have been set up, increasing the capital available to local residents and businesses and allowing people to invest in their neighbors and their community rather than in distant corporations. These schemes enable small businesses to obtain cheap start-up loans of the kind that banks typically offer only to large corporations.

Buy local campaigns

These campaigns help local businesses survive even when pitted against heavily subsidized corporate competitors. Buying local not only helps keep money from leaking out of the local economy but also helps educate people about the hidden costs — to the environment and to the community — of purchasing artificially cheaper distantly produced products. Around the world, grassroots organizations have emerged in response to the intrusion of huge corporate marketing chains into rural and small town economies. For example, the McDonald's Corporation — which opens about five new restaurants each day[7] — has met with grassroots resistance in at least two dozen countries. In the United States, Canada and the UK, the rapid expansion of Wal-Mart, the world's largest retailer, has spawned a whole network of citizens groups to protect jobs and the fabric of their communities from these sprawling superstores. A way of guaranteeing that money stays within the local economy is through the creation of *local currencies* that are only recognized by community members and local participating businesses. Similarly, Local Exchange Trading Systems (LETS) are, in effect, large-scale local barter systems. People list the services or goods they have to offer and the amount they expect in return. Their account is credited for goods or services they provide to other LETS members, and they can use those credits to purchase goods or services from anyone else in the local system. Thus, even people with little or no so-called real money can participate in, and benefit from, the circulation of credit within the local economy.

Community supported agriculture, subscription farming and farmers' markets

In the community supported agriculture (CSA) movement, consumers in towns and cities link up directly with a nearby farmer. Consumers usually have a chance to visit the farm where their food is grown and in many cases their help on the farm is welcomed. CSAs provide small farmers with a constant and reliable market while providing consumers with produce that is fresher and healthier than what they could buy at the supermarket. While small farmers linked to the industrial system continue to fail every year at an alarming rate, CSAs are allowing small-scale diversified farms to thrive in growing numbers. CSAs have spread rapidly throughout Europe, North America, Australia and Japan. In the United States, the number of CSAs has climbed from only two in 1986 to 200 in 1992, and was closer to 1,000 in 2000.[8]

Another model called *subscription farming* provides the farmer even more security because consumers share risk by paying in advance for a whole year's supply of food or even buying a share in the farm.

By connecting farmers directly with urban consumers, *farmers' markets* similarly benefit local economies and the environment. The number of farmers' markets in the US has grown substantially, from 1,755 in 1994 to over 2,600 in 1998.[9] Interest in this form of

Harvesting bulbs with volunteers

VICTORIA STEVENS

marketing has grown elsewhere as well. In the UK, the number of farmers' markets went from zero in 1996 to 270 in the year 2000.[10]

Organic food

Related to the enthusiasm for CSAs and the spread of farmers' markets is the growing general interest in local organic food. Outbreaks of BSE (Mad Cow Disease) as well as increasing incidences of *E. coli*, salmonella and even dioxin poisoning have resulted in major food scares in several parts of the world, most notably in Europe. The demand for more natural, unprocessed and organically grown foods has grown exponentially; close to 10% of agricultural land in some European countries now being cultivated organically.[11] Despite the fact that some large-scale producers oriented towards export have tapped into this burgeoning segment of the food market, organic agricultural methods are most conducive to small-scale, diversified, local production for local consumption. If chemical-intensive, industrial agriculture continues to give way to organic methods, the potential for truly sustainable local food systems will increase dramatically.

Eco-villages

The eco-village movement aims at creating a complete antidote to dependence on the global economy. Around the industrialized world, people are building communities that attempt to get away from the waste and pollution, competition and violence of contemporary life. Many rely on renewable energy and are seeking to develop more cooperative local economies. These efforts provide a significant alternative to the Western consumer model now being imposed on the less-developed parts of the world.[12]

Changing ourselves

The changes discussed above require shifts at the personal level as well. In part, these involve rediscovering the deep psychological benefits — the joy — of living in community. Children, mothers and the aged all know the importance of being able to feel they can depend on others. The values that are the hallmarks of today's fast-paced global economy, on the other hand, are those of a *teenage boy culture*. It is a culture that demands mobility, flexibility and independence. It induces a fear of growing old, of being vulnerable and dependent.

Another fundamental shift involves re-instilling a sense of connection with the place where we live. The globalization of culture and information has led to a way of life in which the nearby is treated with contempt. We get news from China, the Middle East or Washington, DC but remain ignorant about what is going on in our own backyard; at the touch of a button on a TV remote control we have access to all the wildlife of Africa, and our immediate surroundings consequently seem dull and uninteresting by comparison. A sense of place means helping ourselves and our children to see the living environment around us: reconnecting with the sources of our food, perhaps even growing some of our own and learning to appreciate the cycles of seasons and the characteristics of local flora and fauna and forests.

Ultimately, this shift in direction involves a spiritual awakening that comes from making a connection with others and with nature. It requires us to see the world within us — to experience more consciously the great interdependent web of life of which we ourselves are part.

Afterword: Where We Are Going

Wes Jackson

Imagine you're reading this 100 years from now.

Early May: Rain. Three days in a row now, and into the night it kept coming. The south bottom is flooded. Half-Day Creek was over its banks and had spread into the east pasture this morning when Dad moved the yearlings. More rain is in the forecast.

It's calving time. Eight have arrived, and there are four more to come. This is the family's concern. It is not soil erosion or muddy washes or replanting corn after such weather. All of these are memories held in family lore.

The rain is relentless but welcome. The two-year drought is over. Last year's precipitation, less than half the average, has been recouped with rains of the past month.

The drought had not seriously cut last year's yields. Farmers now have mixtures of perennial plants whose varying root architectures are nature's designs to handle drought, absorb water and manage nutrients efficiently. Some reach ten feet down and more; they use water stored earlier. Now, in a downpour, those roots hold the soil, and everybody

in the house this morning knows that the soils on the farm are weatherproof.

It was not always so. They knew of the 50-year transition their grandparents made on this land. Gone from the rolling Midwestern countryside are the monocultures of annual crops. Corn, soybeans, wheat and other former annuals have been perennialized and are grown in mixtures. And with the perennial root mixtures anchoring grain crops now, for the first time in 10,000 years farmers are not forced to roll dice against gravity.

Farmers had won rarely. Less than a century before, the farmer who stayed with it was like the gambler who stays at the casino betting against the house. Because wind and rain are the norm, anyone with annual crops on sloping land lost soil. And no matter how deep, there was only so much good soil to lose.

Farming with annual plants like corn and soybeans, there was little living cover from fall to mid-spring to stop soil erosion. And with loss of soil went loss of fertility. The annual crops with their often small and temporary roots leaked nitrogen fast. Naturally occurring nitrogen, and then the artificial substitute that fed unsustainably high yields, ran off in streams to both create and expand scores of *dead zones* in the seas, even when minimum or no till methods had become widespread.

Controlling erosion and runoff became a major challenge as prices for liquid fossil fuels escalated. No matter that farmers had priority to use such fuels once food was seen as a necessity instead of a commodity or weapon. As incentive increased to reduce input costs, decreased application of chemicals revealed the industrial era's impoverishment of natural soil fertility. Replenishment would require time, natural processes and better practices.

Late October: The combine whines through harvest, mowing a mixture of nearly even heights of perennial corn, sorghum, sunflower and soybeans. The shelling of the corn ears creates a rasping sound. A digital readout in the cab tells the farmer-operator that the bin is full. She signals her teenage son, waiting in the pickup, to pull the wagon alongside. With a lurch, the combine's auger starts and pours the grain into the wagon. The farmer returns to harvest, and the boy heads to the local co-op where a combination of shaking screens and the centrifugal force of a rotating drum separates seeds into a bin for each kind. By Thanksgiving, all of the fields of these modern domestic prairie patches will have been harvested. The sunflower seeds are pressed for oil, refined for on-farm diesel engines. The farm makes its own fuel.

What makes this a different agriculture is not the aboveground drama at harvest, which is still industrial. It is the shift of attention to processes below the land's surface.

With the perennial polyculture arrangement, farmers and agricultural scientists alike have combined the skills of naturalist, ecologist and farmer. This new agriculture arose when ecologists forcefully emphasized that the land before agriculture was mostly covered with perennials in mixtures — the story for millions of years. Soil abuse began when agriculture was introduced, reversing the land's cover to short-lived annual plants. Scientists recognized the need for grains' plentiful calories to feed large populations. But to sustain them would require perennial roots. They committed themselves to a challenge whose practical results would not come in their lifetimes. They teased their colleagues by wearing T-shirts that read, "If you expect to finish your work in your lifetime, you're not thinkin' big enough."

Genetics and plant breeding recovered; both disciplines had been in decline. This new generation of geneticists and breeders first perennialized sorghum, followed by sunflower and wheat and later corn and more. Domesticated were wild perennial legumes — Illinois bundleflower and chickpea and members of the wild composite genus *Silphium*.

Other disciplines joined the effort — plant ecologists, soil ecologists, landscape ecologists and students of environmental history. As perennial crops were being developed, ecologists worked with analogs and prototypes of the various species in combinations. Later they and their intellectual and philosophical descendents worked with the perennialized crop plants themselves. The need to know the vegetative history of various landscapes across the ecological mosaic turned environmental history into one of the most practical of all disciplines.

Biographers' attempts to derive psychological profiles of these agricultural pioneers were unsatisfying. These pioneers did believe that it was within their power to help solve humanity's oldest environmental problem.

They knew that sustainability in agriculture had to come first, because standing behind agriculture were the disciplines of ecology and evolutionary biology. The industrial sector, a product of human cleverness and lots of non-renewable, energy-rich carbon, had no such discipline. Finally, they knew how to begin, and they did. It amounted to a history-making change in collective will.

Historians have explored this shift that began about the year 2000:

- Culture at large became conscious that ten millennia ago most of the land of the planet had been covered with perennial plant mixtures. Such ecosystems tend to preserve ecological capital.

- Discoveries of new oil deposits no longer kept pace with increased demand. A person born in 1936, who had lived two-thirds of a century by 2003, had been alive while 97.5% of all the oil ever pumped had been burned. No alternative technology could match the quantity and convenience of liquid fossil fuels. The food supply of humanity depended to a large degree on such fuels. Many of the young concluded that agriculture needed a new paradigm. They began to explore the efficiencies inherent in the natural integrities of *wild ecosystems*, aiming for these efficiencies to offset the fossil fuel energy then being used for traction, fertilizers and pesticides.

- The biodiversity of the planet was crashing as more human mouths arrived. Some ecologists argued that to save biodiversity, humans would have to intensify agriculture "where the land is already screwed up," as one put

it. Others insisted on bringing processes from wild diversity to the farm and changing the agricultural landscape. Rather than trying to subdue nature, the promoters of the new paradigm posed three questions to land use: *What was here? What will nature require of us here? What will nature help us do here?*

These questions led students to systematically examine landscapes between the extremes of ecological and historical determinism. Ecological determinism must prevail in the most fragile environments. To farm there loses ecological capital, so the original vegetative structure must prevail. But in valley agriculture where flooding replaces fertility and erosion is not beyond replacement levels (such as the Nile before Aswan Dam) annual monocultures grown in rotation can work. Unfortunately, very little land is in this latter category. Farmers had to begin learning where on the continuum their land lay.

Forest meets the sea

VICTORIA STEVENS

Another story is what was happening back then in *the movement to restore and save wild land and forests* — not only for their own sake but because human well-being needs access to such places. The spirit of this land movement is put well by the remarks made by Peter Forbes in a number of talks given at the many gatherings of the land trust movement. He wrote:

All of our religions and philosophies and all of our scientific understandings acknowledge change. The land will change, by our own hands or not, and some of the places we love will be lost, but if our relationships to the earth are ever gaining in insight and leading us to new awareness, we can restore portions of what has been lost. We can make amends. If we can accept the idea of impermanence — that all life does change — we might be better prepared to focus on our relationship to land as much as we focus on the land itself. In this new light, land conservation would have as part of its mission

Rhododendron forest

VICTORIA STEVENS

the notions of sympathy, building health and well being, and reducing suffering much more than the goal of keeping land the same.

Here are five themes that might guide "Land and People" conservation:

Diversity

We need biological diversity on the planet for the same reasons we need all forms of diversity. Diversity creates empathy, stability and morality. Simply put, we cannot know unity without first knowing diversity. Land conservation strikes an essential chord of meaning and fairness when it explicitly promotes diversity of all types: biological, cultural, racial and socio-economic. To live by a credo of diversity, conservationists must work in diverse geographies, serve diverse peoples, be sympathetic to diverse relationships with the land, seek to work beyond the boundaries of their mission, and be constituted of diverse peoples. Through our work, we are always transferring to the public not just land but empowerment itself. At the heart of land conservation, by definition, is the obligation that all involved look beyond their immediate families to the needs of the larger community of life. Conservation, therefore, is first and foremost, against self-interest. And if land conservation is about citizenship, then it must equally be about changing existing power structures. Through this fundamental commitment to diversity, conservation builds awareness, strength and principle.

Good work

Whether carried out by a logger in a forest or a lawyer in an office tower, all forms of work ultimately affect the land. In this important sense, no one is divorced from the land and all share equally in its future. The conservation movement is quick to talk about recreation but is most often silent on work. Yet, it is the place where we live and the work that we do that forge many of our beliefs. Good work is fundamental to the human experience and, therefore, a critical component of any conservation philosophy that hopes to influence our culture. For land conservationists to promote good work, we need to use our resources to aid what remains of our land-based culture. Simultaneously, we need to allow examples of good work to thrive on our "protected" landscapes. We need to constantly search for projects that go beyond recreation or leisure to encompass how people provide for themselves. Some conservation organizations are espousing notions of good work by protecting farmland or allowing green timber harvesting on their lands. Others are investing in fishing and farming cooperatives and making small financial loans to build businesses along greenways. These activities build deeper human relationships with the whole land community by demonstrating how all types of work can reinforce people's connection to the land.

Food

What we eat and drink is our most important daily relationship to the land. Given that one-quarter of America's land base is in some form of agriculture and that the far majority of this is industrial and destructive of both land and people, the single most important change that land conservationists can make is to focus on improving how we grow healthy, local food. We can use our skills and resources to better support farmers who use nature as the measure. Land conservation can help good farming by helping to keep farms affordable and intact, by encouraging community-supported agriculture and organic farms. We can support good harvesting practices on land and water by using our money and skills to keep access affordable, to financially support cooperatives of green producers, and to use our land to keep community intact. We can celebrate food that is unique to our regions, food that says something about us and reminds us that ours is like no other place in the world.

Movement

We are a migratory species, and the fullness of our souls is reached when we can see and feel our landscape on our own scale. The ability to walk, bike, ride horseback and canoe the furthest possible distances creates a sense of freedom that is not unlike wildness, even though these activities might take us through a suburb or even a city. And the same need for movement and migration applies to the more-than-human world that needs wildlife corridors. Experiencing the land using our own muscles, moving at a slower pace than we normally do, and engaging our sight and smell and consciousness make us loyal to that place. Largely as result of Benton MacKaye's 1921 vision for a continuous Appalachian Trail from Georgia to Maine, there are now many other footpaths, greenways, ski trails and kayaking and canoe trails that allow Americans to cover hundreds of miles of their native region by their own ingenuity and knowledge of the land.

History

History is the difference between land and place — place being the union of land with people and their stories. By conserving places out of our past, we learn metaphors and stories that help us find our way in the future. Because of this relationship granted to us through an act of conservation, we have the opportunity for pathos, memory and connection. In protecting a 200-year-old boat shop, or one of the last herring smokehouses, or the boyhood home of Dr. Martin Luther King, we interject into the conservation of natural resources the story of social resources. Critical questions emerge that shape and guide us. What is the role of work and way of life to conservationists? What is the connection between civil rights and the environment?

These themes challenge us to think and speak differently about the aspirations for land conservation, and also offer the promise of a much greater impact to our culture. It is an appeal to all of us to consider the health and well being of our place in the world in terms of the quality of the relationships between the land and the people who are there. This is not nostalgic. We must go forward to nature, not back to it. The future of our culture hinges on our ability to understand and explain this statement....

Our concern for the Earth is the same as our concern for own heart and soul. This is why land conservation must search to see the results of its labor in both nature and culture. Our moral response to the events of the day is to rethink the promise of land conservation as the defense of our human relationship with the world of life. This aspiration for land conservation will be not reached alone by how much nature we can put aside, but by how much love and respect for the land we can engender in the greatest number of people. Our greatest achievement is not being able to say "we saved this place," but being able to say, instead, "You belong here. You are home." Land conservation can become the story of how the soul of the land became the soul of our culture, signaling over and over our place in the world.[1]

Endnotes and References

Foreword: Life On Our Planet
Is In Trouble — What Will YOU Do?

1. Millennium Ecosystem Assessment. *Ecosystems and Human Well-Being: Synthesis.* Island Press, 2005, pp. 1 and 4. This report can be read in full online at maweb.org.

Introduction:
Wild Foresting — A Vision Emerges

1. A summary of some of the main principles set forth in the earlier book and assumed in this one appears in Appendix 1.

2. Millennium Ecosystem Assessment. *Living Beyond Our Means: Natural Assets and Human Well-Being.* United Nations Environment Programme, March 2005; Intergovernmental Panel on Climate Change. *Climate Change 2007: Synthesis Report.* Fourth Assessment Report, IPCC Plenary XXVII, November 2007.

3. "Arctic Sea Ice Shatters all Previous Record Lows." National Snow and Ice Data Center Press Release. Cooperative Institute for Research in Environmental Sciences, University of Colorado — Boulder, October 2007.

4. Homer-Dixon, Thomas. *The Upside of Down: Catastrophe, Creativity, and the Renewal of Civilization.* Island Press, 2006.

5. Hawken, Paul. *Blessed Unrest: How the Largest Social Movement in History Is Restoring Grace, Justice, and Beauty to the World.* Viking, 2007; Bill McKibben. *Deep Economy: The Wealth of Communities and the Durable Future.* Times, 2007; David Korten. *The Great Turning: From Empire to Earth Community.* Berrett-Koehler, 2006; Ervin Laszlo. *The Chaos Point: the World at the Crossroads.* Hampton Roads, 2006.

6. Naess, Arne. *Life's Philosophy: Reason and Feeling in a Deeper World.* University of Georgia, 2002, pp 107-108. An earlier version was discussed in a 1996 exchange between Stan Rowe and Naess: J. Stan Rowe. "Deep Ecology Platform: Moving it from Biocentric to Ecocentric." [online]. [cited June 13, 2008]. ecospherics.net/pages/RoDeepEcolPlat.html. Naess and others have done much research on people's views related to these principles. Many organizations use some version of them, whether or not they refer to the deep ecology movement; for example, see different versions of the Earth Charter on the web.

7. These are also teachings of Buddha, Lao Tzu and others.

Chapter 1: Values Deep in the Woods

1. Cullen Bryant, William. "A Forest Hymn."
2. Wordsworth, William. "Tintern Abbey."

Chapter 2: The Place and the Story

1. Roszak, T.; M. Gomes; & A. Kanner, eds. *Ecopsychology: Restoring the Earth, Healing the Mind.* Sierra Club, 1995.
2. Zimmerman, Michael, et al. *Environmental Philosophy: From Animal Rights to Radical Ecology.* 4th ed. Prentice Hall, 2004.
3. Ekins, P. *The Gaia Atlas of Green Economics.* Anchor, 1992.
4. Tucker, M. E. and J. A. Grim, eds. *Worldviews and Ecology: Religion, Philosophy, and the Environment.* Orbis, 1994.
5. Catton, William R. *Overshoot: The Ecological Basis of Revolutionary Change.* University of Illinois Press, 1982; Clive Ponting. *A New Green History of the World, The Environment and the Collapse of Great Civilizations.* Penguin, 2007.
6. Spretnak, C. *States of Grace: The Recovery of Meaning in the Postmodern Age.* Harper, 1991.
7. Goldsmith, E. *The Way: An Ecological World-View.* Chelsea Green, 2008; Fritjof Capra. *The Web of Life: A New Scientific Understanding of Living Systems.* Anchor, 1997.
8. Merchant, Carolyn. *Radical Ecology: The Search for a Livable World.* 2nd ed. Routledge, 2005. This book is a good overview of these movements. Though bioregionalism is actually not included among them I believe that it should be.
9. Sale, Kirkpatrick. *Dwellers in the Land: The Bioregional Vision.* University of Georgia Press, 2000; Van Andruss, et al. *Home! A Bioregional Reader.* New Society, 1990.
10. Mander, Jerry. *In the Absence of the Sacred: The Failure of Technology and the Survival of the Indian Nations.* Sierra Club, 1992.
11. Blake, William. "The Marriage of Heaven and Hell, Plate 11." In Geoffrey Keynes, ed. *Blake: Complete Writings.* Oxford, 1979.
12. Stegner, Wallace. *Where the Bluebird Sings to the Lemonade Springs: Living and Writing in the West.* Modern Library, 2002, p. 202.
13. Swimme, Brian and Thomas Berry. *The Universe Story: From the Primordial Flaring Forth to the Ecozoic Era — A Celebration of the Unfolding of the Cosmos.* Harper, 1994.
14. Sheldrake, Rupert. *The Presence of the Past: Morphic Resonance and the Habits of Nature.* Park Street, 1995.
15. Stafford, Kim. *Places and Stories.* Carnegie Mellon, 1987, p. 11.
16. Eliot, T. S. "Little Gidding" part 5. In *Four Quartets.* Faber, 1996.

Chapter 3: Forests and Sacred Groves

Abbiw, D. K. 1990. *Useful Plants of Ghana: West African Uses of Wild and Cultivated Plants.* Intermediate Technology Publications.

Elder, J. and H.C. Wong. 1994. *Family of Earth and Sky: Indigenous Tales of Nature from Around the World.* Beacon Press.

Porteous, A. 1928. *The Lore of the Forest: Myths and Legends.* Guernsey Press.

Posey, D.A., ed. 1999. *Cultural and Spiritual Values of Biodiversity.* Intermediate Technology Publications on behalf of United Nations Environment Programme (UNEP).

Schama, S. 1995. *Landscape and Memory.* Knopf.

UNESCO 1996. *Sacred Sites — Cultural Integrity, Biological Diversity.* Programme proposal, Paris, 1996.

Vartak, V. D. and M. Gadgil. "Studies on sacred groves along the Western Ghats from Maharashtra and Goa. Role of Beliefs and Folklore." In Jain, S.K. ed. *Glimpses of Indian Ethnobotany.* Oxford & IBH, 1981, pp. 272-278.

Chapter 4: Enrichment Forestry at Windhorse Farm

1. The Acadian Forest is the very rich and diverse forest which lies between the Northern Hardwood Forest of New England and the Northern Boreal Forest. It is mostly within the

Canadian Maritime Provinces of Nova Scotia, New Brunswick and Prince Edward Island. It has been designated as one of six forests in North America that are considered endangered according to the World Wildlife Fund.

2. Leopold, Aldo. *A Sand County Almanac.* Oxford University Press, 1968, London, Oxford & New York.

3. Tegan Wong, one of the reviewers of this chapter, took exception to my claim that the practices have not really changed. She comments, "What has changed in your forestry practices over the years is this respect for nature's timeframe and your experience and deepening relationship with the land. The Windhorse practices may not seem to have changed to an outsider, but I would say they have changed. Every day, each decision is based on the evolving relationship between you and the forest. Even though the timeframe of your stewardship is short, you can feel if something is working or not, and it informs the decisions you make down the road … The practices may change over time, but what seems to be consistent, and what informs the practices, is that each of you valued the relationship with the forest, and this relationship and deepening mutual understanding has allowed you to tap into the generosity of the forest. Indeed it has given more wood than it would have given through successive clearcuts because you respect and love it for much more than its wood!"

4. Linda Pannozzo, author of the *GPI Forest Accounts* (GPI Atlantic, 2001), commented, "I do have one suggestion having to do with the 'economic filter.' It seems to me that our current economic system is the reason behind the unfettered destruction of the world's forests, and that this is only possible because there is no logical link between the economic theory currently in use and the reality of the earth's ecological systems. So, it is this disconnect that allows us to destroy the earth, for the economy.

David Suzuki once commented on this, saying that our economic system should reflect the reality of our natural world. So, when we use GPI or ecological economics, whatever you want to call it, there is a logical connection. I think the economic filter should include mention of this somehow."

Chapter 5: Ecoforestry — Doing the Right Things

1. Drucker, Peter. *The Effective Executive: The Definitive Guide to Getting the Right Things Done.* Rev. ed. Collins, 2006.

2. In the summer of 1993 some 800 people were arrested protesting clearcut logging in British Columbia's Clayoquot Sound on the west coast of Vancouver Island. The protest received both national and international attention. This event proved to be a catalyst in raising the public's awareness that old growth forests are highly complex systems with a spectrum of values that cannot be reduced solely to short-term economic factors.

3. The British Columbia government has moved towards a results-based approach to forest management in which forest companies are given a considerable level of flexibility and control in meeting clearly defined government goals and targets.

Chapter 6: Ecological Principles for Responsible Forest Use

Bateson, Gregory. 1987. "Men are grass." In W. I. Thompson, ed. *Gaia: A Way of Knowing.* Lindisfarne Press.

Cobb, John B. Jr. and David Ray Griffin. 1977. *Process Theology: An Introductory Exposition.* Westminster John Knox Press.

Cooper, W. S. 1926. The fundamentals of vegetational change. *Ecology* 7: 391–413.

Daly, Herman and J. B. Cobb, Jr. 1989. *For the Common Good.* Beacon Press.

Fuller, Buckminster. 1976. Personal Communication.

Gurwitsch, Alexander. 1922. In P.A. Weiss. 1939. *Principles of Development.* Henry Holt.

Hart, Richard. 1994. Personal Communication.

Ho, Mae-Wan and S. W. Fox. 1988. "Processes and metaphors in evolution." In Mae Wan Ho and S. W. Fox, eds. *Evolutionary Processes and Metaphors.* Wiley.

Johnson, Lionel. 1988. "The thermodynamic origin of ecosystems: A tale of broken symmetry." In B. H. Weber et al., eds. *Entropy, Information, and Evolution.* MIT Press.

Koestler, A. and J.R. Smytbies, eds. 1969. *Beyond Reductionism: New Perspectives in the Life Sciences.* Hutchinson.

Margalef, R. 1968. *Perspectives in Ecological Theory.* University of Chicago Press.

Margulis, Lynn. 1991. "Big trouble in biology: Physiological autopoiesis versus mechanistic neo-Darwinism." In John Brockman, ed. *Doing Science.* Prentice Hall.

Maruyama, Magorah. 1978. "Transepistemological Understanding: Wisdom beyond theories." In Donald Knowler, ed. *Cultures of the Future.* Mouton.

Naess, Arne. 1983. Personal communication.

Odum, Eugene P. 1971. *Fundamentals of Ecology.* Saunders.

Perry, David. 1998. Personal communication (Ecoforestry Summer Institute).

Salthe, Stanley N. 1985. *Evolving Hierarchical Systems.* Columbia University Press.

Schneider. 1988. "Thermodynamics, ecological succession, and natural selection: A common thread." In B. H. Weber et al., eds. *Entropy, Information, and Evolution.* MIT Press.

Shepard, Paul. 1981. Personal communication.

Smuts, J.C. 2007. *Holism And Evolution.* Kessinger Publishing.

Thom, Rene. 1994. *Structural Stability And Morphogenesis.* Westview Press.

Varela, F. et al. 1974. "Autopoiesis: The organization of living systems." *Biosystems* 5:187-196.

Waddington, Conrad. 1971. *The Evolution of an Evolutionist.* Cornell University Press.

Weiss, Paul A. 1967. "One Plus One Does Not Equal Two." In *The Neurosciences: A Study Program.* G.C. Quarton et al., eds. Rockefeller University Press.

Whitehead, A. N. 1933. *Adventures of Ideas.* Macmillan.

_____ 1958. *The Function of Reason.* Beacon Press.

_____ 1967. *Science and the Modern World.* Free Press.

Whittacker, E. T. 1951. *Eddington's principle in the philosophy of science* (Arthur Stanley Eddington memorial lecture). University Press.

Wittbecker, Alan E. 1976. *The Poetic Archaeology of the Flesh.* MRW, Ltd.

_____ 1990. "Metaphysical implications from physics and ecology." *Environmental Ethics* 12(3):276-281.

_____ 1990. "Metaphysical principles from ecological foundations." *Pan Ecology* 5(4): 1-16.

Chapter 7:
A Tree is a Quintessential Plant

Fiero, G. William. *Nevada's Valley of Fire.* KC Publications, 1988.

Spielmann, P.J. "Jurassic pine tree found living in a 'lost world' near Sydney." Associated Press in *Corvallis Gazette-Times.* December 15, 1994.

Maser, Chris and James R. Sedell. *From the forest to the sea: The ecology of wood in streams, rivers, estuaries, and oceans.* St. Lucie Press, 1994.

Lyell, Sir Charles. *Principles of geology; or the modern changes of the Earth and its inhabitants.* D. Appleton & Co., 1866.

Emmons, Louise H. "Tropical rain forests: why they have so many species, and how we may lose this biodiversity without cutting a single tree." *Orion* 8 (1989), pp. 8-14.

Associated Press. "10 percent of tree species under threat of extinction." *Corvallis Gazette-Times,* August 26, 1998.

Chapter 11: Buddhism and Global Warming

Batchelor, Stephen. 1997. *Buddhism Without Beliefs: A Contemporary Guide to Awakening.* Riverhead Books.

Evangelical Climate Initiative. *2006. Climate Change: An Evangelical Call to Action.* [online]. [cited June 20, 2008]. npr.org/documents/2006/feb/evangelical/calltoaction.pdf.

Kaza, Stephanie and Kenneth Kraft. 2000. *Dharma Rain: Sources of Buddhist Environmentalism.* Shambhala.

Loori, John Daido. 2007. *Teachings of the Earth: Zen and the Environment.* Shambhala.

Loy, David. 2003. *The Great Awakening: A Buddhist Social Theory.* Wisdom Books.

Chapter 13: Renewing Our Forest Culture — The Art and Practice of Natural Forests

Maloof, J. *Teaching the Trees; Lessons from the Forest.* University of Georgia Press, 2005.

Simey, I. *Ecoforestry* journals. Summer and Fall issues, 2002.

Chapter 19: The Future of Ecoforestry in Western Australia

Abbott, I. and N. Burrows. 2003. *Fire in Ecosystems in South-West Western Australia: Impacts and Management.* Backhuys.

Abbott, I. and P. Christensen. 1994. Application of ecological and evolutionary principles to forest management in Western Australia. *Australian Forestry,* 57(3), 109-122.

Abbott, I. and P. Christensen. 1996. Objective knowledge, ideology and the forests of Western Australia. *Australian Forestry,* 59(4), 206-212.

Beresford, R., et al. 2001. *The Salinity Crisis: Landscapes, Communities and Politics.* UWA Press.

Bradshaw, J. 2005. *Managing Private Forests and Woodlands in the South West of Western Australia: Combining Wood Production and Conservation.* Natural Heritage Trust and Government of Western Australia.

Burbidge, A.A. 2000. "Conservation of the biota of the megadiverse South-west Botanical Province," *Australia. Australian Systematic Botany Society Newsletter,* 102, 25-33.

Burrows, N.D.; B. Ward; & R. Cranfield. 2002. Short-term impacts of logging on understory vegetation in a jarrah forest. *Australian Forestry,* 65(1), 47-58.

Calver, M.C. 2003. "The precautionary principle and ecosystem health: A case study from the jarrah forest, south-western Australia." In D.J. Rapport et al (eds.) *Managing for Healthy Ecosystems* (pp. 935-947). CRC/Lewis Press.

Calver, M.C. and J. Dell 1998. "Conservation status of mammals and birds in southwestern Australian forests. I. Is there evidence of direct links between forestry practices and species decline and extinction?" *Pacific Conservation Biology,* 4, 296-314.

Calver, M.C., et al. "Towards resolving conflict between forestry and conservation in Western Australia." *Australian Forestry,* 61(4), 258-266.

Calver, M.C., et al. 2005. "Why 'A forest conscientiousness'?" In Calver, M. et al. (eds.) *A Forest Conscientiousness,* Proceedings of the 6th National Conference of the Australian Forest History Society (pp xvii – xxiii). Millpress.

Calver, M. and G. Wardell-Johnson. 2004. Sustained unsustainability? An evaluation of evidence for a history of overcutting in the jarrah forests of Western Australia and its consequences for fauna conservation. In D. Lumney (ed.) *The Conservation of Australia's Forest Fauna* (2nd Ed.) (pp. 94-114). Royal Zoological Society of NSW.

Clinebell, H. 1996. *Ecotherapy: Healing Ourselves, Healing the Earth.* Fortress.

CSIRO & Australian Bureau of Meteorology. 2007. *Climate Change in Australia: Technical Report 2007.* CSIRO.

EPA. 2000. *Environmental Protection of Native Vegetation in Western Australia.* Ferguson, I. 1996. *Sustainable Forest Management.* Oxford University Press.

Hobbs, R.J. 1996. "Ecosystem dynamics and management in relation to conservation in forest systems." *Journal of the Royal Society of Western Australia,* 79, 293-300.

Horwitz, P. and M. Calver. 1998. Credible science? Evaluating the Regional Forest Agreement process in Western Australia. *Australian Journal of Environmental Management,* 5, 213-224.

Indian Ocean Climate Initiative. 2002. *Climate Variability and Change in South West Western Australia.*

Lane, M.B. 1999. Regional Forest Agreements: Resolving resource conflicts or managing resource politics? *Australian Geographical Studies,* 37(2), 142-153.

Lee, K.M. and I. Abbott. 2004. "Precautionary forest management: A case study from Western Australian legislation, policies, management plans, codes of practice and manuals for the period 1919-1999". *Australian Forestry,* 67(2), 114-121.

Lindenmayer, D.B. 2000. Using environmental history and ecological evidence to appraise management regimes in forests. In S.Dovers (ed.) *Environmental History and Policy.* Oxford University Press.

Lindenmayer, D.B. and J.F. Franklin. 1997. Re-inventing the discipline of forestry — a forest ecology perspective. *Australian Forestry,* 60(1), 53-55.

Lindenmayer, D.B. and J.F. Franklin, 2002. *Conserving Forest Biodiversity: A Comprehensive, Multi-scaled Approach.* Island Press.

Lindenmayer, D.B. and J.F. Franklin, 2003. *Towards Forest Sustainability.* Island Press.

Lindenmayer, D.B. and H.F. Recher. 1998. Aspects of ecologically sustainable forestry in temperate eucalypt forests — beyond an expanded reserve system. *Pacific Conservation Biology,* 4, 4-10.

McKenna, R.; M. Brueckner; J. Duff; & P. Horwitz. 2006. What are they taking us for? The participatory nature of Western Australia's Regional Forest Agreement process. *Australasian Journal of Environmental Management,* 13(1), 6-16.

National SOE, 2006.

Nature-based Tourism Strategy, 2004.

Norton, T.W. and N.D. Mitchell. 1994. Towards the sustainable management of southern temperate forest ecosystems: Lessons from Australia and New Zealand. *Pacific Conservation Biology,* 1, 293-300.

Pittock, B. 2007. *Dangerous Aspirations: Beyond 3°C Warming in Australia.* World Wide Fund for Nature (Australia).

Ryan, et al, 2002.

Sharp, C. 2005. "Illusive sustainability: An overview of recent experience." In Calver, M. et al. (eds.) *A Forest Conscientiousness,* Proceedings of the 6th National Conference of the Australian Forest History Society (pp 675-680). Millpress.

Shea, S. 2003. *The Potential for Large Scale Sequestration and Landscape and Biodiversity Rehabilitation in Australia.* University of Notre Dame.

Soule, M.E., et al. 2004. "The role of connectivity in Australian conservation". *Pacific Conservation Biology,* 10, 266-279.

Underwood, R. and J. Bradshaw (eds.). 2000. *Conservation and Use of Western Australia's Forests: The Perspectives of WA Foresters.* Institute of Foresters Australia.

Western Australia. *State of the Environment Report 2007.* [online]. [cited June 24, 2008]. soe.wa.gov.au.

Western Australia Conservation Commission. *WA Forest Management Plan 2004-2013.* Available at conservation.wa.gov.au/downloads.htm?docCatID=3&TLCN=Forest+Management+Plan.Western Australia Forest Alliance. 1998.

World Wide Fund for Nature (Australia). 2005. "Woodland Watch Social Impacts Evaluation".

Chapter 21: A First Nations Perspective on Ecosystem Management

Jaenan, C. J. *Documents in Canadian history.* Addison Wesley, 1988.

Saul, John Ralston. *Voltaire's Bastards: The Dictatorship of Reason in the West.* Vintage, 1993.

Webb, Clement. *A History of Philosophy*. Oxford University Press, 1959.

Chapter 22: The Culture of Forests — Haida Traditional Knowledge and Forestry in the 21st Century

1. This is the date when British sovereignty over British Columbia was established through the Oregon Boundary Treaty — an arbitrarily selected cut off point for CMT protection chosen in the revision of the Heritage Conservation Act in the 1980s.

References

Boas, Franz. 1930. T*he Religion of the Kwakiutl Indians*. Columbia University Press (Reprinted in 1969 by AMS Press)

British Columbia, Government of. *Heritage Conservation Act* [RSBC 1996] Chapter 187. Queens Printer qp.gov.bc.ca/statreg/stat/H/96187_01.htm

British Columbia, Province of. *Culturally Modified Trees of British Columbia. A Handbook for the Identification and Recording of Culturally Modified Trees*. Ministry of Small Business, Tourism and Culture, Archaeology Branch, Resources Inventory Committee. (Version 2.0) for.gov.bc.ca/hfd/pubs/docs/mr/Mr091/cmthandbook.pdf] [previously published in 1998 as: Stryd, Arnoud H. *Culturally Modified Trees of British Columbia*. British Columbia Ministry of Forests, 1998.]

Cathedral Grove. 2004-2007. *Cathedral Grove Big Trees & Totem Poles. Haida Gwaii Totem Poles*. Website developed by Karen Wonders, Research Fellow, Institute for the History of Science, University of Göttingen, cathedralgrove.se/text/06-Totem-Poles-4.htm

Clayoquot Scientific Panel (Scientific Panel for Sustainable Forest Practices in Clayoquot Sound). 1995a. *First Nations' Perspectives on Forest Practices in Clayoquot Sound*. Report 3. Cortex Consulting.

Deur, Douglas and Nancy J. Turner (eds). 2005. *"Keeping it Living": Traditions of Plant Use and Cultivation on the Northwest Coast of North America*. University of Washington Press and UBC Press.

Garrick, David. 1998. *Shaped Cedars and Cedar Shaping. A Guidebook to Identifying, Documenting, Appreciating and Learning from Culturally Modified Trees*. Western Canada Wilderness Committee. [Under authority of Wedlidi Speck, Chief Tlokoglass of the Seeinglae Clan, Kwakwaka'wakw First Nation]

Guujaaw. 2003. Letter to Archaeology and Registry Services Branch, Provincial Government, Victoria, BC, indicating non-concurrence with the application for a 'site alteration permit' 21100-20/30A241 from Husby Forest Products to alter archaeological site in block NAD 120. President, Council of the Haida Nation (July 30, 2003).

Haida Tribal Society. 2007. Map showing location of CMTs cut by Husby logging at Naden Harbour, July 2007. Haida Heritage & Forest Guardians. HLV Survey, BCTS – Eden Lake, NAD120. Naden River Watershed Unit 103F097.

Hamashige, Hope. 2005. "Surprise Finds Top List of Best National Parks." *National Geographic News* June 27, 2005. news.nationalgeographic.com/news/2005/Ø6/0627_050627_bestparks.html

Husby [Husby Group of Companies]. *Forest Development Plan*. (Husby Forest Products Ltd. F.L. A16869, Sitkana Timber Ltd. F.L. A16871, Dawson Harbour Logging Co. Ltd. T.S.L. A16873, TimberWest Forest Limited T.L. T0279, represented by the Husby Group of Companies, 6425 River Road), Delta BC. husby.bc.ca/HusbyForestDevPlan.pdf

Mobley, Charles M. and Morley Eldridge. 1992. "Culturally Modified Trees in the Pacific Northwest." *Arctic Anthropology* 29(2): 91-110.

Munt, Leonard. 2007. Rationale – NAD 120 & STA028. District Manager, Queen Charlotte

Islands Forest District. Unpublished document in possession of the Council of the Haida Nation, Skidegate, BC.

Salmón, Enrique. 2000A. "Kincentric Ecology: Indigenous Perceptions of the Human-Nature Relationship". *Ecological Applications* 10(5): 1327-1332.

Salmón, Enrique. 2000B. "Iwígara. A Rarámuri cognitive model of biodiversity and its effects on land management". Pp. 180-203 in: Paul E. Minnis and Wayne J. Elisens (eds). *Biodiversity and Native America*. University of Oklahoma Press.

Senos, René; Frank Lake; Nancy Turner; & Dennis Martinez. 2006. "Traditional Ecological Knowledge and Restoration Practice in the Pacific Northwest. Pp. 393-426, In: *Encyclopedia for Restoration of Pacific Northwest Ecosystems*. (Dean Apostol, editor). Island Press.

Stewart, Hilary. 1984. *Cedar. Tree of Life to the Northwest Coast Indians*. Douglas & McIntyre.

Stryd, Arnoud H. and Vicki Feddema. 1998. *Sacred Cedar. The Cultural and Archaeological Significance of Culturally Modified Trees*. A report of the Pacific Salmon Forests Project, David Suzuki Foundation. davidsuzuki.org/Forests/Publications.asp

Swanton, John R. 1905. *Haida Texts and Myths, Skidegate Dialect*. Bureau of American Ethnology, Bulletin No. 29. Smithsonian Institution.

Turner, Nancy J. 1995. *Food Plants of Coastal First Peoples*. Royal British Columbia Museum: UBC Press.

Turner, Nancy J. 1998. *Plant Technology of British Columbia First Peoples*. Royal British Columbia Museum and UBC Press.

Turner, Nancy J. 2004. *Plants of Haida Gwaii*. Xaadaa Gwaay guud gina k'aws (Skidegate), Xaadaa Gwaayee guu giin k'aws (Massett). Sono Nis Press.

Turner, Nancy J. 2005. *The Earth's Blanket. Traditional Teachings for Sustainable Living*. Douglas & McIntyre and University of Washington Press (Cultures and Landscapes series).

Turner, Nancy J.; Marianne B. Ignace; & Ronald Ignace. 2000. Traditional Ecological Knowledge and Wisdom of Aboriginal Peoples in British Columbia. *Ecological Applications* 10 (5): 1275-1287

Turner, Nancy J. and Barbara Wilson (*Kii'iljuus*). 2006. "To Provide Living Plants for Study: *The Value of Ethnobotanical Gardens and Planning the Qay'llnagaay Garden of Haida Gwaii.*" *Davidsonia* 16 (4): 111-125.

Chapter 23: Plant Teachers as a Source of Healing — Experiences of Interdependent Health from the Peruvian Amazon

1. Takiwasi means *The House that Sings* in the jungle dialect of Quechua. For more information about Takiwasi, see takiwasi.com.
2. Plant teachers which possess healing knowledge and a spirit known to healers as an *anima*.

References

Giove, Rosa. 2002. *La liana de los muertos al rescate de la vida*. Takiwasi-DEVIDA.

Ibacache, J.; L.T. Morros; & M. Trangol. 2002. *Salud Mental y Enfoque socioespiritual y psico-biológico*. mapuche.info/mapuint/sssmap020911.pdf

Nhat Hanh, Thich. 1975. *The Miracle of Mindfulness*. Beacon Press Books.

Chapter 24:
Tree Meditation Meets Shamanism

1. Michael Harner synthesized a program in Core Shamanism and founded the Foundation for Shamanic Studies (shamanism.org). His best known book on Core Shamanism is *The Way of the Shaman*, Bantam, 1986.
2. Lao Tzu, *Tao Te Ching*, Richard Wilhelm and D.C. Lau, translators, Penguin, 1988.

Chapter 25: Wild Humans

1. Canada and even the US seem sadly intent on imitating this example sometimes.
2. The worship of the false god Money, named in theological Latin.

3. It might be fair to say that natural felines don't have complete relationships with much of anything; feline nature is rather solitary.

4. "Any manager who ... did attempt to pay the external costs imposed on others by his firm would be placing himself at a competitive disadvantage and would be risking his own job at the hands of angry stockholders" (Walther 2007: 40). 5. For those who don't read French: "I don't want to see no quack engineer on my land!"

6. See Leviticus 25.

References

Angus, Karl. 2006. Telephone interviews and correspondence on the life of the early *coureurs-de-bois*. February-April. The late Mr. Angus made Métis history his principal intellectual pursuit. For several years he was President of the Port Alberni Métis Association and for one, Executive Director of the BC United Native Nations Society.

Eichenberger, Bob. 2007. "Helping Ecoforestry Grow: A Personal Effort." *Ecoforestry* 20:3&4, Summer/Fall 20-24.

Komarov, Boris. 1980. *The Destruction of Nature in the Soviet Union*. M. E. Sharpe.

Lähde, Erkki. 2007. "Multiple Use Forestry is More Productive Forestry." *Ecoforestry* 20:3&4, Summer/Fall 4-11.

Martin, Davd. 1998. "Homestead Land Tenure: An Option for Better Forestry." *Ecoforestry* 13:2 (September):26-30.

Maser, Chris. 1994. "Ancient Forests: Priceless Treasures." In Pilarski, Michael, ed. (1994) *Restoration Forestry*. Kivaki Press.

Morgan, Elaine. 1973. *The Descent of Woman*. Bantam.

Morgan, Elaine. 1977. *Falling Apart: The Rise and Decline of Urban Civilization*. Stein and Day.

Ontario Ministry of Lands and Forests. 1969. *The Farm Woodlot*. Government of Ontario.

Walther, Chris. 2007. "Ecoforestry is Public Interest Forestry." *Ecoforestry* 20:1 (Winter/Spring) 39-42.

Wilkinson, Mervin. 1996-1997. Personal interviews at Wildwood, his home and demonstration forest.

Chapter 27: The Powerful Link Between Conserving Land and Preserving Health

1. US National Park Service. State Parks, *National Park Service Announce Expanded Statewide Collaboration for Kids in Parks Program*. News Release, April 23, 2008. [online]. [cited July 30, 2008]. emnrd.state.nm.us/PRD/documents/StateParks NationalParkServiceAnnounceCollaboration.pdf.

Additional References

Baranowski T; W.O. Thompson; R.H. DuRant; J. Baranowski & J. Puhl. Observations on physical activity in physical locations: Age, gender, ethnicity, and month effects. *Research Q Exercise Sport* 1993; 64(2):127-33.

Beatley, T. *Green Urbanism: Learning from European Cities*. Island Press, 1999.

Berger, R. Using contact with nature, creativity and rituals as a therapeutic medium with children with learning difficulties: A case study. *Emotional Behav Difficulties* 2006; 11(2):135-46.

Bettmann, J. Changes in adolescent attachment relationships as a response to wilderness treatment. *J Am Psychoanalytic Assoc* 2007; 55(1): 259-65.

Bodin, M. and T. Hartig. Does the outdoor environment matter for psychological restoration gained through running? *Psychol Sport Exercise*. 2003; 4(2): 141-53.

Burdette, H.L. and R.C. Whitaker. Resurrecting free play in young children: Looking beyond fitness and fatness to attention, affiliation and affect. *Arch Pediatr Adolescent Med* 2005; 159: 46-50.

de Vries S.; R.A. Verheij; P.P. Groenewegen; & P. Spreeuwenberg; Natural environments — healthy environments? An exploratory analysis of the relationship between greenspace and health. *Environment and Planning* A 2003; 35: 1717-31.

Diette, G.B.; N. Lechtzin; E. Haponik; A. Devrotes; & H.R. Rubin. "Distraction therapy with nature sights and sounds reduces pain during flexible bronchoscopy: a complementary approach to routine analgesia". *Chest* 2003; 123(3): 941-8.

Easley, AT; J.F. Passineau; & B.L. Driver; compilers. *The Use of Wilderness for Personal Growth, Therapy, and Education.* US Department of Agriculture, Forest Service, Rocky Mountain Forest and Range Experiment Station, 1990.

Eikenaes, I; T. Gude; & A. Hoffart. "Integrated wilderness therapy for avoidant personality disorder". *Nordic J Psychiatry* 2006;60: 275-81.

Epstein, I. "Adventure therapy: A mental health promotion strategy in pediatric oncology". *J Ped Oncol Nursing* 2004;21(2): 103-10.

Faber, Taylor A.; F.E. Kuo; & W.C. Sullivan. "Coping with ADD: The surprising connection to green play settings". *Environ & Behav* 2001;33(1): 54-77.

Fox, S. *John Muir and His Legacy.* Little, Brown, 1981.

Frumkin, H. "Healthy places: Exploring the evidence". *Am J Public Health* 2003;93(9):1451-56.

Gigliotti, C.M.; S.E. Jarrott; & J. Yorgason. "Harvesting health: Effects of three types of horticultural therapy activities for persons with dementia". *Dementia: Internat J Soc Res Pract* 2004;3(2): 161-80.

Ginsburg, K.R.; Committee on Communications; Committee on Psychosocial Aspects of Child and Family Health. "The importance of play in promoting healthy child development and maintaining strong parent-child bonds". *Pediatrics* 2007;119: 182-91.

Greenway, R. "The wilderness effect and ecopsychology". In: Roszak T, Gomes ME, Kanner AD, Eds. *Ecopsychology: Restoring the Earth, Healing the Mind.* Sierra Club, 1995.

Haller, R.L. and C.L. Kramer. *Horticulture Therapy Methods: Making Connections in Health Care, Human Service, and Community Programs.* Haworth Press, 2007.

Heerwagen, J.H. and G.H. Orians. "Humans, habitats, and aesthetics". In: Kellert SR, Wilson EO. *The Biophilia Hypothesis.* Island Press, 1993.

Heerwagen, J.H.; J.G. Heubach; J. Montgomery; & W.C. Weimer. "Environmental design, work, and well being: managing occupational stress through changes in the workplace environment". *AAOHN J* 1995;43(9): 458-68.

Kaplan, R. "The role of nature in the urban context". In: Altham I, Wohlwill J, Eds. *Behavior and the Natural Environment.* Plenum, 1983.

Kaplan, R and S. Kaplan. *The Experience of Nature: A Psychological Perspective.* Cambridge University Press, 1989.

Kaplan, S. "The restorative benefits of nature: Toward an integrative framework". *J Environ Psychol* 1995;15: 169-82.

Klesges, R.C.; L.H. Eck; C.L. Hanson; C.K. Haddock; & L.M. Klesges. "Effects of obesity, social interactions, and physical environment on physical activity in preschoolers". *Health Psychol* 1990; 9(4): 435-49.

Kuo, F.E. "Coping with poverty: Impacts of environment and attention in the inner city". *Environment & Behavior* 2001;33(1): 5-34.

Kuo, F.E. and W.C. Sullivan(a). "Environment and crime in the inner city: Does vegetation reduce crime?" *Environment and Behavior,* 2001;33(3): 343-367.

Kuo, F.E. and W.C.Sullivan (b). "Aggression and violence in the inner city: Effects of environment via mental fatigue". *Environment and Behavior,* 2001;33(4): 543-71.

Kuo, F.E. and Taylor A. Faber. "A potential natural treatment for Attention-Deficit/Hyperactivity Disorder: Evidence from a national study". *Am J Public Health* 2004; 94(9): 1580-86.

Louv, R. *Last Child in the Woods: Saving our Children from Nature-Deficit Disorder.* Algonquin Books, 2005.

Maas, J.; R.A. Verheij; P.P. Groenewegen; S. de Vries; & P. Spreeuwenberg. "Green space, urbanity, and health: How strong is the relation"?

J Epidemiol Community Health 2006; 60: 587-92.

Manuel, P.M. "Occupied with ponds: Exploring the meaning, bewaring the loss for kids and communities of nature's small spaces". *J Occup Science* 2003; 10:31-39.

Marcus, C.C. and M. Barnes. *Healing Gardens: Therapeutic Benefits and Design Recommendations.* Wiley, 1999.

Pastor, S. and M.C. Straus, Eds. *Horticulture as Therapy: Principles and Practice.* Food Products Press, 1997.

Pretty, J; J. Peacock; M. Sellens; & M. Griffin. "The mental and physical health outcomes of green exercise". *Int J Environ Health Research* 2005; 15(5): 319-37.

Readdick, C.A. and G.R. Schaller. "Summer camp and self-esteem of school-age inner-city children". *Perceptual & Motor Skills* 2005; 101(1): 121-30.

Sallis, J.F.; P.R. Nader; S.L. Broyles; C.C. Berry; J.P. Elder; T.L. McKenzie; & J.A. Nelson. "Correlates of physical activity at home in Mexican-American and Anglo-American preschool children". *Health Psychol* 1993;12(5): 390-8.

Söderback, I; M. Söderström; & E. Schälander. "Horticultural therapy: The "healing garden" and gardening in rehabilitation measures at Danderyd Hospital Rehabilitation Clinic, Sweden". *Pediatr Rehab* 2004; 7(4): 245-60.

Taylor, A.F.; F.E. Kuo; & W.C. Sullivan. "Views of nature and self-discipline: Evidence from inner city children". *J Environ Psychol* 2002; 22(1-2): 49-63.

Ulrich, R.S. "View through a window may influence recovery from surgery". *Science* 1984; 224: 420-21.

van den Berg, A.E.; T. Hartig; & H. Staats. "Preference for nature in urbanized societies: Stress, restoration, and the pursuit of sustainability". *J Social Issues* 2007; 63(1): 79-96.

Wichrowski, M.; J. Whiteson; F. Haas; A. Mola A.; & M.J. Rey. "Effects of horticultural therapy on mood and heart rate in patients participating in an inpatient cardiopulmonary rehabilitation program". *J Cardiopulm Rehab* 2005; 25(5): 270-4.

Wilson, E.O. "Biophilia and the conservation ethic". In: Kellert SR, Wilson EO. *The Biophilia Hypothesis.* Island Press, 1993.

Chapter 28: Creating a New Land Movement with Children

1. Pyle, Robert Michael. *The Thunder Tree: Lessons from an Urban Wildland.* Houghton Mifflin, 1993, p. 147.

Chapter 35: Earth's Greatest Crisis

1. Arrhenius, Svent. See smso.net/Arrhenius.
2. "A World Imperiled: Forces Behind Forest Loss." *Mongabay.* [online]. [cited July 2, 2008]. rainforests.mongabay.com/0801.htm.
3. UN FAO. *Global Forestry Resource Assessment 2005.* [online]. [cited June 17, 2008]. fao.org/forestry/fra2005/en/.
4. "Researchers Link Wildfires, Climate Change." *Associated Press,* July 21, 2006.
5. "Will Forests Adapt to a Warmer World?" *IPS,* November 20, 2006.
6. Taylor, Rob. "World faces megafire threat." *Reuters,* January 19, 2007. [online]. [cited June 17, 2008]. truthout.org/article/world-faces-megafire-threat.
7. May, Elizabeth. *At the Cutting Edge: the Crisis in Canada's Forests.* Key Porter, 2005, p.44.
8. *Global Forestry Resource Assessment 2005,* p. 95.
9. UN FAO says 25%; Nature Conservancy says 20%; CIFOR says 20-25% from land use changes in general, most of which is deforestation.
10. Lynas, Mark. *Six Degrees: Our Future on a Hotter Planet.* National Geographic, 2008.
11. "Gore 'deeply honored' by Nobel win." *USA Today,* October 15, 2007.
12. Environmental Systems of America, Inc. *Rainforest Factoids.*
13. "Deforestation: The hidden cause of global warming." *Independent,* May 14, 2007.

14. Leahy, Stephen. "Environment: Biofuels Boom Spurring Deforestation." *IPS*, March 21, 2008. [online]. [cited July 3, 2008]. ipsnews.net/news.asp?idnews=37035.

15. "Experts: parks effectively protect rainforest in Peru." *Mongabay*, August 9, 2007. [online]. [cited June 17, 2008]. news.mongabay.com/2007/0809-peru.html.

16. "New study confirms continuing forest loss in most countries." *Mongabay*, November 13, 2006.

17. Forest Stewardship Council, October 2007.

18. Personal information from Merv Wilkinson, Wildwood Forest.

19. Almanor Forest. [online]. [cited July 2, 2008]. collinswood.com.

20. Hawken, Paul and Amory and Hunter Lovins. *Natural Capitalism*. Little Brown, 1999.

21. SATO FlagTagSolution™ Selected for Pallet Labeling at RFID Lab of Germany's REWE Group. Brussels, September 15, 2005.

22. Natural Resources Defense Council, Society of American Foresters, *Natural Capitalism*, American Forests.

23. "*Shinrin-yoku* (forest-air bathing and walking) effectively decreases blood glucose levels in diabetic patients." *International Journal of Biometeorology*, Volume 41#3 (February, 1998).

Resources

Earth's Tree News: olyecology.livejournal.com
EcoForestry Institute: ecoforestry.ca
Forest Certification Resource Center: certifiedwood.org
Forest Protection Portal: forests.org
Forest Peoples Programme: forestpeoples.org
Forest Stewardship Council: fsc.org
FSC Canada: fsccanada.org
FSC UK: fsc-uk.org
FSC US: fscus.org
Forest World: forestworld.com
Global Forest Alliance: worldwildlife.org/alliance
Greenpeace Ancient Forests Campaign: greenpeace.org/~forests
Merve Wilkinson's Wildwood, BC: ecoforestry.ca/Wildwood.htm
Mongabay (a great resource base): mongabay.com
Natural Resources Defense Council: nrdc.org/land
Perverse Habits: The G8 and Subsidies that Harm the Forests & Economies: wri.org/forests/g8.html
Rainforest Action Network: ran.org
Rainforest Alliance: rainforest-alliance.org
Society of American Foresters: safnet.org
The Collins Companies: collinswood.com
World Rainforest Movement: wrm.org.uy
World Resources Institute: wri.org/forests

Chapter 36: Forests in Our Future — Contemplating Climate Change and the Importance of Management to British Columbia Forests

1. Pacific Climates Impact Consortium. *Climate Impacts — Introduction.* [online]. [cited June 30, 2008]. pacificclimate.org/resources/climateimpacts/rbcmuseum/.

2. Pacific Climates Impact Consortium. *Cedar - Baseline.* [online]. [cited June 30, 2008]. pacificclimate.org/resources/climateimpacts/rbcmuseum/index.cgi?cedar.

3. Pacific Climates Impact Consortium. *Oak - Baseline.* [online]. [cited June 30, 2008]. pacificclimate.org/resources/climateimpacts/rbcmuseum/index.cgi?oak.

References

Austin, M.A.; D.A. Buffett; D.J. Nicolson; G.G.E. Scudder; & Stevens, Eds. 2008. *Taking Nature's Pulse: The Status of Biodiversity in British Columbia.* Biodiversity BC. 268 pp. [online]. [cited July 25, 2008]. biodiversitybc.org/assets/pressReleases/BBC_StatusReport_Web_final.pdf.

Brown, K.J. and R.J. Hebda. 2002. Origin, development, and dynamics of coastal temperate conifer rainforests of southern Vancouver Island, Canada. *Canadian Journal of Forest Research* 32:353-372.

Carroll, A.L.; J. Regniere; J.A. Logan; S.W. Taylor;

B.J. Bentz; & J.A. Powell. 2006. Impacts of Climate change in range expansion by the mountain pine beetle. *Natural Resources Canada Mountain Pine Beetle Initiative Working Paper 2006-14.* 20 pp.

Easterling, W.E.; P.K. Aggarwal; P. Batima; K.M. Brander; L. Erda; S.M. Howden; A. Kirilenko; J. Morton; J.F. Sousssana; J. Schmidhuber; & F.N. Tubiello. 2007. Food, fibre and forest products. *Climate Change 2007: Impacts, Adaptation and Vulnerability. Contribution of Working Group II to the Fourth Assessment Report of the Intergovernmental Panel on Climate Change.* Parry, M.L., Canziani, O.F., Palutikof, J.P., van der Linden, P.J. and Hanson, C.E., Eds., Cambridge University Press, pp 273-313.

Fischlin, A.; G.F. Midgely; J.T. Price; R. Leemans; B. Gopal; C. Turley; M.D.A. Rounsevell; O.P. Dube; J. Tarazona; & A.A. Velichko. 2007. Ecosystems, their properties, goods and services. In *Climate Change 2007: Impacts, Adaptation and Vulnerability. Contribution of Working Group II to the Fourth Assessment Report of the Intergovernmental Panel on Climate Change.* Parry, M.L., Canziani, O.F., Palutikof, J.P., van der Linden, P.J. and Hanson, C.E., Eds., Cambridge University Press, pp 211-272.

Fraser Basin Council. 2004. *Invasive plant strategy for British Columbia.* 30 pp. [online]. [cited July 25, 2008]. invasiveplantcouncilbc.ca/compendium/.

Hamann, A. and T. Wang. 2006. Potential effects of climate change on ecosystem and tree species distribution in British Columbia. *Ecology* 87: 2773-2786.

Harewell, M.A.; V. Myers; T. Young; A. Bartuska; V. Gassman; J.H. Gentile; C.C. Harwell; A. Appelbaum; J. Barko; B. Causey; C. Johnson; A. McLean; R. Smola; P. Templet; & S. Tosini. 1999. A framework for ecosystem integrity report card. *Bioscience* 49: 543-556.

Hebda, R.J. 1994. Future of British Columbia's flora. In L.E. Harding and E McCullum (editors). *Biodiversity in British Columbia: Our Changing Environment.* Environment Canada, Canadian Wildlife Service. Pp 343-352.

Hebda, R.J. 1995. British Columbia vegetation and climate history with focus on 6 KA BP. *Geographie Physique et Quaternaire* 49:55-79.

Hebda, R.J. 1997. Impact of climate change on bio-geoclimatic zones of British Columbia. In Taylor, E. and B. Taylor. *Responding to Global Climate Change in British Columbia and Yukon: Volume 1 of the Canada Country Study: Climate Impacts and Adaptation.* Environment Canada and British Columbia Ministry of Environment, Lands and Parks, 13:1-15.

Hebda, R. 2007. Ancient and Future Grasslands: Climate Change and Insights from the Fossil Record and Climate Models. *BC Grasslands* 11: 14-16.

Hebda, R.J. 2007. Museum, Climate Change and Sustainability. *Museum Management and Curatorship* 22:329-336.Kurz, and Apps. 1999. A 70-Year Retrospective of Carbon Fluxes in the Canadian Forest Sector. *Ecological Applications.* 9: 526-547.

Meidinger, D. and J. Pojar. 1991 *Ecosystems of British Columbia.* British Columbia Ministry of Forests.

Ministry of Forests and Range. 2006. *Preparing for Climate Change: Adapting to impacts on British Columbia's forest and range resources.* British Columbia Ministry of Forests, 79 pp.

Nabuurs, G.J.; O. Masera; K. Andrasko; P. Benitez-Ponce; R. Boer; M. Dutschke; E. Elsiddig; J. Ford-Robertson; P. Frumhoff; T. Karjalainen; O. Krankina; W.A. Kurz; M. Matsumoto; W. Oyhantcabal; N.H. Ravindranath; M.J. Sanz Sanchez; & X. Zhang. 2007. Forestry. In *Climate Change 2007: Mitigation. Contribution of Working Group III to the Fourth Assessment Report of the Intergovernmental Panel on Climate Change* [B. Metz, O.R. Davidson, P.R. Bosch, R. Dave, L.A. Meyer (eds)], Cambridge University Press.

Scientific Panel for Sustainable Forest Practices in Clayoquot Sound. 1995. *Sustainable ecosystem management in Clayoquot Sound: planning and practices.* Cortex Consultants Inc.

Wilson, S.J. and R. Hebda. 2008. *Mitigating and Adapting to Climate Change through the Conservation of Nature.* Prepared for The Land Trust Alliance of British Columbia. ·

Zhang, Q.B. and R.J. Hebda 2005. Abrupt climate change and variability in the past four millennia of the southern Vancouver Island, Canada. *Geophysical Research Letters.* L16708.

Chapter 37: Aboriginal Forests, Innu Culture and New Sustainable Economics

1. Benton, Raymond. 1990. "A hermeneutic approach to economics: if economics is not science, and if it is not merely mathematics, what could it be?" in Samuels, Warred, ed. *Economics as Discourse: an analysis of the language of economists.* Kluwer; Heilbroner, R. and Milberg, W. 1995. *The Crisis of Vision in Modern Economic Thought.* Cambridge University Press.

2. From "Big Yellow Taxi," lyrics by Joni Mitchell (1970).

3. As ecological economist Clive Spash has pointed out, in a global warming context the economic efficiency lens of cost benefit studies results in economists balancing the climate change-induced loss of lives by those who earn but two dollars a day (and who are hence economically insignificant) against projected increases in golfing opportunities for the rich.

4. Society can, using new technologies, become more efficient (the lay not the economist's version of efficiency) at using resources so that resource consumption per unit of output declines. Nevertheless, with perpetual growth, even with improvements in technological efficiency ever more resources are consumed. For a more extensive treatment, see Chapter 11 of Daly, H. E. 2007. *Ecological Economics and Sustainable Development: Selected Essays of Herman Daly.* Edgar Elgar Publishing.

5. Some proponents of privatization such as economist Peter Pearse seek to address the problem of the private manager focusing on fiber production by creating property rights to non-timber forest resources and by expanding the use of market transactions to mediate between uses and users and achieve the optimal outcome: Pearse, Peter 1998. "Economic Instruments for Promoting Sustainability: Opportunities and Constraints," in Tollefson, Chris (ed.) *Markets, Regulation and Sustainable Forestry.* UBC Press. Other contributors to the volume, in particular Rod Dobell and Michael M'Gonigle, point to the shortcomings of Pearse's narrow neoliberal perspective.

6. Agarwal, Bina. 1986. *Cold Hearths and Barren Slopes: The Woodfuel Crisis in the Third World.* Zed Books.

7. van Kooten, G.C. and E.H. Bulte. 1999. "How Much Primary Coastal Temperate Rainforest Should Society Retain? Carbon Uptake, Recreation and Other Values," *Can. J. of Forest Research* 29(12): 1879-90

8. The author laments that many ecological economists have gotten into the valuation game without being sufficiently critical of the assumptions underlying efficiency analysis and the limitation of valuation itself.

9. Layard, Richard. 2005. *Happiness: Lessons from a New Science.* Penguin.

10. Dr. Seuss. 1971. *The Lorax.* Random House.

11. Karl Polanyi's analysis of how societies react to protect themselves from the corrosive influence of self-regulating markets is very insightful: Polyani, Karl. 1957. *The Great Transformation.* Beacon Press. For a readable, updated exploration of this tendency and the opportunity it presents, see Beneria, Lourdes. 2003. *Gender, Development and Globalization: Economics as if All People Mattered.* Routledge.

12. Editors' note: Neoliberalism in economics is used mainly outside the United States to describe

economic policies brought into prominence during the Reagan and Thatcher years. They emphasize deregulation, privatization, rule of the market, welfare reforms that cut spending, trade liberalization, labor and tax reform and placing greater stress on individual responsibility rather than programs for the common public good. This is a political philosophy and not economics as science. Milton Friedman is one of the main economists associated with neoliberalism in the US. These policies have become part of the practices of the IMF and the World Bank. Its value system is very narrowly based on human pursuit of wealth defined in narrow terms such as growth in profits and continuing growth in GDP. *Development* and *progress* have been defined and measured by these policies rather than more enduring values based on social good, integrity of place and ecological sustainability.

13. For some innovative thinking in this regards see Barnes, Peter. 2006. *Capitalism 3.0.* Berrett-Koehler Publishers.

14. Stiglitz, Joseph. 2006. *Making globalization work.* Norton, p. xiv.

15. Beneria, p. 168.

16. Heithaus, M.R.; A. Frid; A.J. Wirsing; & B. Worm. 2008. "Predicting ecological consequences of marine top predators declines." *Trends in Ecology and Evolution* 23:202-210. Full reports available online at: myweb.dal.ca/bworm/.

17. Forsyth, Jay; Keith Deering; Larry Innes; & Len Moores. 2003. *Forest Ecosystem Strategy Plan For Forest Management District 19 Labrador/Nitassinan 2003-2023.* March 10, 2003. Innu Nation and Department of Forest Resources & Agrifoods, Government of Newfoundland and Labrador.

Chapter 38: Creating Institutions of Care — The Case for Democratic Forest Trusts

Banighan, Jeffrey Thyson. 1990. "Intentional Communities and Land Stewardship Trusts". *The Trumpeter: Journal of Ecosophy* (Winter 1990).

_____. 1997. An Ecoforestry Land Stewardship Trust Model. In Alan Drengson and Duncan M. Taylor, eds. *Ecoforestry: The Art and Science of Sustainable Forest Use.* New Society.

Best, Constance. 2003. "Values, Markets, and Rights: Rebuilding Forest Ecosystem Assets". In James K. Boyce and Barry G. Shelley, eds. *Natural Assets: Democratizing Environmental Ownership.* Island Press.

Blomquist, William. 1992. *Dividing the Waters: Governing Groundwater in Southern California.* Institute of Contemporary Studies.

Brewer, Richard. 2003. *Conservancy: The Land Trust Movement in America.* University Press of New England.

Brick, Phil; Donald Snow; & Sarah Van de Wetering, eds. 2001. *Across the Great Divide: Explorations in Collaborative Conservation and the American West.* Island Press.

Brighton, Deborah. 2003. "Land and Livelihoods in the Northern Forest". In James K. Boyce and Barry G. Shelley, eds. *Natural Assets: Democratizing Environmental Ownership.* Island Press.

Cornuelle, Richard C. 1993. *Reclaiming the American Dream: The Role of Private Individuals and Voluntary Associations.* Transaction.

Danks, Cecilia. 2003. "Community-Based Stewardship: Reinvesting in Public Forests and Forest Communities". In James K. Boyce and Barry G. Shelley, eds. *Natural Assets: Democratizing Environmental Ownership.* Island Press.

Davis, Thomas. 2000. *Sustaining the Forest, the People, and the Spirit.* SUNY Press.

diZerega, Gus. 1998. "Saving Western Towns: A Jeffersonian Green Proposal". In Karl Hess and John Baden, eds. *Writers on the Range.* University of Colorado Press.

Dwyer, Janet and Ian Hodge. 1996. *Countryside in Trust: Land Management by Conservation, Recreation and Amenity Organisations.* Wiley.

Forbes, Peter. 2001. *The Great Remembering: Further Thoughts on Land, Soul, and Society.* Trust for Public Land.

Gregory, H. E. and K. Barnes. 1939. *North Pacific Fisheries, with Special Reference to Alaska Salmon.* Studies of the Pacific No. 3. American Council, Institute of Pacific Relations.

Hardin, Garrett. 1968. "The Tragedy of the Commons". *Science,* 162(1968):1243-1248.

Hess, Karl, Jr. 1993. *Rocky Times in Rocky Mountain National Park: an Unnatural History.* University Press of Colorado.

Kaufman, Herbert. 1967. *The Forest Ranger: A Study in Administrative Behavior.* Resources for the Future.

Kemmis, Daniel. 2001. *This Sovereign Land: A New Vision for Governing the West.* Island Press.

Langston, Nancy. 1995. *Forest Dreams, Forest Nightmares: The Paradox of Old Growth in the Inland West.* University of Washington Press.

Little, Jane Braxton. 2005. "Saving Maidu Culture, one seedling at a time". *High Country News,* 37:6, April 4, 2005.

Matthews, Mark. 2000. "Libby's Dark Secret". *High Country News,* March 13, 2000.

Montgomery, David. 2003. *King of Fish: The Thousand-Year Run of Salmon.* Westview.

Moskowitz, Karyn and Randal O'Toole. 1993. *Transitions: New Incentives for Rural Communities.* Cascade Holistic Economic Consultants.

Nijhuis, Michelle. 2003. "Digging Through the Dust of Libby". *High Country News,* September 1, 2003.

Ostrom, Elinor. 1990. *Governing the Commons: The Evolution of Institutions for Collective Action.* Cambridge University Press.

Ostrom, Vincent. 1991. *The Meaning of American Federalism: Constituting a Self-Governing Society.* Institute for Contemporary Studies Press.

O'Toole, Randal. 1995. Testimony of Randal O'Toole on Forest Management and Ownership. Forests and Public Land Management Committee, Senate Energy and Natural Resources Committee. November, 1995. ti.org/Testimony.html.

_____. 1988. *Reforming the Forest Service.* Island Press.

Polanyi, Michael. 1951. *The Logic of Liberty: Reflections and Rejoinders.* University of Chicago Press.

Ray, Paul H. and Sherry Ruth Anderson. 2000. *The Cultural Creatives: How 50 Million People are Changing the World.* Harmony.

Snyder, Gary. 1990. *The Practice of the Wild.* North Point.

Souder, Jon and Sally Fairfax. 1995. "Forestry on State Trust Lands". *Different Drummer* (summer).

Tang, Shui Yan. 1992. *Institutions and Collective Action: Self-Governance in Irrigation.* Institute of Contemporary Studies.

Williamson, Alex. "Forthcoming. Seeing the Forest and the Trees: The Natural Capital Approach to Forest Service Reform". *Tulane Law Review.*

Wilson, James Q. *Bureaucracy: What Government Agencies Do and Why They Do It.* Basic. 1989.

Chapter 39: Transforming Ourselves, Renewing the Earth

Berkes, Fikret; Johan Colding; & Carl Folke, eds. 2008. *Navigating Social-Ecological Systems: Building Resilience for Complexity and Change.* Cambridge University Press.

Cloke, Kenneth. 2001. *Mediating Dangerously: The Frontiers of Conflict Resolution.* Jossey-Bass.

Daly, Herman. 2005. "Economics in a Full World." *Scientific American.* 293(3): 100-107.

Davis, Wade. 2001. *Light at the Edge of the World.* Douglas & McIntyre.

Earth Charter Initiative 2000. *The Earth Charter Preamble.* Available at earthcharterinaction.org/2000/10/the_earth_charter.html, accessed on June 16, 2008.

Gunderson, Lance and C.S. Holling. 2002. *Panarchy: Understanding Transformations in Human and Natural Systems.* Island Press.

Laszlo, Ervin and Jonas Salk. 1987. *Evolution: The Grand Synthesis.* Shambhala Publications.

Madron, Roy and John Jopling. 2003. *Gaian Democracies: Redefining Globalisation and People Power.* Green Books.

Milanovic, Branko. 2005. *Worlds Apart: Measuring International and Global Inequality.* Princeton University Press.

Norberg-Hodge, Helena. 2002. "The Pressure to Moderize and Globalize." In Jerry Mander and Edward Goldsmith, eds., *The Case Against the Global Economy.* Sierra Club Books, pp. 33-46.

Poncet, Sandra. 2006. *The Long Term Prospects of the World Economy: Horizon 2050.* Available at cepii.fr, accessed on December 7, 2006.

Sivaraksa, Sulak. 2002. "Alternatives to Consumerism." In Allan Hunt Badiner, ed., *Mindfulness in the Marketplace — Compassionate Responses to Consumerism.* Parallax Press, p. 135.

Tainter, Joseph. 1988. *The Collapse of Complex Societies.* Cambridge University Press.

Tidwell, John. 2006. "Global Warming Capable of Sparking Mass Species Extinctions." Posted online at *Conservation International.* Available at conservation.org, accessed on April 11, 2006.

United Nations Department of Economic and Social Affairs. 2006. *World Population Prospects: the 2006 Revision Population Database.* Available at esa.un.org/unpp/, accessed on December 19, 2006.

World Commission on Environment and Development. 1987. *Report of the World Commission on Environment and Development,* p. 1. Available at un.org/documents/ga/res/42/ares42-187.htm, accessed on August 15, 2004.

World Conservation Union, United Nations Environment Program & World Wide Fund For Nature. 1991. *Caring for the Earth: a strategy for sustainable living: summary,* p. 10. Available at coombs.anu.edu.au/~vern/caring /caring.html [accessed Sept. 30, 2008].

World Wildlife Fund. 2006. *Living Planet Report 2006,* p. 1. Available at panda.org.

Chapter 40: Shifting Direction to Local Interdependence

1. Vidal, John. "eco soundings." *The Guardian* (London and Manchester), September 6, 2000, "Society" section, p. 8.

2. Slater, Rodney E., Secretary of Transportation. Letter to Al Gore, March 12, 1997, p. 2. "Highlights of the FY 1997 Transportation Budget," US Department of Transportation, 1997.

3. "Ten Questions on TENs." European Federation for Transport and Environment, Brussels, Belgium, pp. 3-6.

4. "Loan & Credit Summary" (projects approved at World Bank's December 1996 board meeting). worldbank.org.

5. Ministry of Agriculture, Fisheries and Food. *Agriculture in the United Kingdom.* MAFF, The Stationary Office, 1999, pp 9:1-9:8.

6. The US-based group Redefining Progress has been working to expose the shortcomings of conventional economic yardsticks and to promote the use of an alternative set of measures: Clifford Cobb, Ted Halstead and Jonathan Rowe. "If the GDP Is Up, Why Is America Down?" *Atlantic Monthly,* October 1995.

7. McDonald's Corporation. "McDonald's Reports Record Global Results." Press release, January 26, 2000.

8. Center for Integrated Agricultural Systems. *Research Brief #21: Community supported agriculture: growing food ... and community.* University of Wisconsin, 2000.

9. United States Department of Agriculture. *National Directory of Farmers' Markets.* Agricultural Marketing Service, November 1998.

10. Personal correspondence, Jenny Hey, National Association of Farmers' Markets, September 8, 2000.

11. Lampkin, Nicholas. Welsh Institute of Rural Studies, University of Wales, Aberystwyth, UK. Complete data and charts are given on the Institute's website: wirs.aber.ac.uk/research/.

12. The Global Eco-village Network (GEN) links many of these communities worldwide at gaia.org.

Afterword: Where We Are Going

1. Forbes, Peter. "Another Way of Being Human." The Trust for Public Land — Center for Land and People. [online]. [cited July 21, 2008]. tpl.org/tier3_cd.cfm?content_item_id= 5482&folder_id=831.

Appendix 1: Industrial and Ecological Approaches

Alan Drengson and Duncan M. Taylor

Our earlier anthology *Ecoforestry: The Art and Science of Sustainable Forest Use* explored in depth the fertile ground of forest use practices employed by people who call themselves ecoforesters. Their forest use methods are based on the ecological processes of those forests. These practitioners have many ways of articulating what they are doing. They are not all doing the same things, partly because they are based in different forest ecosystems, or in places not uniform with foresters sharing their aims. These individuals reject conventional industrial forestry based on an industrial agricultural model that views native forests as old, diseased and inefficient. Ecoforesters value natural forests for their resilience and for the countless trees, animals and plants who inhabit them. They see these creatures, including the trees, as part of a community of forest workers who cooperatively create the whole forest ecosystem.

In *Ecoforestry* we focused primarily on the details of forest use for deriving products from tree stems to edible plants. In this volume we assume responsible ecoforestry practices

and offer more reflections on these, but we also take these explorations into new territories that are encompassed by the words *wild foresting*. This involves anything from walking and journeying in a forest, to simply admiring it from afar, to taking a class of young people there to learn first hand the many benefits of wild forests or doing ecoforestry. Wild forests have energies, wisdom and feelings that inform humans. We need them to face the challenges of the environmental crisis, which includes everything from global warming to serious local and oceanic pollution from a panoply of industrial chemicals never before found in nature. This book guides us to pursue an attuned wholeness of well inner and outer ecology, which can be described as the blossoming of countless *ecosophies* all over the Earth.

Here in summary form are some of the main comparisons that were set forth in our earlier book and are assumed by this one.

These are the main characteristics of industrial development philosophy, contrasted with ecologically responsible approaches.

DRENGSON AND TAYLOR. *ECOFORESTRY.* NEW SOCIETY, 1997, P. 26

1. Business as usual	1. Need new practices
2. Technical fixes for environmental problems	2. Design approaches that prevent problems
3. Nature as raw material, only instrumental value	3. Nature is intrinsically valuable
4. Mechanistic models	4. Whole systems models, community ordered organic ecosystems
5. Isolated objects, subject-object dualisms	5. Fields, processes and inter-relationships; interdependent complexity
6. Technical knowledge suffices	6. Understanding and wisdom are needed
7. Reductionist	7. Holistic/integral
8. Progress defined economically	8. Progress defined by all values: biodiverse, cultural, spiritual, aesthetic, etc.
9. Consumptive lifestyles	9. Low-impact lifestyles

Industrial Philosophy — Ecological Approaches

This is the same industrial approach applied to agriculture contrasted with the emerging ecoagricultural approaches.

DRENGSON AND TAYLOR. *ECOFORESTRY.* NEW SOCIETY, 1997, PP. 26-27

1. Capital-intensive	1. Knowledge and labor-intensive
2. Large-scale monocultures	2. Small-scale, mixed crops
3. Simplifies ecosystem	3. Increases cropland diversity and complexity
4. Imposes management on nature	4. Lets nature *manage*
5. Uses chemicals, GMOs, etc.	5. Uses no biocides or GMOs
6. Ignores biological communities	6. Enhances soil communities
7. High input costs	7. Low input costs
8. Large agri-business industrial farms	8. Small family and community-sized farms
9. Elimination of rural communities	9. Regeneration of communities

Industrial Agriculture — Ecoagriculture

Finally, these are the main contrasts between conventional industrial forestry and ecoforestry.

Industrial forestry	Ecoforestry
1. Trees are seen as products	1. Forests are ecological communities
2. Short-term production goals	2. Long-term sustainability goals
3. Agricultural production model	3. Forest ecosystem model
4. Trees are the only cash crop	4. Diverse forest products and services
5. Trees' survival dependent on humans	5. Self-sustaining, self-maintaining and self-renewing
6. Chemicals	6. No chemicals
7. Clearcuts	7. Harvesting surplus wood and selective removal
8. Same age stands of trees	8. All ages of trees
9. Monoculture of single or few species	9. All native species of trees
10. Simplified ecosystem	10. Natural biodiversity and complexity
11. Capital-intensive and corporate-based	11. Labor-intensive and locally based
12. Redesigning nature	12. Accepting nature's design
13. Life span: 60-100 years	13. Life span: millennia
14. Loss of the sacred	14. Sense of the sacred and mysterious
15. Older traditions, aboriginal knowledge outdated	15. Older traditions and aboriginal knowledge are sources of wisdom

Industrial forestry — ecoforestry

Methods for attaining these ecoforestry goals follow.

1. Retention must be the first consideration in any planned removal of trees from a stand. Emphasize what must be left and protect such things as rare species, sites of native cultural significance, riparian zones (that is, watercourses, lakeshores, etc.).

2. Leave riparian zones intact. No tree removal should take place in the most sensitive areas. Protect water quality by minimizing alterations to natural drainage patterns.

3. Maintain composition and structures to support fully functioning forests. Important forest structures such as large old trees, snags and large fallen trees are maintained by letting a minimum of 20-30% of overstory trees (well-distributed spatially and by species) grow old and die in any timber extraction area. ☛

4. Use the lowest impact removal methods possible. Avoid building roads and compacting forest soils as much as possible — all roads should be small-scale, contour, low-grade roads requiring a minimum of blasting.

5. Plan in terms of the needs of the larger watershed, even if owner does not control or own the watershed. A watershed zone plan must designate areas where tree removal is not permitted and those where different levels and types of removal are possible.

6. Prohibit clearcutting as currently practised and utilize ecologically appropriate partial cutting methods that maintain the canopy structure, age distribution and species mixtures found in healthy natural forests of a particular ecosystem type.

7. Select trees as candidates for removal by considering how abundant and redundant their structures and functions are to the rest of the forest as a whole, leaving potential wildlife trees to become snags and large woody debris.

8. Allow the forest to regenerate trees through seeds from trees in the logged area. Tree planting will generally not be required because a diverse, fully functioning forest is always maintained, assuring natural regeneration.

9. Maintain ecological succession to protect biological diversity. The process of brush control will be avoided. Over time, all forest phases must occupy every forest site, even on sites managed solely for timber.

10. Prohibit slash burning. Fire is an acceptable tool in landscapes that have a history of naturally occurring fires, but use with caution.

11. Prohibit pesticide use. Disease, insects and shrub/herb vegetation are essential parts of a fully functioning forest.

12. Maintain and restore topsoil quality by leaving sufficient large and small debris.

13. Maintain beauty and other natural aesthetic qualities in the visual, sound and odour landscapes.

14. Always look at the forest as a whole and how each part contributes to the needs and health of the whole in which it resides.

15. Rely as much as possible on local people and markets. Engage in full-cost accounting.

16. Remember that wisdom begins with recognizing our limitations and ignorance. When in doubt, don't!

DRENGSON AND TAYLOR. *ECOFORESTRY.* NEW SOCIETY, 1997, PP. 28-29

Principles of ecoforestry

We respect, hold sacred and learn from the ecological wisdom of natural forests and their multitudes of beings.

We protect the integrity of full-functioning forests.

We do not use industrial agricultural practices on forests.

We remove from forests only values that are in abundance to meet vital human needs.

We remove specific forest values only when this does not interfere with full-functioning forests; when in doubt, we do not.

We minimize the effects of our actions in forests by using only appropriate, low-impact technologies.

We use only non-violent resistance (such as Gandhian methods) to protect our forests.

We do good work and uphold the Ecoforester's Way as a sacred duty and trust.

DRENGSON AND TAYLOR, ECOFORESTRY: NEW SOCIETY, 1997, P. 275

The EcoForester's Oath

1. *Environmental:* e.g. biodiversity, climate moderation, clean air and water, wildlife, healthy soils.

2. *Scientific:* e.g. research, knowledge of species, taxonomy, studies of diversity, knowledge of deep past such as long range weather patterns.

3. *Productive:* e.g. timber, poles, medicines, chemicals, edibles, firewood, ornamentals, wood fiber.

4. *Recreational:* e.g. camping, hunting, fishing, hiking, skiing, canoeing, mountain climbing, bird watching.

5. *Aesthetic:* e.g. natural beauty, painting, drawing, photography, artistic inspiration, poetry, storytelling, natural history, craft traditions, florist supplies.

6. *Spiritual:* e.g. tranquillity, communion with nature, reconnection to our natural self, ecological wisdom from forests, connections with whole communities of living beings, contact with the spontaneous creative powers of nature and the inherent values of the Earth.

7. From the whole forest ecosystem we get *whole cultures:* e.g. BC Aboriginal coastal Haida cultures and Norwegian fjord-forest cultures.

DRENGSON AND TAYLOR, ECOFORESTRY: NEW SOCIETY, 1997, P. 242

Categories of forest values recognized by wild foresting

Appendix 2: Resources for Supporting and Learning About Wild Foresting

Here is an annotated list of website addresses relevant to the topics covered in this book. The lists of references and the citations provided by the contributors of each article offer additional resources for readers who want to be more involved and want to know more.

Agroforestry.net. Host to the *The Overstory* e-journal with a wealth of information about agroforestry and its relationship to other practices and values.

Alice-miller.com. A website rich in material organized by Alice Miller, who is a leader in healing the traumas and injuries of childhood so that people of all ages can become whole and happy as the self they were meant to be. Whole people then can be enlightened witnesses to others and help their journey to their authentic self. Much of our consumerism is driven by deep dissatisfactions that arise out of childhood injuries, and only healing those injuries solves this endless cycle of craving.

Amritapuri.org. Nature care and sacred groves in India in the state of Kerala, which has more sacred groves than any other place in India.

Ancientforests.org. A wealth of global information about ancient forests around the world with links to wonderful examples.

Arcworld.org. Alliance of religious and conservation organizations with lots of info on sacred forests and groves.

Bestfutures.org. The world as we know it is about to be transformed. Why? Because our economic system is based on continuous growth, and unlimited material growth cannot be sustained on a planet with finite resources. Best Futures explores global issues, trends and options and provides new tools for developing sustainable solutions.

Big-picture.tv. Streams free video clips of leading experts, thinkers and activists in environmental and social sustainability. They offer a general audience analysis and commentary from a growing number of world leaders including scientists, journalists, economists, businessmen, designers and politicians.

Biologicaldiversity.org. This Center provides extensive links and information about the state of biodiversity and its importance to culture and human health, as well as programs to encourage support for protection of diversity and the wild.

Bioone.org. An online journal with readily available scholarly and scientific material related to forests, ecology and other biological subjects.

Ceres.org/ceres. The largest coalition of investors, environmental and public interest organizations in North America.

Childrenandnature.org. A website rich in resources and links devoted to reconnecting children with the natural world.

Conbio.org. The Society for Conservation Biology (SCB) is an international professional organization dedicated to promoting the scientific study of the phenomena that affect the maintenance, loss and restoration of biological diversity.

Conservationinstitute.org. The Conservation Science Institute is devoted to quality science for knowledge of the earth and its ecological processes, especially as relevant to conservation and restoration.

Earthwatch.org. Global organization devoted to active research and education related to earth caring and knowledge.

Ecoforestry.ca. A society devoted to ecoforestry practices, also publisher of the *Ecoforesty Journal*.

Ecostery.org. A generic ecosophy website for those wanting to create their own wise living practices and harmonious place as an ecostery (from *eco* and *stery* as in monastery).

Ecotippingpoints.org. An ecotipping point is a key part of an eco-social system that can reverse the direction of change. The point is catalytic — a lever that can turn the environment from decline to health and sustainability. This website provides information about ecotipping points and how one can work in positive ways to set off cycles of improvement rather than downward spirals.

Edugreen.teri.res.in. Sacred groves of India are featured with accounts of their variety and specific features.

Fanweb.org. Forest Action Network is devoted to defending ancient forests.

Footprintnetwork.org. Devoted to using the footprint method to help us assess what our impact is on our local and global environment. This provides invaluable tools for gaining knowledge of how to mitigate our personal and family impacts.

Livingheritage.org. The Living Heritage Trust is a nonprofit devoted to the living heritage of Sri Lanka.

Nature.com. Website for *Nature* magazine.

Opalcreek.org. A center in Portland, Oregon devoted to education on forests with programs for children.

Orionmagazine.org. One of the most valuable websites for nature oriented educational resources and one of the leading publishers of materials related to place based education for deep connections to the land and ecosystems.

Panda.org/news. Source for the online journal of the World Wildlife Fund.

Peopleandplanet.net. Devoted to people and forests and the health and well-being of both.

Raincoast.com. Offers a wealth of ancient forest friendly books, catalogs and good stories for children and adults about wild forests and other species.

Resalliance.org. A network of individuals and small groups dedicated to integrating ecological resilience into social organizations for new paradigm self-organization, instead of top down control.

Rprogress.org. Redefining progress is key to quality of life and ecosystem planning, for it is related to how we define and measure progress. This site offers valuable links and other information about the state of this art.

Sacredforests.org. Religiously oriented site with lots of links to sacred forests.

Sacredland.org. Information on Earth Island Institute's film and other projects, educational resources for all ages.

Sacredsites.com. Resources for locating sacred sites, pilgrimages and other connections with details for places around the world.

Shinto.org. Information about Shinto Shrines of Japan and their connections with forests.

Trumpeter.athabascau.ca. *The Trumpeter: Journal of Ecosophy* is an outstanding resource and is now available online with all back issues free to use. It covers all aspects of ecosophies from theoretical to practical, poetic to philosophical.

WiserEarth.org. A generic website with powerful search capabilities connecting people with resources for sustainable, wiser living and restoration.

The websites below have names that are self explanatory.

Alliance for Zero Extinction: zeroextinction.org

Anew New Zealand: anewnz.org.nz

Club of Budapest: clubofbudapest.org

Club of Rome: clubofrome.org

Conservation International: conservation.org

Convention on Biological Diversity: cbd.int/

David Suzuki Foundation: davidsuzuki.org

Earth Charter Initiative: earthcharter.org

Earth Policy Institute: earth-policy.org

Ecojustice (formerly the Sierra Legal Defense Fund): ecojustice.ca

Equator Principles: equator-principles.com

Evangelical Climate Initiative: christiansandclimate.org

Extractive Industries Transparency Initiative: eitransparency.org

Forest Stewardship Council: fsc.org/en

Friends of the Earth: foe.co.uk

Future Foundation: futuresfoundation.org/au

www.greenbeltmovement.org

Green Cross International: gci.ch/

Green Institute: greeninstitute.net

Honey Bee Network: knownetgrin.honeybee.org/honeybee.htm

Jane Goodall Institute: janegoodall.org

Massive Change: massivechange.com

Mayors for Climate Protection: icleiusa.org/success-stories/cool-mayors

Pembina Institute: pembina.org

Oxfam International: oxfam.org

Rainforest Alliance: rainforest-alliance.org

Rocky Mountain Institute: rmi.org. Amory Lovins' alternative energy research Institute.

Sierra Club: sierraclub.org

Slow Food: slowfood.com

Sustainable Scale Project: sustainablescale.org

Sustainability Research Institute: sustainability-research.org.au

Trees for Life: treesforlife.org.uk

Wetlands International: wetlands.org

Whole Communities: wholecommunities.org

Worldchanging: worldchanging.com

World Wildlife Fund (WWF): worldwildlife.org

Worldwatch: worldwatch.org

Index

About the Contributors

RICHARD ATLEO, Ph.D., is an instructor in the First Nations Studies Department at Vancouver Island University, Nanaimo, Canada. He served as co-chair of the Clayoquot Sound Scientific Panel on Sustainable Forest Practices. He spoke on the theme of this article in September 1999 at the Forests for the Future conference in Nanaimo and at Wildwood. The conference was organized by the Ecoforestry Institute Society.

BRENDA BECKWITH, Ph.D., was born and raised in the oak savannahs near Sacramento, California. Brenda moved to Victoria, British Columbia, in 1997 to pursue doctoral studies on the landscape reconstruction and ethnoecological restoration of the blue camas and oak ecosystems of western Canada. She is currently working as the Senior Laboratory Instructor for the School of Environmental Studies, University of Victoria, and is an ecological gardening and land stewardship consultant.

GONZALO BRITO is a clinical psychologist, having graduated from the Pontificia Universidad Católica of Chile. From 2005 to 2007 he worked as an individual and group psychotherapist at Takiwasi Center, focusing on mindful therapy and yoga workshops with patients.

GUY DAUNCEY is Executive Director of The Solutions Project, and author or co-author of several books, including *Stormy Weather: 101 Solutions to Global Climate Change*, *Cancer: 101 Solutions to a Preventable Epidemic* and other titles. He is President of the BC Sustainable Energy Association (bcsea.org), and Co-chair of Prevent Cancer Now (preventcancernow.ca). He lives in Victoria, BC, Canada. His home page is earthfuture.com.

BILL DEVALL, Ph.D., is Emeritus Professor of Sociology at Humboldt State University, Arcata, California. He is the author of numerous books and articles on the deep ecology movement. Some of his books are *Deep Ecology: Living as if Nature Mattered* and *Simple in Means, Rich in Ends: Practicing Deep Ecology*. He practices meditation at a local Zen Center.

GUS DiZEREGA, Ph.D., is Visiting Assistant Professor of Government, Department of Government, St. Lawrence University, Canton, NY 13617 USA. He is an artist, healer and author of many publications. E-mail: gdizerega@stlawu.edu.

ALAN DRENGSON, Ph.D., is Emeritus Professor of Philosophy and Adjunct Professor of Environmental Studies at the University of Victoria in Canada. He is the author of many articles and books (for example, *The Practice of Technology* and *Beyond Environmental Crisis*). He is the founding editor of *The Trumpeter: Journal of Ecosophy* and *Ecoforestry*, and the coeditor of four anthologies, *The Philosophy of Society*, *The Deep Ecology Movement*, *The Ecology of Wisdom: Writings by Arne Naess,* and *Ecoforestry: The Art and Science of Sustainable Forest Use.* He is the Associate Editor for the *Selected Works of Arne Naess,* a ten volume collection of Naess's work published by Springer in 2005. See ecostery.org for some of his work. E-mail: alandren@uvic.ca.

JIM DRESCHER is an enrichment forester who lives on Windhorse Farm in Nova Scotia, Canada. His use of the forest tends to the benefit of natural forests. He considers Windhorse a small farm, geared especially for horses, where they practice and teach enrichment forestry and sustainable, organic agriculture. The Windhorse Farm School is an experiment based on four disciplines: stillness, study, contemplation and work. Their website address is windhorsefarm.org.

ALAN WATSON FEATHERSTONE is the founder and Executive Director of the award winning Scottish charity Trees For Life. He travels internationally, giving talks and writing articles about trees, forests and ecological restoration. He is also an accomplished nature photographer.

BRENDA FEUERSTEIN is a former music teacher and health consultant, as well as the present director of Traditional Yoga Studies. She has recently coauthored with Georg Feuerstein the book *Green Yoga*.

GEORG FEUERSTEIN, Ph.D., M.Litt., is the author of more than 30 books, including the award-winning *Shambala Encyclopedia of Yoga*, *Structures of Consciousness*, *Lucid Waking* and *Connecting the Dots*.

PETER FORBES is a long time land activist who now works with Whole Communities (wholecommunities.org). He is the author of many articles and books and has been active in the land trust movement for years.

HOWARD FRUMKIN, M.D., Ph.D., is Director of the National Center for Environmental Health/Agency for Toxic Substances and Disease Registry, US Centers for Disease Control and Prevention.

CHRIS GENOVALI is executive director of the Raincoast Conservation Foundation. For further information contact: raincoast.org.

TOM GREEN is an ecological economist who has worked on forestry, resource and economic development issues in BC since 1996. He was environmental advisor and assistant to the chief negotiator for Innu Nation in Labrador from 1991-1994 and Director of Socio-economics for the Rainforest Solutions Project from 2003-2007. Currently, he is pursuing a Ph.D. at the University of British Columbia examining how to reform the undergraduate economics curriculum in order to incorporate sustainability.

NITYA HARRIS works on the development of transitional infrastructure, institutions and strategies; the implementation of practical solutions and the promotion of changes in behavior that will move our societies to live sustainably in the future. She is presently developing (when not traveling!) a solar energy program for British Columbia.

BOB HAY, Ph.D., lives in Perth, Western Australia and is an Adjunct Senior Research Fellow in the Department of Environmental Biology at Curtin University. He formerly worked in the Department of Environment as a Policy Officer.

RICHARD J. HEBDA, Ph.D., received his doctorate in botany from the University of British Columbia and has been a curator (specializing in botany and earth history) at the Royal British Columbia Museum for more than 25 years. Richard has also taught biology, earth and ocean sciences and environmental studies at the University of Victoria. His research areas include vegetation and climate history of BC, ethnobotany of BC First Nations, climate change, restoration of natural systems and processes, grass botany and the ecology/origins of Garry oak and alpine ecosystems.

WES JACKSON, Ph.D., is President and founder of The Land Institute which is dedicated to research into the development of sustainable agricultures based on perennial polycultures. He established and served as chair of one of the country's first environmental studies programs at California State University - Sacramento. His many books include *New Roots for Agriculture* and *Becoming Native to This Place.* He was a

Coastal forest

VICTORIA STEVENS

1990 Pew Conservation Scholar, in 1992 became a MacArthur Fellow and in 2000 received the Right Livelihood Award (sometimes called the Alternative Nobel Prize).

SARAH LAIRD is an independent consultant with a focus on the commercial and cultural context of biodiversity and forest conservation. Recent books include *Biodiversity and Traditional Knowledge: Equitable Partnerships in Practice* (2001) and co-authorship of *The Commercial Use of Biodiversity* (1999). Sarah Laird can be reached at sarahlaird@aol.com.

RICHARD LOUV is the author of *Fly-Fishing for Sharks: An Angler's Journey Across America* (Simon & Schuster, 2001) and *Last Child in the Woods: Saving Our Children from Nature-Deficit Disorder* (Algonquin, 2005). He is also a columnist for The San Diego Union-Tribune and chairman of the Children & Nature Network (cnaturenet.org). For more information about his books, go to richardlouv.com.

DAVD MARTIN [Ph.D., Sociology, University of Washington, 1966] has studied small group self-organization, forest carrying capacity, success and failure of communities and the methodology of social and socio-ecological data collection and analysis. He retired to editing the journal *Ecoforestry,* so current editor Irv Penner can have time with his family and still do his day job. Martin has been Associate Editor of the *Canadian Journal of Statistics* and co-organizer of the 1986 Small Scale Forestry Symposium which convened Canadian, Finnish, Scandinavian and a few Third World foresters and social animators. He had "a few dozen" publications in social science journals before gradually migrating to ecoforestry. "I think of my life as a story-for-Creator, and only the

deeds are included. Words only count as deeds when they reach other people." When not working on the journal or writing, Martin is likely to be forest-keeping, fixing up an old house and learning a new ecosystem northeast of Miramichi, NB, Canada.

WANGARI MAATHAI is the founder of the *Green Belt Movement* and Africa's first woman Nobel Peace Prize Laureate. She was Kenya's Assistant Minister for Environment and Natural Resources. She is also a recipient of the Right Livelihood Award.

GERALD MARTEN, Ph.D., is an ecologist at the East-West Center in Honolulu (eastwestcenter.org) whose main project is the ecotipping study.

CHRIS MASER, M.S., is an international consultant in forest ecology and sustainable forestry practices. He has spent over 25 years as a research scientist in natural history and ecology in forest, shrub steppe, subarctic, desert, coastal and agricultural settings. As well, he has been a research ecologist with the US Department of the Interior, Bureau of Land Management for thirteen years (1974-1987) — the last eight studying old-growth forests in western Oregon — and a landscape ecologist with the Environmental Protection Agency for one year (1990-1991). Currently Chris is an independent author and international lecturer and a facilitator in resolving environmental conflicts, vision statements and sustainable community development.

RALPH METZNER, Ph.D., has been exploring consciousness and transformational practices since he was a graduate student at Harvard. He is now a psychotherapist and professor at the

California Institute of Integral Studies in San Francisco. He is the author of numerous books and articles. His website is at greenearthfound.org.

ALICE MILLER, Ph.D., is a well known psychotherapist and author of an impressive number of books and articles. She has focused much of her work on the healing of trauma, especially childhood trauma which results from *poison pedagogy* and abusive parenting. Her website address is alice-miller.com.

ARNE NAESS, Ph.D., is one of the founders of the Deep Ecology Movement and one of Norway's best known philosophers. He is Professor Emeritus at the University of Oslo and has been working with The Center for Development and Environment (SUM) in Oslo, Norway since 1991. For a collection of his writings in English see the ten-volume *Selected Works of Arne Naess* published in 2005 by Springer. There is also a series on his writings in the archives of *The Trumpeter: Journal of Ecosophy*. He has received numerous awards including the Nordic Council Award for Nature and Environment and was most recently granted the Star of St. Olav by the King of Norway.

HELENA NORBERG-HODGE is a linguist by training and is fluent in six languages. She is the founder and director of the International Society for Ecology and Culture, a non-profit organization dedicated to the protection of biological and cultural diversity, and education for action. ISEC runs programs on four continents aimed at strengthening ecological diversity and community with emphasis on local food and farming. She is a co-founder of the International Forum on Globalization (ifg.org), an alliance of 60 leading activists, scholars, economists, researchers and writers formed to stimulate new thinking, joint activity and public education in response to economic globalization. She is also involved with the Global Ecovillage Network and directs the Ladakh Project, renowned for its groundbreaking work in sustainable development on the Tibetan plateau. She is a recipient of the Right Livelihood Award and author of many books and articles.

BRIONY PENN, Ph.D., is an adjunct professor in the School of Environmental Studies at the University of Victoria, Canada. A geographer from Saltspring Island, she is best known for her award-winning illustrated *Wild Side* columns in various regional publications and hosting the TV magazine show *Enviro/Mental* with CHUM-TV. The program was nominated one of the top three magazine shows in Canada.

JAY RASTOGI has been practicing ecoforestry at Wildwood and as a consultant since 1997. He has a special interest in the preservation of natural and rural landscapes as well as in sharing with others the wonders of the natural world.

CAROLINA READ, CSP, works as an Integrative Heath practitioner in Devon, UK. She writes poetry that blends her skills working with Nature spirits with the eloquence of the human body.

TOM REIMCHEN, Ph.D., is currently an adjunct Associate Professor with the Department of Biology, University of Victoria. His research includes: (1) pursuit and manipulation failures of predators in relation to prey morphology; (2) evolutionary radiation of threespine stickleback on the Queen Charlotte Islands (Haida Gwaii), BC, (3) resolving glacial refugia hypotheses in Haida Gwaii using morphological and molecular markers of endemic vertebrates from western North America, (4) diurnal and nocturnal foraging behavior of black bear during salmon spawning migration and (5) stable nitrogen isotopes in tree rings as historical indicators of marine-derived nutrient transfer into coastal forests.

HOLMES ROLSTON III, Ph.D., is considered to be one of the founders of Environmental Ethics as a discipline. He is a University Distinguished Professor of philosophy at Colorado State University. He has written six books that have been acclaimed in both professional journals and the national press. He was named the 2003 Templeton Prize laureate. The award, which is valued at more than one million dollars, is given each year to a living person to encourage and honor those who advance spiritual matters.

Forest path

VICTORIA STEVENS

CLAIRE SIEBER received her M.A. in anthropology from the University of Victoria, in British Columbia, Canada. Her thesis, *Enseñanzas y Mareaciones: Exploring Intercultural Health Through Experience and Interaction with Healers and Plant Teachers in San Martín, Peru,* was based upon her experiential fieldwork through Takiwasi from May to November of 2006.

ILIFF SIMEY is the owner/carer of a 20 acre old-growth ancient forest in Wales. Forty years of misguided advice and government grants prompting the collapse of the forest industry in Britain has led him to observe how the natural forest can be self-sustaining, productive and to the conviction that we must take advantage of this enforced rest period to restore to holistic health to our woods and forests.

DOUG SKEATES is a retired forester living in Loretto, Ontario, Canada.

DAVID SOBEL, M.Ed., is director of the teacher certification program at Antioch New England Graduate School and author of *Children's Special Places: Exploring the Role of Forts, Dens, and Bush Houses in Middle Childhood* (Zephyr Press, 1993) and many other books and articles. His most recent book is *Childhood and Nature: Design Principles for Education* (Stenhouse Publishers, 2008). He was the winner of the 1991 Education Press Award.

AMANDA SUUTARI is an environmental journalist based in Vancouver, Canada.

DUNCAN M. TAYLOR, Ph.D., teaches at the School of Environmental Studies, University of Victoria, Canada. His research applies complex systems theory to the understanding of individual as well as societal and biophysical interactions and transformations. In turn, he has focused on integral worldviews, BC forest issues, community and environmental restoration and the value of wilderness and adventure therapy. He is the coeditor of *Ecoforestry: The Art and Science of Sustainable Forest Use* and author of *Off Course: Restoring Balance Between Canadian Society and the Environment.*

GRAEME M. TAYLOR, M.A., coordinates BEST Futures (bestfutures.org), a project researching and modeling societal change and evolution. Based in Brisbane, Australia, he is the author of *Evolution's Edge: the Coming Collapse and Transformation of Our World.*

NORAH TRACE, Ph.D., is a psychologist in private practice and has taught graduate courses at the University of Victoria for 17 years. Ecotherapy is a big part of her life and work.

RAY TRAVERS, RPF, is a forestry consultant and chair of the Ecoforestry Institute of Canada, based in Victoria, BC, Canada.
E-mail: rtravers@islandnet.com.

NANCY J. TURNER, Ph.D., is a Distinguished Professor in the School of Environmental Studies at the University of Victoria. As an ethnobotanist she has been collaborating for many years with indigenous elders and other cultural specialists in British Columbia, documenting cultural knowledge of plants and environments. She has published widely in the areas of ethnobotany and ethnoecology.

BARBARA WILSON (Kii'iljuus) is a Haida cultural specialist and matriarch of the Cumshewa Eagle clan, living in Skidegate on Haida Gwaii.

A Parks Canada cultural heritage specialist, she works for Gwaii Haanas National Park Reserve and Haida Heritage Site. Barbara received her formal Cultural Resource Management education from the University of Victoria — graduating in 1999. Nancy and Barbara have been friends and collaborators for many years, and Barbara has adopted Nancy into her clan.

ALAN WITTBECKER, Ph.D., has worked as an ecologist for many different institutions including G.P. Marsh Institute and Central Balkan National Park. He was the Director and Senior Ecologist at Ecoforestry Institute in Portland, Oregon. He coordinated the management of nine forests in Oregon, Idaho and Washington and was also the editor of the journal *Ecoforestry*. He is the author of numerous books and articles including *Good Forestry: From Good Theories and Good Practices; REviewing REthinking REturning: Essays on Life, Ecology and Design* and *Eutopias or Outopias: Choosing to Design and to Make Good Places*. He has worked in the Peace Corps and conducted field research in wildlife ecology in Eastern Europe, Norway and the US. He is currently a faculty member at Ringling College of Art and Design in Sarasota, Florida.

GEORGE WUERTHNER, M.A., is an ecologist, longtime wildlands activist and wilderness visionary whose interests include conservation biology and conservation history. He is a full-time freelance writer and photographer with 33 books to his credit. His work has won numerous awards. He most recently was the editor of *Wild Fire: A Century of Failed Forest Policy,* and *Thrillcraft.* Samples of his work can be viewed at wuerthnerphotography.com.

If you have enjoyed *Wild Foresting* you might also enjoy other

BOOKS TO BUILD A NEW SOCIETY

Our books provide positive solutions for people who want to
make a difference. We specialize in:

Sustainable Living • Green Building • Peak Oil • Renewable Energy

Environment & Economy • Natural Building & Appropriate Technology

Progressive Leadership • Resistance and Community

Educational and Parenting Resources

New Society Publishers

ENVIRONMENTAL BENEFITS STATEMENT

New Society Publishers has chosen to produce this book on Enviro 100, recycled
paper made with **100% post consumer waste**, processed chlorine free, and old
growth free.

For every 5,000 books printed, New Society saves the following resources:[1]

41	Trees
3,728	Pounds of Solid Waste
4,102	Gallons of Water
5,350	Kilowatt Hours of Electricity
6,777	Pounds of Greenhouse Gases
29	Pounds of HAPs, VOCs, and AOX Combined
10	Cubic Yards of Landfill Space

---

[1]Environmental benefits are calculated based on research done by the Environmental Defense Fund and
other members of the Paper Task Force who study the environmental impacts of the paper industry.

For a full list of NSP's titles, please call **1-800-567-6772** *or check out our website at:*

www.newsociety.com

NEW SOCIETY PUBLISHERS